The Economics of Antitrust Injury and Firm-Specific Damages

Edited by
Kevin S. Marshall

Contributors

Stephen H. Kalos
Lawrence Kolbe
Christopher R. Leslie
John E. Loptka
Kevin S. Marshall
Michele Molyneaux
William H. Page
William B. Tye

Lawyers & Judges Publishing Company, Inc.

This publication is designed to provide accurate and authoritative information in regard to the subject matter covered. It is sold with the understanding that the publisher is not engaged in rendering legal, accounting, or other professional service. If legal advice or other expert assistance is required, the services of a competent professional person should be sought.

—From a Declaration of Principles jointly adopted by
a Committee of the American Bar Association
and a Committee of Publishers and Associations.

Lawyers & Judges Publishing Company, Inc.

P.O. Box 30040 • Tucson, AZ 85751-0040
(800) 209-7109 • FAX (800) 330-8795
e-mail: sales@lawyersandjudges.com
www.lawyersandjudges.com

Library of Congress Cataloging-in-Publication Data

The economics of antitrust injury and firm-specific damages / edited by Kevin S. Marshall ; contributors, Stephen H. Kalos ... [et al.].
p. cm.
Includes bibliographical references and index.
ISBN-13: 978-1-933264-45-5 (pbk. : alk. paper)
ISBN-10: 1-933264-45-4 (pbk. : alk. paper)
1. Antitrust law--Economic aspects--United States. 2. Damages--United States. I. Marshall, Kevin Scott, 1960- II. Kalos, Stephen H.
KF1652.E265 2007
343.73'0721--dc22

2007041527

ISBN 10: 1-933264-45-4
ISBN 13: 978-1-933264-45-5
Printed in the United States of America
10 9 8 7 6 5 4 3 2 1

About the Editor

Kevin S. Marshall, Ph.D., M.P.A., J.D. is an Associate Professor of Law at the University of La Verne College of Law in Ontario, California where he teaches *Antitrust* and *Law & Economics*. Dr. Marshall also serves as an Adjunct Professor at the University of La Verne College of Business and Public Administration where he teaches graduate courses in finance and economics.

Dr. Marshall received the degree of Bachelor of Arts, *cum laude*, Phi Beta Kappa, with a major in Economics from Knox College in May 1982. Upon graduating from Knox College, he attended Emory University's School of Law in Atlanta, Georgia, where he was conferred the degree of Juris Doctorate in May 1985. After graduating from law school, Dr. Marshall practiced law for approximately twenty years in Dallas, Texas. The concentration of his practice was in the areas of state/federal civil procedure and commercial litigation, as well as domestic and international competition law. In the fall of 1989, he enrolled in the political economy program at the University of Texas at Dallas. In May 1991, he received the degree of Master of Public Affairs from the University of Texas at Dallas. In December of 1993, he completed his doctoral dissertation entitled *Administered Protection: The Political Economy of U.S. Countervailing and Antidumping Laws* and earned the degree of Doctor of Philosophy in Political Economy from the University of Texas, Dallas.

Additionally, Dr. Marshall is certified in Quantitative Methods and Economic Analysis by the University of Texas at Dallas' School of Social Sciences for his academic achievement and coursework in Descriptive and Inferential Statistics, Costs-Benefits Analysis, Social Science Research Methods, Regression Analysis, Advanced Regression Analysis, and Econometrics. In 1993, he opened the Law Offices of Kevin S. Marshall and continued to actively practice law until the summer of 2004 when he accepted a tenured track position with the University of La Verne's College of Law in Ontario, California where he teaches trade regulation, antitrust, contracts, remedies and law & economics.

Dr. Marshall is also a practicing economist and serves as a Senior Fellow at the Institute for Policy Studies and Information Services (IPSIS), a for-profit organization founded for the purpose of promoting, preserving and enhancing the integrity of scientific methodology in the policy-making process. In 2002, Dr.

Marshall also serves as the Editor of *The Earnings Analyst*, the annual publication of the American Rehabilitation Economics Association dedicated to the publication of peer-reviewed, quality manuscripts dealing with substantive research and practice issues in the areas of forensic vocational and economic evaluation and testimony. Dr. Marshall has served as both a testifying and consulting economic expert with respect to economic damages in Robinson-Patman, antitrust, breach of contract, class-action fairness hearings, wrongful termination, employment discrimination, personal injury, and wrongful death cases.

In addition to his above professional pursuits, Dr. Marshall has served through the years as an Adjunct Professor at various college institutions including Texas Wesleyan University's School of Law, the Economic Department for Southern Methodist University's Dedman College, the University of Texas at Dallas' Business School and School of Social Sciences, and Our Lady of the Lake's Graduate School of Business teaching both graduate and undergraduate courses in *Antitrust Law and Regulation, the Regulation of International Trade and Economic Relations, International Business Transactions, International Trade Policy, Business Law, International Trade, Forensic Economics, Law and Economics, Quantitative Methods & Statistics for Management and Economics, Costs & Benefits Analysis, Law and Data Analysis, Managerial Economics, Microeconomics, Price Theory, International Economics, Real Estate Economics and Investment and Macroeconomics*. Dr. Marshall has published and presented numerous articles involving the interdisciplinary workings of law and economics.

Dr. Marshall may be contacted at the University of La Verne College of Law, 320 East D. Street, Ontario California, 91764. Ph: 909-460-2030. E-mail: kmarshall@ulv.edu

Contributors

Stephen H. Kalos, Ph.D.
Vice President of CRA International and Consultant in Economics, Finance and Business Strategy.

A. Lawrence Kolbe, Ph.D.
Economic Consultant and Founding Principal of *The Brattle Group*, an International Economic Consulting Firm.

Christopher R. Leslie, M.P.P., J.D.
Professor of Law,
Chicago-Kent College of Law.

John E. Loptka, J.D., L.L.M.
A. Robert Noll Distinguished Professor Law,
Penn State Dickenson School of Law.

Kevin S. Marshall, J.D., M.P.A., Ph.D.
Associate Professor of Law & Adjunct Professor of Economics and Finance, University of La Verne Colleges of Law, Business Administration and Public Administration.

Michele A. Molyneaux, J.D.
Associate Attorney,
Sanders & Parks, P.C.

William H. Page, J.D., L.L.M.
Marshall M. Criser Eminent Scholar,
University of Florida Levin College of Law.

William B. Tye, Ph.D.
Economic Consultant and Founding Principal of *The Brattle Group*, an International Economic Consulting Firm.

Dedication

*This book is dedicated to all who have furthered, are furthering, and/or will further the development of the interdisciplinary study of law and economics.**

* To encourage the continued development of the study of law and economics, the author has assigned all royalties due from the sale of this book to the University of La Verne College of Law for the purpose of establishing an endowed scholarship dedicated to qualified students who demonstrate a genuine interest in the interdisciplinary study of law and economics. If you would like to make an additional contribution to the scholarship fund, please remit your gift to the ULV-COL Scholarship in Law & Economics, c/o Associate Dean of Development, 320 East D. Street, Ontario, California 91764. All gifts to the scholarship fund are tax-deductible.

Table of Contents

Acknowledgments

I hereby express my sincerest appreciation to my research assistants, Alisha Leuer, Manuela Todorut, Kyle Claussen, Michael Luther, and Shanna Burkholder. Their assistance and dedication to this project was critical in getting it to press. I express my further appreciation to the University of La Verne College of Law for its support of this project through its 2007 Summer Research and Scholarship Grant Program. Finally, I thank each of the contributing authors for their participation in this project. Understanding the economics of competition is essential to antitrust analysis; it is essential in determining whether the law has been violated in the first instance; and it is equally essential in determining an appropriate remedy.

—Kevin S. Marshall

Preface

Teaching Antitrust: In Search of an Optimal Interdisciplinary Approach

Kevin S. Marshall, J.D., M.P.A., Ph.D.

Since the emergence of the "Chicago School" in the 1970s, U.S. antitrust policy has been evolving into a legal body of increasing economic sophistication. Gone are the days in which courts employ impressionistic assessments of competitive harm in construing challenged business practices. Promoting the welfare of the consumer, economically defined, appears to have emerged as the sole legitimate goal of the antitrust laws.[1]

Consequently, the art of teaching antitrust law lies not only in one's ability to lead the student, business client, and/or judge through a historical morass of evolving common law doctrine, but also in one's ability to relate the applicability of microeconomic theory to the subject matter in question. While the integration of law and economics is essential to the teaching of antitrust law, successfully accomplishing such a task is often problematic, especially given the breadth and depth of both fields, and the time constraints imposed by a law school's semester system or by a judge in the administration of his or her docket. The key to finding an optimal and rewarding balance, whether in the classroom, law office or courtroom, is to focus the accompanying economic instruction (through repetition and application if possible) on the fundamental underlying assumptions of the economic model of perfect competition. A thorough understanding of these assumptions is achievable despite often arbitrarily imposed time constraints. It also provides critical insight regarding anticompetitive conduct as it is identified by the common law. More importantly, such an understanding provides the student, practitioner, business client and/or judicial officer with an efficient, analytical tool for identifying suspected anticompetitive conduct.

The Sherman Act states that it is unlawful to engage in conduct that "restrains" or constitutes an "attempt to monopolize" or that "monopolizes" trade or commerce. The Federal Trade Commission Act furthers states that it is unlawful to engage in conduct that constitutes "unfair methods of competition." The typical antitrust classroom/practice experience requires the student/jurist to traverse the common law landscape of jurisprudential analysis, providing the student/jurist with the classic case-by-case method of unraveling the meaning of these statutory texts. Through dissection of often complex commercial fact patterns and accompanying judicial analysis, anticompetitive conduct is ultimately identified and revealed to the student/jurist. The many precedents illuminate and demonstrate the meaning and reach of such constructs. Although somewhat inefficient, statutory meaning is derived from the cumbersome effort of learning to recognize precedent and its relevant fact patterns.

Learning the fundamental assumptions (or the requisite preconditions) underlying the model of perfect competition not only greatly simplifies the task of understanding antitrust precedent, it also prepares the student/jurist to identify anticompetitive conduct independent of such precedent. Once the student/jurist understands what conditions must exist for competition to thrive, the student/jurist is in a superior position to analyze anticompetitive conduct that may trigger statutory liability, without having to resort to his or her command of common law precedent. A working knowledge of these underlying economic assumptions (or requisite preconditions) of the model of perfect competition is a powerful tool for students/jurists to take with them as they continue to engage in, and/or counsel and consult with respect to competitive markets worldwide.

The underlying assumptions of the model of perfect competition consist of:

1. the existence of numerous buyers and sellers, each acting independently and rationally;
2. each buyer and seller consuming or producing such a negligible amount of the total output that no one buyer or seller can influence price by the amount they either consume or produce;
3. there being no entry or exit barriers with respect to consumer or producer markets;
4. all market participants, that is, all buyers and sellers, being fully informed;
5. all products being homogenous, and constituting interchangeable substitutes for each other; and
6. the forces of supply and demand being free to determine the quantity of output in a relevant market, as well as determine a market-clearing, competitive price with respect to the same.

Microeconomic theory teaches that if the above conditions are met, the model of perfect competition will create efficiencies in consumption, production, and allocation. And it is through the creation of such efficiencies that a perfectly competitive market promises the greatest social opportunity for wealth creation. Or, in antitrust parlance, it promises greater output at lower prices.

If the above assumptions (or conditions) must be met in order for the perfectly competitive market to thrive, then clearly any market conduct or activity that impairs, threatens, suppresses, or jeopardizes any one or more of these assumptions (or conditions) must be discouraged as a matter of policy. Unreasonable restraints of trade and/or unfair methods of competition are proscribed by antitrust policy, and thus one of the primary goals of any antitrust course is to teach the student to be able to identify conduct that constitutes an unreasonable restraint of trade or an unfair method of competition. It is in this context that the referenced underlying assumptions provide a powerful analytical paradigm for identifying market conduct or activity that may likely constitute an unreasonable restraint of trade or an unfair method of competition.

For example, cartel behavior threatens assumptions one, two, and three, in that (1) sellers are no longer acting independently but rather interdependently; (2) such interdependence, to the extent it is successful, may result in a cartel powerful enough to influence price; and (3) thereby result in a cartel powerful enough to create barriers to entry by rival cartels. Price-fixing violates assumptions one and two, given that (1) it requires interdependent and collusive behavior to consummate an agreement; and (2) once consummated, the agreement by design influences market prices. Monopoly violates assumptions one, two, and three, in that (1) there are no longer numerous sellers, but only one; (2) that one seller can set the price since it is the only supplier of the good or service; and (3) it may further have sufficient power to create absolute or relative barriers to entry. Willful acquisitions and/or maintenance of monopoly power can be defined as that conduct specifically designed to jeopardize any one of the above assumptions. The false disparagement of a rival's product violates assumption four, as well as assumption one because such conduct creates information asymmetries which impair the ability of market participants to act rationally. Each assumption provides insight with respect to whether certain conduct may rise to the level of constituting an unreasonable restraint of trade or an unfair method of competition. Mastery of these underlying assumptions undoubtedly complements the analytical lessons filtered through the case law.

The study of antitrust law is an interdisciplinary endeavor. While the traditional case method approach provides a solid introductory foundation for the law and business student/jurist interested in the regulation of competition, such an approach, absent any applied economic theory, will likely result in a stale, task-oriented classroom and/or jurisprudential environment, primarily devoted to categorizing an evolving common law history. However, by teaching the law and business student and/or jurist the operational foundations of price theory, i.e., the underlying assumptions (or requisite preconditions) of the perfect competition model, through repetition and application to the cases discussed throughout the term, one can expect inspired, innovative, and energetic classroom participation. Given the arbitrarily imposed time constraints imposed by an institutional semester or an administrative judge, one cannot expect to teach or learn all the intricacies of microeconomics, but since an understanding of microeconomics fundamentals will result from an understanding of the underlying assumptions of the model of perfect competition, one can expect to achieve a certain level of competence in their application.

The focus of this text is to teach and/or illustrate the fundamentals of microeconomics as it relates to the administration and enforcement of antitrust laws both domestically and internationally. The following chapters instruct as to the fundamental economic constructs relevant to the analysis of antitrust injury (or more generally, competitive injury), as well as address both legal and economic issues with respect to the measurement of antitrust damages. Each chapter provides the student, practitioner, consultant and/or judicial officer critical insight with respect to the analysis and measurement of competitive injury and any resulting business damages. This book is designed to serve as 1) a companion text in any antitrust law class; 2) a supplemental text in any managerial economics class; and 3) a resource to practitioners and consultants in the field of antitrust and industrial organization.

Each of the contributing authors is recognized for his or her scholarship and/or expertise in the antitrust regulatory field. Professor Leslie is a professor of law at the Chicago-Kent School of Law in Chicago, Illinois where he teaches antitrust law. Professor Leslie brings to this publication years of antitrust scholarship, as well as private practice experience in antitrust and complex commercial litigation. Michele Molyneaux is engaged in the practice of law in Phoenix, Arizona, where she is involved in commercial litigation. Drs. William B. Tye, Stephen H. Kalos and A. Lawrence Kolbe have each served as testifying and consulting experts in both the private and public sectors, each providing expertise in economics, finance and business strategy. Professor Loptka is the A. Robert Noll Distinguished Professor of Law at Penn State Dickinson School of Law where he teaches antitrust law. Professor Page is a Marshall M. Criser Eminent Scholar at the University of Florida Levin College of Law where he teaches antitrust law as well. Like Professor Leslie, both Professors Loptka and Page bring to this publication years of antitrust scholarship, as well as private practice experience in antitrust.

I am honored that each of the above authors agreed to participate in this book project. The totality of their varied backgrounds and experiences not only illustrates the robust nature of the contents that hereto follow, but also illustrates the profound interdisciplinary nature of regulating competition in the markets of the world.

Endnote

1. Alan Devlin, A Neo-Chicago Perspective on the Law of Product Tying, 44 American Business Law Journal 521 (Fall 2007) citing Stephen Ross, Network Effects and the Limits of GTE Sylvannia's Efficiency Analysis, 68 Antitrust L.J. 945-945-65 (2001); *Rieter v. Sonotone Corp,* 442 U.S. 330, 343 (1979) (holding that the Sherman Act creates a "consumer welfare prescription"); Robert Bork, The Antitrust Paradox: A Policy at War with Itself, 427 (2d ed. 1993) (arguing that the sole purpose of the antitrust laws is to promote consumer welfare); William J. Kolasky, U.S. and EU Competition Policy Cartels, Mergers, and Beyond (2002), http://www.usdoj.gov/atr/public/speeches./9848.pdf (noting that "the ultimate goal of any sound competition policy must be consumer welfare, which competition advances through lower prices, higher output and enhanced innovation."); Howard H. Ghang, et. al, *Has the Consumer Harm Standard Lost its Teeth? in* High-Stakes Antitrust: The Last Hurrah? 72 (Robert W. Hahn, ed. 2003) ("[C]onsumer welfare is the fundamental standard for evaluating competitive effects.") *See generally,* Robert H. Lande, *Consumer Choice as the Ultimate Goal of Antitrust* 62 U.Pitt. L. Rev. 503 (2001).

Chapter 1

The Economics of Competitive Injury

Kevin S. Marshall, J.D., M.P.A., Ph.D.

Synopsis

> *Indeed, the plaintiff who is not threatened with the kind of injury that antitrust law is designed to prevent may not be seeking to vindicate the public interest as a private attorney general at all...The antitrust injury concept thus requires the antitrust plaintiff to show that its own injury coincides with the public detriment tending to result from the alleged violation. This requirement increases the likelihood that public and private enforcement of the antitrust laws will further the same goal of increased competition*[1]

1.1 Introduction

In addition to establishing a firm specific injury, proving an "antitrust injury" is essential in private antitrust actions under virtually all antitrust laws.[2] According to the United States Supreme Court, an antitrust injury is an "injury of the type the antitrust laws were intended to prevent."[3] Such jurisprudential circularity necessitates an inquiry as to the fundamental purpose of the U.S. antitrust laws. In this regard, the antitrust laws are generally regarded to be "a set of laws designed to promote competition and, therefore, economic efficiency."[4] Thus, it is no surprise that antitrust injury has been said to be synonymous with "injury to competition."[5] As Judge Easterbrook of the Seventh Circuit proclaimed, "[a]ntitrust law condemns practices that drive up prices by curtailing output."[6] Although the term has jurisprudential origins, precision with respect to its meaning is driven by economic constructs. The purpose of this chapter is to foster a robust and thorough understanding of what it means to "injure competition" from a purely economic perspective.

Section 1.2 of this chapter begins by reviewing and discussing the development of the common law requirement that an antitrust plaintiff not only prove an injury-in-fact, but also prove antitrust injury. That Section will demonstrate that the assessment of competitive injury is a question for microeconomics and not jurisprudential precedence. In Section 1.3, this chapter presents an economic analysis of competitive injury. To understand "injury to competition," it is necessary to understand the fundamental underpinnings of microeconomics' theoretical model of perfect competition. Although the term "antitrust injury" may be characterized as an action that results in curtailed output and higher prices, the following analysis demonstrates that the term is much richer; it illustrates that whenever market conduct impairs one or more of the requisite antecedent conditions of the perfectly competitive economic model, *competition* is thereby injured. Finally, Section 1.4 concludes by proffering an analytical paradigm for assessing whether market conduct is likely to result in injury to competition, one of the essential *prima facie* elements of a federal antitrust cause of action.

1.2 Antitrust Injury—Brunswick and its Progeny

In *Brunswick Corp. v. Pueblo Bowl-O-Mat, Inc.,*[7] the United States Supreme Court vacated the Court of Appeals' decision and rendered judgment in favor of the defendant (Brunswick) with respect to the plaintiffs' antitrust damages claim.[8] The Supreme Court reasoned that the plaintiffs' damages were caused not by a reduction in competition, but rather by the continuation of competition.[9] In reaching its conclusion, the Supreme Court observed that "[t]he antitrust laws... were enacted for the '*protection of competition not competitors,*'"[10] Accordingly, the Supreme Court "christened"[11] the following prima facie element of any antitrust claim for damages:

Plaintiffs must prove *antitrust injury*, which is to say injury of the type the antitrust laws were intended to prevent and that flows from that which makes defendants' acts unlawful. The injury should reflect the anticompetitive effect either of the violation or of anticompetitive acts made possible by the violation.[12]

The Court's ruling is best understood within the factual context of the case. At the time of the litigation, the defendant, Brunswick, was one of the two largest manufacturers of bowling equipment in the United States.[13] The plaintiffs were three of the ten bowling centers owned by Treadway Companies, Inc.[14] Since 1965, Brunswick had acquired several bowling centers, six of which were in the plaintiffs' markets.[15] The plaintiffs initiated an antitrust cause of action contending that Brunswick's acquisitions violated various provisions of the antitrust laws.[16]

Brunswick's acquisition and operation of the six bowling centers within the plaintiffs' respective markets resulted from Brunswick's strategic decision to acquire and operate bowling centers that were in default under their equipment purchase agreements with Brunswick.[17] The plaintiffs initiated their cause of action alleging that these acquisitions might substantially lessen competition or tend to create a monopoly in violation of Section 7 of the Clayton Act.[18] Pursuant to Section 4 of the Clayton Act,[19] the plaintiffs sought damages for three times the reasonably expected profits to be made by Brunswick from the operation of their acquired bowling centers.[20]

To establish damages, the plaintiffs attempted to demonstrate that had Brunswick not acquired and operated the defaulting bowling centers in their respective markets (but rather simply had repossessed its equipment and closed the defaulting centers), the plaintiffs' market shares, as well as their profits, would have increased.[21] The plaintiffs' damage claims essentially were premised upon the continuation of competition within their respective markets. But for Brunswick's acquisition and operation of the subject bowling centers, the plaintiffs would have profited from the inevitable closing of the defaulting centers, resulting in the curtailment of output and its inverse effect on price.

It is within this factual context that the Supreme Court clarified that an antitrust plaintiff not only has the burden of establishing an injury-in-fact, but also of proving an antitrust injury; that is, an injury to *competition*. To the extent that Brunswick maintained the competitive environment in each of the plaintiffs' relevant markets,[22] society benefits from the efficiencies that result. These efficiencies include lower prices, more choices, and perhaps better service. To find an antitrust violation in such a situation would be antithetical to microeconomic theory and the tenets of its perfectly competitive economic model.

Approximately nine years after *Brunswick*, the Supreme Court reiterated its requirement that a private plaintiff seeking antitrust relief must show a threat of antitrust injury in *Cargill, Inc. v. Monfort of Colorado, Inc.*[23] The Court in *Cargill,* supplementing its holding in *Brunswick*, instructed that "a showing of loss or damage due merely to increased competition does not constitute [a threat of antitrust] injury."[24] In *Cargill*, the nation's fifth largest beef packer brought an action under the Clayton Act to enjoin a merger between the second and third largest beef packers.[25] The plaintiff claimed that after the merger, the defendant firm would lower its prices to some level at or slightly above costs in order to compete with the other packers for market share.[26] The plaintiff argued that the defendant firm would be in a position to do so because of the multi-plant efficiencies its acquisition of another firm would provide.[27] Although the plaintiff conceded that the merger would not drive it out of business, it argued that to remain competitive, it would necessarily be required to compete on price (for instance, lower its prices) and suffer losses in profitability.[28] Consequently, the issue before the Court was "whether [the plaintiff's] loss of profits in such circumstances constitut[ed] antitrust injury.[29] To resolve this issue, the Court looked to *Brunswick*.[30]

Fortifying its holding in *Brunswick*, the *Cargill* Court explained:

> *Brunswick* holds that the antitrust laws do not require the courts to protect small businesses from the loss of profits due to continued competition, but only against the loss of profits from practices forbidden by the antitrust laws. The kind of competition that Monfort alleges here, competition for increased market share, is not activity forbidden by the antitrust laws. It is simply, as petitioners claim, vigorous competition. To hold that the antitrust laws protect competitors from the loss of profits due to such price competition would, in effect, render illegal any decision by a firm to cut prices in order to increase market share. The antitrust laws require no such perverse result, for '[i]t is in the interest of competition to permit dominant firms to engage in vigorous competition, including price competition.' The logic of *Brunswick* compels the conclusion that the threat of loss of profits due to possible price competition following a merger does not constitute a threat of antitrust injury.[31]

With its ruling in *Brunswick* and *Cargill*, the Supreme Court made it clear that the existence of an antitrust injury (separate and apart from an antitrust plaintiff's proof of specific damages) is a required element of proof in most, if not all, private federal antitrust lawsuits.[32] In *Brunswick,* the Supreme Court specifically mandated that antitrust plaintiffs

> must prove antitrust injury, which is...injury of the type the antitrust laws were intended to prevent and that flows from that which makes defendants' acts unlawful. The injury should reflect the anticompetitive effect either of the violation or of anticompetitive acts made possible by the violation.[33]

In *Cargill,* by reiterating its ruling in *Brunswick,* the Supreme Court conclusively established that "a private plaintiff must allege threatened loss or damage 'of the type the antitrust laws were designed to prevent.'"[34] Because "[t]he antitrust laws... were enacted for the 'protection of *competition,*'"[35] an antitrust "injury should reflect [an] anticompetitive effect."[36] Simply put, it should reflect a structural injury to a perfectly competitive model as it is understood within the field of economics.

1.3 The Perfectly Competitive Model—A Paradigm for Identifying Conduct Injurious to Competition[37]

The Sherman Act informs that it is unlawful to engage in conduct that "*restrains,*" "*monopolize[s],*" or constitutes an "*attempt to monopolize*" trade or commerce.[38] The Federal Trade Commission Act further provides that it is unlawful to engage in conduct that constitutes "*unfair methods of competition.*"[39] When confronted with allegations of anticompetitive conduct, it is common for the jurist and antitrust practitioner to traverse the common law landscape of jurisprudential analysis in pursuit of a precedential indication whether such conduct might fall within the meaning of the referenced statutory texts. The dissection of complex commercial fact patterns and accompanying judicial analysis is the method by which anticompetitive conduct may or may not be identified. The myriad of precedential outcomes illuminates and demonstrates the meaning of such constructs. Although perhaps somewhat inefficient, statutory meaning is derived from the cumbersome recognition of precedent and its relevant fact patterns. Thus, as Professors Areeda and Hovenkamp suggest, "applying antitrust law is very difficult."[40]

Instruction on the fundamental assumptions (or stated differently, the requisite antecedent conditions)

> Underlying the perfectly competitive model not only dramatically simplifies the task of understanding antitrust precedent, but also provides an analytical framework for identifying anticompetitive conduct independent of precedential constraint. Once the requisite antecedent conditions for competition to thrive are identified and understood, the jurist, the antitrust practitioner and the economic analyst is in a superior position from which to analyze anticompetitive conduct that may trigger statutory liability.[41]

The underlying assumptions (or rather the antecedent conditions) of the perfectly competitive model[42] essentially include the following:[43]

1. There exists numerous buyers and sellers,[44] each acting independently[45] and rationally;[46]

2. Each buyer and seller consumes or produces such a negligible amount of the total output such that no one buyer or seller can influence price by the amount they either consume or produce;[47]
3. There are no barriers to entry or exit with respect to consumer or producer markets;[48]
4. All market participants, that is all buyers and sellers, are fully informed of all relevant economic and technological data;[49]
5. All products are homogeneous, or rather, constitute interchangeable substitutes for each other;[50]
6. The forces of supply and demand are free to determine the quantity of output in a relevant market as well as determine a market-clearing, competitive price with respect to that output.[51]

Microeconomic theory teaches that if these assumptions hold true, or rather, if the above conditions are met, "the perfectly competitive model will create efficiencies in consumption, production, and allocation."[52] "[I]t is through the creation of such efficiencies that a perfectly competitive market promises the greatest social opportunity for wealth creation," or in "antitrust parlance, it promises greater output at lower prices."[53]

If the above assumptions (or conditions) must be met in order for the perfectly competitive market to thrive, then (from a purely economic perspective) "it follows that any market conduct or activity that impairs, threatens, suppresses or jeopardizes any one or more of such underlying" assumptions (or conditions) "must be discouraged as a matter of public policy."[54] It is in this context that the referenced underlying assumptions "provide a powerful analytical paradigm for identifying market conduct or activity that may likely constitute an unreasonable restraint of trade, an unfair method of competition, [as well as] *competitive injury*."[55]

For example, cartel behavior threatens the first, second, and third assumptions above in that 1) sellers are no longer acting independently but rather interdependently; 2) such interdependence, to the extent it is successful, may result in a cartel power sufficient to influence price; and 3) such interdependence, to the extent it is successful, may also result in cartel power sufficient to create barriers to entry with respect to cartel rivals. Price fixing violates the first two assumptions in that 1) it requires interdependent and collusive behavior to consummate an agreement, and 2) once that agreement is consummated, it influences market prices by its design. A monopoly violates the first three assumptions in that 1) there are no longer numerous sellers, but rather one; 2) that single seller can necessarily set prices since it is the only supplier of the good or service; and further, 3) that single seller may have sufficient power to create absolute or relative barriers to entry. Willful acquisition and/or maintenance of monopoly power can be defined as conduct that is specifically designed to jeopardize any one of the above assumptions. The false disparagement of a rival's product violates the fourth assumption, as well as the first assumption, in that such conduct creates information asymmetries, which impair the ability for market participants to act rationally. The examples are endless. Each assumption provides insight with respect to whether certain conduct may rise to the level of constituting a restraint of trade, an unfair method of competition, or even whether such conduct is likely to result in *injury to competition*. Mastery of these underlying assumptions undoubtedly compliments the analytical lessons filtered through case law.

A. Efficiency—The Objective of Perfect Competition and the U.S. Antitrust Laws

"Economic theory has long acknowledged that the given environment within which society functions is constrained by scarcity," and that this "scarcity is the fundamental source of social and political conflict."[56] "Given such scarcity, all societies are confronted with the problem of determining 1) what and how much, to produce; 2) how to produce; and 3) for whom to produce."[57] "The field of microeconomics has demonstrated that the adoption of the perfectly competitive model provides a remarkable social mechanism with which to [administer] the social problems generated by scarcity. The perfectly competitive model ultimately nurtures, if not [assures], efficiencies in the allocation, production and distribution of scarce resources."[58] As Figure 1.1 demonstrates, the unfettered forces of supply and demand determine an efficient quantity of production for any given good or service (Q_e), as well as a market-clearing price with respect to the same (P_e). Thus, perfect competition minimizes waste in that the risk of under- or over-production is minimized; supply equals demand; and resources are allocated and distributed to those who value them most.

Figure 1.1 illustrates the market demand and supply curves for a given good in a competitive market. It is important to note that a firm's individual supply curve is derived from its marginal cost curve. As long as the market price for a given good equals or exceeds the marginal cost to produce that good, a firm will produce and supply the given good.[59] The market or industry supply curve is derived from the horizontal summation of all the marginal cost curves of the competing individual firms (for example, the horizontal summation of their individual firm supply curves).[60] The industry or market supply curve reflects the schedule of prices at which firms are willing to supply a given quantity of any good or service. As price increases, rational firms are willing to supply more and more, and thus the more the market or industry is willing to supply. Given the positive relationship between the price of a good or service and the quantity supplied, the slope of the market or industry supply curve is also positive.

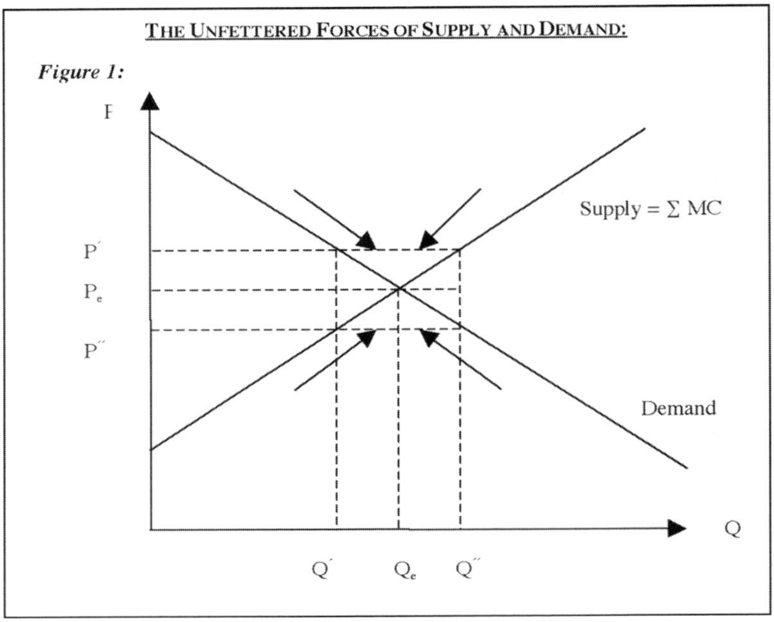

Figure 1.1

The industry or market "demand curve can be viewed as a schedule of the marginal *willingness-to-pay* of customers."[61] In Figure 1.1, the competitive equilibrium price (P_e) equals the industry's marginal cost of production at the equilibrium output (Q_e).[62] Should the market only produce Q′ units of the good or service in question, economic waste results because the marginal willingness-to-pay exceeds the marginal cost to produce additional units of the good or service. Should the market produce Q″ units of the good or service in question, economic waste results because the marginal cost to produce Q″ units exceeds the marginal willingness-to-pay. Figure 1.1 ultimately demonstrates that the unfettered forces of supply and demand in a perfectly competitive market determines a market-clearing quantity (Q_e) and a corresponding price (P_e), thereby answering the profound political and economic question of what and how much society should produce of a given good or service given the constraints of scarcity. It is no wonder that "[e]conomists generally view antitrust as a set of laws designed to promote competition and, therefore, economic efficiency."[63] Accordingly, to the extent commercial conduct impedes, obstructs, or eliminates any of the necessary operational conditions of the perfectly competitive model, injury to competition results.

B. The Perfectly Competitive Model and Its Condition of Rationality

The theory of rational choice drives the economic constructs of the perfectly competitive model:

> Central to the perfectly competitive model is the assumption that all market participants are rational, with rational action being defined by the principle of utility-profit maximization.[64] Any act of consumption or production that fails to maximize the utility or profit of an individual or firm is considered to be irrational economic behavior.... Consequently, in order to act rationally, all market participants must be fully informed of all costs and benefits associated with their respective economic activities. Once informed of all...costs and benefits [associated with a certain activity], an economically rational actor will weigh his or her costs and benefits, and if the benefits exceed or equal [his or her] costs, he or she will engage in such activity.[65]

Moreover, it is observed that:

> Economic rationality necessarily requires that all costs and benefits be considered when exercising economic choices.... To the extent all such costs and benefits are not considered (i.e., they are external to the rational decision-making process), non-utility/profit-maximizing choices will be made, resulting in unacceptable market inefficiencies.[66]

Rationality further requires that market participants be fully informed with respect to all relevant economic and technological data.[67] In this regard, consumers must have access to accurate information regarding the goods and services they contemplate consuming in order to act rationally. Access to accurate information regarding the benefits and costs associated with such goods and services is necessary for a consumer's choice in a utility-maximizing manner.

As previously observed, misinformation and deception obstructs rationality in the marketplace. Accordingly, conduct intentionally disseminating misinformation or grounded on deception impedes the operational efficiencies of the perfectly competitive model. For example, falsely disparaging a rival or a rival's goods or services may likely create externalities to the extent that such conduct "interferes with the consumer's ability to identify all the benefits and/or costs associated with the purchase of the rival's goods or services."[68] Additionally, and more directly, such inaccurate information may likely create inefficient distortions in the marketplace consisting of the "under-production of the disparaged product [or service] and/or the over-production of the disparager's product [or service]."[69]

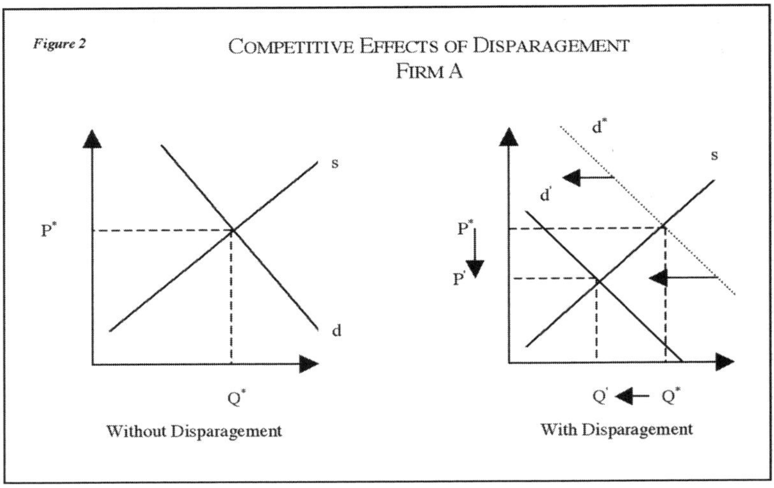

Figure 1.2

Figure 1.2 "illustrates the distortions that might result from deceptive and false disparagement practices. The demand function for Firm A's product is a statement of the relation between the quantity demanded, Q, and all factors that affect that quantity," including "the price of the good or service under analysis, the price of other goods" (namely complements and substitutes), "the number of buyers in the market, the relative income of consumers, consumer tastes and preferences, general marketplace expectations," as well as other possible influences.[70]

> To the extent the disparagement distorts the price[71] of the product or negatively influences the taste and preferences of the consumer with respect to Firm A's product, the demand for the product [or service] may likely shift to the left from d to d′, curtailing output of Firm A's product [or service] from Q^* and Q'.[72]

"Additionally, the disparagement practice may not only distort the market for the disparaged product," but it may distort the market for the product's substitutes.[73] For example in Figure 1.3 below, "Firm B, by and through its disparaging practices, may capture market share from Firm A," which results "in an increase in Firm B's output from Q^* to Q' as consumers substitute Firm B's [product] or services for Firm A's.[74]

Finally, "[a] successful campaign of disparagement may also jeopardize and threaten other [requisite] conditions necessary for competition to thrive" to the extent that disparagement creates entry barriers and/or leads to oligopoly and/or monopoly.[75] To the extent that a firm adopts a campaign to falsely disparage "its competitors and their respective products for the purpose of forcing them to exit the market," or through creating a barrier to the firm's competitors' entry or re-entry, and such a campaign proves to be successful, it will result in an injury to competition.[76] Such practices will "drive up prices by curtailing output"[77] as demonstrated in Figure 1.4 below.

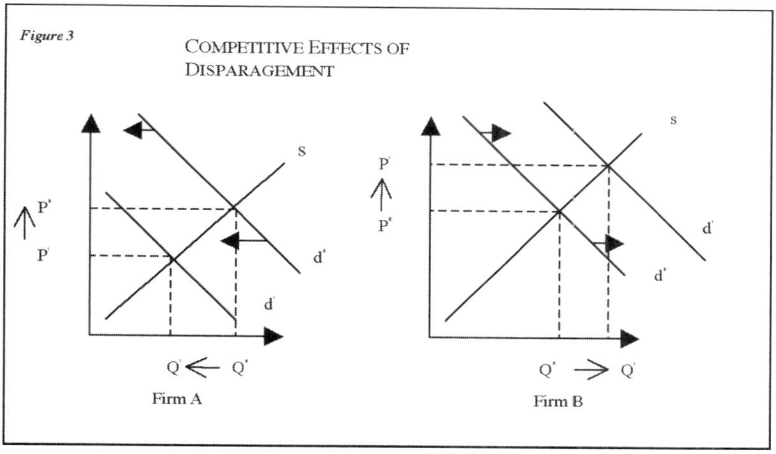

Figure 1.3

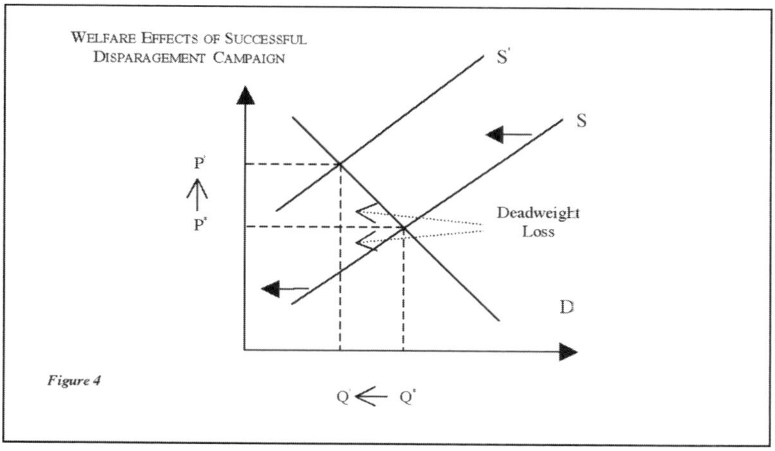

Figure 1.4

"The market supply function, S, for a given product is a statement of the relation between the quantity supplied and all factors affecting that quantity," including "the price of the good in question, the price of a supplier's related goods, the number of sellers producing the good, input prices, the current state of technology," as well as general market expectations.[78]

> As rival firms are driven from the market as a result of false disparagement, the market supply curve, S, shifts to S′, thereby resulting in a curtailment of output (Q^* decreases to Q′) and an increase in price (P^* increases to P′) , all of which results in a deadweight loss[79] to society as designed on the above graph.[80]

In short, as demonstrated above, conduct that impairs rationality in the marketplace causes injury to competition. Intentional conduct falsely disparaging a competitor's goods or services clearly has the propensity of impairing rationality. Such conduct impedes an operational condition necessary for efficient exchange. Such an impediment constitutes a restraint on trade.[81] It is in this vein that "it injures competition."[82]

C. The Perfectly Competitive Model and Its Condition of Numerous, Price-Taking Buyers and Sellers

Competition thrives in a market environment involving numerous buyers and sellers.[83] Ambiguity with respect to the meaning of "numerous" is resolved by the perfectly competitive model's assumption that all market participants are *price takers*.[84] The *numerosity* condition is satisfied when there is a sufficient number of buyers and sellers such that each buyer and seller consumes or produces a negligible amount of the total output; and given the negligible magnitude of their consumption or production, no one buyer or seller can influence or affect price.[85] In this regard, conventional economic theory instructs:

> In a perfectly competitive market, the large number of sellers and buyers of a good ensures that no single seller or buyer can affect its price. The market forces of supply and demand determine price. Individual firms take the market price as a given in deciding how much to produce and sell, and consumers take it as a given in deciding how much to buy.[86]

Market power is derived from one's ability to influence market price.[87] A firm with the ability to raise its price relative to the competitive price level is observed to possess market power.[88] Conduct that results in the creation of market power (that is, the power to influence price) diminishes the efficiencies of competition. The wielding of such power is typically exemplified in the economic literature by *monopoly*, the polar opposite of perfect competition.

Under conditions of perfect competition, market participants (individual buyers and sellers) cannot affect price by the amount they either consume or produce. Sellers perceive a perfectly elastic demand curve,[89] that is, they can sell as many products as they can produce at the market price. Figure 1.5 reiterates the essential features of the perfectly competitive economic model discussed in conjunction with Figure 1.1. A firm in perfect competition, given its lack of market power, must accept the price set by the market, in this case price P_c. For every unit sold, a firm will generate incremental income equal to the unit price of the product or service. Such incremental income, in economic parlance, constitutes *marginal revenue*.[90] As a rational actor, a firm will produce at Q_f, where its marginal costs[91] equal its marginal revenue.[92] At Q_f a firm will maximize its profits. To produce and sell a quantity at less than Q_f is irrational given that the benefits of producing an additional unit exceeds the additional costs associated with the same.[93] Likewise, to produce and sell a quantity that exceeds Q_f is irrational given that the costs of producing an additional unit exceed the benefits associated with the same.[94] As previously noted, the firm's marginal cost curve (mc_f) is essentially the firm's supply curve.[95]

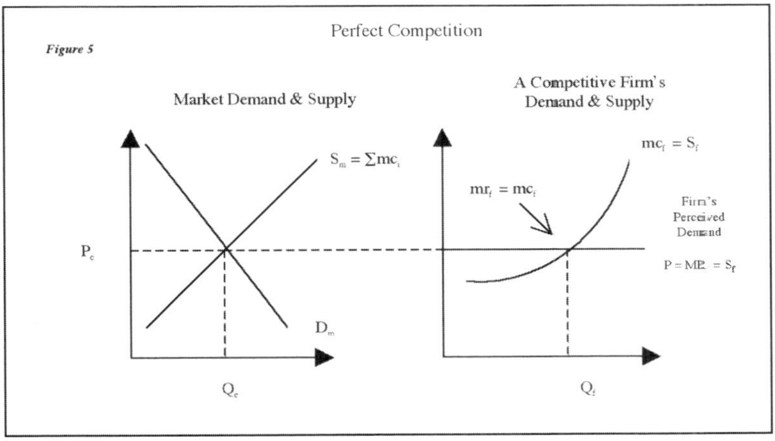

Figure 1.5

Recall that the market demand and supply curves are derived by horizontally summing all of the individual demand and supply curves of all market participants and are denoted as S_m and D_m.[96] In competition, the forces of supply and demand determine a market-clearing quantity of output (Q_c) of the product or service in question as well as a market price (P_c). As stated above, in competition, there is no waste. No more and no less is produced then that which society determines to be optimal, at a price set by the autonomous forces of supply and demand. As determined by the forces of supply and demand, Q_c units are produced and sold at price P_c.

The polar opposite of perfect competition, as stated above, is monopoly. A monopoly is defined as "a market that has only one seller but many buyers."[97] A monopolist is the sole producer of a product, and, therefore, the monopolist faces a demand curve that is the market demand curve (in contrast with the perceived demand curve facing a producer in perfect competition). In Figure 1.6, the market demand curve ($D_{monopoly}$) "relates the price that the monopolist receives to the quantity it offers" to sell.[98] The market supply curve is the monopolist's marginal cost curve.[99] Assuming rationality, a monopolist's profit maximization output is Q_m at price P_m where its marginal revenue equals its marginal costs.

The welfare effects of monopoly are illustrated in Figures 1.6 and 1.7. By superimposing for comparison purposes the economic models of monopoly and perfect competition, it is demonstrated that as a market evolves and concentrates into monopoly, less is produced at higher prices. In Figure 1.7, perfect competition will produce Q_c units at price P_c, where $D_c = P_c = MR_c$ intersects S_c. In contrast, a market controlled by a monopolist will produce a lesser quantity of Q_m units at a higher price of P_m, where $MR_{m\,=}\,S_m$.[100] Because of resulting higher prices and a curtailment of production, monopoly creates a deadweight loss to society. Antitrust laws were clearly intended to prevent losses of this type.

Accordingly, conduct that decreases the number of sellers (or buyers, in the case of monopsony), and thereby increases a seller's ability to influence price, jeopardizes the requisite conditions necessary for competition to thrive. To the extent such conduct violates the first and second assumptions above, an injury to competition results. This is not to suggest that making the determination of whether a firm actually constitutes a monopoly under Section 2 of the Sherman Act is a simple task. Rather, the focus of this chapter is limited to whether conduct creates an antitrust injury, that is, an injury to competition. And as this chapter demonstrates, determining whether an "injury to competition" exists necessitates a thorough understanding of microeconomics' model of perfect competition.

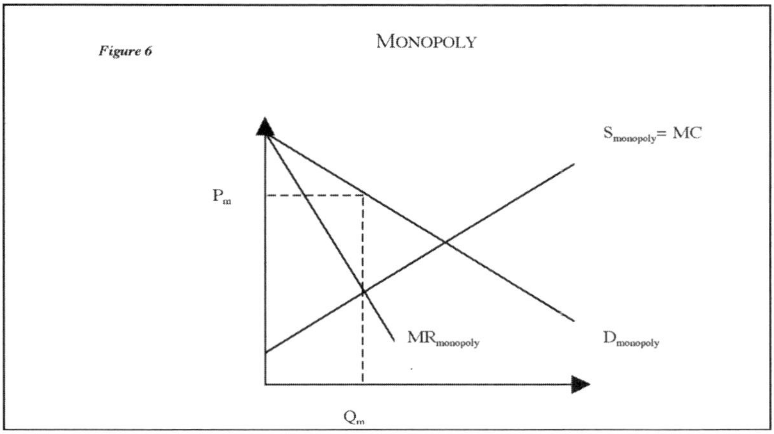

Figure 1.6

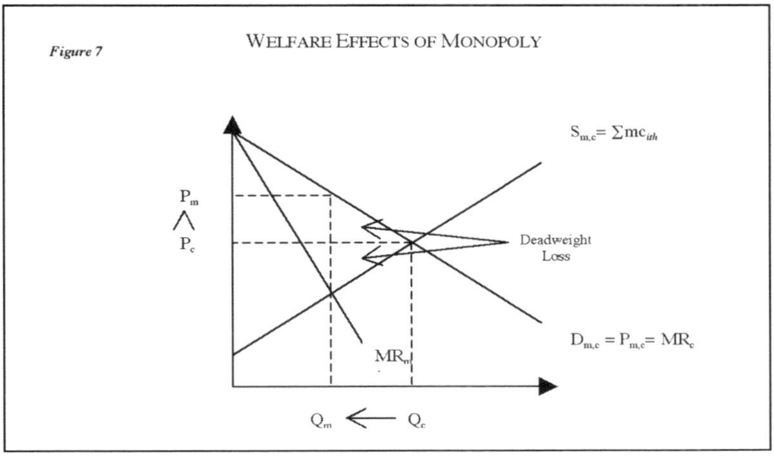

Figure 1.7

D. The Perfectly Competitive Model and Its Condition of Independence

The perfectly competitive model is characterized by *independence*. The efficiencies of the model depend upon market participants acting independently of one another. To the extent that buyers and sellers coordinate their market activities, the requisite independent character of competition is jeopardized and threatened, if not destroyed. For example, if all sellers in the marketplace collaborated with respect to their output decisions, their joint efforts would generate an aggregate market power capable of influencing price. As the number of buyers and sellers diminish, the opportunity for them to coordinate their market activities increases.[101]

Conventional microeconomic theory defines oligopoly as: "a small number of firms in an industry so that, in any decision it makes, each firm must take into account the expected reaction of other firms. Oligopolistic firms are mutually *interdependent* and can be collusive or noncollusive."[102]

Economics has long recognized the injurious nature of cartel behavior. A cartel is "a group of firms that, through some type of explicit agreement, collude to jointly determine the values of strategic variables such as price and output."[103] Oligopolies have a strong incentive to *cartelize* their industry and act as a single monopolist by restricting output to a level that maximizes profit to the combination of the firms.[104] It merits noting that the "price-taking assumption" becomes increasingly threatened as an industry increasingly concentrates into a few firms. Each firm recognizes that its output decisions have an obvious effect on price. Consequently, "firms as a group recognize they can affect price and manage to coordinate their decisions so as to achieve monopoly profits."[106]

In Figure 1.8 (which assumes that marginal costs are constant over all output ranges), equilibrium in a perfectly competitive market is denoted at point C. As an industry concentrates and thereby reduces the number of sellers in the market, the antecedent condition of *independence* (in perfect competition) is gradually transformed into a condition of *interdependence* (as the market evolves from perfect competition to oligopoly). Assuming the remaining oligopolistic firms continue to zealously compete, they may maintain a quasi-competitive equilibrium at point C. The market equilibrium under oligopoly, however, can occur at many points along the demand curve between points C and M, depending on the firms' strategic interrelationships. Point M is the cartel's equilibrium resulting from its agreement to act as a single firm with respect to its output and pricing decisions. Whether by cartel (firms operating with a formal agreement to fix prices and output) or collusion (a covert, informal agreement among firms in an industry to fix prices and output levels), injury results similar to that observed in monopoly. Accordingly, coordinated market activities jeopardize the first and second assumptions above to the extent that such market activity eliminates *independence* and *price-taking*.

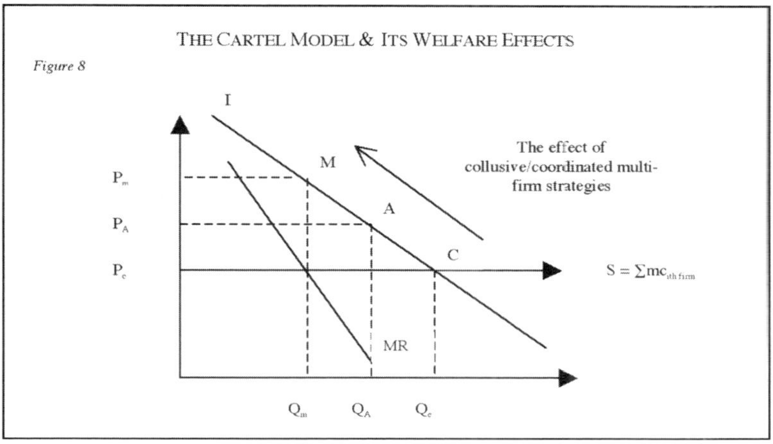

Figure 1.8 *Adopted from Walter Nicholson,* Microeconomic Theory, Basic Principles and Extensions *(9th ed. 2005), p. 417, Fig. 14.1.*

Consequently, it is no surprise that the United States Supreme Court has summarily condemned coordinated conduct in the form of price fixing as per se unlawful.[107] In delivering the Supreme Court's opinion in *United States v. Trenton Potteries Co.*,[108] Justice Stone maintained:

> The aim and result of every price-fixing agreement, if effective, is the elimination of one form of competition. The power to fix prices, whether reasonably exercised or not, involves power to control the market and to fix arbitrary and unreasonable prices. The reasonable price fixed today may through economic and business changes become the unreasonable price of [tomorrow]. Once established, it may be maintained unchanged because of the absence of competition secured by the agreement for a price reasonable when fixed. Agreements which create such potential power may well be held to be in themselves unreasonable or unlawful restraints, without the necessity of minute inquiry whether a particular price is reasonable or unreasonable as fixed and without placing on the government in enforcing the Sherman Law the burden of ascertaining from day to day whether it has become unreasonable through the mere variation of economic conditions. Moreover, in the absence of express legislation requiring it, we should hesitate to adopt a construction making the difference between legal and illegal conduct in the field of business relations depend upon so uncertain a test as whether prices are reasonable—a determination which can be satisfactorily made only after a complete survey of our economic organization and a choice between rival philosophies.[109]

In *United States v. Socony-Vacuum Oil Co.*[110] Justice Douglas further observed that:

> [F]or over forty years [the Supreme Court] has consistently and without deviation adhered to the principle that price-fixing agreements are unlawful per se under the Sherman Act and that no showing of so-called competitive abuses or evils which those agreements were designed to eliminate or alleviate may be interposed as a defense.[111]

Recently in *FTC v. Superior Court Trial Lawyers Ass'n,*[112] the Supreme Court reiterated Justice Douglas's observation in a footnote in his *Socony Vacuum Oil* opinion:

> 'Price-fixing agreements may or may not be aimed at complete elimination of price competition. The group making those agreements may or may not have power to control the market. But the fact that the group cannot control the market prices does not necessarily mean that the agreement as to prices has no utility to the members of the combination. The effectiveness of price-fixing agreements is dependent on many factors, such as competitive tactics, position in the industry, the formula underlying pricing policies. Whatever economic justification particular price-fixing agreements may be thought to have, the law does not permit an inquiry into their reasonableness. They are all banned because of their actual or potential threat to the central nervous system of the economy.[113]

Interdependent activity is clearly a threat to the "nervous system" of an economy driven by the perfectly competitive model. Thus, coordinated activity with respect to price-fixing, boycotts,[114] territorial allocations,[115] as well as information-sharing,[116] threaten, if not violate, the assumption of *independence* and will likely result in a discernable injury to the perfectly competitive model.

E. The Perfectly Competitive Model and Its Condition of No Entry or Exit Barriers

The perfectly competitive model requires that there be no entry or exit barriers. Barriers to entry are "social, political, or economic impediments that prevent firms from entering a market."[117] Entry barriers may permit "existing firms [to] earn above-normal profit without inducing entry."[118] A barrier to exit is "any restriction on the ability of incumbents to redeploy assets from one industry or line of business to another."[119] Additionally, economists have observed that "[a]n important aspect of competitive strategy...is finding ways to create barriers to entry—conditions that deter entry by new competitors."[120]

In its simplest application, the absence of entry barriers generates competitive prices and outputs. For example, in Figure 1.9, the entry of a producer shifts the market supply curve from S^* to S', resulting in an expansion of output from Q^* to Q' and a corresponding decrease in price from P^* to P'. Ultimately, more is produced at lower prices, thereby increasing societal welfare. Correspondingly, ease of exit is also important in that it provides for the efficient allocation of societal resources, that is, it allows firms to exit certain markets and devote their resources to more profitable ventures in other markets. The absence of entry barriers ultimately protects the market from monopoly. As long as there are no entry barriers, the ability of firms to reduce output and charge supra-competitive prices is held in check. Monopoly rents will always attract entry.

Entry barriers may be classified as either natural or artificial. An entry barrier is "natural" if it is an inherent operational condition of the market.[121] For example, scale economies, product differentiation, high initial investment constraints, risk, cost of capital, advertising, extent of vertical integration or vertical contracting, and government intervention by regulation may be inherently characteristic of certain product markets. An entry barrier is "artificial if it is strategically erected by incumbent firms in order to make entry more difficult."[122] Certain practices such as limit pricing,[123] patent accumulation,[124] solicitation of governmental regulation, and even vertical integration or contracting (exclusive dealing arrangements) can be designed to deter entry.[125]

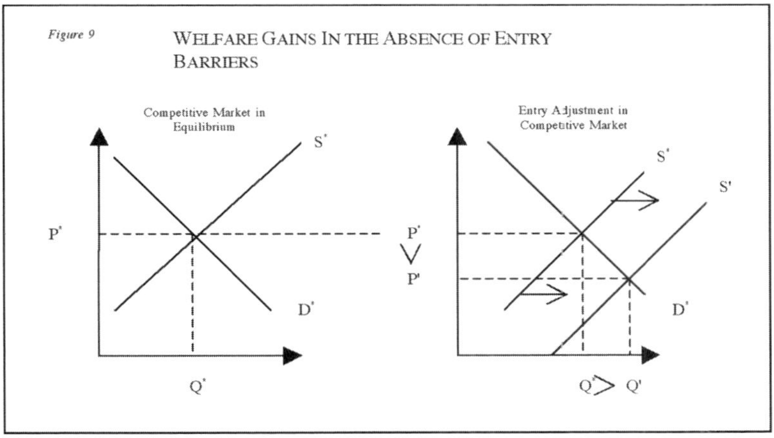

Figure 1.9

For example, exclusive dealing arrangements designed to deter entry obstruct the autonomous forces of supply and demand from determining a competitive output level at a corresponding competitive price. "In its simplest form, an exclusive dealing arrangement is a contract between a [supplier] and a buyer forbidding the buyer from purchasing the contracted good from any other seller, or requiring the buyer to take all of its needs in the contracted good from that [supplier]."[126] Related practices such as quantity or market share discounts (which reward dealers for selling relatively more of a particular seller's brand),[127] or even covenants not to compete,[128] also have the effect of deterring entry. The anticompetitive nature of such conduct lies in the arrangement's propensity to create an artificial barrier to entry. As observed by Professors Hovenkamp and Areeda, "[t]he most frequently given rationale for condemning exclusive dealing arrangements is that they limit the access of upstream rivals to downstream firms, thus reducing upstream competition and creating or perpetuating lower output and higher prices."[129]

Conduct that impedes or obstructs the third assumption (or condition) above mandating freedom of entry and exit results in *injury to competition*. Artificial barriers to entry impede the efficiencies of the perfectly competitive economic model. From this perspective it can be said that artificially created entry barriers "[injure] competition" in that they result in the artificial curtailment of output and higher prices. This loss in societal surplus or welfare is of a nature the antitrust laws were intended to prevent.

F. The Perfectly Competitive Model and Its Condition of Product Homogeneity

Product homogeneity, assuming all other conditions of the perfectly competitive model are present, ensures that no one seller may affect product price. To the extent that a supplier has a uniquely differentiated product, that supplier likely may have the ability to determine price with respect to his or her product. In fact, in the "extreme case of product differentiation[,] the differentiated product may be a relevant market unto itself."[130] In such extreme cases, the competitive model may suffer injury similar to that experienced with monopoly.[131]

Product differentiation is typically associated with monopolistic competition, a market structure consisting of many firms where entry by new firms is not restricted.[132] Each firm is said to sell "a brand or version of the product that differs in quality, appearance, or reputation, and each firm is the sole producer of its own brand."[133] Monopolistic competition is characterized as "a market structure in which just enough product differentiation exists to support elements of both monopoly and perfect competition."[134] Accordingly, "[t]he amount of monopoly power the firm has depends on its success in differentiating its product from those of other firms."[135] Examples of monopolistic markets abound: facial soaps, carbonated beverages, cereals, household cleaning supplies, packaged coffee, and toothpaste are just a few such markets.[136] Although each brand name supplier has a limited power to determine the price for the differentiation of its product, such power is constrained by the absence of entry barriers and the competitive environment with respect to the differentiation in question. Consequently, the obstruction of the perfectly competitive model's condition of product homogeneity creates little concern, especially in the absence of entry barriers. The absence of product homogeneity, however, can accentuate a firm's ability to affect product price in the presence of entry barriers, or if the product differentiation is so extreme that it creates a monopoly market, or both.

For purposes of this discussion, product differentiation is mentioned for completeness. Product homogeneity is an operational condition of the perfectly competitive model. Although product differentiation poses a slight threat of injury to competition (in that each seller has some power over the price of its brand-differentiated product), such a threat is of little import provided that none of the other operational conditions of the model are implicated. If any of the other antecedent conditions of the perfectly competitive model are implicated, product differentiation aggravates the resulting injury to competition.

G. The Perfectly Competitive Model and Its Unrestricted Forces of Supply and Demand—Maximizing Output at Minimum (Competitive) Prices

The last assumption, or antecedent condition, of the perfectly competitive model is essentially a catch-all component. The violation or obstruction of any one or more of the model's preceding assumptions of antecedent conditions restricts the forces of supply and demand. Additionally, it has long been acknowledged that government intervention in the form of price controls (price ceilings and/or floors) or subsidies constrain the autonomous forces of the market from determining a socially optimal, competitive output at competitive prices. Whether through government intervention, or by the anticompetitive conduct of private firms, market activity that imposes artificial restrictions on the forces of supply and demand ultimately *injures competition.*

The classic microeconomic textbook example of government intervention that restricts the forces of supply and demand involves the imposition of a price ceiling.[137] Figure 1.10 illustrates that, in the absence of governmentally imposed price controls, a perfectly competitive market will determine a market clearing equilibrium price and quantity P_0 and Q_0. With an imposed maximum price P_{max}, the quantity supplied falls to Q_s, and the quantity demanded increases to Q_D, creating a shortage equal to Q_D minus Q_S. Of course, a governmentally imposed price floor set above the market price of P_0 results in a surplus (that is, at such a price the quantity supplied exceeds the quantity demanded).

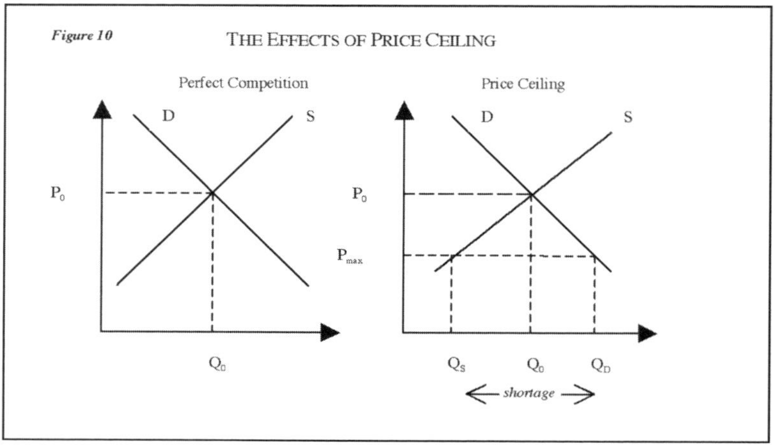

Figure 1.10

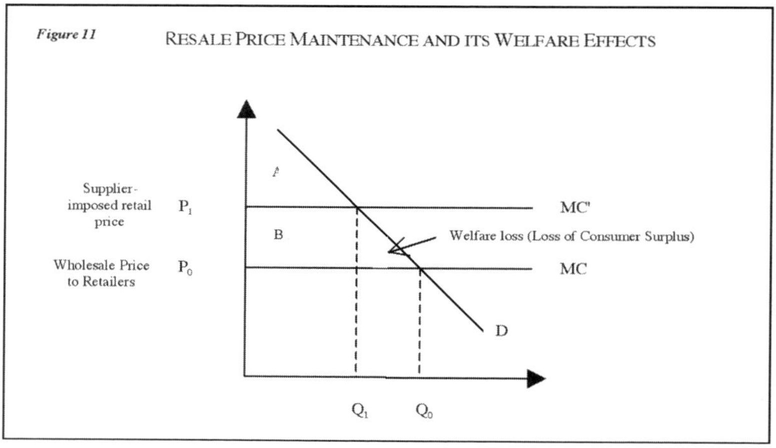

Figure 1.11

Resale price maintenance, although it may impair several of the other requisite conditions of the perfectly competitive model, illustrates private firm conduct that essentially imposes a price control in an otherwise competitive market, thereby restricting the autonomous forces of supply and demand. Resale price maintenance is "the practice by which a manufacturer attempts to control the prices at which its products are resold by dealers and distributors."[138] The impact on the dealer market suggests a welfare loss. For example, in Figure 1.11, assume that a supplier provides its product at a wholesale price of P_0, and that is the only cost that retailers have with respect to this product. If the demand curve is D, then under perfect competition the quantity sold is Q_0, and consumers' surplus is equal to the sum of A + B + C. If the supplier maintains a resale price of P_1, and the quantity sold is Q_1, then consumers' surplus is reduced to A, B is reallocated as producer surplus, and A is the deadweight loss in consumer surplus.[139]

A supplier's mandated resale price essentially constitutes vertical price fixing (which also implicates the *independence* assumption, or condition, of the model). It imposes a minimum (or even a maximum)[140] price at which a good may be sold in the competitive dealer's market. Such a price imposition ultimately restricts the forces of supply and demand, resulting in either a shortage or surplus as observed with governmentally-imposed price controls. Figure 1.12 illustrates the market distorting impact of resale price maintenance practices.

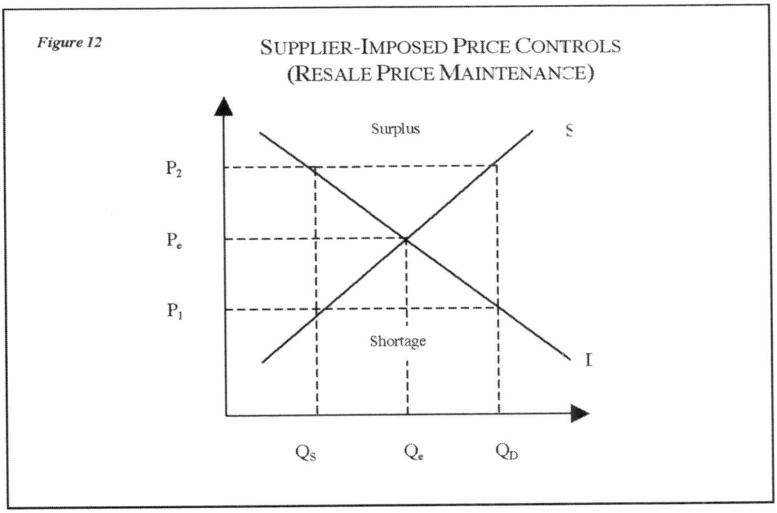

Figure 1.12

Since 1911 and until recently, minimum resale price maintenance has been held to be a per se violation of Section 1 of the Sherman Act.[141] In *Dr. Miles Medical Co. v. John D. Park & Sons,*[142] the Dr. Miles Medical Company required firms distributing its products to enter into restrictive agreements establishing minimum resale prices for the products.[143] The defendant, John D. Park, refused to enter into any such restrictive agreement, especially since he could purchase Dr. Miles' products from other wholesalers at discounted prices.[144] Dr. Miles initiated a lawsuit seeking to restrain Park from inducing Dr. Miles' distributors to break their contracts with Dr. Miles, which obligated them not to sell D. Miles' goods below a certain price.[145] The Supreme Court affirmed the lower court's dismissal of Dr. Miles' claim, holding that "agreements or combinations between dealers, having for their sole purpose the destruction of competition and the fixing of prices, are injurious to the public interest and void."[146]

In support of its opinion, the Court reiterated English Common law:

> 'The true view at the present time,' said Lord Macnaghten in Nordenfelt v. Maxim Nordenfelt Guns & Ammunition Co. [1894] A.C. p. 565, 6 Engl. Rul. Cas. 413, 'I think, is this: The public have an interest in every person's carrying on his trade freely: so has the individual. All interference with individual liberty of action in trading, and all restraints of trade of themselves, if there is nothing more, are contrary to public policy, and therefore void.'[147]

Lord Macnaghten's observation (ultimately shared by the Supreme Court in *Dr. Miles*) that "[a]ll interference [in] individual liberty of action in trading... [is] contrary to public policy" echoes the import of this last assumption (or condition) of the perfectly competitive model.[148] Any and all interferences with the autonomous forces of supply and demand are contrary to the public policy because ultimately they are injurious to competition.

Although the U.S. Supreme Court recently reversed its long-standing practice of judging resale price maintenance practices as being *per se* unlawful,[149] such practices are nonetheless extremely suspect from an economic perspective in that they threaten and/or obstruct one of the operational conditions of the perfectly competitive model, i.e., all market participants are price-takers.

1.4 An Analytical Paradigm

To understand what constitutes an antitrust injury, or rather an injury to competition, one must understand the core features of competition. The perfectly competitive model explains the core features of competition. Competition thrives only in an environment in which its underlying assumptions or conditions are satisfied. Conduct that threatens, jeopardizes, and ultimately impairs any of the model's assumptions or conditions is injurious to the model. The magnitude of the injury is relative to the magnitude of the impairment or obstruction. In its purest form, any impairment or obstruction is injurious to competition. While jurisprudential economics seems to relate *injury to competition* to market activity that results in a "curtailing of output and higher prices," theoretical economics illustrate that *injury to competition* relates to a much broader spectrum of market activities, all of which have the effect of constraining the underlying operational conditions of the perfectly competitive model.

A thorough understanding of the model's operational conditions is thus necessary for one to analyze and identity competitive injury. Such an understanding simplifies the analysis. Searching for judicial precedence that might identify injury by analogy is cumbersome, imprecise, and often requires an act of jurisprudential contortion of conventional economic theory.

The perfectly competitive model's underlying assumptions (or conditions) constitute the model's nervous system. An attack on the model's nervous system results in injury. As Figure 1.13 suggests, certain market activities may attack only one assumption (or condition), while others may attack multiple assumptions (or conditions). Conduct that obstructs multiple assumptions (or conditions) compounds the injury. The more assumptions (or conditions) threatened, jeopardized, or impaired by certain conduct, the greater the magnitude of injury. Consequently, when analyzing whether certain conduct is injurious to competition, the analysis must start with microeconomics' model of perfect competition, and not jurisprudential precedent.

As Figure 1.14 indicates, systematic campaigns for market share involving conduct that impairs or obstructs several of the perfectly competitive model's operational conditions can be expected to compound and aggravate the *injurious effect* of such conduct. For example, catastrophic antitrust injury (that is, injury to competition) would result from an oligopolistic wholesaler engaged in a multitude of anticompetitive acts, such as a horizontal limit price fixing scheme, a product disparagement campaign supported by a horizontal territorial market division agreement, and a resale dealer price maintenance program. Thus, the more assumptions or conditions impacted by market conduct, the greater the injury.

Figure 13

Injurious Conduct and its Potential Relationship to the
Underlying Assumptions (or Antecendent Conditions) of Pefect Competition Model.

Conduct	Numerous buyers and sellers	Rationality	Independence	Price taker	No barriers to entry or exit	Full Information	Unrestricted Forces of Supply and Demand
Product Disparagement		√			√	√	√
Monopoly	√			√	√		√
Duopoly	√		√	√	√		√
Oligopoly	√		√	√	√		√
Price Fixing			√	√	√		√
Output Agreements							√
Boycott			√	√	√		√
Information Exchanges			√	√			√
Territorial Allocations	√		√	√	√		√
Exclusive Dealing	√		√		√		√
Predatory Pricing		√		√	√		√
Resale Price Maintenance			√	√			√
Tying	√		√	√	√		√

Figure 1.13

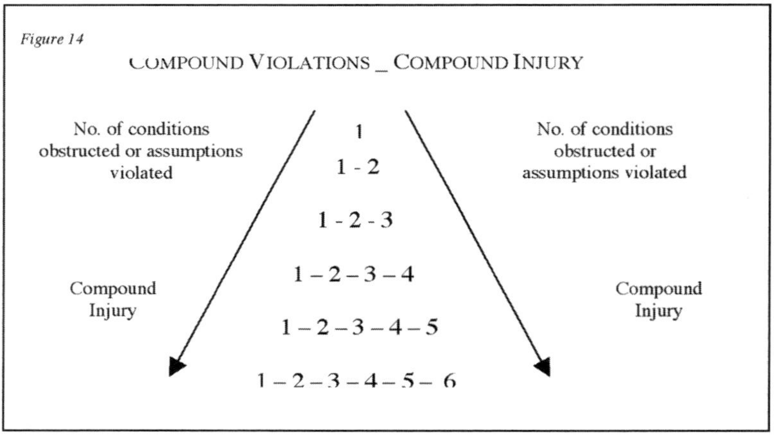

Figure 1.14

1.5 Conclusion

It has long been settled that one of the goals of the antitrust laws is to nurture, foster, and cultivate a socio-economic environment within which competition will thrive. The requirement that a plaintiff establish an "antitrust injury" increases the likelihood that the public and private enforcement of the antitrust laws will further such a goal, especially since "antitrust injury" is regarded to be synonymous with "injury to competition." In order to discern whether there exists an "injury to competition," one must understand what is meant by the term "competition." To understand "competition," one must look to the field of microeconomics and its economic model of perfect competition.

The term "antitrust injury" means an action that impairs the operational conditions of the perfectly competitive model that may ultimately lead to the curtailment of output and higher prices. The perfectly competitive model's operational conditions essentially constitutes the "central nervous system" of the competitive market place.[150] Conduct, therefore, that attacks and vitiates any of the model's underlying conditions (or assumptions) poses an actual threat to the central nervous system of the economy. It is from this perspective that this chapter proffers an analytical framework from which to assess and analyze conduct that will likely result in an injury to competition. When assessing and analyzing the existence of "antitrust injury," the jurist or analyst is instructed to refer first to the theoretical constructs of microeconomics, rather than common law precedent. Such a first step is free from the institutional prejudices of stare decisis. More importantly, such a first step simplifies the initial analysis with respect to the determination of an "antitrust injury."

This chapter is not intended to suggest that the above proposed analytical framework will ferret out all market activity that should be proscribed as a matter of law. Moreover, this chapter does not attempt to identify each and every market activity that might perceivably threaten or impair one or more of the operational conditions of the perfectly competitive model. Such practices as predatory pricing, tying, the artificial raising of a rival's costs, as well as several other practices that might clearly threaten several of the underlying operational conditions of the model were not discussed. To consider each and every potential act that might result in antitrust injury is beyond the scope of this chapter. Rather, this chapter specifically addresses the substantive meaning of "antitrust injury," one element of a prima facie antitrust claim under the Sherman, Clayton, and Federal Trade Commission Acts. The substantive meaning of such a term is best explained by the fundamental tenets of microeconomics, and thus the determination of "antitrust injury" should proceed first and foremost from a purely microeconomic perspective.

Endnotes

1. PHILLIP E. AREEDA & HERBERT HOVENKAMP, FUNDAMENTALS OF ANTITRUST LAW § 3.03(b), at 3-31 (3d ed. 2006).

2. HERBERT HOVENKAMP, FEDERAL ANTITRUST POLICY: THE LAW OF COMPETITION AND ITS PRACTICE 605 (3d ed. 2005).

3. *Brunswick Corp. v. Pueblo Bowl-O-Mat, Inc.*, 429 U.S. 477, 489 (1977).

4. W. KIP VISCUSI, JOSEPH E. HARRINGTON, JR., & JOHN M. VERNON, ECONOMICS OF REGULATION AND ANTITRUST 70 (4th ed. 2005).

5. *Healow v. Anesthesia Partners*, 92 F.3d 1192 (9th Cir. 1996)(unpublished table decision)(holding anesthesiologist had no antitrust injury... because the underlying market structure did not support any inference of "*injury to competition*" (emphasis added)).

6. *Sanderson v. Culligan, Int'l Co.*, 415 F.3d 620, 623 (7th Cir. 2005); *see* also *NCAA v. Univ. of Okla.*, 468 U.S. 85, 103-07 (1984); *Broadcast Music, Inc. v. CBS, Inc.*, 441 U.S. 1, 19-20 (1979); William H. Page, *The Chicago School and the Evolution of Antitrust; Characterization, Antitrust Injury, and Evidentiary Sufficiency,* 75 VA. L. REV. 1221, 1268-73 & 1308 n.253 (1989).

7. 429 U.S. 477 (1977)

8. *Id.* at 491.

9. *Id.* at 488.

10. *Id.* (emphasis added) (quoting *Brown Shoe Co. v. United States*, 370 U.S. 294, 320 (1962)). "Taken as a whole, the legislative history illuminates congressional concern with the protection of *competition,* not *competitors*, and its desire to restrain mergers only to the extent that such combinations may tend to lessen competition." *Brown Shoe,* 370 U.S. at 320.

11. 1 AREEDA & HOVENKAMP, *supra* note 1, § 3.03(a), at 3-28 ("Although *Brunswick* christened this requirement 'antitrust injury,' the concept is older. It is reflected in criticism of the lower court decision in *Brunswick* itself, as well as in some applications of the 'target area' test for standing."); *see also* Kevin. S. Marshall, *Product Disparagement Under the Sherman Act, Its Nurturing and Injurious Effects to Competition, and the Tension Between*

Jurisprudential Economics and Microeconomics, 46 SANTA CLARA L. REV. 231, 233 & n.13 (2006).

12. *Brunswick*, 429 U.S. at 489.

13. *Id.* at 479.

14. *Id.*

15. *Id.*

16. *Id.* at 480.

17. *Id.* at 479-80. "During the seven years preceding the trial in this case, [Brunswick] acquired 222 centers, 54 of which it either disposed of or closed. These acquisitions made [Brunswick] by far the largest operator of bowling centers, with over five times as many centers as its next largest competitor. [Brunswick's] net worth in 1965 was more than eight times greater... than the total for the 11 next largest bowling chains. Nevertheless, [Brunswick] controlled only 2% of the bowling centers in the United States. *Id.* at 480.

18. *Id.* at 480; *see also* Clayton Act § 7, 15 U.S.C. § 18 (2000).

19. Clayton Act § 4, 15 U.S.C. § 15 (2000).

20. *Brunswick*, 429 U.S. at 480-81. It merits noting that the plaintiffs also sought a divesture order, injunction, and "such 'other further and different relief' as might be appropriate under § 16 of the Act." *Id.* at 481.

21. *Id.*

22. It is conceivable that the acquisition and continued operation of each of the bowling centers might result in an injury to competition to the extent that Brunswick operated such centers at a loss. Such conduct would be irrational in the short run in that it was not a profit-maximizing act. However, in the long run it would be predatory to the extent it would likely result in driving other competitors out of the market.

23. 429 U.S. 104, 109 (1986). Subsequent to the Court's decision in *Brunswick* and prior to its decision in *Cargill*, the Court confirmed the importance of showing antitrust injury under section 4 of the Clayton Act. In *Blue Shield of Virginia v. McCready,* 457 U.S. 465 (1982), the Court found that "a health-plan subscriber suffered antitrust injury as a result of the plan's 'purpose-

fully *anticompetitive scheme*' to reduce competition for psychotherapeutic services by reimbursing subscribers for services provided by psychiatrists but not for services provided by psychologists." *Cargill,* 479 U.S. at 110 (quoting *Blue Shield,* 457 U.S. at 483 (1982)). The Court further noted that antitrust injury "as analyzed in *Brunswick*, is one factor to be considered in determining the redressability of a particular form of injury under § 4." *Blue Shield,* 457 U.S. at 489 n.19. Similarly, in *Associated General Contractors of California, Inc. v. California State Council of Carpenters,* the Court applied "the *Brunswick* test" and held that the petitioner had failed to allege such an injury. 459 U.S. 519, 540 (1983).

24. *Cargill, Inc.,* 469 U.S. at 122.

25. *Id.* at 106-07.

26. *Id.* at 114-15.

27. *Id.*

28. *Id.* at 115. *See also id.* at 115 n. 10 ("In this case, Monfort has conceded that its viability would not be threatened by Excel's decision to lower prices: 'Because Monfort's operations were as efficient as those of Excel, only below-cost pricing would remove Monfort as an obstacle.'")

29. *Id.* at 115.

30. *Id.*

31. *Id.* at 116 (quoting *Arthur S. Langenderfer, Inc. v. S.E. Johnson Co.,* 792 F.2d 1050, 1057 (6th Cir. 1984)).

32. 1 AREEDA & HOVENKAMP, *supra* note 1, § 3.03(a), at 3-24 to 3-26.

33. *Brunswick Corp. v. Pueblo Bowl-O-Mat, Inc.,* 429 U.S. 477, 489 (1977).

34. *Cargill,* 479 U.S. at 113 (quoting *Brunswick,* 429 U.S. at 489).

35. *Brunswick,* 429 U.S. at 488 (quoting *Brown Shoe Co. v. United States,* 370 U.S. 294, 320 (1962)); *see also supra* note 10.

36. *Id.* at 489; *see also supra* note 12.

37. *See generally* Marshall, *supra* note 11 (introducing the perfectly competitive model as a paradigm for identifying conduct injurious to competition for the limited purpose of analyzing the (anti)competitive effects of disparagement practices and whether such practices may constitute a violation of the Sherman Antitrust Act).

38. Sherman Antitrust Act, 15 U.S.C. §§ 1,2 (emphasis added).

39. Federal Trade Commission Act, 15 U.S.C. § 45 (emphasis added).

40. 1 AREEDA & HOVENKAMP, *supra* note 1, § 3.03(a), at 3-31.

41. *See* Marshall, *supra* note 11, at 235-36.

42. *See* DAVID C. COLANDER, MICROECONOMICS 242 (5th ed. 2004) (outlining the "necessary conditions for perfect competition" to thrive).

43. *See* Marshall, *supra* note 11, at 236-37.

44. *See* ROBERT S. PINDYCK & DANIEL L. RUBINFELD, MICROECONOMICS 327 (5th ed. 2001) ("In a perfectly competitive market, the large number of sellers and buyers of a good ensures that no single seller or buyer can affect its price. The market forces of supply and demand determine price.") EDWIN MANSFIELD & GARY YOHE, MICROECONOMICS: THEORY/APPLICATION 356-57 (11th ed. 2004) ("The firm in a perfectly competitive market has so many rivals that competition becomes impersonal in the extreme…A competitive firm faces so little of the market demand that its effective demand curve is horizontal at whatever price the market will bear. A competitive firm can decide only the output that it would like to supply to the market given that price.")

45. *See* PINDYCK & RUBINFELD, *supra* note 44, at 430 ("In [competitive] markets, each firm could take price or market demand as given and largely ignore its competitors. In an oligopolistic market, however, a firm sets price or output based partly on strategic considerations regarding the behavior of its competitors."); MANSFIELD & YOHE, *supra* note 44, at 426, 433-34 ("Unlike the case of…competition, the supply side of an oligopoly market is composed of a few firms. Conditions in oligopolistic industries tend to promote collusion, since the number of firms is small and the firms recognize their interdependence. The advantages to the firms of collusion seem obvious; increased profits, decreased uncertainty, and a better opportunity to prevent others' entry.")

46. STEVEN E. LANDSBURG, PRICE THEORY & APPLICATIONS 634 (6th ed. 2005) ("[T]he economist assumes that people are *rational*."); *see also infra* note 64 (discussing rational choice as an equimarginal principle).

47. *See* PINDYCK & RUBINFELD, *supra* note 44, at 252 ("Because *each individual firm sells a sufficiently small proportion of total market output, its decisions have no impact on market price*...The assumption of price taking applies to *consumers* as well as firms."); MANSFIELD & YOHE, *supra* note 44, at 290 ("[P]erfect competition requires that each *participant in the market, whether a buyer or a seller, be so small in relation to the entire market that he or she cannot affect the product's price.*")

48. *See* PINDYCK & RUBINFELD, *supra* note 44, at 253 ("[F]ree entry (exit) means that there are no special costs that make it difficult for a new firm either to enter an industry and produce or to exit if it cannot make a profit. *As a result, buyers can easily switch from one supplier to another, and suppliers can easily enter or exit a market.*"); MANSFIELD & YOHE, *supra* note 44, at 290 ("Perfect competition also requires that *all resources be completely mobile*. Each resource must, in other words, be able to enter or leave the market with ease and to switch from one use to another without fuss or bother.")

49. *See* PINDYCK & RUBINFELD, *supra* note 44, at 595 ("[W]e have assumed that consumers and producers have complete information about the economic variables that are relevant for the choices they face."); MANSFIELD & YOHE, *supra* note 44, at 290-91 ("[P]erfect competition requires that consumers, firms, and resource owners have *perfect knowledge of the relevant economic and technological data*. Consumers must be aware of all prices. Laborers and owners of capital must be aware of how much their resources will bring in all possible uses. Firms must know prices of all inputs and the characteristics of all relevant technologies. And in its purest sense, perfect competition requires that all of these economic decision-making units have an accurate knowledge o the past, the present, *and the future*.")

50. *See* PINDYCK & RUBINFELD, *supra* note 44, at 252-53 ("Price-taking behavior typically occurs in markets where firms produce identical, or nearly identical, products. When *the products of all of the firms are perfectly substitutable with one another* – that is, when they are *homogeneous* – no firm can raise the price of its product above the price of other firms without losing most or all of its business.") MANSFIELD & YOHE, *supra* note 44, at 405 (stating that, in perfectly competitive situations, "[t]here are a large number of firms producing and selling...goods that are...completely homogeneous.")

51. *See* PINDYCK & RUBINFELD, *supra* note 44, at 55 ("The market mechanism is the tendency for supply and demand to equilibrate i.e., for price to move to the market-clearing level, so that there is neither excess demand nor excess supply."); MANSFIELD & YOHE, *supra* note 44, at 347-48 ("We have seen that a perfectly competitive economy maximizes the total net gain of consumers and producers. We then showed... how deadweight losses – reductions in economic efficiency – result if the government [obstructs the forces of supply and demand by imposing a price ceiling[,]...a price floor[,]...a tariff, a quota, or an excise tax." *see also* Marshall, *supra* note 11, at 236-37.

52. Marshall, *supra* note 11, at 237-38.

53. *Id.* at 238.

54. *Id.*

55. *Id.* (emphasis added).

56. *Id.*; *see also* COLANDER, *supra* note 42, at 4-5.

57. Marshall, *supra* note 11, at 238; *see also* COLANDER, *supra* note 42, at 4-5.

58. Marshall, *supra* note 11, at 238.

59. *See* VISCUSI ET AL., *supra* note 4, at 80 ("The individual firms' supply curves are their marginal cost curves; hence we can think of the supply curve [above] as the industry's marginal cost curve."); PINDYCK & RUBINFELD, *supra* note 44, at 263 ("[T]he firm's supply curve is *the portion of its marginal cost curve that lies above the average economic cost curve*."); COLANDER, *supra* note 42, at 247 fig. 11-3 ("Since the marginal cost curve tells the firm how much to produce, the marginal cost curve is the perfectly competitive firm's supply curve.")

60. VISCUSI ET AL., *supra* note 4, at 80 ("The competitive industry's supply curve is found by horizontal aggregation of the supply curves of individual firms."); *see also,* PINDYCK & RUBINFELD, *supra* note 44, at 283 ("The short-run...supply curve is the horizontal summation of the supply curves of the firms in an industry."); COLANDER, *supra* note 42, at 254 ("In the short run when the number of firms in the market is fixed, the market supply curve is just the *horizontal sum of all the firms' marginal cost curves, taking account of any changes in input prices that might occur*.")

61. VISCUSI ET AL., *supra* note 4, at 81.

62. *Id.*

63. *Id.* at 70.

64. Marshall, *supra* note 11, at 238; *see also* COLANDER, *supra* note 42, at 242 ("[F]irms are profit-maximizing entrepreneurial firms...."); *Id.* at 181 ("The analysis of rational choice is the analysis of how individuals choose goods within their budget in order to maximize total utility, and how maximizing total utility can be accomplished by considering marginal utility. That analysis begins with the premise that rational individuals want as much satisfaction as they can get from their available resources. The term *rational* in economics means, specifically, that people prefer more to less and will make choices that give them as much satisfaction as possible."); LANDSBURG, *supra* note 46, at 634 ("The economist assumes that people act according to the principle of equimarginality. This is often expressed by saying that the economist assumes that people are *rational*. Indeed, it has been said that a student becomes a true economist on the day when he fully understands and accepts the principle that people equate costs and benefits at the margin."); MANSFIELD & YOHE, *supra* note 44, at 44 (stating that given the consumer's tastes, it is assumed that he or she is rational in the sense that he or she tries to *maximize utility*); STEPHEN A. MATHIS & JANET KOSCIANSKI, MICROECONOMIC THEORY: AN INTEGRATED APPROACH 2 (2002) ("[M]aking rational choices is a matter of choosing the amount(s) of some decision, or independent, variable(s) such that the extra benefit received from the last unit chosen is just equal to its extra cost. In economics, the process of measuring and comparing the extra benefits and extra costs associated with a rational decision is known as marginal analysis."); PINDYCK & RUBINFELD, *supra* note 44, at 254 ("The assumption of *profit maximization* is frequently used in microeconomics because it predicts business behavior reasonably accurately and avoids unnecessary analytical complications.")

65. Marshall, *supra* note 11, at 239; *see also* ANTHONY E. BOARDMAN ET AL., COST-BENEFIT ANALYSIS: CONCEPTS AND PRACTICE 30 (3d ed. 2006) ("Choose the combination of [goods and/or inputs] that maximizes net benefits.")

66. Marshall, *supra* note 11, at 239; *see also* MANSFIELD & YOHE, *supra* note 44, at 675 ("[P]roducers act in ways that cause harm to others without paying the full cost of the damage. In these and other, similar cases, the pursuit of private gain will not necessarily promote the social welfare.")

67. *See* PINDYCK & RUBINFELD, *supra* note 44, at 595 ("[W]e have assumed that consumers and producers have complete information about the economic variables that are relevant for the choices they face.")

68. Marshall, *supra* note 11, at 240.

69. *Id.* at 241. *See generally* Marshall, *supra* note 11, at 231-54 (discussing in depth the anticompetitive effect of a firm engaging in the intentional disparagement of a competitor and/or its products).

70. *Id.* at 241; *see also* MARK HIRSCHEY, MANAGERIAL ECONOMICS 67-68 (10th ed. 2003) (stating a demand function may be expressed in functional form as $Q_{x\text{-demanded}} = f(P_{good}, P_{comp/subst}, I_{ncome}, \#\ buyers, T_{astes}, E_{xpectations}, X_i \ldots X_n)$)

71. Price distortion will necessarily result from the consumer's under-evaluation of the benefits provided by the product, or from the over-evaluation of the costs associated with the product.

72. Marshall, *supra* note 11, at 242. In this illustration, and the illustrations that follow in this subsection, the disparagement conduct is exhibited in a highly competitive monopolistic market characterized by product differentiation. *See* PINDYCK & RUBINFELD, *supra* note 44, at 424 ("A monopolistically competitive market has two key characteristics: 1)Firms compete by selling differentiated products that are highly substitutable for one another but not perfect substitutes…2) There is *free entry and exit*" it is relatively easy for new firms to enter the market with their own brands and for existing firms to leave if their products become unprofitable.")

73. *See* Marshall, *supra* note 11, at 242.

74. *Id.*

75. *Id.* at 244.

76. *Id.*

77. *Sanderson v. Culligan, Int'l Co.,* 415 F.3d. 620, 623 (7th Cir. 2005).

78. *Id.* at 245; *see also* HIRSCHEY, *supra* note 70, at 74 (stating a supply function can be expressed in functional form as: $Q_{x\text{-supplied}} = f(P_x, P_{related\ goods}, \#\ suppliers, P_{inputs}, T_{echnology}, E_{xpectations}, X_i \ldots X_n)$).

79. *See* COLANDER, *supra* note 42, at 272 (defining deadweight loss as "the net cost to society from the existence of monopoly").

80. Marshall, *supra* note 11, at 245.

81. *Id.* at 243.

82. *Id.*

83. *See supra* text accompanying notes 44-46.

84. *See supra* text accompanying notes 47.

85. *See supra* note 47 and accompanying text.

86. PINDYCK & RUBINFELD, *supra* note 44, at 327.

87. *See* LANDSBURG, *supra* note 46 at 329 ("Market power [is the] ability of a firm to affect market prices through its actions.")

88. *See* ABA SECTION OF ANTITRUST LAW, MARKET POWER HANDBOOK 2 (2005); *see also* U.S. Dep't of Justice Merger Guidelines, 49 Fed. Reg. 26,823 (June 29, 1984), *reprinted in* 4 Trade Reg. Rep. (CCH) ¶ 13,103 (defining market power as "[the] ability of one or more firms profitably to maintain prices above competitive levels for a significant period of time"). Although the 1984 guidelines were superseded in 1992, the new guidelines continue to acknowledge this basic principle. *See* U.S. Dep't of Justice & Federal Trade Comm'n, Horizontal Merger Guidelines, 57 Fed. Reg. 41,552 (Apr. 2, 1992), *reprinted in* 4 Trade Reg. Rep. (CCH) ¶ 13,104.

89. *See* COLANDER, *supra* note 42, at 132-33 ("The most commonly used elasticity concept is price elasticity of demand and supply. Price elasticity of demand is *the percentage change in quantity demanded divided by the percentage change in price*..."). The horizontal demand curve depicted in the referenced diagram [Figure 1.5] demonstrates that a change in price above or below P^c results in an infinitely large increase in quantity demanded. *See id.* at 137 ("This curve is perfectly elastic, reflecting the fact that *quantity responds enormously to changes in price* ($\varepsilon = \infty$).")

90. *See id.* at 245-46 ("Since profit is the difference between total revenue and total cost, what happens to profit in response to a change in output is determined by marginal revenue (MR), *the changes in total revenue associated with a change in quantity*.... Since a perfect competitor accepts the market price as given, marginal revenue is simply the market price.")

91. *See id.* at 211 ("Marginal cost is *the increase (decrease) in total cost from increasing (or decreasing) the level of output by one unit.*")

92. *See id.* at 246 ("[T]o maximize profit, a firm should produce where marginal cost equals marginal revenue.")

93. At any point to the right of Q_f, $mr_f > mc_f$. A rational producer, therefore, will produce and sell additional units until it reaches Q_f, where $mr_f = mc_f$.

94. At any point to the left of Q_f, $mr_f < mc_f$. In other words, the marginal costs exceed the marginal revenue for a quantity in excess of Q_f.

95. *See* COLANDER, *supra* note 42, at 247 ("Because the marginal cost curve tells us how much of a produced good a firm will supply at a given price, *the marginal cost curve is the firm's supply curve*.").

96. The market supply curve is derived by summing all of the individual supply curves of the sellers competing in the market. Since the firm's supply curve is essentially its marginal revenue curve, the market supply curve is derived by horizontally summing all of the seller's marginal revenue curves ($Sm = \sum mc_{\text{ith firms}}$).

97. PINDYCK & RUBINFELD, *supra* note 44, at 327. Although this Article will not address monopsony, it merits noting nonetheless. Monopsony is a "market with many sellers [and] only one buyer." *Id.* Monopsony is closely related to monopoly and its existence similarly results in injury to competition. *Id.*; *see also* COLANDER, *supra* note 42, at 264 ("Monopoly is a *market structure in which one firm makes up the entire market*."); MANSFIELD & YOHE, *supra* note 44, at 356 ("A monopoly exists whenever there is a single source of supply.")

98. PINDYCK & RUBINFELD, *supra* note 44, at 327; *see also* COLANDER, *supra* note 42, at 267-68 ("Since the demand curve tells us what consumers will pay for a given quantity, to find the price a monopolist will charge you must extend the quantity line up to the demand curve."); MANSFIELD & YOHE, *supra* note 44, at 364-65 ("The demand curve shows that the market would bear a price of *P* if *Q* units of output were delivered to its customers, and so it should charge *P* per unit.")

99. *See supra* notes 59, 60, 96, and accompanying text. Remember that the market supply curve is derived from the horizontal summation of all the individual supply curves in the market. Further, recall that a firm's individual supply curve is essentially its marginal cost curve. In monopoly, the horizontal summation of all the individual marginal cost curves consists of identifying the single marginal cost curve of the monopolist. Thus the market supply curve

in monopoly is the monopolist's marginal cost curve. *See* COLANDER, *supra* note 42, at 267-68; MANSFIELD & YOHE, *supra* note 44, at 360-66; PINDYCK & RUBINFELD, *supra* note 44, at 329-333.

100. *See* ABA SECTION OF ANTITRUST LAW, MARKET POWER HANDBOOK 2 (2005); COLANDER, *supra* note 42, at 268-69; HIRSCHEY, *supra* note 70, at 378-93; LANDSBURG, *supra* note 46, at 336; MATHIS & KOSCIANSKI, *supra* note 64 at 383-407; WALTER NICHOLSON, MICROECONOMIC THEORY: BASIC PRINCIPLES AND EXTENSIONS 385-94 (9th ed. 2005); PINDYCK & RUBINFELD, *supra* note 44, at 347-48; VISCUSI ET AL., *supra* note 4, at 295; MICHAEL E. WETZSTEIN, MICROECONOMIC THEORY: CONCEPTS & CONNECTIONS 372-88 (2005).

101. *See* George J. Stigler, *A Theory of Oligopoly,* 721 J. POL. ECON. 44 (1964), *reprinted in* GEORGE J. STIGLER, THE ORGANIZATION OF INDUSTRY 39 (1968); *see also* Gregory J. Werden, *Economic Evidence on the Existence of Collusion: Reconciling Antitrust Law with Oligopoly Theory*, 71 ANTITRUST L.J. 719, 728 (2004) (explaining that one implication of Stigler's oligopoly model is "that collusion is more likely to be sustainable the smaller the number of competitors.")

102. COLANDER, *supra* note 42, at 294 (emphasis added); *see also* HIRSCHEY, *supra* note 70, at 428-29; MATHIS & KOSCIANSKI, *supra* note 64 at 444-45; PINDYCK & RUBINFELD, *supra* note 44, at 429-30; PAUL A. SAMUELSON & WILLIAM D. NORDHAUS, ECONOMICS 185-87 (17th ed. 2001); VISCUSI ET AL., *supra* note 4, at 106; WETZSTEIN, *supra* note 100, at 481.

103. MATHIS & KOSCIANSKI, *supra* note 64 at 445 (emphasis added); *see also* COLANDER, *supra* note 42, at 329 ("[A] *cartel*... is a combination of firms in which the firms haven't actually merged but nonetheless act essentially as a single entity."); MANSFIELD & YOHE, *supra* note 44, at 434; ("Open and formal collusive arrangements are called cartels."); PINDYCK & RUBINFELD, *supra* note 44, at 451 ("Producers in a *cartel* explicitly agree to cooperate in setting prices and output levels.")

104. COLANDER, *supra* note 42, at 294.

105. NICHOLSON, *supra* note 100, at 417.

106. *Id.* at 417 fig. 14.1.

107. *See United States v. Trenton Potteries Co.,* 273 U.S. 392 (1926).

108. 273 U.S. 392 (1926).

109. *Id.* at 397-98.

110. 310 U.S. 150 (1940).

111. *Id.* at 218.

112. 493 U.S. 411 (1990).

113. *Id.* at 435 (quoting *Socony-Vacuum Oil*, 310 U.S. at 224 n.59); *see also Arizona v. Maricopa County Med. Soc'y*, 457 U.S. 332, 351 & n23 (1982); 7 PHILLIP E. AREEDA & HERBERT HOVENKAMP, ANTITRUST LAW ¶ 1509, at 400-01 (2d ed. 2003) ("In sum, price-fixing cartels are condemned per se because the conduct is tempting to businesspersons but very dangerous to society. The conceivable social benefits are few in principle, small in magnitude, speculative in occurrence, and always premised on the existence of price-fixing power that is likely to be exercised adversely to the public. Moreover, toleration implies a burden of continuous supervision for which the courts consider themselves ill-suited. And even if power is usually established while any defenses are not, litigation will be complicated, condemnation delayed, would-be price fixers encouraged to hope for escape, and criminal punishment less delayed, would-be price fixers encouraged to hope for escape, and criminal punishment less justified. Deterrence of a generally pernicious practice would be weakened. The key points are the first two. Without them, there is no justification for categorical condemnation.")

114. *See* 1 AREEDA & HOVENKAMP, *supra* note 1, § 22.02 n.1 (Supp. 2006) (citing *e.g.*, *Maricopa County Med. Soc'y*, 457 U.S. at 344 n.15 (stating in dicta: boycotts "unlawful…of themselves"); *Federal Maritime Comm'n v. Aktiebolaget Svenska Amerika Linien*, 390 U.S. 238, 250 (1968) (stating in dicta: "any agreement by a group of competitors to boycott a particular buyer or group of buyers is illegal per se"); *United States v. Sealy*, 388 U.S. 350, 358 n.5 (1967) (group boycotts illegal per se); *United States v. General Motors Corp.*, 384 U.S. 127, 146 (1966) (stating agreement among automobile dealers persuading GM to refuse to sell cars to discounting dealers unlawful per se: "where businessmen concert their actions in order to deprive others of access to merchandise which the latter wish to sell to the public, we need not inquire into the economic motivation underlying their conduct"); *Silver v. NYSE*, 373 U.S. 341, 347 (1963) (stating "group boycott" is illegal per se); *Radian Burners, Inc. v. Peoples Gas Light & Coke Co.* 364 U.S. 656, 659 (1961) (stating allegations of antitrust competitive standard-setting process stated claim for per se unlawful concerted refusal); *N. Pac.*

Rwy. Co. v. United States, 356 U.S. 1, 5 (1958) (stating in dicta that group boycotts are unlawful per se); *Com-Tel, Inc. v. Dukane Corp.*, 669 F.2d 404, 408 (6th Cir. 1982) ("Group boycotts fall within one of the forbidden per se categories."); *Williams v. St. Joseph Hosp.*, 629 F.2d 448, 452 (7th Cir. 1980) (stating group boycotts are "unlawful in and of themselves"); *Webb v. Utah Tour Brokers Ass'n.*, 568 F.2d 670, 675 (10th Cir. 1977) (stating boycott of established tour brokers against new entrant unlawful per se); *Yoder Bros., Inc. v. California-Florida Plant Corp.*, 537 F.2d 1347, 1366 (5th Cir. 1976) (stating chrysanthemum grower's patent licensing arrangements designed to sustain monopoly of all future variations amounted to per se unlawful group boycott).

115. *See* 1 AREEDA & HOVENKAMP, *supra* note 1, § 22.07a n.1 (Supp. 2005) (citing *Palmer v. BRG of Ga.*, 498 U.S. 46 (1990) (per curiam)); *see also United States v. Brown*, 936 F.2d 1042, 1045 (9th Cir. 1991) (affirming conviction after rivals divided markets for billboard sites and agreed not to compete for one another's sites); *United States v. Suntar Roofing, Inc.*, 897 F.2d 469, 473 (10th Cir. 1990) (affirming conviction upon unlawful per se horizontal customer allocation among roofers); *United States. V. Coop. Theatres of Ohio, Inc.*, 845 F.2d 1367, 1373 (6th Cir. 1988) (holding motion picture "split" was illegal per se); *Affiliated Capital Corp. v. City of Houston*, 700 F.2d 226, 236 (5th Cir. 1983) (holding agreement among municipal cable television companies dividing the city into geographic regions unlawful per se), *rev'd en banc on other grounds*, 735 F.2d 1555 (5th Cir. 1984); *United States v. Capitol Serv., Inc.*, 756 F.2d 502, 507 (7th Cir. 1985) (holding motion picture split agreement unlawful per se); *Serv. Merch. Co., Inc. v. Boyd Corp.*, 722 F.2d 945, 950 (1st Cir. 1983)(holding agreement among distribution of microwave ovens diving their territories was per se unlawful); *Engine Specialties, Inc. v. Bombardier Ltd.*, 605 F.2d 1, 7-11 (1st Cir. 1979) (holding market division agreement between manufacturer of minicycles and potential entrant per se unlawful); *Gainesville Utils. Dep't v. Fla. Power & Light Co.*, 573 F.2d 292, 300 (5th Cir. 1978) (holding geographic market division between two utilities covering wholesale power unlawful per se); *United States v. Consol. Laundries Corp.*, 291 F.2d 563, 574 (2d Cir. 1961) (holding horizontal customer allocation scheme among linen supply companies per se unlawful); *Bascom Food Prods. Corp. v. Reese Finer Foods, Inc.*, 715 F. Supp. 616, 630-32 (D.N.J. 1989) (holding market arrangement unlawful notwithstanding some doubt about whether the arrangement was actually horizontal).

116. *See e.g., Am. Column & Lumber Co. v. United States,* 257 U.S. 377, 411-12 (1921) (striking down a trade association program which mandated compliance with several restrictive requirements, including immediate report-

ing of price changes and the filing of daily reports on sales, production and purchases); *Sugar Inst. v. United States,* 297 U.S. 553, 581 (1936) (holding that it was an antitrust violation for the trade association members to refrain from changing an announced price through a secret price concession); *United States v. Container Corp. of America,* 393 U.S. 333, 336-37 (1969) (holding that a reciprocal exchange of prices to stabilize prices though at a downward level had "an anticompetitive effect in the industry, chilling the vigor of price competition.")

117. COLANDER, *supra* note 42, at 242 (emphasis omitted); *see also* MANSFIELD & YOHE, *supra* note 44, at 475; ("Firms…try to discourage entrants from invading their turf.… [E]ntry of new firms into a market can reduce the profits of existing firms."); PINDYCK & RUBINFELD, *supra* note 44, at 346 ("[B]arriers to entry [are] conditions that deter entry by new competitors.")

118. VISCUSI ET AL., *supra* note 4, at 168; *see also* HOVENKAMP, *supra* note 2, § 1.6 at 39 ("[A] barrier to entry [is] 'the extent to which, in the long run, established firms can elevate their selling prices above minimal average costs of production and distribution … without inducing potential entrants to enter the industry.'" (quoting J. BAIN, INDUSTRIAL ORGANIZATION 252 (1968))).

119. HIRSCHEY, *supra* note 70, at 381.

120. PINDYCK & RUBINFELD, *supra* note 44, at 346.

121. HOVENKAMP, *supra* note 2, § 1.6 at 42.

122. *Id.*

123. *See* VISCUSI ET AL., *supra* note 4, at 181, 183 ("The price at which fringe expansion is zero is called the *limit price*.… *Limit pricing* is the use of price by established firms to deter entry.")

124. *See* 1 AREEDA & HOVENKAMP, *supra* note 1, § 7.01 (Supp. 2006); *see also* *Walker Process Equip., Inc. v. Food Machinery & Chem. Corp.,* 382 U.S. 172, 174 (1965) (holding that the "enforcement of a patent procured by fraud on the Patent Office may be violative of § 2 of the Sherman Act"); *see also* 1 AREEDA & HOVENKAMP, *supra* note 1, § 7.02 (Supp. 2006) ("Wrongfully brought infringement actions can be based on fraudulently obtained patents, and in those cases the fraud in obtaining the patent establishes the impropriety of the subsequent infringement action—one who acted fraudulently in obtaining a patent necessarily knows its patent is unenforceable. But infringement actions can also be qualifying exclusionary practices under

§ 2 when they are based on valid patents that are known by the infringement plaintiff to be unenforceable as a result of improprieties in procurement, or on valid patents but where the infringement plaintiff knew or should have known that the infringement defendant was not an infringer.")

125. 1 AREEDA & HOVENKAMP, *supra* note 1, § 18.01a (Supp. 2005).

126. *Id.*

127. *See id.*

128. *See id.*

129. *Id.* § 18.02; *see also Interface Group v. Mass. Port Auth.*, 816 F.2d 9, 11 (1st Cir. 1987) ("Exclusive dealing arrangements may *sometimes* be found unreasonable under the antitrust laws because they may place enough outlets, or sources of supply, in the hands of a single firm (or small group of firms) to make it difficult for new, potentially competing firms to penetrate the market.")

130. 1 AREEDA & HOVENKAMP, *supra* note 1, § 18.02d7 (Supp. 2005); *see also, e.g.*, Coca-Cola Co., Trade Reg. Rptr. ¶ 23,625, at 23,332 (June 13, 1994) (finding relevant market of name-brand carbonated soft drinks); MANSFIELD & YOHE, *supra* note 44, at 405.

131. *See Eastman Kodak Co. v. Image Technical Serv., Inc.*, 504 U.S. 451, 482 (1992) (holding "in some instances one brand of product can constitute a separate market"); *see also NCAA v. Bd. of Regents of the Univ. of Okla.*, 468 U.S. 85, 101-02, (1984); *Int'l Boxing Club of N.Y., Inc. v. United States*, 358 U.S. 242, 249052, (1959); *Int'l Bus. Mach. Corp. v. United States*, 298 U.S. 131 (1936).

132. *See supra* note 97.

133. *See* PINDYCK & RUBINFELD, *supra* note 44, at 423.

134. MANSFIELD & YOHE, *supra* note 44, at 405.

135. PINDYCK & RUBINFELD, *supra* note 44, at 423.

136. *Id.*

137. *See* COLANDER, *supra* note 42, at 167; *see also* LANDSBURG, *supra* note 46, at 252-55; NICHOLSON, *supra* note 100, at 320-322, 481; PINDYCK &

RUBINFELD, *supra* note 44, at 422; SAMUELSON & NORDHAUS, *supra* note 102, at 79-82.

138. Pauline M. Ippolito, *Resale Price Maintenance: Empirical Evidence from Litigation,* 34 J.L. & ECON. 263, 263 (1991).

139. *See* E. THOMAS SULLIVAN & HERBERT HOVENKAMP, ANTITRUST LAW, POLICY AND PROCEDURE: CASES, MATERIALS, AND PROBLEMS 436-39 (5th ed. Supp. 2005) (discussing the economic arguments for and against the inefficiencies of resale price maintenance practices).

140. *Id.* at 447 (noting that in *Albrecht v. Herald Co.,* 390 U.S. 145 (1968), a newspaper publisher attempted to set the maximum price at which independent carriers could sell its paper at retail; the Court held that such a combination constituted an illegal restraint of trade "when the newspaper combined with a subscription solicitor and route carrier to [coerce] the independent carrier into following the newspaper's suggested RPM").

141. *See, Dr. Miles Medical Co. v. John D. Park & Sons,* 220 U.C. 373 (1911) (holding resale price maintenance per se unlawful under the Sherman antitrust laws); *See also, Leegin Creative Leather Products v. PSKS, Inc. d.b.a. Kay's Kloset,* 2007 WL 1835892 (U.S.) (holding "*Dr. Miles* is overruled and vertical price restraints are to be judged by the rule of reason.")

142. 220 U.S. 373 (1911).

143. *Id.* at 375-376.

144. *Id.* at 381-82.

145. *Id.*

146. *Id.* at 384-85; *see also People v. Sheldon,* 34 N.E. 785 (N.Y. 1893); *Judd v. Harrington,* 34 N.E. 790 (N.Y. 1893); *People v. Milk Exch.*, 39 N.E. 1062 (N.Y. 1895); *United States v. Addyston Pipe & Steel Co.,* 85 F. 271 (6th Cir. 1898); *W.W. Montague & Co. v. Lowry,* 193 U.S. 38 (1904); *Chapin v. Brown,* 48 N.W. 1074 (Iowa 1891); *Craft v. McConoughy*, 79 Ill. 346 (Ill. 1875); *W.H. Hill Co. v. Gray & Worcester*, 127 N.W. 803 (Mich. 1910).

147. *Dr. Miles,* 220 U.S. at 406.

148. *Id.*

149. *See, Leegin Creative Leather Products v. PSKS, Inc. d.b.a Kay's Kloset*, 2007 WL 1835892(2007).

150. In *United States v. Socony Vacuum Oil Co.*, Justice Douglas explained that price fixing agreements are "all banned because of their actual or potential threat to the central nervous system of the economy." 310 U.S. 150, 224 n.23 (1940); *see also supra* note 115 and accompanying text.

Chapter 2

Antitrust Damages and Deadweight Loss

Christopher R. Leslie, M.P.P., J.D.

Synopsis

The study of economics is now part and parcel of antitrust analysis. But despite the infusion of economics into antitrust law, some core economic truths have not wound their way into antitrust doctrine. This [chapter] examines an important way in which antitrust law still ignores the core reason that economists condemn monopoly and price fixing: deadweight loss. Deadweight loss is a form of inefficiency associated with reduced output. When a monopolist—or a cartel—reduces sales in order to increase price, socially beneficial transactions do not occur. This injures both the excluded consumers and the economy more broadly as inefficient substitution takes place.

Part 2.1 [of this chapter] provides a brief overview of basic economics and the concept of deadweight loss. It explains how antitrust violations create deadweight loss. It also notes the consensus of concern about deadweight loss among antitrust scholars.

Part 2.2 discusses how antitrust law fails to consider deadweight loss in the calculation of damages. Courts in consumer antitrust suits base damages on the amount of the overcharge imposed by the antitrust defendant. This measure of damages neglects non-purchasers who have been excluded from the market altogether. Part 2.2 also explains why treble damages do not address the problem of deadweight loss.

Part 2.3 considers the ramifications of antitrust's failure to remedy deadweight loss. The primary goals of antitrust law are compensating the victims of antitrust violations and deterring future violations. Both goals are undermined by omitting deadweight loss considerations from damages calculations. Further, this omission means that antitrust violators are not held accountable for all of the injuries that they have inflicted on society and the economy.

Part 2.4 considers how to incorporate deadweight loss concerns into antitrust litigation. Two major issues must be addressed. First, is it possible to adequately measure deadweight loss? Second, who should be able to sue to recover damages based on deadweight loss? Part 2.4 answers the first question in the affirmative. It then explores possible plaintiffs, including current class action members, excluded consumers as private plaintiffs in either individual or class lawsuits, and state attorneys general suing as parens patriae. Part 2.4 argues that state attorneys general are in the best position to sue for deadweight loss damages without creating too many ancillary problems. Finally, Part 2.5 concludes that the presence of deadweight loss should counsel against efforts—which are periodically in vogue, including now—to detreble antitrust damages.

2.1 Monopolies, Cartels, and Deadweight Loss

Economic models posit two basic types of markets, competitive and monopolized. The competitive market model assumes that there are multiple sellers who compete against each other without colluding on price. In a monopolized market, one firm sets the market price, unconstrained by competition. Most product markets fall somewhere in between these two extremes on a continuum of market concentration. Despite the rarity of true monopolies and perfect competition, these constructs still help explain what occurs in many real-world markets and the consequences of diminished competition in these markets.

In a perfectly competitive market, the market clears where the marginal consumer purchases the last unit at a price equivalent to the marginal cost of producing this last unit. That price is the reservation price of the marginal consumer and will be the market price for all consumers, even those with a higher reservation price. The fact that these inframarginal consumers pay a lower price than they are willing to pay creates consumer surplus. The total consumer surplus is the area ABC in Figure 2.1.

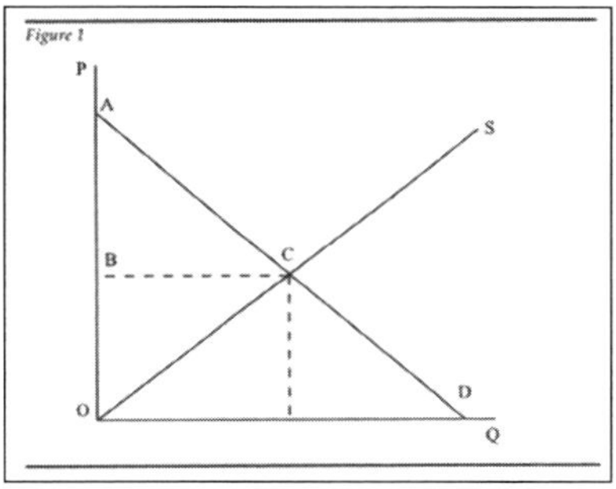

Figure 2.1

There are two primary mechanisms by which a market can shift along the continuum from relatively competitive to relatively noncompetitive. First, a dominant firm can acquire monopoly power (either legally or through illegitimate means). Second, the many sellers in a market can agree to stop competing against each other and to operate as a cartel. Both have similar deleterious effects on consumers and market efficiency.

Monopolies increase their profits by reducing output and increasing price. While monopolies sell fewer units of product, they sell them at a supra-competitive price to those consumers with relatively high reservation prices. Of course, a monopolist can only do this if it does not face competitors who bid the price down toward the competitive price. While having monopoly power does not violate the antitrust laws, using anticompetitive conduct to exclude actual and potential competitors can violate section 2 of the Sherman Act.

Cartels increase collective profits by pursuing the monopolist's strategy of limiting production in order to increase price. But cartels face problems that monopolists do not. First, there are coordination issues. These formerly competing firms must now agree on total output and market allocation.[1] Second, cartels may have less ability to charge the same profit-maximizing price as a similarly situated monopolist. Both the monopolist and the firms in a cartel must worry that setting the supra-competitive price too high may induce new competitors to enter the market.[2] But cartels have an additional concern that monopolists do not: cheaters. If the cartel raises its price too high, then it increases the incentive for cartel members to cheat on the cartel agreement.[3] Thus, while the monopolist need only worry about new firms entering the market, cartels must worry about both outsiders and the enemy within.

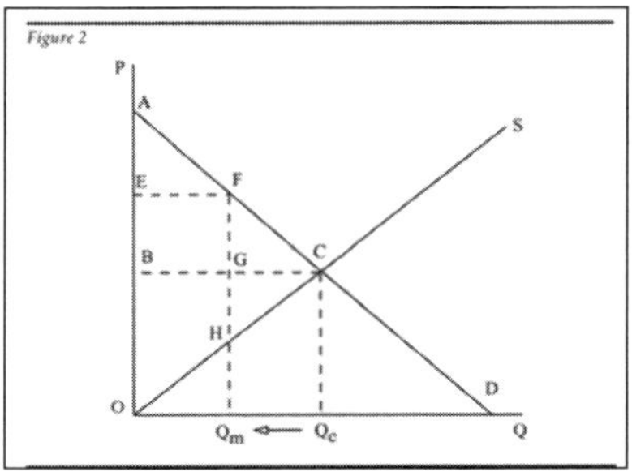

Figure 2.2

In short, both monopolization and cartelization attempt to generate profit by raising prices that consumers pay, which—absent the ability to price discriminate—requires a reduction in output. Figure 2.2 reflects this.

There are two major effects of reduced quantity and higher price. First, there is a transfer of wealth from consumers to producers, represented by rectangle BEFG in Figure 2.2. Not all antitrust commentators agree that this transfer represents a harm that antitrust law should care about. Theorists associated with the Chicago school believe this transfer is efficiency-neutral and, therefore, should be of no concern to antitrust. Other scholars who view antitrust law as concerned about consumer protection see the wealth transfer as a real harm.

Second, by reducing supply in order to increase price, monopolists and cartel participants also create deadweight loss.[4] Any antitrust violation that reduces output below the efficient equilibrium causes deadweight loss. The total deadweight loss is represented by triangle HFC.

Of this total deadweight loss, the smaller triangle GFC represents lost consumer surplus; triangle GCH is lost producer surplus. In contrast to the debate about the welfare effects of wealth transfers, there is no disagreement about the deleterious effects of deadweight loss.

This is one area of antitrust theory where there is relative unanimity: deadweight loss should be avoided. The framers of the Sherman Act were concerned with monopolists and cartelists restricting supply because some consumers would not get necessary goods. Although the concept of deadweight loss did not exist as such, congressional concern about undersupply was essentially a desire to address what economists later denominated as deadweight loss.[5] Chicago school theorists and more mainstream jurists all recognize that deadweight loss is inefficient[6] because antitrust violators could profitably increase production, and the social benefits of the incremental additional units would be greater than the cost of producing those marginal units. In sum, all scholars agree that monopolies and cartels inflict harmful deadweight loss on society.[7]

2.2 Antitrust Law Fails to Award Damages Based on Deadweight Loss

While antitrust theory recognizes the problem of deadweight loss, antitrust doctrine does not meaningfully incorporate the concept of deadweight loss. Monopolization and cartelization are condemned in part because they cause deadweight loss. But the plaintiff has no burden to prove such harm in any given case: the presence of deadweight loss is not an element of liability. It is generally not explicitly discussed in the case law. More importantly, deadweight loss plays no meaningful role in antitrust damages. Economists and legal scholars have invested much time developing a literature on deadweight loss. But antitrust courts have barely even mentioned the concept of deadweight loss, let alone applied it to determine the appropriate level of damages in monopolization or price-fixing cases.

Those consumers who suffer from the deadweight loss caused by an antitrust violation because they are unable to purchase products cannot bring antitrust claims. While a few courts have recognized that antitrust violations can cause deadweight loss,[8] even courts that recognize deadweight loss in theory deny standing to plaintiffs attempting to recover damages based on the deadweight loss.[9] Professor Hovenkamp has observed that "the courts have not been kind to damages actions by nonpurchasers—people who claim that they would have purchased at the competitive price but responded to the monopoly price by buying something else."[10] Indeed, Robert Lande has noted that "there does not appear to have been even a single instance in which a plaintiff has recovered for any allocative inefficiency effects of market power."[11] In short, excluded consumers generally do not have standing to initiate antitrust litigation to recover damages based on deadweight loss.[12]

The language in court opinions provides anecdotal support for the conclusion that antitrust courts do not sufficiently consider the concept of deadweight loss in their analysis of either liability or damages. A Westlaw search of all federal courts opinions for "deadweight loss" returned a mere fifteen (15) cases.[13] Eleven (11) of the cases referring to deadweight loss were not antitrust cases.[14] The remaining four cases referred to the concept of deadweight loss in antitrust litigation. However, two courts simply recognized in passing that antitrust violations can cause deadweight loss.[15] Another opinion referred to scholarship "arguing that antitrust injury includes more than just the deadweight loss from reduced output and increased price."[16] None of the cases actually incorporated deadweight loss into the antitrust analysis. None discussed whether a plaintiff should be able to recover damages based on deadweight loss. The results of this search are clearly not conclusive because courts can discuss or apply the underlying concept of deadweight loss without actually using the term as such. But given the widespread use of the term in antitrust scholarship, it is nevertheless surprising to see the term so little used in antitrust jurisprudence.

The primary reason that courts pay little attention to the concept of deadweight loss in the analysis of antitrust damages is that the current damages inquiry in consumer-initiated antitrust litigation focuses exclusively on overcharges. The test for calculating damages in antitrust actions brought by consumers is based on the overcharge: the difference between the price that the consumers actually paid and the price that they would have paid but for the violation.[17] As a result, the sole purpose of damages in consumer-initiated suits is seen as remedying this overcharge. For example, the Supreme Court has described treble damages "as a means of protecting consumers from overcharges resulting from price fixing."[18] The implicit assumption is that only those consumers who paid the overcharge will bring antitrust litigation.[19]

To rely exclusively on actual purchasers to litigate antitrust violations means that deadweight loss is not part of antitrust damages because the purchasers who are bringing private lawsuits do not suffer the deadweight loss. The deadweight loss reflects the inefficiency from the sales that did not take place. The direct burden of deadweight loss is suffered by non-purchasers, those prevented from making purchases because of the antitrust violation. While a traditional plaintiff can suffer both from overcharges and deadweight loss damages if he reduces his purchases, under current law he gets no recovery on the forgone purchases and only recovers the overcharge on the products that he did buy.[20] In sum, the problem is that the current damages measure was designed to deal exclusively with overcharges, but when purchasers sue for overcharges, deadweight loss is not taken into account.

It may seem that firms found liable for illegal monopolization or cartelization already pay damages that include a measure for deadweight loss because actual damages are automatically trebled. Some scholars have suggested that, given the difficulty of measuring deadweight loss,[21] "trebling actual damages may serve as a surrogate measure, exacting from perpetrators a rough measure of the harm inflicted by their wrongdoing."[22] The logic appears to be that the two-thirds of overall damages award beyond the compensatory amount are more than the deadweight loss caused by the violation. Thus, the defendant is, in effect, paying for the deadweight loss implicitly.

While it is tempting to believe that the automatic trebling of damages punishes the antitrust violator for any deadweight loss caused by its violations, there are many reasons not to find complete solace in trebling. First, the stated goals of trebling do not include providing a proxy for deadweight loss. Treble damages serve a variety of interconnected goals. From the plaintiffs' perspective, treble damages ensure a sufficient remedy for the victims of antitrust violations.[23]

More importantly, treble damages are meant to provide a sufficient incentive for private plaintiffs to investigate and bring suit and to compensate for the fact that most antitrust violators will probably not be brought to justice since many violations are difficult to detect.[24] From the violators' perspective, the trebling of damages disgorges ill-gotten gains and thus serves "to deprive violators of 'the fruits of their illegality.'"[25] Some courts reason that the additional two-thirds of the overall damage award beyond actual damages "is not remedial and inevitably presupposes a punitive purpose."[26] Through disgorgement and punishment, treble damages should deter future violations of the antitrust laws.[27] In short, treble damages serve a number of goals.[28] But none of the goals traditionally articulated for treble damages is tethered to deadweight loss. None of the congressmen who adopted the treble damages provision proffered trying to capture deadweight loss as a justification for the trebling of antitrust damages. Treble damages were not intended to force defendants to pay for the deadweight loss created by their antitrust violation.[29]

Second, most antitrust cases settle so trebling is not actually performed. Settlement amounts generally do not provide full compensation for the higher prices faced by those consumers who continued to purchase the product, let alone any amount of money to represent the deadweight loss suffered by consumers forced out of the market. In antitrust class actions, cases are settled for pennies on the untrebled dollar. Courts do not even consider the trebling of damages when approving proposed settlements as reasonable; instead, the defendant's settlement offer is compared to the class members' single damages.[30] Furthermore, neither class counsel nor judges consider the deadweight loss imposed by the defendant's conduct when negotiating and approving settlements. In short, much antitrust litigation—even some that can be characterized as successful—does not result in plaintiffs receiving trebled damages and, thus, trebling cannot be relied upon to make antitrust violators pay for the deadweight loss that they have created.

Finally, most antitrust awards—even after trebling—generally represent little more than single damages. Robert Lande has explained how the lack of prejudgment interest, the statute of limitations constraints, and tax consequences may mean that even those antitrust violators found liable for their misdeeds may end up paying less than single damages.[31] Indeed, "[e]ven the cartels that have paid the most in history—the Vitamin cartels—have paid less than one times their overcharges in damages and fines total, and this does not even adjust for lack of prejudgment interest."[32] In short, the promise of trebled antitrust damages is hardly ever realized.[33]

For these reasons, trebling does not seem to compensate for the facts that excluded consumers cannot bring suit and that deadweight loss is not included in damages analysis.

2.3 The Harms of Not Providing a Remedy for Deadweight Loss

This section explains why it matters that antitrust damages do not take account of deadweight loss. It may seem of little consequence. After all, antitrust cases are still being brought and damage awards, including settlements, are occasionally stratospheric.[34] But the cases that make headlines do not tell the entire story.[35]

Antitrust law is designed to compensate victims of anticompetitive conduct.[36] Taking this compensation purpose seriously requires considering deadweight loss and the impact of antitrust violations on non-purchasers as well as on those consumers compelled to pay a higher price. The absence of deadweight loss from the antitrust damage calculation does not simply deny some compensation to antitrust plaintiffs who are currently bringing antitrust litigation and are compensated by other measures. Instead, failing to include deadweight loss as a feature of antitrust damages means denying illegally excluded consumers all compensation for their injuries. Because the current antitrust damage formulas assume that the antitrust plaintiff has purchased the product,[37] excluded consumers who have made no purchases receive no recovery.

Excluded consumers though are injured by antitrust violations just as much as—if not more than—those consumers who pay a higher price. After all, most purchasers still get some consumer surplus,[38] whereas excluded consumers get none.[39] Moreover, the population of excluded consumers may represent a more vulnerable segment of the population than those who simply pay a higher price. For example, excluded consumers may be more likely to be poor and have fewer alternatives, and thus be forced to do without altogether.

Antitrust law should compensate those who actually suffer the harm associated with deadweight loss. These excluded consumers suffer antitrust injury and are entitled to some form of recovery. It seems odd that the one form of injury that everyone agrees antitrust violations cause is the one injury for which antitrust provides no damages.

Of course, deadweight loss not only harms excluded consumers; it causes injury to society more broadly by creating a misallocation of resources. Being priced out of the market may mean that some consumers must go without, even though they could have and would have purchased the product at the competitive price. The deadweight loss also means that the consumers may demand substitutes, whose production may represent a less efficient use of inputs than would be the case if the monopolist or cartel members produced the quantity at which marginal costs equal marginal revenue.[40] Antitrust violations also cause waste in the form of expenditures invested in securing supra-competitive profits[41] and of executive time spent investigating, pursuing, and defending against antitrust claims.[42] Forgone consumption, compelled substitution, and nonproductive uses of labor all represent different aspects of inefficiency from the deadweight loss caused by antitrust violations that are unaccounted for in traditional measures of antitrust damages.

If antitrust violators are not held accountable for the deadweight loss that they inflict, then insufficient deterrence could result. One major goal of the American antitrust regime is to deter anticompetitive conduct.[43] Rational firms are willing to break the law if their violations are cost-beneficial. If the punishment for a particular violation is less than the expected benefit, then a profit-maximizing firm—at least one that puts little independent weight on being law-abiding—may knowingly violate the law.

One could argue that sufficient deterrence already exists even without adding damages specifically tethered to deadweight loss. But there are reasons to believe that under-deterrence is a problem. First, much scholarship shows that antitrust damages are often too low to completely disgorge ill-gotten gains.[44] There is not sufficient disgorgement in many—perhaps most—cases. Second, it is becoming progressively more difficult for plaintiffs to prevail in antitrust litigation as courts remove more conduct from the per se category.[45] The courts have also made it more difficult for plaintiffs to prove an agreement in section 1 cases.[46] By reducing the probability of liability in these ways, antitrust jurisprudence is simultaneously decreasing the deterrent effects of treble damages that are imposed only after a finding of liability. Third, Congress and antitrust enforcement officials have taken some small steps to replace automatic treble damages with single damages in some situations where firms engage in cooperative arrangements.[47]

It is difficult to know with certainty whether or not the current antitrust damages regime has approached the level of optimal deterrence. In order to answer the question, we would need to know more about the underlying population of actual and would-be antitrust violations, which we do not. But there is strong anecdotal evidence of under-deterrence in that price-fixing conspiracies are being discovered at an increasing rate.[48] This suggests that making price-fixers pay additional damages based on deadweight loss would move us closer toward the optimal deterrence.

Even independent of deterrence theory, respect for the virtue of accountability requires that antitrust damages analysis include some consideration of deadweight loss. Currently, antitrust violators are not paying for all of the harm that they impose on society. Neither settlements nor damage awards incorporate any measure of deadweight loss. This seems inappropriate because the law generally seeks to compel those who break the rules to pay for the damage that they inflict on society. Antitrust law should compel violators to take responsibility for the full impact of misdeeds.

2.4 Issues in Incorporating Deadweight Loss Concerns into Antitrust Litigation

Given the consensus among antitrust commentators that deadweight loss constitutes a serious harm, it seems surprising that antitrust law does not sufficiently recognize or address this species of harm. While some scholars have noted the irony that courts routinely fail to wrestle with damages associated with deadweight loss,[49] no meaningful effort has been undertaken to educate federal judges about deadweight loss or how to incorporate such concerns into antitrust jurisprudence. Two goals should be kept in mind. First, firms that are found liable for illegal monopolization or cartelization need to be made to pay damages for the deadweight loss. Second, antitrust law should find a mechanism to compensate the victims who suffer the brunt of the deadweight loss: excluded consumers.

Conceptually, it makes sense that antitrust law should address deadweight loss. But two major issues preclude easy incorporation of deadweight loss into antitrust litigation. First, is it possible to measure deadweight loss with sufficient accuracy? Second, who should have standing to pursue damages based on deadweight loss?

A. Measuring Deadweight Loss

This section makes three arguments. First, the legal standard for proving antitrust damages allows for some uncertainty. Second, while deadweight loss cannot be easily measured with precision, it can be estimated with reasonable accuracy. Third, courts and Congress can find ways to compensate for the uncertainty associated with quantifying deadweight loss.

The damages analysis in antitrust litigation has two distinct steps, each with its own evidentiary standard. In order to recover damages after proving liability, the antitrust "plaintiff must first prove the fact of antitrust damages, some 'element of actual damages caused by the defendant's violation of the antitrust laws.'"[50] The fact of damages must be proven by a traditional preponderance of evidence standard.[51]

Once the fact of damages is proven, then the "plaintiff is held to a less rigid standard of proof with respect to the amount of damage caused by an antitrust violation, because economic harm is intangible and difficult to quantify."[52] The plaintiff's burden is lowered on the amount of damages inquiry for at least three reasons. First, the specific amount of damages caused by an antitrust violation is too difficult to ascertain with certainty. The Supreme Court has noted that "[t]he vagaries of the marketplace usually deny us sure knowledge of what the plaintiff's situation would have been in the absence of the defendant's antitrust violation."[53] Second, the defendant is generally responsible for this difficulty and thus any uncertainty should weigh against the defendant, not the plaintiff. The

Supreme Court long ago recognized that a "wrongdoer is not entitled to complain that [damages] cannot be measured with the exactness and precision than would be possible if the case, which he alone is responsible for making, were otherwise."[54] This warrants a "relaxed standard" for proving the amount of damages since "if there is uncertainty, the defendant should bear the burden of that uncertainty because his unlawful actions created it."[55] Finally, maintaining differential standards for fact of damages and amount of damages strikes the proper balance between making the plaintiff prove damages and not making the hurdle too high given the inherent imprecision in quantifying damages.[56]

The legal standard for quantifying antitrust damages allows for approximation. The Supreme Court has reasoned that the plaintiff's calculation need only "show the extent of the damages as a matter of just and reasonable inference, although the results be only approximate."[57] As a result, lower federal courts have accepted that a plaintiff's damage calculation in antitrust litigation may suffer from "minor imperfections."[58]

But this relaxed standard for quantifying damages still has teeth. There must be a reasonable basis for assumptions employed in the plaintiff's damages model.[59] Speculation is not sufficient.[60] Thus, courts will affirm jury damages awards in antitrust cases so long as they are not based upon "speculation or guess-work."[61]

Given these standards, can deadweight loss provide a basis for antitrust damages? While it is easy to see conceptually how antitrust violations create deadweight loss, it can be exceedingly difficult to convert the concept into a workable legal test for antitrust damages. In *Illinois Brick Co. v. Illinois*,[62] the Court suggested that measuring demand elasticity is a "serious problem."[63] Many commentators, too, have warned about the difficulties inherent in attempting to quantify deadweight loss in antitrust litigation.[64] While such concerns are well-taken, damage estimates are rarely precise. The issue is not whether estimates of deadweight loss will be precise, but rather whether they will be reasonable. This section argues that this threshold of reasonableness can be achieved.

In order to calculate the amount of total deadweight loss associated with an antitrust violation, courts must estimate five elements of a deadweight loss calculation:

1. the market output with the violation (QM);
2. the amount of the overcharge;
3. what the market output would have been but for the violation (QC);
4. the price that would have been charged but for the violation; and
5. the shape of the demand between QM and QC.

This list excludes one obvious factor: the shape of the supply curve. It is not necessary to know the shape of the supply curve between QM and QC because the defendant should not be responsible for paying antitrust damages based on the lower part of the deadweight loss triangle. The deadweight loss triangle is composed of lost consumer surplus and forgone producer surplus. The shape of the bottom part of the triangle need not be defined at all because deadweight loss damages should not include lost producer surplus. The defendant has already paid for this by not collecting the profits on the sales it decided to forgo.[65] This makes the estimation process easier because we can make the deadweight loss calculation as though the marginal cost curve were horizontal.

The five listed variables are both necessary and subject to reasonable approximation. First, the market output while the violation was taking place establishes the left-hand side of the deadweight loss triangle. This should be easy to prove; it is the quantity that was actually sold.

Second, it is necessary to know the amount of the overcharge in order to know the upper left boundary of the deadweight loss triangle. Calculating the amount of the overcharge does not represent a problem for antitrust courts; they must do this in traditional consumer-initiated suits where the damages are measured exclusively by the overcharge.

Third, courts must estimate the market output that would have occurred but for the violation in order to determine the right-hand boundary of the deadweight loss triangle. While we may not know this with certainty—as we do the post-violation market output—it can be reasonably estimated using traditional economic methods.[66] It may be easier to secure sufficient data to more accurately estimate this variable in some markets, such as those with comprehensive scanner data or those involving commodities, than in others.

Fourth, it is also necessary to estimate the competitive price in order to establish the right-hand boundary of the deadweight loss triangle. Traditional antitrust plaintiffs already have to prove what price would have prevailed absent the antitrust violation. This is necessary in order to prove the amount of illegal overcharge. Courts generally do this by examining the market price before the violation and then controlling for other variables besides the antitrust violation that would have affected the price.

Finally, courts need to have a sense about the slope of the demand curve between the quantity that was sold and the quantity that would have been sold but for the antitrust violation. The shape of the demand curve will be the most difficult fact to prove. It is possible for economists to estimate demand curves.[67] Indeed, some economists argue that the calculations lead to relatively precise derivations of consumer surplus and the deadweight loss associated with price increases.[68] Estimating the demand curve does not necessarily require more speculation than estimating lost profits, probable market shares, or counterfactuals necessary to calculate damages for traditional antitrust plaintiffs.[69]

While these five factors will be difficult to prove with true precision, hired economists can debate the precise amount of deadweight loss created by a defendant's actions in any particular case. Economists are now well used to debating models and damage estimates in front of antitrust juries and judges. And, whether jurors are sufficiently trained in the basics of economics or not, for decades we have allowed them to pick winners in these trial-staged economists' debates. Although deadweight loss cannot be calculated with pinpoint accuracy, reasonable estimates are possible.[70] And that is all that the standard for antitrust damages requires.[71]

If the concern is about judicial competence or wasting judicial resources, the proper response is to standardize the deadweight loss calculation in a way that solves these problems, not to ignore the real injuries associated with deadweight loss. It may be difficult to prove deadweight loss with precision, but consider what we know before we get to the point that calculation is necessary. We know: (1) that the defendant(s) violated the antitrust laws; (2) that (absent inelastic demand) the violation caused deadweight loss; and (3) that absent an attempt at estimating the deadweight loss associated with the violation, the defendant will not pay any penalty for a harm that we know it has inflicted on consumers and the economy more broadly. These facts provide the critical context for any debate about whether antitrust jurisprudence should award damages based on deadweight loss. If we know for a fact that the defendant has imposed injury through illegal conduct, but that the damages are difficult to measure with precision, the response should be to award a damage amount that is as fair as possible given our limitations, not to abandon the category of damages altogether. The wrongdoer should bear the costs of damages uncertainty. As the Supreme Court recognized long ago, "[a]ny other rule would enable the wrongdoer to profit by his wrongdoing at the expense of his victim. It would be an inducement to make wrongdoing so effective and complete in every case as to preclude any recovery, by rendering the measure of damages uncertain."[72] Yet, to date, courts have taken this condemned approach in dealing with deadweight loss.

Courts should develop a mechanism to address the uncertainty associated with deadweight loss instead of excising this consideration from antitrust damages analysis entirely. The primary, and most important, source of uncertainty is the shape of the relevant arc of the demand curve. There are many possible ways to eliminate litigation debates over demand elasticity. For example, antitrust could provide fixed statutory damages for deadweight loss. Such a one-size-fits-all approach is probably inappropriate for antitrust litigation, where the variance in the deadweight loss inflicted by different antitrust violations can be enormous. Bearing this in mind, one approach to standardizing damages could be to measure deadweight loss based on the dollar volume of commerce affected by the violation. Such dollar volumes already serve as the basis for criminal sentencing and fines in antitrust cases. The larger the volume of commerce affected, the greater the amount of deadweight loss likely generated by the antitrust violation. Consequently, this provides a rough approximation of the likely size of the deadweight loss.

Alternatively, courts could simplify the deadweight loss calculation by presuming, as a matter of law, that the relevant part of the demand curve is linear. The plaintiff would still need to establish, through expert testimony, the causal reduction in quantity and what the price would have been at the competitive quantity, as well as the output but for the antitrust violation. But because the shape of the demand curve is the most arduous part of the estimation, assuming linearity would eliminate much of the measurement debate. The assumption of a straight demand curve may not reflect reality in many markets, but an antitrust plaintiff must make some assumptions in calculating damages.[73] This question is whether it is worse to assume a linear demand curve or not to hold antitrust violators responsible for damages that we know with certainty they are inflicting on consumers and the economy. Surely the latter is the greater offense.

Whatever standard for estimating deadweight loss is chosen, there are ways to minimize the effects of measurement error. Courts must consider the relative risks of underestimation and overestimation of the amount of deadweight loss. Any miscalculation of the amount of deadweight loss caused by an antitrust violation will result in either overestimation or underestimation of actual damages. The possibility of trebling should inform how we perceive and treat the relative risks of underestimating and overestimating damages. On the one hand, a trebling of damages would more than compensate for an underestimation of deadweight loss damages. In contrast, any overestimation error would be magnified by a subsequent trebling of damages. Thus, trebling could either mitigate or magnify estimation errors. In the context of awarding additional antitrust damages based on deadweight loss, it would be preferable to err on the side of underestimating damages because any award of damages for deadweight loss would definitely move us closer to the appropriate levels of both compensation and deterrence.

Because trebling creates a non-negligible risk of over-deterrence, Congress could provide that damages based solely on deadweight loss should not be trebled. If the award were limited to single damages, then so long as the jury's damage estimate were not more than three times greater than the actual deadweight loss damages, the defendant would still be paying significantly less than treble damages on an accurate damage calculation. The defendant would likely pay an amount that at least approximates the deadweight loss associated with the defendant's antitrust violation. Allowing only single damages for deadweight loss would not harm the overall structure of antitrust enforcement. Treble damages would remain for all current private antitrust plaintiffs, such as competitors and direct purchasers. Further, single damages are not unprecedented.[74] For example, in civil cases, the federal government can sue only for single damages.[75] In short, allowing single damages for deadweight loss is a reasonable compromise.[76]

B. Who Should Recover Deadweight Loss Damages

If antitrust jurisprudence were to attempt to include deadweight loss in damage calculations, this would raise the question of who should be able to recover for the deadweight loss associated with a proven antitrust violation. Possible candidates are: the purchaser class action plaintiffs who currently bring antitrust class action litigation against monopolists and price fixers; individual non-purchaser consumers who were actually excluded from the market; excluded consumers as class action litigants; and state attorneys general bringing parens patriae suits.

1. Current antitrust plaintiffs

The easiest approach would be to give current antitrust class action members the right to recover damages based on the deadweight loss imposed on non-purchasers. Instead of encouraging new litigation by a new class of plaintiffs, perhaps a deadweight loss measure of damages could be included in already-existing litigation. There are already dozens of antitrust class actions brought every year. These cases do not currently seek any damages based on deadweight loss. But they could. Courts could adjust the current damage measures to award more money to current plaintiffs based on estimates of how much deadweight loss was caused by the defendants' antitrust violation. Some commentators have argued that "the direct purchaser, rather than the would-be consumer, is the preferable choice to recover damages for consumer deadweight loss."[77]

Simply allowing current consumer-plaintiffs to seek additional recovery based on deadweight loss would have one major advantage: efficiency.[78] If the plaintiffs prove liability, then additional damages could be added to the traditional damages award. Conversely, a rule could be adopted that if the defendant could win on summary judgment or at trial just once, it would eliminate claims from both classes of consumers, excluded and non-excluded.

But there are important problems with simply awarding deadweight loss damages to current antitrust plaintiffs. First, there would be no compensation for the excluded consumers who actually suffer the harms of deadweight loss. If the goal of incorporating deadweight loss into antitrust damage analysis is simply to make defendants bear the cost of inefficiency that they have created, then it should not matter who receives the money. In his *Illinois Brick* dissent,

Justice Brennan noted that "from the deterrence standpoint, it is irrelevant to whom damages are paid."[79] However, to the extent that one reason to address deadweight loss is to afford some measure of compensation to excluded consumers, this approach does not succeed.

Second, if the claims are simply given to purchaser-class members, it is not clear that defendants will actually pay more money out. Most class actions brought by purchaser-plaintiffs settle for pennies on the dollar; class members are unlikely to get more money simply because the litigation also disposes of claims of the non-purchaser class, who are absent from the litigation. If consumer-plaintiffs do not actually extract more money from defendants, then no additional penalty is assessed for the deadweight loss imposed by illegal monopolization or cartelization.

In short, this alternative may provide no compensation to excluded consumers and no additional deterrence. As a result, relying exclusively on traditional purchaser-plaintiffs may not change the status quo at all.

2. Private individual suits

The most obvious way to insure compensation for the excluded consumers is to allow them to sue to recover damages based on the deadweight loss that they suffered as a result of the antitrust violation. But before a federal court would allow non-purchasers—or any antitrust plaintiffs—to recover antitrust damages, the claimants must clear several hurdles, the most important of which is antitrust standing. In order to have standing to pursue antitrust litigation, a plaintiff must prove that it has suffered antitrust injury. Antitrust injury is "injury of the type the antitrust laws were intended to prevent and that flows from that which makes the defendants' acts unlawful. The injury should reflect the anticompetitive effect either of the violation or of anticompetitive acts made possible by violation. It should, in short, be the type of loss that the claimed violation would be likely to cause."[80] While limiting, the concept of antitrust injury is large enough to encompass harms beyond the mere increase of price to consumers.[81]

Excluded consumers suffer antitrust injury. First, antitrust injury is not narrowly confined to actual purchasers. The Supreme Court has noted that the Sherman Act "does not confine its protection to consumers, or to purchasers, or to competitors, or to sellers...The Act is comprehensive in its terms and coverage, protecting all who are made victims of the forbidden practices by whomever they may be perpetrated."[82] Thus, non-purchasers are not automatically excluded from antitrust protection. Second, many courts have explained that antitrust injury essentially requires that the plaintiff's "loss come from acts that reduce output or raise prices to consumers."[83] Similarly, the Seventh Circuit has opined that antitrust injury "means injury from higher prices or lower output, the principal vices proscribed by the antitrust laws."[84] Excluded consumers suffer harm from reduced output. Indeed, they are the consumers most directly harmed by the lower output associated with antitrust violations. This qualifies as antitrust injury.[85]

However, not all antitrust injuries provide standing to victims of antitrust violations. For jurisprudential reasons, courts deny standing to some who have suffered harm as a result of an antitrust violation. If every firm, consumer, or employee negatively affected by an antitrust violation could recover treble damages, there might be too much enforcement and unnecessary, redundant litigation.[86] Thus, courts impose limits on antitrust standing beyond the injury requirement alone. These additional limits are constructed as standing factors, associated with Associated General Contractors,[87] including "(1) the nature of the plaintiff's alleged injury; that is, whether it was the type the antitrust laws were intended to forestall; (2) the directness of the injury; (3) the speculative measure of the harm; (4) the risk of duplicative recovery; and (5) the complexity in apportioning damages."[88] Also important is "the existence of more direct victims."[89] None of the factors is determinative; instead courts engage in balancing on a case-by-case basis.[90]

Excluded consumers can satisfy most of the Associated General Contractors factors. First, non-purchasers suffer antitrust injury. The nature of the injury—deadweight loss—experienced by excluded consumers is the type of harm that antitrust laws were intended to deter and remedy.[91] Thus, the first factor is satisfied.

Second, the plaintiff's injury must be direct. This means that the plaintiff must prove "'a causal connection between the defendant's actions violative of the Sherman Act and the actual injury to the plaintiff's business.'"[92] Part of this directness inquiry asks whether other potential plaintiffs have suffered a more direct, intervening injury.[93] Thus, courts "are more likely to find no standing if the plaintiff's injury both derives from and is measured by another's more direct injury."[94] Plaintiffs whose claims are derivative of others' claims are denied standing because the alleged antitrust injury is not directly caused by the antitrust violation.[95]

Excluded consumers suffer direct injury. First, the monopolist's or cartel's decision to reduce output is the direct cause of consumers' inability to purchase products that would have otherwise been available. Second, the injuries of excluded customers are not derivative of the claims of those consumers who paid a higher price. While some courts have denied standing to non-purchasers because "actual purchasers exist who were more directly injured by the conspiracy,"[96] actual purchasers have not been more directly injured than excluded consumers. They have just been differently injured. Suppose that a firm has two units of a product and there are two buyers, each of whom wants to purchase one unit. The firm says that it will sell only one unit (not both) to the highest bidder, and then proceeds to have an auction. After the firms bid against each other and one outbids the other, they have both been injured directly by the firm's decision to limit its sales. The purchaser is injured by paying a higher price and the non-purchaser is injured by being denied access to the product. The purchaser's injury may be easier to calculate but the injuries are equally direct. Neither's injury is derivative of the other's injury.

Also related to the directness of injury, some courts have limited standing to plaintiffs who are within the "target area" of the alleged antitrust violation.[97] Under the target area test for standing, courts "focus on the area affected by the anticompetitive conduct, requiring that the plaintiff be within the area of the economy which was endangered by a breakdown of competition and that plaintiff's injury be a direct result of the lessening of that competition."[98] Non-purchasers should satisfy this test as well. Excluded consumers are targets of an antitrust violation that reduces output and are "person[s] against whom the conspiracy was aimed"[99] because the defendants know that they are going to stop sales to this group of consumers in order to charge a higher price to the remaining consumers with higher reservation prices.

The multiplicity of potential plaintiffs affects the standing inquiry. Courts have held that they "have a legitimate interest in...avoiding the 'risk of duplicate recoveries on the one hand or the danger of complex apportionment of damages on the other.'"[100] With respect to damage apportionment, scarce judicial time and resources are not well spent attempting to allocate a pool of damages among competing plaintiffs, especially when one group has been more directly injured than another. Similarly, courts may deny standing if allowing a particular category of plaintiffs would create a risk of duplicate recoveries. In *Illinois Brick Co. v. Illinois,*[101] the Supreme Court ruled that indirect purchasers do not have standing to sue to recover overcharges because direct purchasers already had standing and to allow both direct and indirect purchasers to sue for the same overcharge would result in duplicative recoveries. Some courts and commentators have argued that *Illinois Brick* precludes standing for nonpurchasers.[102]

These factors, associated with *Illinois Brick*, do not counsel against standing for excluded consumers. First, there is no problem of allocating damages between non-purchasers and traditional antitrust plaintiffs because deadweight loss is a different injury. For example, while both competitors and actual purchasers are traditional plaintiffs in section 2 litigation, neither competitors nor actual purchasers suffer damages associated with deadweight loss. Competitors' damages are based on lost sales, whereas consumer-plaintiffs are injured by the higher prices paid on products actually purchased.[103] Because no current antitrust plaintiffs recover damages based on the deadweight loss, allowing damages for precisely those losses creates no allocation problems between purchasers and non-purchasers (or between non-purchasers and competitors). There is, however, a problem with allocating among the non-purchasers, as will be discussed below.

Second, there is no risk of redundant or duplicative recoveries because excluded consumers would be suing for a different injury that is independent of the overcharge. While some scholars have stated that one purpose of the standing doctrine "is to assign the right to sue for antitrust injury to the most efficient plaintiff,"[104] the excluded consumer is the most efficient plaintiff for the particular injury associated with deadweight loss.

Third, *Illinois Brick* itself does not preclude standing for non-purchasers. The primary import of *Illinois Brick* is that indirect purchasers cannot sue, not that only direct purchasers have standing to sue. *Illinois Brick's* holding precluding suits by indirect purchasers is largely irrelevant to the issue of whether excluded consumers should have standing because there is no indirect non-purchaser. The injury suffered by excluded consumers is not derivative of the injuries of other victims of the violation. As a result, *Illinois Brick* is of no moment

The final standing factor is much more problematic. In order to receive standing, the antitrust plaintiff's injury cannot be speculative. Applying this factor, courts may deny standing "if damages 'rest at bottom on some abstract conception or speculative measure of harm.'"[105] Thus, state attorneys general do not have standing to pursue damages based on economy-wide harms, in part because such harms are necessarily speculative and difficult to measure.[106]

The damage claims of excluded consumers appear to be speculative for three reasons.[107] First, it is hard to determine with certainty who the excluded consumers are, that is, which consumers would actually have purchased the product but for the antitrust violation. For traditional consumer-plaintiffs, it is relatively easy to determine if they bought the product and thus suffered from an overcharge. It is harder for consumers to prove that they did not purchase a product solely due to the illegally elevated price (or unavailability). If a plaintiff made consistent purchases over time before the violation, but ceased its purchases after the price hike—and not for reasons unassociated with the higher price—then there may be a basis for inferring what purchases would have occurred, but did not, during the period of the antitrust violation.[108] But absent a meaningful prior course of dealing, this factor will be difficult to prove without speculation.[109] In many cases, the necessary evidence will be unavailable.[110]

Second, even if courts could identify with confidence those consumers who did not make purchases because of the antitrust violation, it would be difficult to know how many units each individual consumer forwent purchasing. This creates a problem of proof at trial because, as Frank Easterbrook has observed, "a large number of people did not buy an infinite amount."[111] For the individual non-purchaser, this element "almost always...involves a great deal of speculation—more than attends the computation of an actual purchaser's overcharge injuries."[112]

Third, each excluded consumer has suffered a different quantum of damages depending on how much he valued the product that he was unable to purchase because of the antitrust violation. Because excluded consumers have different damages depending on their reservation prices, it would be too hard for courts or juries to estimate the harm to each individual plaintiff who brings suit to recover the deadweight loss associated with exclusion from the market.

While total deadweight loss can be estimated, the calculation is an aggregate measurement, not an individualized one. This will be a significant problem in the litigation context. Traditional plaintiffs all suffer the same amount of damages per unit purchased; the overcharge is essentially a constant. The only variable among purchaser-plaintiffs is the number of units purchased at the illegally inflated price—a variable that is generally subject to definitive proof. In contrast, the damages suffered by excluded consumers lack any meaningful homogeneity. First, excluded consumers do not share any uniformity in damages. Each individual's actual damages are a function of that individual's reservation price. Second, in addition to varying reservation prices, different consumers face different damages based on the number of units of the product that they would have purchased but for the antitrust violation. Unlike actual purchases, this is less susceptible to meaningful proof.

In sum, although deadweight loss can be estimated in the aggregate, the precise amount of deadweight loss is hard to measure for each particular consumer. The lack of verifiable, individual damage calculations makes deadweight loss an inappropriate damages measure for suits brought by individual private plaintiffs.[113] But antitrust law should not automatically preclude non-purchasers from seeking recovery for losses associated with their being denied access to products in a competitive market. At most, it should preclude standing to individual excluded consumers. Because aggregate damages are not prohibitively speculative—and non-purchasers can satisfy the other factors for antitrust standing—collective litigation that seeks damages based on the total deadweight loss caused by the violation should not be ruled out.

3. Class action litigation

If individual suits by non-purchasers are inappropriate because individual damages are too difficult to quantify, then perhaps the answer is class action litigation. Traditional antitrust class actions define the class as those consumers who purchased the product during a certain time period. But deadweight loss deals with those consumers who did not buy the product, so they are excluded from traditional class actions. A separate class could be comprised of those consumers excluded from the market by the defendants' antitrust violation.

There are at least three major problems with relying on non-purchaser class actions. First, it may be hard to find a proper representative plaintiff. In traditional antitrust class actions, the representative is generally a consumer who has purchased the product at the inflated price. But for a class action designed to address deadweight loss, is there such a thing as a typical non-purchaser? Some purchasers may have been unwilling to pay the heightened price; some may have been unable to find the product at all. Some may have purchased a substitute product; some may have had to buy the product on a secondary market, e.g., eBay, at a price even above the monopoly or cartel price; some may have had to do without the product or a substitute altogether. Depending on their response to the product scarcity and their reservation prices, the class members will suffer different damages. In contrast to purchasers who generally suffer the same damages, no nonpurchaser is particularly typical. Second, it may be hard to limit the class for the same reason that it would be difficult to limit individual antitrust suits to recover damages based on deadweight loss. If there is money involved, then anybody could say that he would have purchased the product if the price had been a little lower. Third, there is a risk of frivolous suits. There is already a great deal of concern that class counsel abuse the class action process to extort large settlements. Creating a new class of antitrust plaintiffs could exacerbate the problem. In short, there is reason not to trust private enforcers to show the appropriate restraint.

4. Parens patriae suits

Because of concerns about effectiveness and the potential for abuse in class action litigation, parens patriae suits represent the most appropriate vehicle to address the issue of deadweight loss. With the Hart-Scott-Rodino Act, Congress amended the antitrust laws to allow state attorneys general to pursue antitrust claims on behalf of natural persons in their states. Congress intended these parens patriae actions to satisfy the three underlying goals of the Sherman Act: "(1) compensation of victims of antitrust violations; (2) disgorgement of profits by the offenders; and (3) deterrence of future anticompetitive actions."[114] Parens patriae suits have been growing in popularity and state attorneys general have brought such antitrust suits involving "a broad range of consumer items including automobiles, automotive products, food processors, real estate, milk, consumer electronics, footwear, toys, cemetery plots, petroleum products, garbage carting, and cable television services."[115]

However, state attorneys general do not currently bring parens patriae suits to recover damages based on deadweight loss. There is no legal impediment to such claims. There can be parens patriae suits for a class defined as consumers excluded from the market because of the antitrust violation. The consumers whose rights the state is vindicating must have suffered antitrust injury.[116] But that is not a problem here because excluded consumers have suffered antitrust injury, as discussed above.[117]

There are many advantages to using the parens patriae vehicle. State attorneys general can be trusted to vigorously pursue appropriate cases. Parens patriae actions have already proven to be a valuable asset in the enforcement regime to detect and remedy antitrust violations. States have initiated antitrust investigations and have litigated them to meaningful conclusion, either settlement or liability.[118]

While state enforcement officials have brought much litigation, they are unlikely to bring frivolous parens patriae lawsuits. Unlike private class counsel, government attorneys are not motivated to bring a high volume of litigation in order to generate quick settlements. State actors may make more judicious decisions than private attorneys because "given the limited resources available to public enforcement agencies, the government presumably is better able to take into account relevant enforcement costs and prosecute only those matters which are truly in the public interest."[119] The risks of frivolous litigation are reduced because prevailing defendants can get attorneys' fees if the court finds that a state attorney general "has acted in bad faith, vexatiously, wantonly, or for oppressive reasons."[120] State attorneys general are also accountable at the settlement stage because the court must approve any dismissal or settlement of a parents patriae antitrust action.[121] Of course, in pursuing a parens patriae suit, the state can hire private attorneys to assist in investigation and litigation.[122] However, the state would still provide the critical brake against meritless suits.[123]

Allowing such parens patriae actions would insure some level of accountability for the deadweight loss imposed by antitrust violations. While it is hard to identify the injured consumers, defendants who create deadweight loss should be held responsible for the harm that they inflict. Just because courts cannot readily identify the victims does not mean that antitrust law should not provide a remedy. Parens patriae suits may help eliminate the problem of having to identify the actual consumers who suffered the deadweight loss.

There is efficiency in relying on state attorneys general to recover damages based on deadweight loss because in some cases the state antitrust authorities are already bringing an antitrust suit seeking traditional damages. In those cases, they should be allowed to add a damages claim for deadweight loss. Because a major concern is that in cases of known antitrust violations the penalties are not sufficiently high to disgorge ill-gotten gains, state attorneys general could seek additional damages based on the estimated deadweight loss caused by the defendant's violation. But government attorneys should not be limited in seeking deadweight loss damages only to those cases in which they have brought the initial antitrust litigation. In those situations in which either a competitor or class action has already established liability, the state could bring a follow-on suit to recover damages based on the deadweight loss caused by the violation. There is precedent for the government pursuing follow-on litigation in the wake of private antitrust litigation.[124] Such follow-on suits should be very efficient as there is no need to prove liability, since an earlier suit has established liability and collateral estoppel should preclude re-litigation of liability issues.

The final advantage of using parens patriae suits instead of individual private litigation is that the damages in a successful action would represent total deadweight loss, saving courts from having to adjudicate the claims of individual consumers. The federal parens patriae statute specifically provides that "damages may be proved and assessed in the aggregate by statistical or sampling methods, by the computation of illegal overcharges, or by such other reasonable system of estimating aggregate damages as the court in its discretion may permit without the necessity of separately proving the individual claim of, or amount of damage to, persons on whose behalf the suit was brought."[125] Congress eliminated the necessity of proving individual damages "because the proof of individual claims and amounts would be impracticable and virtually impossible."[126] This is certainly the case with claims of excluded consumers. However, while individual deadweight loss damages would be prohibitively difficult to measure, total deadweight loss is subject to reasonable estimation.[127]

However, the issue remains as to what the state authorities should do with the antitrust damages that they collect in a parens patriae suit to recover deadweight loss. The damages secured in a parens patriae suit "shall (1) be distributed in such manner as the district court in its discretion may authorize; or (2) be deemed a civil penalty by the court and deposited with the State as general revenues…"[128] From the standpoint of deterrence, all that matters is making the antitrust violator pay for the deadweight loss that it has created. Regardless of where the money ultimately goes, awarding damages based on deadweight loss increases deterrence by making antitrust defendants internalize more of the social costs of their violations. Thus, even if a state were to channel the damage award to state coffers, deterrence would be enhanced.

But state officials should at least attempt to achieve the compensatory goal as well. This requires funneling the damage award to those who actually suffered as a result of the deadweight loss caused by the antitrust violation. For the purposes of compensation, state attorneys general could take several tacks. First, they could allow individuals to file claims for a share of the recovery as is done following class action settlements and trials. Second, they could attempt to construct a cy pres distribution.

In order to provide compensation, antitrust law might allow excluded consumers to make claims against a common fund created as a result of successful litigation to recover damages based on deadweight loss. In some class actions under current law, after the common fund is established, the class members must go through a claim process in which they prove that they qualify for class membership and are entitled to money from the settlement fund. But in traditional class actions, membership in the class is relatively objective. For example, if the person made the required purchase in the relevant time frame, then she is a member of the class; if not, she is not a member of the class.[129] For class members who have suffered a deadweight loss injury, the question is not so black and white. They must show that they would have made a purchase but for the increased price. For the same reason that it would be difficult to identify the individuals who would have standing to bring an antitrust suit in their own names to recover deadweight loss damages, it would be impractical for successful state attorneys general and their staff to funnel any monetary award to the specific consumers priced out of the relevant market.

Because the individual nonpurchasers may not step forward or may be impossible to identify with sufficient certainty, the state should consider a cy pres distribution. This entails the court distributing the funds to third parties in a manner that approximates the compensatory goal of antitrust litigation. Cy pres distributions make sense when there are a great number of victims who are hard to locate and the cost of administering individual recoveries would be prohibitively high.[130] Cy pres distributions are relatively common in parens patriae antitrust suits.[131] In the case of deadweight loss damages, the money could go to create pro-consumer antitrust initiatives, to aid existing public interest groups that support consumer interests,[132] or to fund state antitrust enforcement efforts.[133] These allow at least indirect benefits to the excluded consumers,[134] in part by helping to prevent future violations of the antitrust laws. With a cy pres approach, there is no problem with identifying which precise members of the class did not purchase the product because of the illegal activity.

Cy pres distributions almost always represent a second-best solution, but they are better than the alternative of continuing the status quo. Whether a damage award based on deadweight loss is distributed through a claims process or a cy pres mechanism, allowing recovery of deadweight loss with parens patriae suits would represent a comparative advantage over the current damages regime that does not recognize deadweight loss at all. For the purposes of deterrence, it does not matter where the money goes; it could escheat to the state. But the cy pres approach allows the possibility of proxy compensation for the injured consumers. Actions to recover damages based on deadweight loss represent precisely the type of scenario that the parens patriae mechanism is designed to address: many consumers are injured; it would be hard to identify and locate the affected consumers; and only aggregate damages can be reliably estimated.

2.5 Deadweight Loss and Detrebling

There is a continuing effort to replace treble damages with single damages in antitrust litigation generally. The detrebling movement hit its stride during the Reagan administration when legislation was introduced to detreble damages for most antitrust violations. While that effort failed, today the Antitrust Modernization Commission is again considering detrebling damages, in this case for section 2 violations. The apparent justification put forward is that antitrust damages are too high and thus create a risk of over-deterrence.

Understanding the role of deadweight loss in many antitrust violations should counsel against detrebling antitrust damages. If violators pay only single damages, then they will almost definitely inflict more harm on consumers than they are being held responsible for. That results in a suboptimal fine because the optimal antitrust fine should include a measurement for the deadweight loss caused by the violation.[135] The Areeda and Hovenkamp treatise explains:

> The rationale for equating damages with the sum of the monopoly overcharge plus deadweight loss is this: recovery of the monopoly overcharge alone takes away precisely the violator's gains. But if the violation produces any efficiency gain at all, it will still be profitable, notwithstanding that the resulting deadweight loss from monopoly exceeds the efficiency gains. As a result, setting damages equal to the overcharge alone represent insufficient deterrence.[136]

Replacing treble damages with single damages would be a mistake. Even the monopolist who is caught and held liable would be inflicting more harm on society than he is being forced to pay back.[137] Furthermore, monopolists and price fixers may profit from their antitrust violations, especially in the absence of prejudgment interest.[138] In short, the presence of deadweight loss should counsel against single damages. At a minimum, any movement toward a single-damages regime for section 2 violations should provide for the defendant to also pay the cost of the deadweight loss that it created.

2.6 Conclusion

Antitrust violations, such as illegal monopolization and cartelization, create inefficiency and social harm in the form of deadweight loss. Antitrust theorists recognize that deadweight loss represents antitrust harm because consumers are being denied the ability to purchase a product even though they are willing and able to pay a price that is greater than the cost of production and because additional units would be available at or below a price that consumers could afford if the product were sold in a competitive market.

Despite the widespread recognition of deadweight loss as an antitrust injury, antitrust jurisprudence fails to consider this injury as an element of antitrust damages. The current treble-damage schema provides no compensation for excluded consumers. While treble damages could theoretically punish antitrust violators for the deadweight loss caused by artificially reduced supply, they cannot possibly provide any compensation for those consumers who were compelled to forgo efficient purchases due to the inflated price.

However, there are two problems with awarding damages based on deadweight loss, both relating more to practicality than to legal or economic philosophy. First, there is the standing problem: it is too hard to identify the true victims who suffer the injury. Second, it is too difficult to estimate the precise amount of deadweight loss.

Both of these problems can be addressed, short of omitting deadweight loss from the antitrust damages equation altogether. It may be easier for courts to determine total harm but not allocate the harm among individual consumers. If courts can measure deadweight loss broadly but not individually, this counsels in favor of parens patriae lawsuits with cy pres distributions. Through these lawsuits, antitrust violators will still be held responsible for the harm that they inflict on the economy and will not be able to escape responsibility simply because individual consumers are unable to prove either their exclusion from the market due to the violation or their actual injury. The estimation problem can be addressed by not trebling damages based solely on deadweight loss.

The result is not perfection, but it should represent an improvement over current jurisprudence. If deadweight loss is the primary harm that antitrust laws are intended to deal with, then antitrust law should find some way to compensate those injured by the deadweight loss. The difficulty of proving deadweight loss damages with precision should not mean that firms found to have violated antitrust laws should be completely unaccountable for the harms that they have inflicted on consumers priced out of the market.

Endnotes

1. See Christopher R. Leslie, Trust, Distrust, and Antitrust, 82 TEX. L. REV. 515, 555-57 (2004).

2. The presence of barriers to entry enhances the ability of monopolists and cartels to raise price with less fear of price-reducing competitors' coming into the market.

3. Leslie, supra note 1, at 553-54.

4. There is no deadweight loss if there is perfect price discrimination. KEITH N. HYLTON, ANTITRUST LAW: ECONOMIC THEORY AND COMMON LAW EVOLUTION 14 (2003). But perfect price discrimination is difficult to achieve. For the purposes of this article, I will assume no price discrimination. This assumption is reasonable because price discrimination is difficult to accomplish and often entails significant costs to prevent arbitrage.

5. Herbert Hovenkamp, Antitrust's Protected Class, 88 MICH L. REV. 1, 21 (1989) ("While the economic concepts of allocative efficiency and social cost were unknown to them, some members of Congress realized that monopoly yielded both high prices and reduced output").

6. William M. Landes, Optimal Sanctions for Antitrust Violations, 50 U. CHI. L. REV. 652, 653 (1983) ("The standard economic rationale for making a cartel illegal is not that it charges too high a price or that it redistributes income from consumers to cartel members, but that it restricts output, causing a deadweight or efficiency loss... — a loss to consumers without an offsetting gain to producers"); Hovenkamp, supra note 5, at 14 ("For those who believe that efficiency is the exclusive goal of the antitrust laws, the wealth transfer is not a policy problem, for it represents no efficiency loss. For them, the antitrust problem is the deadweight loss triangle"); STEPHEN BREYER, REGULATION AND ITS REFORM 16 (1982) ("The result is waste: Consumers compare the high monopoly price of the monopolized product with the relatively cheaper prices of competitively produced products and buy more of the latter even though (1) they may prefer more of the former and (2) it costs society less in terms of real resources to produce more of the former and less of the latter").

7. LAWRENCE A. SULLIVAN & WARREN GRIMES, THE LAW OF ANTITRUST: AN INTEGRATED HANDBOOK 12 (2d ed. 2006) ("If there is universal agreement on one antitrust goal, it is that antitrust should strive for the efficient allocation of society's available goods and services"). There is

a debate, however, about how much deadweight loss is caused. See ROGER D. BLAIR & DAVID L. KASERMAN, ANTITRUST ECONOMICS 37-39 (1985).

8. See, e.g., In re Western Liquid Asphalt Cases, 487 F.2d 191, 200 (9th Cir. 1973) ("[T]he amount of the overcharge is not necessarily the total amount of harm to plaintiffs. Purchasers may also have been damaged by being forced to turn to substitute goods, or to discontinue purchasing the price-fixed product"); *Ball Memorial Hosp. v. Mutual Hosp. Ins.,* 784 F.2d 1325, 1334 (7th Cir. 1986) (noting injury in the form of lower output).

9. *Montreal Trading Ltd. v. Amax Inc.*, 661 F.2d 864, 866 (10th Cir. 1981). Montreal Trading is atypical because "the defendants maintained that Montreal Trading could claim no damages from any inability to purchase potash since it intended to resell to customers in North Korea in violation of the Foreign Assets Control Regulations, 31 C.F.R. [section] 500.201(b)." Id. In the context of higher prices and reduced quantity caused by a cartel agreement, at least one court has allowed excluded consumers to sue on a boycott theory. See, e.g., *Amey v. Gulf Abstract & Title*, 758 F.2d 1486 (11th Cir. 1985).

10. Hovenkamp, supra note 5, at 31.

11. Robert H. Lande, Are Antitrust "Treble" Damages Really Single Damages? 54 OHIO ST. L.J. 115, 152 (1993); see also David C. Hjelmfelt & Channing D. Strother, Jr., Antitrust Damages for Consumer Welfare Loss, 39 CLEV. ST. L. REV. 505, 505 n.4 (1991) ("In an unreported decision, the U.S. District Court for the Central District of California granted defendant's motion to exclude any reference before the jury to damages based on the loss of consumer welfare") (citing *City of Vernon v. S. Cal. Edison Co.,* No. 83-8137 (C.D. Cal. May 23, 1989)).

12. ABA ANTITRUST SECTION, MONOGRAPH No. 13, TREBLE DAMAGES REMEDY 42 (1986).

13. This search included "deadweight loss," "dead-weight loss," and "dead weight loss."

14. *Minn. Milk Producers Ass'n v. Glickman*, 153 F.3d 632 (8th Cir. 1998) (milk producers challenging federal milk pricing program); *Newman-Green, Inc. v. Alfonzo-Larrain R.,* 854 F.2d 916 (7th Cir. 1988) (jurisdictional issue in trademark dispute over royalty payments); *United States v. BNS Inc.,* 848 F.2d 945 (9th Cir. 1988) (Beezer, J., dissenting) (arguing that district court abused its discretion in granting preliminary injunction to target in takeover

battle because preventing efficient transfers creates deadweight loss); *Olympia Equip. Leasing Co. v. W. Union Tel. Co.*, 786 F.2d 794 (7th Cir. 1986) (bankruptcy can cause deadweight loss); *Am. Hosp. Supply Corp. v. Hosp. Prods. Ltd.*, 780 F.2d 589 (7th Cir. 1986) (same); *Adventures Plus, Inc. v. City of Dallas*, 2001 WL 1018732 (N.D.Tex. 2001) (challenge to constitutionality of zoning); In re Caere Corp. Sec. Litig., 837 F.Supp. 1054 (N.D. Cal. 1993) (securities fraud); *Rintel v. Wathen*, 806 F.Supp. 1467 (C.D. Cal. 1992) (securities fraud); *United States v. Bogan*, 788 F.Supp. 433 (N.D. Cal. 1992) (amending criminal sentences of armed robbers); In re Verifone Sec. Litig., 784 F.Supp. 1471 (N.D. Cal. 1992) (securities); *National Treasury Employees Union v. Horner*, 1987 WL 10106 (D.D.C. 1987) (order granting stay in labor case).

15. *Brown v. Pro Football, Inc.*, 50 F.3d 1041 (D.C. Cir. 1995) (Wald, J., dissenting) ("according to the economists, there is a dead-weight loss associated with imposition of monopsony pricing restraints"); *Telecor Commc'ns, Inc. v. Sw. Bell Tel. Co.*, 305 F.3d 1124 (10th Cir. 2002) (quoting Wald dissent in Brown).

16. *Consol. Metal Prods., Inc. v. Am. Petroleum Ins.*, 846 F.2d 284, 293 n.26 (5th Cir. 1988) (discussing Lawrence A. Sullivan, The Viability of the Current Law on Horizontal Restraints, 75 CALIF. L. REV. 835, 840-51 (1987)); see also *Univ. of Okla. v. NCAA*, 707 F.2d 1147 (10th Cir. 1983) (plaintiffs granted standing despite fact that "many of the injuries alleged by the plaintiffs are in the nature of vertical restraint injuries rather than the allocative efficiency/deadweight loss classically attributed to cartelization").

17. Plaintiffs who have been charged too much money because of either a price-fixing cartel or illegal monopolization will prove their actual damages based on the amount of the overcharge and that amount will be trebled by the court.

18. *Reiter v. Sonotone Corp.*, 442 U.S. 330, 343 (1979).

19. See *Warner Mgmt. Consultants, Inc. v. Data Gen. Corp.*, 545 F. Supp. 956, 963 (N.D. Ill. 1982). However, there is still a limit on even those consumers who paid "too much" because of the antitrust violation. Although antitrust violations may cause other suppliers (who have not either illegally monopolized a market or participated in a cartel) to raise their prices, most courts hold that only those consumers who paid the inflated price to the actual violator may recover antitrust damages. Lande, supra note 11, at 147 ("Courts are split over whether customers of the violator's competitors can successfully sue the offenders on the theory that the offenders were responsible for

"umbrella" effects. As a practical matter, however, umbrella effect damages are rarely awarded against an offending cartel or monopoly, largely because of proof problems").

20. Landes, supra note 6, at 676 ("One criticism of this damage computation is that it does not compensate for the deadweight loss. That is, customers who reduce their purchases or make none at all do not recover on the units they would have purchased if price had been lower").

21. See infra notes 50-73 and accompanying text.

22. Edward D. Cavanagh, Detrebling Antitrust Damages: An Idea Whose Time Has Come?, 61 TUL. L. REV. 777, 786 (1987).

23. *Andrx Pharm., Inc. v. Biovail Corp. Int'l*, 256 F.3d 799, 805 (D.C. Cir. 2001); *Montreal Trading Ltd. v. Amax Inc.,* 661 F.2d 864, 867 (10th Cir. 1981).

24. *Kelco Disposal, Inc. v. Browning-Ferris Indus.,* 845 F.2d 404, 410-11 (2d Cir. 1988) ("A plaintiff that undertakes the role of private attorney general and recovers treble damages, is awarded attorneys' fees for safeguarding paramount and pervasive values that are protected by federal law"); see also Phillip Areeda, Antitrust Violations Without Damage Recoveries, 89 HARV. L. REV. 1127, 1127 (1976) ("Treble damages also punish wrongdoers and enlist private plaintiffs in the work of detecting, punishing, and thereby deterring wrongdoing") (citing *Zenith Radio Corp. v. Hazeltine Research, Inc.,* 395 U.S. 100, 130-31 (1969); *Lehrman v. Gulf Oil Corp.,* 500 F.2d 659, 667 (5th Cir. 1974)).

25. Montreal Trading, 661 F.2d at 867 (quoting *Ill. Brick Co. v. Illinois*, 431 U.S. 720, 746 (1977)).

26. *Lyons v. Westinghouse Elec. Corp.,* 222 F.2d 184, 189 (2d Cir. 1955).

27. See Joseph Gregory Sidak, Rethinking Antitrust Damages, 33 STAN. L. REV. 329, 330 (1981) ("The purposes of treble damages are twofold: to compensate plaintiffs for their injury and to punish the defendant in order to deter future violations") (citing *Pfizer, Inc. v. Gov't of India,* 434 U.S. 308, 314 (1978); Illinois Brick, 431 U.S. at 746; *Brunswick Corp. v. Pueblo Bowl-O-Mat, Inc.,* 429 U.S. 477, 485-86 (1977); and Zenith Radio, 395 U.S. 100 at 130-31.

28. See Cavanagh, supra note 22 at 783 ("The private treble damages provision fosters four interrelated goals: (1) compensation of victims; (2) deterrence of violators; (3) forfeiture of ill-gotten gains; and (4) punishment for wrong-

doing"); Hjelmfelt & Strother, supra note 11, at 508 ("[T]he Supreme Court has held that the purpose of the trebling provision is intentionally a mixed one") (citing *Am. Soc. of Mech. Eng'rs, Inc. v. Hydrolevel Corp.,* 456 U.S. 556, 575-76 (1982)).

29. Hjelmfelt & Strother, supra note 11, at 509 ("There is no basis for assuming that recovery of the deadweight loss is subsumed within treble damages. As indicated previously, while trebling of damages is intended to accomplish several purposes, recovery of deadweight consumer welfare loss is not one of them").

30. *City of Detroit v. Grinnell Corp.*, 495 F.2d 448, 458 (2d Cir. 1974) ("[T]here are strong reasons why trebling is improper when computing a base recovery figure which will be used to measure the adequacy of a settlement offer").

31. See Lande, supra note 11, at 118.

32. Robert H. Lande, Why Antitrust Damage Levels Should Be Raised, 16 LOY. CONSUMER L. REV. 329, 341 n.48 (citing Brief of Amici Curiae of Professors Darren Bush, et al. at 4, Empagran, S.A. v.F. Hoffman-LaRoche, Ltd., No. 03-724 (U.S. Mar. 15, 2004), 2004 WL 533933 ("This research demonstrates that the international vitamin cartel generated the largest total of antitrust fines and penalties in history, which are calculated to be between $4.4 and $5.6 billion. But the cartel's monopoly profits in all areas of the world were $9 to $13 billion").

33. See Robert Pitofsky, Antitrust At The Turn Of The Twenty-First Century: The Matter of Remedies, 91 GEO. L.J. 169, 171 (2002) ("Studies show that treble damages really amount approximately to single damages in most circumstances"); Joseph F. Brodley, Antitrust Standing In Private Merger Cases: Reconciling Private Incentives And Public Enforcement Goals, 94 MICH. L. REV. 1, 23 n.91 (1995) ("In fact, treble damages turn out to be closer to single damages when current losses, litigation costs, and future recovery are discounted to present value").

34. See, e.g., In re Visa Check/MasterMoney Antitrust Litig., 297 F. Supp. 2d 503, 508 (E.D.N.Y. 2003) ($3.4 billion settlement); *Conwood Co. v. U.S. Tobacco Co.,* 290 F.3d 768 (6th Cir. 2002) ($1.05 billion damages award against antitrust defendant).

35. Antitrust plaintiffs also face greater problems with ever-tightening standards for liability rather than problems with the standards or formulas for calculating damages.

36. Lande, supra note 11, at 122 ("The legislative history and case law indicate that compensation is a goal, perhaps even the dominant goal, of antitrust's damages remedy"); Roderick G. Dorman, The Case for Compensation: Why Compensatory Components are Required for Efficient Antitrust Enforcement, 68 GEO. L.J. 1113, 1116-19 (1980).

37. See supra notes 17-19 and accompanying text.

38. This is the difference between their reservation price and the monopoly (or cartel) price that they paid.

39. They may get some consumer surplus from the substitute products if they purchase a substitute, but they would receive more in the market where the antitrust violation occurred.

40. ABA ANTITRUST SECTION, MONOGRAPH NO. 13, TREBLE DAMAGES REMEDY 26 (1986) ("Deadweight loss constitutes an economic inefficiency in that resources that would have been used to produce additional units of the monopolist's goods are diverted to the production of substitute goods valued less by consumers. In an economic sense, therefore, resources are less efficiently utilized").

41. Landes, supra note 6, at 665 ("It has been argued recently that the social cost of monopoly is far greater than just its deadweight loss. Because firms spend resources to monopolize a market and to maintain their monopoly position, part of the aggregate overcharge to consumers is transformed into a resource expenditure...Because these expenditures produce nothing of value, they add to the social cost of a monopoly").

42. See Lande, supra note 11, at 142-43 ("The 225 officials who responded reported spending an average of 203 hours of executive time per case. This figure does not include administrative or nonexecutive time, corporate overhead or direct expenses, Board of Directors time, in-house counsel time, time wasted because of disruption of employees routine, or time spent by employees discussing the case").

43. Hovenkamp, supra note 5, at 6. Deterrence is one of the reasons behind the treble damage scheme. Lande, supra note 11, at 125 ("Congress's decision to award treble damages could also imply that at least part of their purpose is the deterrence of undesirable behavior").

44. See supra notes 31-33 and accompanying text. See also Hjelmfelt & Strother, supra note 11, at 507 ("One mathematical model predicts that, at commonly

encountered inflation rates, treble damages provide insufficient deterrence even if detection and successful prosecution is assumed to be certain") (citing ABA ANTITRUST SECTION, MONOGRAPH NO. 13, TREBLE DAMAGES REMEDY 43 (1986)). Disgorgement plays an important role in deterrence, in that the law must minimize the expected benefits of illegal conduct in order to render violations not cost-beneficial. The Supreme Court has recognized that "[o]nly by requiring violators to disgorge the 'fruits of their illegality' can the deterrent objectives of the antitrust laws be fully served." *Blue Shield of Va. v. McCready,* 457 U.S. 465, 473 n.10 (1982) (citation omitted). Of course, having defendants pay the amount of the deadweight loss caused by their antitrust violations is not a form of disgorgement. Disgorgement means calculating the gains that the defendant received from its illegal conduct and forcing the defendant to pay those back. Incorporating deadweight loss into antitrust damages is not disgorgement because antitrust violators do not gain from the deadweight loss directly. *Montreal Trading Ltd. v. Amax Inc.,* 661 F.2d 864, 867 (10th Cir. 1981) ("Here, we note that while nonpurchasers may be considered victims of the conspiracy, the alleged conspirators gained no "fruits" from nonsales except to the extent that sales volume had to decline if they were to succeed in charging inflated prices"). That is what makes the loss total—it is not a transfer of wealth from consumer to producers.

45. See, e.g., *Texaco Inc. v. Dagher*, 126 S. Ct. 1276 (2006); *State Oil Co. v. Khan,* 522 U.S. 3 (1997); *Bus. Elecs. Corp. v. Sharp Elecs. Corp.,* 485 U.S. 717 (1988); *Broad. Music, Inc. v. Columbia Broad. Sys., Inc.,* 441 U.S. 1 (1979).

46. See *Matsushita Elec. Indus. Co., Ltd. v. Zenith Radio Corp.,* 475 U.S. 574 (1986) and its progeny.

47. See National Cooperative Research & Production Act (providing single damages for some joint ventures); Standards Development Organization Advancement Act of 2004 (providing single damages for some standard setting organizations); Antitrust Criminal Penalty Enhancement and Reform Act of 2004 (providing for single damages for the first cartel member to confess under the government's amnesty program).

48. Of course even the optimal deterrent will not successfully deter all misconduct, but the number of suspected and convicted price-fixers is sufficiently high to believe that the current regime has not achieved optimal deterrence. These numbers do not reflect the recent increases in antitrust penalties. See also Lande, supra note 32, at 330 ("There is no convincing evidence that the aggregate of direct purchaser damages, indirect purchaser damages, and the

like produces damage levels so high that they have led to real duplication or overdeterrence").

49. Hovenkamp, supra note 5, at 30-31 ("Ironically, even though the traditional deadweight loss triangle is the oldest recognized and least controversial of monopoly's social costs, the existing rules of antitrust standing rarely permit the deadweight loss to become the basis of a damages action"). There are scholars who advocate bringing deadweight loss considerations into antitrust damages analysis. See ABA ANTITRUST SECTION, MONOGRAPH NO. 13, TREBLE DAMAGES REMEDY 33-35 (1986).

50. *Eleven Line, Inc. v. N. Tex. Soccer Assoc., Inc.,* 213 F.3d 198, 206-207 (5th Cir. 2000) (quoting *Multiflex, Inc. v. Samuel Moore & Co.,* 709 F.2d 980, 989 (5th Cir. 1983)).

51. *J.T. Gibbons, Inc. v. Crawford Fitting Co.,* 704 F.2d 787, 791 (5th Cir. 1983).

52. *Copper Liquor, Inc. v. Adolph Coors Co.,* 624 F.2d 575, 580 (5th Cir. 1980) (citations omitted).

53. *J. Truett Payne Co., Inc. v. Chrysler Motors Corp.,* 451 U.S. 557, 566 (1981).

54. *Story Parchment Co. v. Paterson Parchment Paper Co.,* 282 U.S. 555, 563 (1931); ABA SECTION ON ANTITRUST LAW, SAMPLE JURY INSTRUCTIONS IN CIVIL ANTITRUST CASES (1999 ed.) at F-8 ("A defendant's violations of antitrust laws often create a situation in which it is hard to determine the precise amount of damages suffered by the plaintiff").

55. *Malcolm v. Marathon Oil Co.,* 642 F.2d 845, 864 (5th Cir. 1981).

56. *Pierce v. Ramsey Winch Co.,* 753 F.2d 416, 434-35 (5th Cir. 1985).

57. Story Parchment, 282 U.S. at 563; ABA ANTITRUST SECTION, MONOGRAPH NO. 13, TREBLE DAMAGES REMEDY 11 (1986) ("The damages awarded need only be an approximation; lack of certainty of amount or precision in calculation are not grounds for denying recovery").

58. *Hobart Brothers Co. v. Malcolm T. Gilliland, Inc.,* 471 F.2d 894, 903 (5th Cir. 1973).

59. ABA SECTION ON ANTITRUST LAW, SAMPLE JURY INSTRUCTIONS IN CIVIL ANTITRUST CASES (1999 ed.) at F-8 ("Plaintiff's right to be fairly compensated should not be affected by any difficulty you may have in determining the precise amount of the recovery so long as there is a reasonable basis in the evidence for your award").

60. *Pierce v. Ramsey Winch*, 753 F.2d at 438 ("We are careful to note, however, that, even under the relaxed standard, a jury verdict based on speculation alone cannot stand").

61. *Bigelow v. RKO Radio Pictures*, 327 U.S. 251, 264 (1946).

62. 431 U.S. 720 (1977).

63. Id. at 742.

64. See ABA SECTION OF ANTITRUST LAW, PROVING ANTITRUST DAMAGES 196 (1996) ("there are obvious practical problems associated with proving what purchases would have been but were not made"); Cavanagh, supra note 22, at 834 ("The economic measure of loss—lost opportunity cost—is always difficult to determine"); Frank Easterbrook, Detrebling Antitrust Damages, 28 J.L. & ECON. 445, 450 (1985) ("Finding [the sum of the monopoly overcharge and the welfare triangle]…is no mean feat. The court needs to know the elasticities of supply and demand over the entire range of output, and it also needs to compute a hypothetical market price for a market characterized by different costs of production"); ROBERT BORK, THE ANTITRUST PARADOX 108 (1978) ("We do not know in any actual case the slope of the demand curve, the location of the initial cost curve, the distance (if any) the cost curve will shift, or the amount (if any) the output will change").

65. Landes, supra note 6, at 678 ("The optimal penalty should equal the net harm to persons other than the offender").

66. Steven C. Salop in A Reassessment of Antitrust Remedies, Panel Discussion, 55 ANTITRUST L.J. 123, 127 (1986).

67. See, e.g., Jerry A. Hausman, Exact Consumer's Surplus and Deadweight Loss, 71 AM. ECON REV. 662, 673-74 (1981) ("While it has been known that use of the compensated demand curves lead to the appropriate welfare measures, it has not been generally recognized how straightforward it is to derive the compensated demand curves from observed market demand curves").

68. See id. at 663 ("From an estimate of the demand curve, we can derive a measure of the exact consumer's surplus, whether it is the compensating variation, equivalent variation, or some measure of utility change. No approximation is involved"); Jerry A. Hausman & Whitney K. Newey, Nonparametric Estimation of Exact Consumers Surplus and Deadweight Loss, 63 ECONOMETRICA 1445 (1995); Robert D. Willig, Consumer's Surplus Without Apology, 66 AM. ECON. REV. 589 (1976) ("I derive precise upper and lower bounds on the percentage errors of approximating the compensating and equivalent variations with consumer's surplus. These bounds can be explicitly calculated from observable demand data, and it is clear that in most applications the error of approximation will be very small"); see also Pascal Lavergne, Vincent Requillart & Michel Simioni, Welfare Losses Due to Market Power: Hicksian Versus Marshallian Measurement, 83 AM. J. OF AGRIC. ECON. 157 (2001) (noting that "Hausman…shows how theoretical variation of consumer surplus can be exactly derived when only one price changes"); Robert H. Haveman, Mary Gabay, and James Andreoni, Exact Consumer's Surplus and Deadweight Loss: A Correction, 77 AM. ECON. REV. 494, 494 (1987) ("Jerry Hausman's 1981 paper…is a clear demonstration that Hicksian-based estimates of welfare change can be measured exactly from an empirically estimated demand or supply curve"); ANDREU MAS-COLELL, MICHAEL D. WHINSTON, & JERRY R. GREEN, MICROECONOMIC THEORY 84-87, 385-86 (1995).

69. See Hjelmfelt & Strother, supra note 11, at 511 ("Based upon that determination, lost profits would be calculated. Calculations for market share growth obviously involve many more assumptions than does estimating demand elasticity").

70. Id. at 514 ("There is nothing inherently speculative about the computation of damages based on deadweight loss. If the calculation is carefully performed with adequate record support for its assumptions, such a damage study should not be rejected on grounds that damages cannot be calculated").

71. See supra notes 52-58 and accompanying text.

72. *Bigelow v. RKO Radio Pictures,* 327 U.S. 251, 264-65 (1946); see also *Andrx Pharm., Inc. v. Biovail Corp. Int'l,* 256 F.3d 799, 815 (D.C. Cir. 2001) (quoting Bigelow, 327 U.S. at 265); *Story Parchment Co. v. Paterson Parchment Paper Co.,* 282 U.S. 555, 562 (1931) ("Although damages may be difficult to quantify, '[t]he most elementary conceptions of justice and public policy require that the wrongdoer shall bear the risk of the uncertainty which his own wrong has created'").

73. This is particularly true when estimating lost future profits. *Hobart Brothers Co. v. Malcolm T. Gilliland, Inc.*, 471 F.2d 894, 904 (5th Cir. 1973).

74. See supra note 47.

75. See ABA ANTITRUST SECTION, MONOGRAPH No. 13, TREBLE DAMAGES REMEDY 20 (1986) (explaining rationale).

76. This is not an argument for detrebling antitrust damages more generally. Trebling still serves a valuable function in traditional suits. If the purpose of treble damages is to encourage private investigation and litigation, such enticement is not necessary for deadweight loss claims, which are likely to be follow-on lawsuits. There is no need for extensive investigation and little risk of losing the liability determination in litigation, as collateral estoppel should resolve the core issues against the defendant.

77. Hjelmfelt & Strother, supra note 11, at 507.

78. Id. ("Additionally, it is more efficient to permit the direct purchaser to recover for all losses caused by the violation").

79. *Ill. Brick Co. v. Illinois*, 431 U.S. 720, 760 (1977) (Brennan, J., dissenting).

80. *Brunswick Corp. v. Pueblo Bowl-O-Mat, Inc.*, 429 U.S. 477, 489 (1977).

81. *Blue Shield of Va. v. McCready*, 457 U.S. 465, 482-83 (1982) ("[W]hile an increase in price resulting from a dampening of competitive market forces is assuredly one type of injury for which [section] 4 potentially offers redress, that is not the only form of injury remediable under [section] 4") (citation omitted).

82. Id. at 472.

83. *Bob Nicholson Appliance, Inc. v. Maytag*, 883 F. Supp. 321, 324 (S.D. Ind. 1994) (emphasis added) (citing *Stamatakis Indus., Inc. v. King*, 965 F.2d 469, 471 (7th Cir. 1992) (quoting *Chi. Prof'l Sports Ltd. P'ship v. Nat'l Basketball Ass'n*, 961 F.2d 667, 670 (7th Cir. 1992)); see also *O.K. Sand and Gravel v. Martin Marietta Corp.*, 819 F. Supp. 771,787 (S.D.Ind. 1992)).

84. *Nelson v. Monroe Reg'l Med. Ctr.*, 925 F.2d 1555, 1564 (7th Cir.1991) (emphasis added).

85. Reduced output must qualify as antitrust injury; otherwise the consumer victims of illegal boycotts would be unable to seek compensation.

86. Cavanagh, supra note 22, at 806 ("Posner, on the other hand, points out that the private remedy by itself may lead to too much enforcement because the plaintiffs' bar 'cannot be relied upon to exercise appropriate self-restraint'"); *Andrx Pharm., Inc. v. Biovail Corp. Int'l,* 256 F.3d 799, 806 (D.C. Cir. 2001) ("The Supreme Court, however, has recognized that 'the potency of the remedy implies the need for some care in its application' and does not construe the section 4 language to allow suit by every party affected by an antitrust violator's 'ripples of harm.' McCready, 457 U.S. at 476-77, 102 S. Ct. 2540").

87. *Associated Gen. Contractors, Inc. v. Cal. State Council of Carpenters*, 459 U.S. 519 (1983).

88. *Amarel v. Connell*, 102 F.3d 1494, 1507 (9th Cir. 1996) (citing Associated Gen. Contractors, 459 U.S. at 535).

89. Andrx Pharmaceuticals, 256 F.3d at 806 ("Additional factors to be considered in determining whether the plaintiff has 'antitrust standing' include: the directness of the injury, whether the claim for damages is 'speculative,' the existence of more direct victims, the potential for duplicative recovery and the complexity of apportioning damages") (citations omitted).

90. See Amarel, 102 F.3d at 1507.

91. See supra notes 82-84 and accompanying text.

92. *Instructional Sys. Dev. Corp. v. Aetna Casualty & Surety Co.*, 817 F.2d 639, 650 (10th Cir. 1987) (quoting *King & King Enters. v. Champlin Petroleum Co.,* 657 F.2d 1147, 1156 (10th Cir. 1981)).

93. See *Hahn v. Rifkin/Narragansett S, Fla. CATV Ltd. P'ship*, 941 F.Supp. 1196, 1200 (S.D. Fla. 1996).

94. Andrx Pharmaceuticals, 256 F.3d at 816.

95. See, e.g., *Midwest Gas Servs., Inc. v. Ind. Gas Co.*, 317 F.3d 703, 710-11 (7th Cir. 2003).

96. *Montreal Trading Ltd. v. Amax Inc.,* 661 F.2d 864, 868 (10th Cir. 1981) ("Given these problems and uncertainties, and that actual purchasers exist

who were more directly injured by the conspiracy and who could be expected to police the conspiracy as 'private attorneys general,' see *Hawaii v. Standard Oil Co.,* 405 U.S. 251, 262, 92 S.Ct. 885, 891, 31 L.Ed.2d 184 (1972), we believe nonpurchasers should be denied standing to sue, at least when they lack a past course of dealing with the conspirators").

97. Some courts treat the "target area" test as an alternative to the "direct injury" test. See, e.g., *Warner Mgmt. Consultants, Inc. v. Data Gen. Corp.,* 545 F.Supp. 956, 963 n.6 (N.D. Ill. 1982) ("In *Repp v. F.E.L. Publications, Ltd.,* 688 F.2d 444 at 441-45 (7th Cir. 1982), the court of appeals indicated that this circuit had not yet chosen between the 'target area' and the 'direct injury' tests").

98. In re Indus. Gas Antitrust Litig., 681 F.2d 514, 516 (7th Cir. 1982); see also *Arthur S. Langenderfer, Inc. v. S.E. Johnson Co.,* 917 F.2d 1413 (6th Cir. 1990) ("We have also looked to see whether the injury claimed is arguably within the zone of interests protected by the antitrust laws").

99. *Calderone Enters. v. United Artists Theatre Circuit*, 454 F.2d 1292, 1295 (2d Cir. 1971).

100. Langenderfer, 917 F.2d at 1438 (quoting Associated General Contractors, 459 U.S. at 543-44).

101. 431 U.S. 720 (1977).

102. See, e.g., Sidak, supra note 27, at 338 n.32 ("Alternatively, it is arguable on economic and legal grounds that the parties most entitled to damages are consumers whose diverted purchases constituted the actual deadweight loss. But such a rule is barred by the Supreme Court ruling that indirect purchasers may not recover damages from antitrust violators. *Illinois Brick Co. v. Illinois,* 431 U.S. 720 (1977)"); *Montreal Trading Ltd. v. Amax Inc.,* 661 F.2d 864, 868 (10th Cir. 1981).

103. Similarly, when cartels raise prices, purchasers and nonpurchasers suffer different damages for different injuries—overcharges and deadweight loss, respectively.

104. Roger D. Blair & William H. Page, "Speculative" Antitrust Damages, 70 WASH. L. REV. 423, 434 (1995).

105. *Andrx Pharm., Inc. v. Biovail Corp. Int'l,* 256 F.3d 799, 815 (D.C. Cir. 2001) (quoting *Blue Shield of Va. v. McCready*, 457 U.S. 456, 475 n.11).

106. See *Hawaii v. Standard Oil Co.,* 405 U.S. 251 (1972). There is also a risk of duplicative recoveries. See *Warner Mgmt. Consultants, Inc. v. Data Gen. Corp.,* 545 F.Supp. 956, 962 (N.D. Ill. 1982).

107. See Hovenkamp, supra note 5, at 31.

108. See *Montreal Trading Ltd. v. Amax Inc.,* 661 F.2d 864, 868 (10th Cir. 1981) ("When the non-purchaser can show a regular course of dealing with the conspirators, injury may not be inherently speculative").

109. See id. ("But when, as here, the non-purchaser has no prior course of dealing with any defendant, we will remain unsure about many things, including: whether the purchase would have been made from one of the conspirators or from one of their competitors; what quantity would have been purchased; what price would have been paid; and at what price resale would have occurred").

110. For consumers who had not purchased the product in the past but would have participated in the market at the competitive price, they will have no evidence of their injury despite the fact that they were an actual and intended victim of the antitrust violation.

111. Frank H. Easterbrook in A Reassessment of Antitrust Remedies, Panel Discussion, 55 ANTITRUST L.J. 123, 126 (1986); see also HYLTON, supra note 4, at 61 ("Each consumer who has purchased two widgets at the monopoly price could potentially claim that he would have purchased three widgets at the competitive price. But how can courts determine the validity of such claims? They cannot, so courts do not permit consumers to recover on such speculative components of injury").

112. Hovenkamp, supra note 5, at 31.

113. Blair & Page, supra note 104, at 425 ("Any practical adaptation of the private damage remedy to antitrust policy requires an effective mechanism for the proof of individual harm").

114. Susan Beth Farmer, More Lessons from the Laboratories: Cy Pres Distributions in Parens Patriae Antitrust Actions Brought By State Attorneys General, 68 FORDHAM L. REV. 361, 377 (1999).

115. Id. at 362-64 (citations omitted).

116. *Commonwealth v. Milk Indus. Mgmt. Corp.,* 812 F.Supp. 500 (E.D. Pa. 1992).

117. See supra notes 82-85 and accompanying text.

118. See Remeron End-Payor Antitrust Litig., 2005 WL 2230314, *16 (D.N.J. 2005) (citing cases).

119. Cavanagh, supra note 22, at 807.

120. 15 U.S.C.A. [section] 15c(d)(2).

121. 15 U.S.C.A. [section] 15c(c).

122. See Edward Brunet, Improving Class Action Efficiency by Expanded Use of Parens Patriae Suits and Intervention, 74 TULANE L. REV. 1919, 1932 (2000) (noting states' employment of private counsel in tobacco litigation).

123. See id. at 1932-33 (noting that state attorneys general's offices can monitor private counsel hired to litigate parens patriae actions, including limiting attorneys' fees).

124. See, e.g., Arthur M. Kaplan, Antitrust as a Public-Private Partnership: A Case Study of the NASDAQ Litigation, 52 CASE W. RES. L. REV. 111 (2001).

125. 15 U.S.C.A. [section] 15d.

126. Farmer, supra note 114, at 382 n.145 (quoting H.R. Rep. No. 94-499, at 14-15 (1976), reprinted in 1976 U.S.C.C.A.N. 2572, 2584).

127. There may be an issue of calculating deadweight loss on a per state basis. Joint litigation with several state attorneys general may help resolve such issues.

128. 15 U.S.C.A. [section] 15e.

129. Though objective, it may be hard to prove class membership because consumers often do not retain proof of purchase.

130. See *New York v. Salton, Inc.*, 265 F. Supp. 2d 310 (S.D.N.Y. 2003).

131. See SULLIVAN & GRIMES, supra note 7, at 948 ("Although states have received substantial damage awards in some parens patriae actions, the awards often have cy pres (substitutes for direct payments to the injured

buyer) characteristics, for example discount coupons for future purchases or payments channeled to relevant charitable causes").

132. See, e.g., *New York v. Reebok Int'l, Ltd.*, 903 F. Supp. 532, 537 (S.D.N.Y. 1995), aff'd 96 F.3d 44 (2d Cir. 1996).

133. See Farmer, supra note 114, at 398-99 ("The residual funds resulting from class action or statutory parens patriae antitrust litigation or settlements have been used to fund antitrust enforcement by state Attorneys General in a number of cases") (citing cases); see, e.g., *New York v. Nintendo of Am., Inc.*, 775 F. Supp. 676, 679 (S.D.N.Y. 1991).

134. See Farmer, supra note 114, at 394.

135. Landes, supra note 6, at 656 ("The rule for determining the optimal fine or damage award is simple to state: the fine should equal the net harm to persons other than the offender. In our example this harm is $150, the $100 overcharge plus the $50 deadweight loss"). Not surprisingly, however, basing damages solely on the deadweight loss caused by an antitrust violation would be too small to deter anticompetitive conduct. Hovenkamp, supra note 5, at 6 ("One might think that the optimum penalty for antitrust violations must be based on the deadweight loss, since that loss represents the 'social cost' of monopoly. But clearly a penalty equal to the deadweight loss would be too small").

136. PHILLIP E. AREEDA & HERBERT HOVENKAMP, 1 ANTITRUST LAW 125 n.36 (2d ed. 2000).

137. Cavanagh, supra note 22 at 823-24 ("IT]he accepted measure of damages in monopolization and cartelization cases—overcharges—does not measure the total harm caused by the illegal conduct. In addition to overcharges, there is a net loss to society arising from the misallocation of resources").

138. See Lande, supra note 11, at 169 ("If defendant overcharged by one dollar, defendant would gain more than a dollar because of the time value of money").

Chapter 3

Quality Control of Economic Expert Testimony: The Fundamental Methods of Proving Antitrust Damages

Michele Molyneaux, J.D.

Synopsis

3.1 Introduction

In *Daubert v. Merrell Dow Pharmaceuticals, Inc.*,[1] the Supreme Court stated that under Rule 702 of the Federal Rules of Evidence "the trial judge must ensure that any and all scientific testimony or evidence admitted is not only relevant, but reliable."[2] The proposed expert testimony "must be supported by appropriate validation—i.e., 'good grounds,' based on what is known."[3] The Court explained that trial judges must determine reliability by engaging in "a preliminary assessment of whether the reasoning or methodology underlying the testimony is scientifically valid and of whether that reasoning or methodology properly can be applied to the facts in issue."[4] The Court provided factors that might be relevant to the inquiry, including "whether it can be (and has been) tested," "whether the theory or technique has been subjected to peer review and publication," "the known or potential rate of error," and the "degree of acceptance within [a relevant scientific] community."[5] "The focus, of course, must be solely on principles and methodology, not on the conclusions that they generate."[6] Nonetheless, the Court emphasized that "[t]he inquiry envisioned by Rule 702 is...a flexible one,"[7] and the Court did "not presume to set out a definitive checklist or test."[8]

Furthermore, the Court found that "rule 702's 'helpfulness' standard requires a valid scientific connection to the pertinent inquiry as a precondition to admissibility."[9] Whether the testimony presented by the expert is "sufficiently tied to the facts of the case...has been aptly described...as one of 'fit.'"[10] However, "[s]cientific validity for one purpose is not necessarily scientific validity for other, unrelated purposes."[11]

In its later decision of *Kumho Tire Co. v. Carmichael*,[12] the Supreme Court clarified that the trial courts' gatekeeping function is not limited to 'scientific' expert testimony, but rather applies to all expert testimony.[13] The Court stated that there is not a clear line dividing "scientific" knowledge, "technical" knowledge, or "other specialized" knowledge, and the *Daubert* factors may or may not apply depending on the facts of each case:

> [T]he factors identified in *Daubert* may or may not be pertinent in assessing reliability, depending on the nature of the issue, the expert's particular expertise, and the subject of his testimony...The conclusion, in our view, is that we can neither rule out, nor rule in, for all cases and for all time the applicability of the factors mentioned in *Daubert*, nor can we now do so for subsets of cases categorized by category of expert or by kind of evidence. Too much depends upon the particular circumstances of the particular case at issue.[14]

The objective of the inquiry is to "make certain that an expert, whether basing testimony upon professional studies or personal experience, employs in the courtroom the same level of intellectual rigor that characterizes the practice of an expert in the relevant field."[15] Thus, *Kumho Tire* emphasizes that judges have broad discretion when discharging their gatekeeping function.

Before *Daubert* and *Kumho*,[16] federal courts evaluated economic testimony in antitrust cases using roughly comparable standards. Antitrust damages generally cannot be measured with absolute accuracy. In *Story Parchment Co. v. Paterson Parchment Paper Co.*,[17] the Supreme Court pointed out that "[t]he rule which precludes the recovery of uncertain damages applies to such as are not the certain result of the wrong, not to those damages which are definitely attributable to the wrong and only uncertain in respect of their amount."[18] The Court emphasized:

> [I]t would be a perversion of fundamental principles of justice to deny all relief to the injured person, and thereby relieve the wrongdoer from making any amend for his acts. In such case, while damages may not be determined by mere speculation or guess, it will be enough if the evidence show[s] the extent of the damages as a matter of just and reasonable inference, although the result be only approximate. The wrongdoer is not entitled to complain that they cannot be measured with the exactness and precision that would be possible if the case, which he alone is responsible for making, were otherwise.[19]

As *Story Parchment* indicates, there is a difference between impermissible speculation and permitted inference.[20] Although "[j]uries are allowed to act upon probable and inferential, as well as direct and positive proof,"[21] lest "the wrongdoer...profit by his wrongdoing at the expense of his victim,"[22] the jury is still required to "make a just and reasonable estimate of the damage based on relevant data."[23]

Section 3.2 of this [chapter] reviews the basic methods used by experts, and generally accepted by federal courts, to prove antitrust damages. Section 3.3 discusses the damage estimate admissibility requirement of having an adequate foundation based upon sufficient facts. Finally, Section 3.4 analyzes the *Daubert* notion of "fit." This means that the damage estimate may contain only those damages that flow from an antitrust injury; damages caused by factors other than the antitrust violation must be disaggregated from the damage estimate, and damages caused by more than one antitrust violation must be disaggregated from one another, if possible.

3.2 Methods of Proving Amount of Damages

The objective of antitrust damages is to restore the plaintiff to the economic condition in which it would have been "but for" the violation.[24] The two general classifications for private damage claims are overcharge cases and foreclosure cases.[25] Overcharge cases involve injury sustained by (1) a purchaser paying a monopoly price for an item bought from an illegal cartel or monopoly; (2) "a seller for whom the price was suppressed by a monopsonist[26] or a buyer's cartel"; or (3) the buyer of a product that was illegally tied.[27] The measure of damages is generally calculated as the "difference between the illegal price that was actually charged and the price that would have been charged 'but for' the violation, multiplied by the number of units purchased."[28] In cases of foreclosure, firms perform exclusionary acts that discourage competition, resulting in injury to competitors.[29] Such exclusionary practices include "exclusive dealing contracts, concerted refusals to deal,...mergers, resale price maintenance and nonprice restraints," and tying arrangements where a competitor in the market of the tied product is injured.[30] In these cases, the defendant's illegal actions restrict or eliminate the plaintiff's participation in the market and "an antitrust plaintiff's damages should reflect the difference between its performance in a hypothetical market free of all antitrust violations and its actual performance in the market infected by the anticompetitive conduct."[31]

The fundamental methods for measuring damages are: (1) the yardstick method, (2) the before-and-after method, (3) the market-share method, and (4) the going-concern method. These methods are not mutually exclusive, and often a combination of them is used to establish damages. The available evidence in each case will generally determine the methods used.

A. Yardstick Method

Under the yardstick method of damages, the plaintiff compares its performance to the performance of a substantially similar business, referred to as the "yardstick." The plaintiff uses the yardstick business's performance to draw inferences about how the plaintiff's business would have performed "but for" the antitrust violation. The Supreme Court approved the use of the yardstick method for estimating antitrust damages in *Bigelow v. RKO Radio Pictures, Inc.*[32] In that case, plaintiffs owned the Jackson Park movie theater in Chicago, while the defendants were a group of businesses in the Chicago area that either distributed the movies or owned competing movie theaters.[33] Plaintiffs alleged that the defendants illegally conspired to distribute the films so that the theaters controlled by or affiliated with the defendant distributors received new films several weeks in advance of the plaintiffs.[34] This allowed the defendants to maintain high admission prices in their theaters for the advanced movie showings, and forced the plaintiffs to lower their admission prices since the movies had already been shown in the area for several weeks by the defendants.[35]

Plaintiffs claimed that the delay in distribution led to a competitive disadvantage and lost profits.[36] To estimate damages, plaintiffs compared Jackson Park's earnings over a five-year period with corresponding earnings of one of the defendant competitors, the Maryland Theater.[37] Defendants argued that it was not possible to prove damages because the illegal film distribution system prevented plaintiffs from showing "that other conditions affecting profits would have continued without change unfavorable to them during the critical period if that system had not been established, and [plaintiffs] had conducted their business in a free competitive market."[38] The district court found that although the two theaters were comparable in size, the Jackson Park theater had a better location, better equipment, and was more attractive to customers.[39] Under the conspiracy, the Maryland theater was able to show movies one week before plaintiffs' Jackson Park theater.[40] Over the five-year damage period, the Maryland theater's net receipts exceeded the Jackson Park theater's receipts by roughly $116,000.[41] The Supreme Court upheld the jury's damage award based on the yardstick method.[42] Although *Bigelow* predated *Daubert*, the Supreme Court's approval of the damage analysis was faithful to the spirit of *Daubert* because the damage estimate was sufficiently tied to the facts of the case and the expert properly applied the yardstick methodology to the facts in issue.

The primary difficulty in using the yardstick method is finding a suitable yardstick. The plaintiff must demonstrate that the yardstick is substantially similar to its injured business. Even though allowances can be made for differences between the yardstick and the injured business, the yardstick still must be closely comparable to the plaintiff's business. One authority asserts that to be applicable, the yardstick and the plaintiff must participate in the same product market and be located in different geographic markets.[43] When differences exist, the expert must make adjustments in the damage calculations to account for them. For instance, if there is a difference in labor costs, the expert could "determine the labor cost per unit of output and adjust the 'but for' price for the labor cost difference."[44] However, when there is a significant difference of the type for which the expert cannot adjust, the yardstick method will be rejected.[45]

An illustration of an expert performing this adjustment is found in *Greenhaw v. Lubbock County Beverage Ass'n.*,[46] which involved retailers in Lubbock County fixing the price of liquor from June of 1970 to December of 1974.[47] Plaintiffs consisted of a class of consumers that purchased liquor from the defendants during the conspiracy.[48] Plaintiffs' expert estimated damages by comparing liquor prices in Lubbock County with the competitive market prices in Dallas.[49] First, the expert calculated a ratio reflecting the difference in cost between the markets.[50] Next, the expert used the ratio to estimate the "but for" price of liquor in Lubbock County during the damage period absent the conspiracy.[51] The expert estimated from these prices that the average overcharge during the damage period was about 7.74%.[52] Finally, the expert multiplied the defendants' total liquor sales during the damage period by 7.74% to arrive at the aggregate overcharge.[53] The expert's analysis met the *Daubert* standard, even though this case occurred a decade before *Daubert*. The expert reliably employed the yardstick method by adjusting for differences between the yardstick market and the Lubbock County market by using a valid methodology that was based on what was known. The Fifth Circuit found the expert's damage estimate acceptable.[54]

In another case, *Eleven Line, Inc. v. North Texas State Soccer Ass'n*,[55] plaintiff owned a private soccer facility and claimed that defendant, a not-for-profit soccer association, engaged in exclusionary anticompetitive conduct.[56] Specifically, the plaintiff alleged that the defendant's implementation of a membership rule that required soccer players to restrict their activities to sanctioned facilities put the plaintiff's business, which was not a sanctioned facility, out of business.[57] Plaintiff's expert sought to prove damages by using the plaintiff's other soccer arenas as the yardstick.[58] The court found that the only similarity between these other arenas and the arena in question was that plaintiff owned them all.[59] The expert did not provide any evidence of the "geographical location, size or attractiveness of those facilities, the size and type of the soccer player market that they served, the relative costs of operation, the amounts charged per team, or the number of seasons run."[60]

Because the expert did not provide this evidence, the court had no way of determining if the arenas were comparable to the allegedly damaged arena, and whether the expert should have made adjustments to account for any differences. For instance, if the price charged per team was different, the expert could have adjusted the damage estimate by substituting the price charged by the damaged arena for the price charged by the yardstick arena in the damage computation. The court concluded that the yardstick chosen by the expert could not be used to estimate plaintiff's damages.[61] Although *Eleven Line* occurred after *Daubert* and even after *Kumho Tire*, the opinion does not mention either case. Nonetheless, the opinion in *Eleven Line* is in line with *Daubert*'s scrutiny of expert testimony. The damage analysis of plaintiff's expert was not sufficiently grounded in the facts, and the methodology was improperly applied because the plaintiff did not demonstrate that the yardstick was substantially similar to the damaged arena. Therefore, the damage estimate was not reliable and not helpful to a jury.

B. Before-and-After Method

Under the before-and-after method, the plaintiff estimates damages using its performance before or after the antitrust violation to infer how it would have performed during the damage period. In overcharge cases, plaintiff estimates the prices "but for" the illegal overcharges by using the prices charged before or after the price-fixing or monopolization.[62] In the case of foreclosure, the plaintiff estimates its profits "but for" the illegal practices by using its own economic condition before the antitrust violation.[63]

A simple example is found in *Bigelow*,[64] where the plaintiff presented a comparison between its receipts from the Jackson Park theater during the five-year damage period and the corresponding receipts obtained during the four years prior to the conspiracy.[65] This comparison demonstrated a "falling off" of the Jackson Park's receipts during the five-year damage period totaling over $125,000.[66] The Supreme Court found that the comparison between Jackson Park's receipts before the defendants' illegal practices began and the receipts during the damage period "afforded a sufficient basis for the jury's computation of the damage."[67]

Even though *Bigelow* occurred nearly fifty years before *Daubert*, the Supreme Court's opinion pointed out the *Daubert* notion of the difference between impermissible speculation and permitted inference. The Court stated that the "jury may make a just and reasonable estimate of the damage based on relevant data."[68] Using the terminology in *Daubert*, the plaintiff's expert properly applied the before-and-after methodology to the facts, and the estimate was sufficiently tied to the facts of the case.

Nearly twenty years before *Bigelow*, the Supreme Court approved the use of the before-and-after method in *Eastman Kodak Co. v. Southern Photo Materials Co.*[69] There, the plaintiff sold photographic supplies to professional photographers, while defendant manufactured photographic supplies and sold these supplies to distributors for resale.[70] The defendant imposed price-fixing restrictions on the distributors that prevented them from selling the supplies of defendant's competitors.[71] Plaintiff purchased supplies from the defendant under these restrictions.[72] After defendant's failed attempt to buy plaintiff's business, defendant refused to sell supplies to the plaintiff at regular dealer discounts, but rather required plaintiff to purchase the supplies at higher retail prices.[73] As a result, plaintiff could no longer obtain and sell supplies necessary to its customers and therefore suffered significant loss of business.[74]

Plaintiff claimed as damages the lost profits that it would have obtained had it been able to continue the purchase and sale of defendant's products.[75] To estimate damages during the four-year damage period, plaintiff used its gross profits from its sales of defendant's supplies for the four years before defendant's antitrust violation, subtracting any additional necessary expenses for obtaining and selling defendant's supplies during the four-year damage period.[76] Although this case was nearly seventy years prior to *Daubert*, the Supreme Court expressed *Daubert*'s idea of reliability by stating that the "amount of the damages could not be determined by mere speculation or guess, but must be based on evidence"[77] and that plaintiff's before-and-after analysis "sufficiently showed the extent of the damages, as a matter of just and reasonable inference."[78]

Courts will exclude expert testimony estimating damages when the expert has not properly used the before-and-after method. For instance, a federal court in the district of Kansas excluded economic expert testimony because of several errors in the expert's before-and-after analysis in *In re Aluminum Phosphide Antitrust Litigation*.[79] In that case, class action plaintiffs who purchased aluminum phosphide[80] from defendants alleged that defendants conspired to fix the price of aluminum phosphide from 1988 through 1992 at supra-competitive levels.[81] Prior to plaintiffs' lawsuit, the United States Department of Justice issued subpoenas in its criminal investigation of price-fixing in the industry.[82] Some of the defendants pled guilty, others pled no contest, and the court eventually dismissed the charges against the remaining defendants.[83] To prove damages, plaintiffs' expert witness used the before-and-after method to estimate prices that would have prevailed during the conspiracy period, based on the prices that prevailed during a later non-conspiracy period.[84] In the expert's opinion, the estimated price of aluminum phosphide from 1988 to 1992, "but for" the conspiracy, was the price that prevailed during the ten months from January 1 to October 31, 1993, which was called the "normative" period.[85]

The district court found that the expert's opinion was flawed because the "opinion ignores the before component of the 'before and after' model."[86] Although price information was available for all the defendants during the period from 1986 to 1988, before the alleged conspiracy, the expert did not use the data.[87] The data showed that before the alleged conspiracy, prices were significantly higher than the expert's chosen normative prices following the alleged conspiracy.[88] The district court concluded that the damage estimate fell short of the *Daubert* standard because the economic analysis was not "grounded in the methods and procedures of the science of economics" since the expert failed to account for the higher pre-conspiracy prices.[89]

Furthermore, the district court found that the expert's opinion designating the normative period as following a "sufficient lag time" of fifteen months after the criminal indictments was "based on neither evidence nor science."[90] The expert had not provided the court with an acceptable explanation regarding the necessary lag time for prices of aluminum phosphide to return to normal levels following the alleged conspiracy.[91] The district court found that "[a]bsent a scientifically-supported opinion in this regard, the record suggests no reason why an equally plausible normative period could not commence sometime (any time) before January 1, 1993."[92] To determine whether there was a lag time and if so, its length, the expert could have computed individual regressions for consecutive time periods (e.g., two-month periods) following the alleged conspiracy.[93] If the coefficients of the regressions shifted for successive time periods, then this would be evidence of a lag time in which the prices of aluminum phosphide were returning to competitive levels. Stabilizing coefficients would signal the termination of the lag time and the return of prices to competitive levels.

Moreover, the expert did not provide a reason why he characterized the stable prices during his normative period as "normal" when the industry steadily declined in demand from 1988 through 1993.[94] The expert's regression model should have included a variable representing the declining demand over this time period to reflect this market condition. Using *Daubert*, the district court excluded the expert's before-and-after method because it was "unreliable,"[95] "scientifically unsound and irrelevant under *Daubert*," and "would not assist a trier of fact to determine the fact or amount of plaintiffs' damages."[96]

Under the before-and-after method, the plaintiff must demonstrate that its performance before or after the antitrust violation would reliably predict its performance "but for" the illegal activity. For example, in *R.S.E., Inc. v. Pennsy Supply, Inc.*,[97] plaintiff and defendants were in the road construction and blacktop business.[98] Plaintiff filed an action against defendants alleging conspiracy of a concerted refusal to deal, conspiracy to monopolize, and an attempted monopoly.[99] To prove damages, plaintiff's expert chose plaintiff's most profitable year for each business—road construction and blacktop—to predict plaintiff's performance "but for" the alleged antitrust violation of defendants.[100] This resulted in a different year chosen for each business: "the best year for the blacktop production and the best year for road construction."[101]

The district court rejected the damage estimate because the two different years chosen by the plaintiff for the before period did not provide an adequate foundation for predicting performance in the damage period.[102] The court found that plaintiff's "lost profits damage model, which was prepared using the split years, could not possibly be the basis for a jury to arrive at [a] 'reasoned' damage award, free of guesswork or speculation...where no single year was used but the best portion of two years."[103] Although *R.S.E. v. Pennsy Supply* was decided before *Daubert*, the court rejected the damage estimate by applying the level of scrutiny that *Daubert* requires. In terms of *Daubert*, the damage estimate was not reliable because the expert did not properly apply the before-and-after methodology to the facts and the analysis was not sufficiently tied to the facts of the case. Furthermore, *Daubert* requires that an expert "employ in the courtroom the same level of intellectual rigor that characterizes the practice of an expert in the relevant field."[104] Picking the most profitable years as a basis for a damage estimate is not an acceptable economic practice outside of the courtroom, and therefore it is not acceptable inside of the courtroom.

C. Market-Share Method

Some commentators identify the market-share theory as a third method of establishing damages.[105] However, in most applications the market-share method is not a distinct method, but rather a computational intermediate step within a before-and-after or yardstick method. Nevertheless, in certain situations the market-share method can be applied as a distinct method. Under this approach, a plaintiff computes damages on the basis of lost market share resulting from defendant's antitrust violation. The plaintiff converts its reduction in market share to the quantity of reduced output, and from this quantity calculates the amount of lost profits. This method is applicable in cases where the plaintiff seeks damages resulting from exclusionary practices,[106] and is particularly effective if the entire market experiences external changes during the damage period, while the illegal activity is internal to the market.

An example of using market share as an intermediate measure while applying the yardstick method is found in *National Farmers' Organization, Inc. v. Associated Milk Producers, Inc.*[107] In this case, the Eighth Circuit found that the dairy cooperative, Associated Milk Producers ("AMP"), conspired to eliminate National Farmers' Organization ("NFO") from the milk marketing businesses in ten midwestern states by using price discrimination, coercively disrupting milk supplies, and harassing buyers of NFO milk.[108] By federal regulation, milk was pooled and distributed in distinct geographic regions called "market orders."[109] Statistics on milk marketing were available for each market order.[110] The court found that NFO could recover lost membership dues and checkoff fees because the antitrust violations resulted in NFO losing members and marketing volume in ten market orders during the damage period, from 1971 to 1975.[111]

In its damage estimation, NFO used its performance in market order 68, which was not part of the damaged orders, as a yardstick to measure its "but for" performance in the damaged orders.[112] NFO had a 10.5% market share on order 68 for 1973.[113] NFO claimed that it would have obtained a 10.5% market share on each of the ten damage orders "but for" the defendants' illegal conduct.[114] NFO paid its members the proceeds from the sales of their milk less a checkoff fee for each unit volume, which went towards marketing the milk.[115] To calculate its lost checkoff fees, NFO calculated 10.5% of the total volume of milk on each damaged market order and subtracted the actual volume of milk it pooled on each corresponding market order.[116] Then NFO multiplied the lost volume by the checkoff fee charged for each unit volume, which yielded NFO's lost checkoff fee.[117]

To estimate lost membership dues, NFO obtained the yearly number of milk producers on each damaged market order.[118] It multiplied this number by the 10.5% yardstick, which resulted in an estimate of the number of producers NFO would have pooled in the "but for" world.[119] NFO subtracted from this number the actual number of producers it pooled to yield the number of members it would have added in the "but for" world.[120] Finally, NFO multiplied the number of members that it would have added by the membership dues collected per member to arrive at its lost membership dues.[121] Even though *National Farmers' Organization* occurred before *Daubert*, the Eighth Circuit scrutinized NFO's damage estimate at a level that complies with *Daubert*. The court analyzed issues such as differences between the yardstick market and the market on the damaged orders,[122] calculations for each element of the damage estimate,[123] time of entry on the damaged orders,[124] time to achieve mature market share on the damaged orders,[125] the combination of some of the federal orders and post computational figures,[126] and adjustments to reflect lawful competition.[127] In line with *Daubert*, the court stated that damage estimates must allow the fact finder to "make a just and reasonable estimate [of the damage that is] not based on speculation or guesswork."[128] The court concluded that although NFO's yardstick was not perfect, it was "sufficiently comparable to the other damage orders that extrapolation of NFO's performance on that order to the other damage orders would provide a just and reasonable estimate of NFO's damage."[129]

An example of using market share as an intermediate measure in the before-and-after method is found in *Rangen, Inc. v. Sterling Nelson & Sons, Inc.*[130] There, both plaintiff and defendant were in the business of manufacturing fish food.[131] Plaintiff claimed antitrust damages resulting from defendant's illegal acts of bribing Idaho's fish and game department officials to select defendant to supply fish food for the state.[132] To estimate damages, plaintiff presented evidence that it was one of four companies seeking the Idaho business during the damage period.[133] Also, in the year after the damage period, plaintiff was one of four suppliers that bid for Idaho's business and successfully received the bid.[134] Plaintiff reasoned that after the illegal conduct, it obtained 25% of the market share in Idaho for fish food.[135] From this, plaintiff estimated that "but for" the illegal practice, plaintiff would have maintained a 25% market-share during the damage period.[136] The Ninth Circuit found that plaintiff's assumption that it would have been the low bidder on one fourth of Idaho's business was "not susceptible to tangible proof."[137] However, the court concluded that plaintiff's strong position in the fish food industry and success in bidding after the damage period justified the assumption.[138] Even though Rangen occurred nearly three decades before *Daubert*, the court analyzed the damage estimate as *Daubert* would have required. The estimate was reliable because it was sufficiently tied to the facts of the case in that it was based upon what was known, and the expert properly applied the before-and-after methodology to the facts. The Ninth Circuit accepted plaintiff's analysis and upheld an award for lost profits based on plaintiff's lost sales volume during the damage period.[139]

An example of a situation using the pure market-share method without the before-and-after or yardstick methods can be demonstrated in a hypothetical. Suppose that the plaintiff is one of several companies producing safety widgets for large buildings. These companies compete by placing bids with potential customers to obtain business, and the safety widgets are certified by a national safety agency. At some point, the plaintiff designs a super safety widget that is equal in effectiveness to the regular safety widget. Also, the super safety widget is priced less than the regular safety widget for larger sized buildings. Plaintiff begins to place parallel bids for both the regular safety widget and the super safety widget. In addition, the plaintiff applies to the national safety agency for certification of the super safety widget. However, because of an antitrust violation on the part of the national safety organization, plaintiff's application is rejected. In plaintiff's antitrust lawsuit, it attempts to establish damages by using the market-share method. The plaintiff's expert reasons that if the national safety organization had certified the super safety widget, customers would have chosen the super safety widget over the regular safety widget whenever the super safety widget had a lower price. The expert estimates plaintiff's lost market share by comparing plaintiff's parallel bids over the damage period. The expert calculates that in 60% of the parallel bids, the bid price of the super safety widget is less than the bid price of the regular safety widget. Therefore, the expert concludes that the super safety widget would comprise 60% of the safety widget market "but for" the antitrust violation. Next, the expert converts the 60% market share to lost revenue during the damage period. Finally, the expert uses the plaintiff's marginal costs to convert the lost revenue to lost profits.

D. Going-Concern Method

As with the market-share method, some commentators designate the going-concern value of a business as a method.[140] However, a business's going-concern value is a measure of what the injured business was worth to a reasonable buyer before sustaining injury from an antitrust violation. Essentially, it is "the present value of its profits, plus its salvageable assets."[141] This measure of damage is used only when the plaintiff is completely driven out of business. Factors considered when measuring the going-concern value of a business are those that might influence a prospective purchaser:

1. What profit has the business made over and above an amount fairly attributable to the return on the capital investment and to the labor of the owner?
2. What is the reasonable prospect that this additional profit will continue into the future, considering all circumstances existing and known as of the date of the valuation? [142]

Any profit potential of the business that is not transferable to a purchaser is not included in the going-concern value of the business.[143]

The expert may estimate the value of plaintiff's salvageable assets by several methods.[144] The expert may adjust the historical book values of the tangible assets to reflect fair market value, and then subtract the plaintiff's liabilities to arrive at the fair market value of the plaintiff's net worth.[145] Alternatively, the expert may employ an appraiser to estimate the fair market value of the plaintiff's assets. The expert then adds the present value of plaintiff's future profits[146] to the fair market value of plaintiff's assets to arrive at the going-concern value.

Another means of estimating the going-concern value is by using the value of the plaintiff's goodwill.[147] Using this approach, the expert first subtracts opportunity costs[148] from the plaintiff's cash flow that occurred before the antitrust violation, to arrive at excess earnings.[149] Next, the value of excess earnings is capitalized to arrive at a measure of the plaintiff's goodwill. Finally, the expert adds the plaintiff's goodwill to the value of its tangible assets to arrive at an approximation of the value of plaintiff's company.[150]

The value of a business as a going-concern is an alternative measure of antitrust damages to lost future profits.[151] The Eighth Circuit found in *Albrecht v. Herald Co.*[152] that a projection of future earnings is inherent in the determination of the fair market value of a particular business.[153] In that case, plaintiff was a newspaper carrier for the defendant newspaper publisher.[154] Plaintiff charged his subscribers a higher price than the publisher's suggested retail price.[155] After receiving customer complaints, the publisher attempted to convince plaintiff to lower his price to the suggested retail price.[156] After the attempts failed, the publisher started soliciting plaintiff's subscribers and competing against plaintiff on his route.[157] Plaintiff eventually had to sell his business as a result of defendant's illegal actions.[158]

The Eighth Circuit explained that in awarding damages, the district court considered (1) damages arising before plaintiff sold its business, which represented lost profits resulting from the defendant's competition; (2) the difference between the going-concern value of the business at the time of sale and the actual price plaintiff received; and (3) lost future profits after plaintiff sold the business.[159] Reversing the district court, the Eighth Circuit held that plaintiff could not receive complete compensation for his business and receive future profits that the business may have obtained.[160] Since potential future profits are inherent in the going-concern value of the business, damages of future profits and going-concern are duplicative.[161] The discounted value of "future profits is one method of figuring present value, but this does not mean that a person is entitled to present value plus future profits."[162] Therefore, the court concluded that plaintiff was only entitled to receive damages for lost profits before the sale, and "the full market value on the sale of [the business] as a going-concern, free of the restrictive practices." [163]

3.3 Analysis Must be Based on Sufficient Facts

Regardless of methodology, all damage estimates must be "based upon sufficient facts or data."[164] "The language 'facts or data' is broad enough to allow an expert to rely on hypothetical facts that are supported by the evidence."[165] Furthermore, a trial court is not authorized "to exclude an expert's testimony on the ground that the court believes one version of the facts and not the other" when there are competing versions of the facts.[166] As a result, the expert must ensure that his or her analysis of antitrust damages is based upon sufficient facts and data.

This challenge rises to a new level when a plaintiff alleges that defendants engaged in antitrust activity that caused the plaintiff to go out of business. The estimated "but for" performance of the plaintiff is more uncertain when the plaintiff was not even in business during the damage period. An example of this type of damage estimate that the court accepted as based upon a reasonable foundation is found in *Rossi v. Standard Roofing, Inc.*[167] Plaintiff Rossi was a distributor of roofing and siding products who purchased products from manufacturers and resold them in large volumes.[168] Defendants were several distributors and one manufacturer of roofing and siding products.[169] Rossi worked as a manager for one of the defendant distributors, Standard, and eventually was promoted to vice president.[170] Standard fired Rossi because, according to Rossi, he would not participate in price-fixing activities with other defendants.[171] Nonetheless, Rossi had a reputation for "extremely competitive pricing, excellent service, and reliability" within the industry.[172] After being fired, Rossi pursued his own business as a distributor.[173] However, his company closed in less than a year after having problems acquiring roofing and siding supplies.[174] Apparently Rossi's aggressive pricing annoyed some of his competitors, who in turn pressured the major supplier of roofing and siding products not to sell to Rossi.[175] American Builders and Contractors (ABC) bought the assets of the company and most of the employees stayed on to work for ABC, with Rossi as branch manager.[176]

Rossi brought an action claiming that defendants conspired to drive him out of business in violation of the antitrust laws.[177] The damage expert's analysis was based on the yardstick method and had two primary assumptions.[178] First, the expert assumed that Rossi's distributor business would have attained the same sales revenues during the damage period that ABC's branch distributorship achieved with Rossi managing the branch.[179] The Third Circuit found that this assumption was reasonable because it was based upon the actual sales that Rossi achieved "competing against the same firms, selling the same products at the same location to the same customers under the actual business conditions that existed at the time."[180] Second, the expert assumed that Rossi would have managed his own distributorship the same way he managed Standard's branch before he was fired.[181] The expert used Standard's financial data to calculate averages for "cost of sales, payroll expenses, equipment expenses, and administrative expenses" over a fourteen-year period and used these averages in the damage estimate.[182] Although *Rossi* occurred after *Daubert*, the Third Circuit's opinion does not cite *Daubert*. Nonetheless, the court's opinion is compatible with the spirit of

Daubert in its finding that Rossi's damage estimate incorporated actual data and therefore was based upon a "reasonable foundation."[183] Also, the jury would not be required to engage in "speculation or guess work" in basing its verdict on the damage estimate.[184] In the terms of *Daubert*, the damage estimate was reliable because the analysis "fit" the facts of the case and Rossi's expert applied the yardstick methodology properly to the facts in issue.

At the other extreme, courts will reject an expert's damage estimate when it is based upon unreasonable and unrealistic assumptions. A blatant example of this is *Southern Pacific Communications Co. v. AT&T,*[185] where the district court pointed out numerous "imaginary" assumptions in Southern Pacific Communications Company's (SPCC) damage analysis.[186] SPCC filed suit against AT&T and the Bell System operating companies alleging that the Bell System monopolized and conspired to monopolize the private phone line market and conspired to restrain trade in that market.[187] To prove damages, SPCC's experts presented a "but for" model of SPCC and the market absent the alleged illegal practices.[188] The district court completely rejected the experts' analysis, specifying egregious unrealistic assumptions, referring to the "but for" company as "imaginary" and "made-for-trial-fiction."[189]

First, the district court rejected the assumption that the "but for" competitors of AT&T would obtain 60% of the market for private lines.[190] SPCC's expert testified that to attract investors, a competitor in the market required a 20% market share in the "but for" world.[191] In rejecting this assumption, the district court pointed out that there were at least eight competitors in the private line market in the actual world, with additional companies planning to enter.[192] Some of these companies possessed a very small market share since these companies also provided switched services and could provide private line service with minimal incremental costs.[193] Moreover, there was nothing in the record that supported the assumption that SPCC would be one of the three remaining "but for" companies out of the eight that actually competed in the market.[194] The court found the entire damage model to be without foundation.[195]

Second, SPCC's damage analysis had increased demand assumptions for private lines.[196] However, the analysis ignored the "sole source" policy of the Department of Defense, the greatest user of private line services, which precluded SPCC from obtaining the business of this customer.[197] Also, the damage analysis did not consider SPCC's business plan to move out of the private line business and into switched services.[198]

Third, the damage analysis assumed that AT&T's competitors in the private line service would set prices 15% lower than AT&T's private line prices during the twenty-year damage period.[199] In the real world, SPCC priced its services at least 30% below AT&T's prices.[200] The district court found the assumption that

AT&T would not take any action to maintain competitive prices when encountered with the possibility of losing almost two-thirds of its private line business "plainly contrary to practical experience and unreasonable on its face."[201]

Finally, the district court questioned numerous other assumptions about the conduct of the "but for" SPCC company. For instance, the damage analysis predicted that SPCC would have constructed a network in the "but for" world that was significantly larger than any other private line network ever constructed or planned by SPCC with dramatically increased profitability.[202] The "but for" SPCC had perfect foresight and always started construction with exactly the necessary lead-time to result in new capacity to serve the "but for" increased demand as it became profitable.[203] The "but for" company never encountered delays in getting construction permits or certificates of public convenience and necessity.[204] The district court concluded that the damage analysis did not provide a reasonable approximation of damages and any damages awarded "could only be based on pure speculation or guesswork."[205] Although *Southern Pacific Communications Co.* occurred before *Daubert*, the court's opinion adheres to the admissibility framework of *Daubert*. The expert testimony was unreliable for a number of reasons, including (1) the analysis was not based upon the facts, but rather on "imaginary facts," and (2) the expert did not apply the level of intellectual rigor that characterizes the economic analysis outside of litigation.

3.4 Analysis Must be Tailored to Antitrust Injury ("Fit")

A. Antitrust Injury

Plaintiffs can recover damages for an injury "proximately caused by an antitrust violation"[206] if the plaintiff suffered an injury "of the type the antitrust laws were intended to prevent and that flows from that which makes defendants' acts unlawful."[207] When a plaintiff does not suffer any injury of the type that antitrust laws were intended to prevent, then the court will deny the claim. In *Brunswick Corp. v. Pueblo Bowl-O-Mat,*[208] the Supreme Court specified the term "antitrust injury" as meaning "injury of the type the antitrust laws were intended to prevent and flows from that which makes defendant's acts unlawful."[209] In that case, plaintiffs consisted of three bowling centers, while defendant was a large manufacturer of bowling equipment.[210] Due to the decline in the bowling industry in the 1960s, defendant had difficulty obtaining payments from bowling centers for equipment.[211] To counter this problem, defendant started acquiring and operating some of the defaulting bowling centers.[212] Plaintiffs alleged that defendant's acquisitions lessened competition or tended to produce a monopoly in violation of the Clayton Act and sought damages for three times "the reasonably expectable profits to be made [by plaintiffs] from the operation of their bowling centers" but for defendant's acquisitions.[213] To establish damages, plaintiffs showed that if defendant had permitted the centers that were defaulting to shut down, plaintiffs would have increased their market share and profits.[214]

The Supreme Court stated that to recover damages, plaintiffs had to establish more than a causal link between the injury and defendant's unlawful market presence.[215]

> Plaintiffs must prove antitrust injury, which is to say injury of the type the antitrust laws were intended to prevent and that flows from that which makes the defendant['s] acts unlawful. The injury should reflect the anticompetitive effect either of the violation or of anticompetitive acts made possible by the violation.[216]

If defendant's acquisitions violated the antitrust laws, they did so because a "'deep pocket' parent" entered "a market of 'pygmies.'"[217] However, plaintiffs' injury still would have occurred if the centers had refinanced or been acquired by "'shallow pocket' parents."[218]

Moreover, plaintiffs claimed that they were deprived of increased market shares resulting from defendant's acquiring and operating the centers and thereby maintaining competition.[219] Plaintiffs intended to recover damages that would give them the "profits they would have realized had competition been reduced. The antitrust laws, however, were enacted for 'the protection of competition, not competitors.'"[220] Thus, the Supreme Court rejected plaintiffs' damage claim because plaintiffs did not suffer any injury of the type that antitrust laws were intended to prevent. Although this case was decided before *Daubert*, the case is in line with the *Daubert* helpfulness standard. The plaintiffs' damage estimate was not sufficiently connected to the pertinent inquiry in that it did not measure the harm caused by an antitrust injury. Therefore, it was not helpful to the jury.

A plaintiff that suffers an "antitrust injury" can recover damages for losses that are proximately caused by an antitrust violation. An illustration is *Greene v. General Foods Corp.*[221] In that case, plaintiff owned and operated a distributorship of General Foods products.[222] After defendant terminated plaintiff's distributorship, plaintiff filed suit claiming that defendant's pricing structure violated the antitrust laws and that defendant terminated him because he did not comply with the pricing structure.[223] Plaintiff sought damages for profits lost prior to his termination as a result of the pricing structure as well as future lost profits.[224] The Fifth Circuit affirmed the jury's verdict to award to plaintiff not only the lost profits resulting from the loss of defendant's product lines, but also proximately caused lost profits from the loss of the other product lines that plaintiff distributed.[225]

Recent courts have followed the requirement of antitrust injury when evaluating recoverable damages and have permitted damage recovery for proximately caused injuries. For example, in *Image Technical Services, Inc. v. Eastman Kodak Co.,*[226] plaintiffs were independent service organizations that serviced Kodak equipment.[227] Plaintiffs claimed that Kodak used its market monopoly of Kodak equipment to produce another monopoly in the market of equipment service in violation of the Sherman Act.[228] Due to increased competition from plaintiffs in servicing defendant's equipment, defendant restricted access to its equipment parts and eventually stopped selling these parts to plaintiffs.[229] Because of defendant's unlawful actions, not only did plaintiffs' business of servicing Kodak equipment suffer, their business of refurbishing and selling used Kodak equipment also suffered.[230] The Ninth Circuit permitted plaintiffs to recover damages for lost profits for service revenues resulting from the defendant's refusal to sell parts to the plaintiffs.[231] The court remanded for new trial on plaintiffs' right to recover damages for lost profits due to reduced sales of plaintiffs' refurbished Kodak equipment.[232]

B. Disaggregation

An economic damage analysis must also account for factors that contributed to plaintiff's damages other than the antitrust practices of the defendant. In general, if plaintiff's damages resulted from both lawful conduct and unlawful conduct of the defendant, the plaintiff is only entitled to recover for the unlawful conduct. Similarly, if factors such as market conditions or plaintiff's own actions caused plaintiff's losses in addition to unlawful conduct of the defendant, plaintiff is only entitled to recover for the unlawful conduct. Consequently, plaintiff's damage analysis must account for these other factors such that the damage estimate is only for the unlawful conduct.

For instance, when an expert employs the before-and-after method and all of plaintiff's damages are due to the illegal actions of defendant, then there are no damages stemming from legal conduct to disaggregate. However, if some of plaintiff's damages are the result of conditions that are separate from defendant's illegal conduct, then this portion of plaintiff's damages must be excluded from the damage estimate. For example, suppose the plaintiff experiences a reduction in sales due to exclusionary practices and seeks to recover lost profits. Experts generally employ regression analysis to identify the factors that determine sales.[233] The factors usually include supply and demand factors, and the expert estimates the data covering both the damage period and the competitive period. In the "dummy-variable"[234] model, there is a dummy variable that represents the illegal activity, which has a value of one during the damage period and zero during the competitive period. This approach assumes that the antitrust violation decreased sales by a certain amount during the damage period, while not affecting sales during the competitive period. Consequently, the expert can isolate the effect of the illegal activity from factors external to the illegal activity if all relevant variables are known.

Alternatively, the expert may use the "residual"[235] model, which uses the data from the competitive period to estimate the "but for" profits. The expert compares the estimated "but for" profits to the actual profits during the damage period to isolate the effect of the illegal activity. Similarly, a damage estimate using the yardstick approach must account for differences if the yardstick is not closely comparable to the plaintiff's damaged business. In most cases, disaggregation is an issue because differences can be attributed to legitimate factors.

The reason for requiring antitrust plaintiffs to disaggregate damages is that, without disaggregation, juries must speculate as to the amount of damages attributable to the defendant's antitrust violation. For example, in *Isaksen v. Vermont Castings, Inc.*,[236] plaintiff distributed woodburning stoves used for heating while defendant manufactured and supplied these stoves.[237] Plaintiff claimed that defendant coerced him into raising the price of the stoves in violation of the antitrust laws.[238] To prove damages, plaintiff used the before-and-after method, comparing his profits before and during the damage period.[239] The Seventh Circuit found the damage estimate flawed because it did not separate the losses caused by defendant's unlawful practices from losses caused by the reduced market demand for the stoves.[240] The court concluded that "[t]he jury pulled the figure of $100,000 out of a hat in which Isaksen's expert witness had done the usual magic tricks; but...there was no evidence of how much the antitrust violation, as distinct from unrelated market forces, contributed to Isaksen's losses."[241] This pre-*Daubert* case is in line with the *Daubert* ideas of sufficiency and helpfulness. Because the damage estimate did not separate the losses caused by defendant's unlawful practices from losses from the reduced demand, the jury was required to speculate. Therefore, in terms of *Daubert*, the damage estimate had an insufficient connection to the pertinent inquiry and therefore was not helpful to the jury.

Disaggregation concerns also arise where a plaintiff alleges that multiple practices employed by the defendant are antitrust violations, but the court finds that some of these practices are lawful. The Ninth Circuit addressed this issue in *City of Vernon v. Southern California Edison Co.*[242] In that case, plaintiff alleged that defendant engaged in anticompetitive practices by disallowing plaintiff's use of defendant's power transmission lines, maintaining rate schedules that were discriminatory, and preventing plaintiff from acquiring power from alternate suppliers.[243] Plaintiff's damage study assumed that "all of [defendant's] acts contributed to the damage figure."[244] However, the court found that some of defendant's acts were lawful and therefore held that the damage estimate was speculative because it "failed to segregate the losses, if any, caused by acts which were not antitrust violations from those that were."[245] Like *Isaksen*, this pre-*Daubert* case rejected a damage estimate having an insufficient connection to the pertinent inquiry and therefore was not helpful to the jury.

3.5 Conclusion

In *Daubert*, the Supreme Court emphasized the role of judges as gatekeepers of evidence and described standards for judges to use in applying Rule 702 to screen scientific expert testimony. *Kumho Tire* established that the *Daubert* standard applies to all expert testimony. However, federal courts have historically scrutinized expert testimony to prove antitrust damages at a comparable level to that outlined in *Daubert*. The basic methods of proving antitrust damages, which federal courts generally accept, include the yardstick method, the before-and-after-method, the market-share method, and the going-concern measure of damages. Regardless of the methodology used by the expert, the damage estimate must have a foundation based on sufficient facts. In addition, the damage estimate can only contain damages that are caused by an antitrust injury. Finally, damages caused by factors other than the antitrust violation must be disaggregated from the damage estimate, and damages caused by more than one antitrust violation must be disaggregated from one another.

Endnotes

1. 509 U.S. 579 (1993). In *Daubert*, two young boys suffering birth defects and their parents sued the manufacturer of Bendectin, an antinausea drug available by prescription, which the boys' mothers had taken during pregnancy. Id. Before trial, the district court excluded plaintiffs' scientific evidence, consisting of structure-activity studies, in vitro or animal cell experiments, in vitro or live animal research, and reanalysis of the epidemiological data, because it did not meet the "general acceptance" standard of admissibility because it "had not been published or subjected to peer review." *Id.* at 583-84. The Ninth Circuit affirmed. *Daubert v. Merrell Dow Pharms., Inc.,* 951 F.2d 1128 (9th Cir. 1985), *rev'd,* 509 U.S. 579 (1993)).

2. *Daubert*, 509 U.S. at 589.

3. *Id.* at 590.

4. *Id.* at 592-93.

5. *Id.* at 593-94 (quoting *United States v. Downing,* 753 F.2d 1224, 1238 (3d Cir. 1985)).

6. *Id.* at 595. The Supreme Court blurred the line between methodology and conclusion in *Joiner v. Gen. Elec. Co.,* 522 U.S. 136, 146 (1997). The Court stated that "conclusions and methodology are not entirely distinct from one another...A court may conclude that there is simply too great an analytical gap between the data and the opinion proffered." *Id.* at 146.

7. *Daubert*, 509 U.S. at 594.

8. *Id.* at 593.

9. *Id.* at 591-92.

10. *Id.* at 591.

11. *Id.*

12. 526 U.S. 137 (1999). In *Kumho Tire*, plaintiffs brought suit against a tire manufacturer and tire distributor in response to a tire failure that caused a fatal accident. Id. at 142. The district court excluded plaintiffs' expert testimony under the *Daubert* standard because the expert's tire failure analysis did not have a "scientific basis." Id. at 146. The Eleventh Circuit reversed, stating that the "*Daubert* analysis applies only where an expert relies 'on the application of scientific principles,' rather than on a skill- or experience-based observation.'" *Id.* (quoting *Carmichael v. Samyang Tire, Inc.,* 131 F.3d 1433, 1435-36 (11th Cir. 1997), rev'd sub nom. *Kumho Tire Co. v. Carmichael,* 526 U.S. 137 (1999)).

13. *Id.* at 147-148.

14. *Id.* at 150 (quotation and citation omitted).

15. *Id.* at 152.

16. For detailed information on the admissibility of expert testimony under the *Daubert-Kumho-Joiner* trilogy and the history of the standard, see D.H. Kaye, *The Dynamics of Daubert: Methodology, Conclusions, and Fit in Statistical and Econometric Studies,* 87 VA. L. REV. 1933 (2001).

17. 282 U.S. 555 (1931). *Story Parchment* arose from defendants' alleged monopolization conspiracy and related exclusionary practices. Id. at 559. The trial court admitted damage evidence and approved a jury verdict for plaintiffs. *Id.* The First Circuit vacated the judgment on the grounds that plaintiffs failed to prove that they suffered recoverable damages. *Story Parchment Co.*

v. Paterson Parchment Paper Co., 37 F.2d 537 (1st Cir. 1930), *rev'd*, 282 U.S. 555 (1931).

18. *Id.* at 562 (citation omitted).

19. *Id.* at 563

20. See Roger D. Blair & William H. Page, *"Speculative" Antitrust Damages*, 70 WASH. L. REV. 423, 425-26 (1995).

21. *Story Parchment*, 282 U.S. at 564.

22. *Bigelow v. RKO Radio Pictures, Inc.*, 327 U.S. 251, 264 (1946).

23. *Id.*

24. *Id.*

25. Phillip E. Areeda et al., Antitrust Law: An Analysis of Antitrust Principles and Their Application ¶ 391a (2d ed. 2000).

26. "A monopsonist is a monopoly buyer rather than a seller." Herbert Hovenkamp, Federal Antitrust Policy: The Law of Competition and Its Practice § 1.2b (2d ed. 1999).

27. Id. ¶ 17.5a, at 658. "A tie-in or tying arrangement is a sale or lease of one product or service on the condition that the buyer take a second product or service as well." *Id.* § 10.1, at 392.

28. Areeda et al., *supra* note 25, § 391a.

29. Hovenkamp, *supra* note 26, § 17.6a, at 666.

30. *Id.*

31. *Nat'l Farmer's Org. v. Associated Milk Producers,* 850 F.2d 1286, 1306 (8th Cir. 1988).

32. 327 U.S. 251, 257-58, 264 (1946).

33. *Id.* at 253-54.

34. *Id.* at 254, 258.

35. *Id.*

36. *Id.* at 254.

37. *Id.* at 257-258.

38. Id. at 260-61. Defendants also argued that because the jury found that the film release system was part of a conspiracy to fix prices, this conspiracy enabled plaintiffs to artificially raise prices and, therefore, plaintiffs benefited from the illegal system. *Id.* at 261.

39. *Id.* at 258.

40. *Id.*

41. *Id.*

42. *Id.* at 266.

43. Areeda et al., *supra* note 25, ¶ 391f.

44. *Id.* ¶ 394b3.

45. *Id.*

46. 721 F.2d 1019 (5th Cir. 1983).

47. *Id.* at 1022.

48. *Id.* at 1022-23.

49. *Id.* at 1026.

50. *Id.*

51. *Id.*

52. *Id.*

53. *Id.*

54. *Id.* at 1029. The Fifth Circuit noted that once antitrust injury is established, the damage estimate "enjoys a relaxed burden of proof if rational, reason-

able, and articulably related to the evidence, a product of inference rather than speculation." *Id.* at 1029.

55. 213 F.3d 198 (5th Cir. 2000).

56. *Id.* at 199.

57. *Id.*

58. *Id.* at 208.

59. *Id.*

60. *Id.*

61. *Id.* at 208-209.

62. Areeda et al., *supra* note 25, § 391e.

63. *Id.*

64. 327 U.S. 251 (1946); see *supra* text accompanying notes 33-42 describing the facts of *Bigelow*.

65. *Id.* at 258.

66. *Id.*

67. *Id.* at 266.

68. *Id.* at 264.

69. 273 U.S. 359 (1927).

70. *Id.* at 368.

71. *Id.*

72. *Id.*

73. *Id.* at 368-369.

74. *Id.* at 369.

75. *Id.*

76. *Id.* at 376.

77. *Id.* at 379.

78. *Id.*

79. 893 F. Supp. 1497, 1507 (D. Kan. 1995).

80. Aluminum phosphide was used as a fumigant to control insects while storing raw agricultural products. *Id.* at 1498.

81. *Id.*

82. *Id.* at 1499.

83. *Id.*

84. *Id.* at 1500-01.

85. *Id.* at 1501. The expert selected this time frame as the normative period because:

> (1) the grand jury issued subpoenas in late summer or early fall of 1991, thereby signaling to defendants that the price-fixing jig was up and triggering a resumption of competitive forces; (2) designating January 1 through October 31, 1993, as the normative period allowed sufficient lag time for prices to return to normal; and (3) data for January 1 through October 31, 1993, was the last portion of the most recent calendar year for which transaction data [were] available.
>
> *Id.* at 1501-02 (citations and quotations omitted).

86. *Id.* at 1502

87. *Id.*

88. *Id.*

89. *Id.* at 1502 n. 11.

90. *Id.* at 1502.

91. *Id.*

92. *Id.*

93. For information on using regression to determine the transition period following a conspiracy, see Michael O. Finkelstein & Hans Levenbach, *Regression Estimates of Damages in Price-Fixing Cases, in Statistics and the Law* 79, 97 (Morris H. DeGroot et al. eds., 1986).

94. In re Aluminum Phosphide Antitrust Litigation, 893 F. Supp. at 1502-03.

95. *Id.* at 1507.

96. *Id.*

97. 523 F. Supp. 954 (M.D. Pa. 1981).

98. *Id.* at 958

99. *Id.*

100. *Id.* at 966.

101. *Id.*

102. *Id.* at 967-68.

103. *Id.* at 968.

104. *Kumho Tire Co. v. Carmichael,* 526 U.S. 137, 152 (1999).

105. E.g., Hovenkamp, *supra* note 26, § 17.6b3, at 671.

106. Exclusionary practices include illegal monopolization, tying arrangements, exclusive dealings, predatory pricing, and refusals to deal.

107. 850 F.2d 1286 (8th Cir. 1988).

108. *Id.* at 1289.

109. *Id.* at 1294 n.9.

110. *Id.*

111. *Id.* at 1291.

112. *Id.* at 1294.

113. *Id.* at 1295.

114. *Id.* at 1298.

115. *Id.*

116. *Id.*

117. *Id.*

118. *Id.* at 1299.

119. *Id.*

120. *Id.*

121. *Id.* at 1300.

122. *Id.* at 1295-97.

123. *Id.* at 1294-1312 (examining the damage estimate elements of checkoff proceeds, membership dues, bargaining expense checkoff fee, and post relief damages).

124. *Id.* at 1301-02.

125. *Id.* at 1302.

126. *Id.* at 1302-03.

127. *Id.* at 1305-06.

128. *Id.* at 1293.

129. *Id.* at 1297.

130. 351 F.2d 851 (9th Cir. 1965).

131. *Id.* at 853.

132. See *id.* at 854-55.

133. *Id.* at 855.

134. *Id.*

135. *Id.*

136. *Id.* at 855-56.

137. *Id.* at 855.

138. *Id.*

139. *Id.* at 855-56.

140. E.g., Hovenkamp, *supra* note 26, § 17.6d, at 674.

141. *Id.*

142. *Standard Oil Co. v. Moore,* 251 F.2d 188, 219 (9th Cir. 1957) (stating that business owner's age, health, and desire to continue in business are not relevant to "going-concern" measurement).

143. *Id.* at 220.

144. See Areeda et al., *supra* note 25, ¶ 396 for a detailed discussion of several ways of measuring the going-concern and fair market value of a business.

145. See *id.* ¶ 396b3, at 568 (rejecting the book value method as a way to calculate the value of a business).

146. Plaintiff's lost profits can be estimated by the before-and-after and yardstick methods.

147. Areeda et al., *supra* note 25, ¶ 396b1, at 567. "Goodwill" is defined as "[a] business's reputation, patronage, and other intangible assets that are considered when appraising the business, esp. for purchase; the ability to earn income in excess of the income that would be expected from the business viewed as a mere collection of assets." Black's Law Dictionary 703 (7th ed. 1999).

148. These opportunity costs include such items as the "required return on similar investments as well as the economic depreciation of capital assets and the amortization of intangible assets." Areeda, et al., *supra* note 25, ¶ 396b1.

149. *Id.*

150. *Id.*

151. *Graphic Prods. Distribs., Inc. v. Itek Corp.,* 717 F.2d 1560, 1580-83 (11th Cir. 1983) (awarding damages based upon lost future profits because the evidence for going-concern value lacked probative value); *Lehrman v. Gulf Oil Corp.,* 500 F.2d 659, 663-64 (5th Cir. 1974) (stating that "going concern value and lost future profits are each viable alternative measures of antitrust damages").

152. 452 F.2d 124 (8th Cir. 1971).

153. *Id.* at 131.

154. *Id.* at 125.

155. *Id.*

156. *Id.*

157. *Id.*

158. *Id.* at 125-26.

159. *Id.* at 126.

160. *Id.* at 131.

161. *Id.*

162. *Id.*

163. *Id.*

164. Fed R. Evid. 702(1). In *Webb v. Utah Tour Brokers Ass'n,* 568 F.2d 670, 678 (10th Cir. 1977), the Tenth Circuit stated that:

> [A]lthough the courts are not strict about the *kind* of foundations or theories which are employed so long as it is credible and substantial...some such foundation must be shown. It will not be rejected

where there is some prior experience with which to make a comparison. With such evidentiary foundation there can be a projection; where, on the other hand, the profits are mere possibilities and are too far removed from reality, they must be held unacceptable. (emphasis added).

165. Fed. R. Evid. 702 advisory committee's note (citation omitted).

166. *Id.*

167. 156 F.3d 452 (3d Cir. 1998).

168. *Id.* at 458-58.

169. *Id.* at 458.

170. *Id.*

171. *Id.*

172. *Id.*

173. *Id.* at 458-59.

174. *Id.* at 459.

175. *Id.* at 456.

176. *Id.* at 460.

177. *Id.* at 456.

178. *Id.* at 485-86.

179. *Id.* at 486.

180. *Id.*

181. *Id.*

182. *Id.*

183. *Id.* at 486-87.

184. *Id.* at 484.

185. 556 F. Supp. 825 (D.D.C. 1982).

186. *Id.* at 1073-74.

187. *Id.* at 850-51.

188. *Id.* at 1073.

189. *Id.* at 1073, 1076.

190. *Id.* at 1076-77.

191. *Id.* at 1077.

192. *Id.* at 1077-78.

193. See *id.* at 1077.

194. *Id.* at 1078.

195. *Id.* at 1079.

196. *Id.*

197. *Id.*

198. *Id.* at 1079-80.

199. *Id.* at 1080.

200. *Id.* at 1081.

201. *Id.* at 1080.

202. *Id.* at 1084.

203. *Id.* at 1085.

204. *Id.*

205. *Id.* at 1098.

206. *Pierce v. Ramsey Winch Co.*, 753 F.2d 416, 436 (5th Cir. 1985).

207. *Brunswick Corp. v. Pueblo Bowl-O-Mat, Inc.*, 429 U.S. 477, 489 (1977). For a detailed discussion on antitrust injury and proximately caused damages, see Maxwell M. Blecher & James Robert Noblin, *The Confluence of Muddied Waters: Antitrust Consequential Damages and the Interplay of Proximate Cause, Antitrust Injury, Standing and Disaggregation*, 13 St. John's J. Legal Comment. 145 (1998).

208. 429 U.S. 477 (1977).

209. *Id.* at 489.

210. *Id.* at 479.

211. *Id.*

212. *Id.* at 479-80.

213. *Id.* at 480-81.

214. *Id.* at 481.

215. *Id.* at 489.

216. *Id.* (emphasis added).

217. *Id.* at 487.

218. *Id.*

219. *Id.* at 488.

220. *Id.* (quoting *Brown Shoe Co. v. United States,* 370 U.S. 294, 320 (1962)) (emphasis added).

221. 517 F.2d 635 (5th Cir. 1975).

222. *Id.* at 639.

223. *Id.*

224. *Id.*

225. Id. at 660-66. The expert included the "margin on products of other manufacturers sold to those accounts." *Id.* at 661.

226. 125 F.3d 1195 (9th Cir. 1997).

227. *Id.* at 1200.

228. *Id.*

229. *Id.* at 1201.

230. *Id.*

231. *Id.* at 1223.

232. *Id.* at 1224.

233. For more information on regression analysis, see Finkelstein & Levenbach, *supra* note 93, at 79, and Areeda et al., *supra* note 25, § 393(a)-(g).

234. Finkelstein & Levenbach, *supra* note 93, at 90-91.

235. *Id.*

236. 825 F.2d 1158 (7th Cir. 1987).

237. *Id.* at 1161.

238. *Id.*

239. *Id.* at 1165.

240. *Id.*

241. *Id.*

242. 955 F.2d 1361 (9th Cir. 1992).

243. *Id.* at 1363.

244. *Id.* at 1373.

245. *Id.* at 1372; see also *Litton Sys., Inc. v. AT&T,* 700 F.2d 785, 825 (2d Cir. 1983) (stating "that damage studies are inadequate when only some of the conduct complained of is found to be wrongful and the damage study cannot be disaggregated").

Chapter 4

Antitrust Damages from Lost Opportunities

William B. Tye, Ph.D. and Stephen H. Kalos, Ph.D.

Synopsis

4.1 Introduction

Economic[1] and legal analysis of alternative approaches to antitrust damages in the antitrust literature is surprisingly sparse.[2] While dozens of articles appear on antitrust liability issues in areas as, say, resale price maintenance, the literature on the law and economics of antitrust damages can almost be counted on a pair of hands.

It would also appear that this neglect of the subject reflects the relative allocation of efforts devoted to damages during the antitrust litigation process. Most antitrust cases are settled, dismissed, or abandoned. Litigation strategy thus may defer a sophisticated study of damages until after all the motions, discovery, settlement conferences and even liability phase of a bifurcated trial are complete. Even without bifurcation, the defense strategy until recently has often been to ignore damages during the liability phase, on the grounds that any other approach was tantamount to an admission of culpability.[3]

In our view, this emphasis on liability issues to the exclusion of damage issues is misplaced. The objective of this article is to fill this void by identifying the basic principles that should govern the determination of antitrust damages.

Common violations of these principles are identified and the issues are illustrated by a recent case of note, *Pennzoil v. Texaco*.[4] Readers interested in formal mathematical demonstration of the cited principles should consult [Chapter 5]...which is not confined to the antitrust arena.[5] The analysis focuses on damages arising from lost opportunities created by market foreclosure, and does not address other antitrust offenses such as price fixing.[6]

4.2 Objectives in Formulating Principles for Determining Damages

The sensible place to start in understanding damages from lost or diminished business opportunities is to ask what the award of damages is to accomplish. Alternative objectives of the award of damages that have been proposed are to:

1. Punish the violator;
2. Deter the potential violator;
3. Compensate the victim;
   a. By "making the victim whole" as of the time of the violation; or
   b. By "making the victim whole" as of the time of trial; and
4. Motivate optimal decisions for private litigants to sue and/or settle.

In implementing these objectives, a number of disputes over appropriate methodology arise because of: (1) time gaps between the violation itself and the compensation for the damages arising from the violation; and (2) uncertainty at any point in time as to future costs to the victim. These methodological issues translate into disputes over the appropriate discount rate for future lost profits and the appropriate role of hindsight in accounting for damages during the period between violation and trial.

In the case of antitrust damages, plaintiffs and defendants often argue for objectives and methodologies that benefit themselves by appeal to a variety of "tie breakers," such as: (1) treble damages (a generalized contingency cited by defendants as purportedly available to offset any choice of methodology that is disadvantageous to the victim); or (2) the guilt of the defender (a generalized appeal to equity cited by plaintiffs, whereby infringers are deprived of any opportunity for ill-gotten gains by giving the benefit of the doubt to their victims).

The presence of treble damages in civil antitrust proceedings does in fact help clarify some of the debate. Without taking a position on whether a multiplier of three (trebling) provides the correct degree of deterrence, we presume that the calculation of antitrust damages seeks chiefly to compensate the victim, not punish the offender. This measure is equivalent in economic principles to what is generally referred to as "compensatory damages" or "indemnification."

Trebling thus plays a role in antitrust proceedings similar to that of punitive damages in other cases of injury.[7] Any other assumption makes either the trebling factor or the guilty verdict a generalized "fudge factor" capable of blessing any fault in the damage calculation by citing an offsetting correction.

The presence of mandatory trebling in an antitrust case thus allows us to elide many of the difficulties that otherwise arise because of possible conflicts among the four above objectives. Because trebling is explicitly designed to reward the successful plaintiff beyond mere indemnification, the debate over conflicts among the objectives can take place in the context of arguments over the appropriate multiplier. This would not be the case in the more general case of a damage award outside the antitrust context.

However, even in theory the notion of indemnification of the victim of an antitrust offense is not necessarily achieved under the current rules. Traditionally, prejudgment interest is excluded from antitrust damages on the grounds that trebling makes such awards unnecessary. Without trebling, such interest would otherwise be included within the damage award if the victim is to be made whole.[8]

"Lost profits" as a measure of damages can arise from a number of legal principles of liability - an antitrust violation resulting in a foreclosure of the plaintiff from a market, a breach of contract that forecloses market access, etc. In theory the general economic principles involved in computing lost profits are invariant to the legal principles that create the liability. In other words, if the defendant's acts have wrongly prevented the plaintiff from investing in a project, the "lost profits" of that opportunity do not depend on the legal characterization of the act. However there may be special circumstances that surround the reason for the damage calculation that must be taken into account.

To distinguish among the various legal theories of liability, we first examine issues surrounding the correct damage methodology when there has been a foreclosure of access to a market outside the antitrust context. One would then eliminate any elements from the damage award that are assumed to be already included in the trebling (to prevent multiple counting) and make any other adjustments deemed distinctive to the antitrust context. The net damage figure would then be trebled. The antitrust victim will necessarily not be made indifferent to the economic consequences of the offense by the award of antitrust damages prior to trebling if trebling is assumed to include any measure of indemnification to the victim.

This leaves us still with a major question as to what point in time the victim should be made whole; at the time of infraction or at the time of trial. Such a distinction can make a large difference in the amount of damages. To clarify the methodological disputes, we assume initially that a one-time violation occurs and detection, judgment, and compensation are immediate. We then introduce the role of opportunity costs, sunk costs, and market imperfections. Throughout, we assume that the victim's recovery of attorneys' fees and litigation expenses are recovered through other means.

In the examples that follow, we assume for the purpose of argument that the defendant has been found liable for damages. Thus the use of the terms "violator" and "victim" flow from the presumption that liability has already been established. Trial on both liability and fact of damage is assumed to have resulted in a verdict in plaintiff's favor, leaving only the issue of the amount of damages.

For the purpose of argument we also assume that damages are paid at the conclusion of the damages phase of the trial. When the complaint and trial come well after the alleged offense, it is assumed that a statute of limitations is not a constraint on the damage period. We address only the issue of a legally enforced damage award and do not address settlement possibilities, while recognizing that the former will affect the latter.

In actual practice, the appropriate procedures for calculating damages may be affected by rulings from the bench and controlling precedents. Precedent or differing circumstances might govern the appropriate objective of the damage estimate, the appropriate methodology to achieve a given objective or appropriate assumptions for a given methodology. (These precedents or rulings should be thoroughly researched by counsel prior to embarking upon any damage study.)

In many cases, however, such precedents may not be helpful and in any case vary considerably across legal jurisdictions.[9] Nor can these precedents be said to always be based on sound principles of economics and finance. We assume, therefore, that the analysis is unconstrained by such precedents (except as identified in the above-mentioned ground rules).

In summary, we therefore make the following assumptions:

1. Damages awards are designed to make violators *expect* to pay the costs of violation(s);
2. Making the victim "whole" means awarding damages sufficient to make the victim indifferent between the damages and the value of the lost opportunity.

4.3 Basic Principles for Estimating Damages

Based upon these assumptions, economic and financial analysis indicates that the following principles should be applied in estimating damages to business opportunities that have been destroyed or devalued:

1. Risks of future uncertainty should be accounted for by examining the full range of alternative scenarios (not just a particular outcome).

2. Future damages may be measured as the net present value of expected cash flows in the "but-for" world that would have existed but for the violation, minus the net present value of expected cash flows in the "actual" world after the violation. The net present value of expected cash flows will be equal to the present value of the cash flows generated by an investment minus the amount of the investment.
3. Future expected after-tax cash flows should be discounted at the appropriate risk-adjusted after-tax opportunity cost of capital to get the current value.
4. Opportunity costs (sometimes equivalent to the lawyer's concept of mitigation) must be accounted for in the damage award.
5. Large damages estimates from lost or diminished business opportunities usually arise from either (1) market imperfections or "economic rent" (the availability of returns in the foreclosed activity in excess of those in the mitigation opportunity); or (2) the presence of sunk costs (the extreme case of zero opportunity costs and no mitigation potential).

4.4 Common Examples of Methodological Errors in Damage Studies

There is clearly great room for honest differences of expert opinion over how to measure costs, expected revenues, and the appropriate discount and interest rates.[10] Such differences exist even in competitive capital markets and will, of course, be exaggerated in the context of litigation with its opportunities for hindsight. However, differences in damage estimation can also arise from clear misapplication of the appropriate methodology. Common examples include:

1. A failure to distinguish between expected values of cash flows and those occurring in a particular hypothesized future state of the world;
2. A failure to incorporate opportunity costs (mitigation possibilities) when costs are not truly sunk; and
3. An unrealistic reliance upon market imperfections.

In practice, differences over assumptions about the facts in the but-for world, the treatment of opportunity costs, and assumptions about market imperfections explain much of the difference in damage estimates in trial situations. We now turn to each of these and provide illustrative examples.

Error No. 1: Discounting estimated cash flow in a particular future scenario instead of an expected value over all future scenarios

Because there are often no objective data on the expected values of future cash flows from a particular opportunity, plaintiffs and defendants sometimes tend to focus on individual potential future scenarios highly favorable to their case. Indeed, one can project with confidence that there is some assumed particular outcome in the future that will justify almost any damage number.

The issue is how to deal with past and future uncertainty, which is especially acute in constructing the "but-for" world. Financial economics tells us that the applicable cash flows are *expected*[11] *values* in the statistical sense, not the "most believable" future scenario.[12] Both upside and downside possibilities must be accounted for to produce an unbiased estimate.

This admonition raises questions as to what to make of discovery materials and objective outside data on the expected cash flows. What the parties believed at the time should be given considerable weight, while recognizing that these beliefs may not be realistic. Most new businesses ultimately fail, for example, but entrants almost invariably believe that they will beat the averages.[13] These potential disagreements over how to construct the data should not obscure the basic point: the risk-adjusted opportunity cost of capital should be applied to the *expected* values, not the "most believable" scenario.

Rather than deal with future uncertainty by estimating expected values over all future states of the world, however, plaintiffs and defendants commonly argue for a single but-for world supportive of their positions. Consider, for example, a hypothetical case based on a matter on which one of the authors recently worked. The plaintiff alleged that but-for a conspiracy on the part of the defendants, it would have successfully introduced a new product several years earlier than it was actually introduced. The plaintiff's expert presented a study that indicated damages well in excess of $100 million. The damage estimate was based on a number of assumptions regarding a specific hypothetical, but-for world quite favorable to the plaintiff but, arguably, very speculative.

Not surprisingly, the damage estimate turned out to be highly sensitive to the particulars of the assumptions. Defendant's expert adopted the plaintiff's methodology but showed that changing only a few key assumptions - about how the but-for world would have turned out - changed the estimated damages to negative numbers.

Victims choosing to estimate future damages based on rosy scenarios thus wield a two-edged sword. It may be easy to estimate large damages, but offenders by the same token may easily show that things could very likely have turned out much worse. Even worse, the whole study may be ruled too speculative because it fails to account explicitly for future uncertainty.

Error No. 2: Failure to incorporate opportunity costs (mitigation possibilities) when costs are not truly sunk

The plaintiff's obligation to mitigate damages is fairly well established in the law.[14] The legal concept of mitigation is closely related to the economist's concept of opportunity costs and sunk costs.[15] From the economist's perspective, all costs are opportunity costs. For every opportunity, therefore, there are likely to be opportunity costs that must be considered. But it is surprising how often damage studies fail to incorporate the principle or do so in an economically inappropriate way.

To illustrate, assume that the victim sold from a moveable hot dog stand and was foreclosed from competing on a corner of a block in New York City. If that seller could at no cost set up a stand down the street without loss of sales despite the market foreclosure, damages would be zero. Indeed, we would say that the plaintiff operated in a perfectly contestable market[16] with zero sunk costs, i e., costs idiosyncratic to the foreclosed opportunity.[17] Lost net revenues do not represent true damages in this case because the lost revenues are offset by opportunity costs of an equal amount. In legal parlance, it may be said that the foreclosed competitor could have mitigated damages by the amount of opportunity costs.[18]

Sunk costs represent the extreme case of an asset whose value is reduced to nothing by the foreclosure because of the complete lack of alternative opportunities. Such costs are potentially a legitimate source of a large damage claim from market foreclosure.

In practice, a number of common errors occur in dealing with opportunity costs (mitigation possibilities):

1. Opportunity costs are ignored entirely,
2. Opportunity costs are overstated or understated, and
3. Fixed costs are incorrectly assumed to be sunk to the foreclosed opportunity.

Plaintiffs frequently claim that the opportunity to invest was eliminated and that they are entitled to all the returns that would have been earned had they not been foreclosed. This is a fallacy. By not investing in the foreclosed opportunity, they had an opportunity to do something else with the money that they would have invested in the project. That alternative investment would have also earned a return. The plaintiffs should only be entitled to the extra return, if any, that they would have earned in the opportunity that was blocked.

Simply recognizing opportunity costs is not enough. There can be serious errors in accounting for them. In one case, the plaintiff claimed that it had lost an opportunity to sell a natural resource due to an alleged attempt to monopolize by a firm that was both a competing supplier of the product and a provider of transportation for the product. Because of the alleged antitrust violations, the plaintiff never invested in planned facilities to produce the product. Plaintiff claimed that it could have earned a 15% rate of return on the investment that it never made. It further claimed that by not investing in the facilities it instead borrowed less and thus saved paying interest at a borrowing rate which was considerably less than 15%. Thus, the plaintiff argued it would have earned 15% minus its borrowing rate, after mitigation.

This argument is flawed. Financial economics teaches us that there is a relationship between risk-taking and expected reward. That is, people and firms must be compensated for taking greater risks by the promise of a greater expected return. This implies that in estimating the opportunity costs to an investment that was not undertaken, it is necessary to take account of the risk of the opportunity that was taken away and all alternative opportunities available to the plaintiff. In the above case, by foregoing additional borrowing, the plaintiff would expect to earn a lower rate of return but also gained the benefit of taking less risk. Moreover, the plaintiff presumably had alternative opportunities to borrow additional funds to make riskier investments with correspondingly greater expected rates of return.

Even where an investment has been made, opportunity costs must still be considered since some investments share alternative uses. Consider the case where a manufacturer of a product sells considerably less of the product as a result of a violation. The manufacturer has excess capacity in its staff, factory and warehouses. It does not lay off management or sales staff. It argues that it could have served the incremental but-for demand without increased warehouse costs, management costs or salaries to sales staff because these employees and facilities were already in place. According to the plaintiff, these costs were fixed and thus should not be allocated to incremental sales.

This argument is not necessarily correct: fixed costs are not necessarily sunk. The warehouse, sales staff, management time, and even factory capacity may have opportunity costs. For example, it may have been possible for the plaintiff to rent out warehouse space that was not used because of the violation. Similarly, management time freed up because of the loss of an opportunity can be turned to other projects that otherwise would not have been undertaken. If there are no such opportunities, managers could be laid off.

Once mitigation possibilities are accounted for, however, the potential for large damage awards arising from sunk costs often turns out to be disappointingly (to plaintiffs) small. Large damage estimates, therefore, generally rely on large market imperfections, to which we now turn.

Error No. 3: Unrealistic reliance upon market imperfections

It has been said that behind every great fortune (at least a new one), there is a great crime. Behind most great damage estimates, there is likely to be a great market imperfection, explicit or implicit. Assumptions of large market imperfections in the foreclosed opportunity are a special case of low opportunity costs because they are assumed to be available only in the foreclosed opportunity.

To illustrate, assume that the plaintiff has few costs sunk to the foreclosed market, i.e., the victim can readily shift "fixed" assets to another venture. Damages would still arise if the foreclosed alternative produced returns in excess of their opportunity costs, and plaintiffs usually claim that such is the case. How does one identify these assumptions and whether they are realistic?

These assumed market imperfections may produce considerable paradoxes for the plaintiff in an antitrust case, because they are in addition to the market imperfections introduced by the antitrust violation. To illustrate, assume that the plaintiff has few costs sunk to the foreclosed market. When opportunity costs (mitigation possibilities) are accounted for, the victim can readily shift assets to another venture. Damages would still arise if the foreclosed alternative produced returns in excess of their opportunity costs, and plaintiffs usually claim that such is the case.

In the absence of special circumstances such as patents, the issue is: What is the rationale for expected profits far in excess of the competitive rate (which by definition is the opportunity cost if costs are not sunk)? In many cases, plaintiffs without further explanation assume that they would earn monopoly profits absent the violation.

A common error is the failure to take account of the expected competitive response. For example, the authors have been involved in a case in which a manufacturer claimed that its attempted entry into a market was thwarted by a breach of contract on the part of a distributor. The manufacturer calculated damages on the theory that it would have captured a certain market share based on its successful entry, at an assumed price, with all incumbent competitors selling the same products, at the same prices as they actually did. This assumption flies in the face of testimony by the president of the largest incumbent firm that, had it begun to lose market share to the new entrant, it would have lowered its prices in response.

A. Sunk Costs and Market Imperfections as Sources of Damages

The above discussion can be summarized in a simple formula[19] that provides a useful framework for damage calculations as of the date of damage.

Damages = (Net Present Value of World that Should Have Been) - (Net Present Value of World that Was)

The general formula for net present value (`NPV') is:

$$NPV = I_0 + PV\ (\text{Future Cash Flows})$$

where
" I_0" is the initial outlay on a given project or investment; and
"PV(Future Cash Flows)" is the value today of the expected future cash flows for this project or investment.

Here it is useful to think of I_0 as the cumulative outlay the victim has made as of the date of damage, including interest at an appropriate rate.[20] Then if we let PV_s represent the value of future cash flows in the world that should have been and PV_w the value in the world that was, the above formula becomes:

$$\begin{aligned} \text{Damages} = \quad & -I_0 + PV_s - (-I_0 + PV_w) \\ & = -I_0 + PV_s + I_0 - PV_w \end{aligned}$$

Clearly the "I_0" [terms] cancel out. Leaving them in, however, provides a ready interpretation for the above principles. If there are no imperfections in the foreclosed market, the project may be a zero net present value investment. $I_0 = PV_s$. If there are good mitigation possibilities (i.e., no sunk costs), the value of the money already invested can be recovered: $I_0 = PV_w$. Sunk costs ($I_0 > PV_w$) can create damages even for a competitive, zero NPV investment ($I_0 = PV_s$), and market imperfections ($PV_s > I_0$) can create damages even if there are no sunk costs ($I_0 = PV_w$).[21] The first pair of terms ($-I_0 + PV_s$) seems to us to correspond approximately to the legal concept of net "lost expectation" damages. The latter pair ($+I_0 - PV_w$) corresponds to the notion of "reliance" damages, i.e., the amount spent less mitigation possibilities.

B. Case Study: *Pennzoil v. Texaco*

Pennzoil v. Texaco provides a dramatic example where a market imperfection implicit in a large damage award was combined with finding low opportunity costs. As shown in Table 4.1, Pennzoil claimed economic damages of \$7.5 billion based on an uncomplicated theory.[22] The theory was that Pennzoil, but for Texaco's conduct, could have obtained an interest in Getty's proven reserves for about \$3.4 billion, whereas it would have taken an expenditure of \$10.9 billion to replicate these reserves through exploration - a difference of \$7.5 billion. That is, Pennzoil argued that it was denied the opportunity to purchase an asset worth \$10.9 billion for a price of only \$3.4 billion, or roughly a third of its value.

Table 4.2 shows that without much difficulty, Texaco could outline a counter theory of damages which would produce a relatively small estimate of damages or even a negative number.[23] First, assume that Pennzoil suffered no damages until it had a valid contract with Texaco. Getty's shareholders presumably sold their shares for what they were worth in a competitive market. If so, then Pennzoil was deprived of no special deal more advantageous than its opportunity costs.[24] In the alternative, Pennzoil should have taken its purchase price and bought another similarly undervalued oil company as soon as it was rebuffed (all oil companies were selling at a fraction of their replacement costs on the stock exchanges at the time).[25] If Pennzoil had done so, its damages would be (1) the administrative and legal costs incurred by it between the time the jury found it had a valid agreement and the time of the tortious interference, plus (2) the transaction costs of striking the deal with Getty (i.e., all costs which are assumed to be sunk to the deal).

Table 4.1
Plaintiff's Theory of Damages: *Pennzoil v. Texaco*

Pennzoil's replacement cost of reserves (@ $10.87/bbl.)	$10.9 billion
Cost of Pennzoil's shares of Getty (@ $3.40/bbl.)	– 3.4 billion
Compensatory damages	= $7.5 billion

Table 4.2
Outline of Possible Defendant's Theory of Damages: *Pennzoil v. Texaco*

Damage Issue	Possible defendant argument
Risk of future scenarios	Pennzoil actually enjoyed negative damages because future oil prices declined
Mitigation/opportunity costs	If the stock market undervalues oil reserves, Pennzoil should have bought another oil company at one-third of its true value
Reliance upon market imperfections	The Getty interests would not sell out for one-third the value of its reserves Plaintiffs theory of damages implies that Texaco would have benefited from the offense despite damages, but it went bankrupt

Even better for Texaco, Pennzoil made no such effort to mitigate and, as it turned out, one can argue that it actually benefited from the offense. Oil prices began declining soon after the end of the agreement, permitting Pennzoil to pursue even more attractive investment alternatives. Consequently, damages actually incurred were negative. Indeed, Pennzoil sought damages, rather than seeking restitution or specific performance in the form of having Getty's assets sold to it at the price in the Pennzoil-Getty agreement.[26] Is there any doubt that in a declining oil market Pennzoil preferred the damage award to the restitution of the property it wanted to buy at the original purchase price?

The magnitude of the market imperfection implicit in the Pennzoil theory can be readily seen. Pennzoil assumed no mitigation behavior was possible, because there was no alternative way to invest at an equal or greater profit the assets that would be used to acquire Getty. While Pennzoil assumed that the Getty oil reserves were grossly undervalued by the market, it also implicitly assumed that no other oil companies were at all undervalued. But if it were true that Getty were such a unique asset, why didn't Getty wake up and triple its price? And why did the stock market grossly undervalue Getty if it was a unique asset worth so much money? Were the Getty interests guilty of imprudence?

The implicit market imperfection in Getty's damage estimate can be seen from yet another perspective. The damages liability imposed on Texaco forced it to declare bankruptcy despite that fact that it acquired all of Getty at close to the bargain per-barrel price implied by the damages award. Yet Pennzoil's offer was to buy only 43% of Getty. If 43% of Getty created a windfall of $7.5 billion for Pennzoil, 100% of Getty would have created a windfall of roughly $17,412 billion to Texaco *even after damages*.[27] If the damages theory were correct, the windfall to Texaco from buying essentially the other half of Getty at less than a third of its value would more than offset the payment of compensatory and even punitive damages to Pennzoil. Pennzoil's theory of damages implied that the tortious interference was highly efficient (Pennzoil, Getty and Texaco should have all benefited). Yet Texaco could not post bond[28] and was judged bankrupt.[29] To believe the Pennzoil damage theory is to believe that there was a market imperfection of mind-boggling proportions that was not recognized by the capital markets even after the highly publicized trial and appeals process. Clearly the stock market did not buy the market imperfection story implicit in the trial verdict.

4.5 Considerations of the Lag Between the Offenses and Damages: The Role of Hindsight

The award of damages long after the date of the offense introduces a difficult problem: the possible availability of far more data on damages than was available at the time of the offense. Indeed, it may even become apparent that the antitrust offender performed the foreclosed victim a favor by preventing him from investing in a money-losing venture, i.e., actual damages as measured at trial may well be negative.[30] What should be done with the information that damages may be perceived differently in light of hindsight?

Different uses of hindsight can produce huge differences in damage awards.[31] *Pennzoil v. Texaco* again provides an extreme but realistic example. Plaintiff's damage estimates at trial were based on certain expectations of the state of oil markets at the time of the offense. By the time of trial, oil prices were declining. What did Getty lose: (1) the opportunity it thought it had at the time of the agreement; or (2) the one it actually lost in retrospect?

Under conditions of economic uncertainty, even an accurate and fair estimate of the sum required to compensate the victim as of the time of trial is likely to differ significantly from an accurate and fair estimate of the sum necessary to compensate the victim as of the date of the offense. Not surprisingly, contending theories have emerged for and against the use of hindsight.[32] The two chief approaches go by many names, as shown in Table 4.3. Table 4.4 summarizes the chief features of the two methods.

Table 4.3
Nomenclature of Alternative Estimation Approaches

No hindsight ex ante	Use of hindsight ex post
Time of impact	Time of trial
Lost going concern value	Lost future profits
Lost expectancy	Lost outcome

Table 4.4
Features of the Alternative Approaches

Ex ante	Ex post
Uses information available at the time of the violation	Makes full use of information available at time of trial (hindsight)
Takes account of full range of possible outcomes	Takes account of actual "but for" outcome
Discounts all future damages to time of violation	Discounts only to time of trial
Relieves the plaintiff of the risk of lost opportunity	Exposes the plaintiff to risks of the lost opportunity to time of trial
Intended to make victim whole at time of violation	Intended to make victim whole at time of trial

The choice of the appropriate date for establishing indifference does not resolve itself either by appeals to legal authority or consensus over economic principles. In the present state of affairs, plaintiffs and defendants are likely to perform the calculations and espouse the most attractive result.

A careful analysis of the properties of the two approaches reveals that assessing damages under the *ex post* methodology will have three main consequences as compared with the *ex ante* approach:

1. In industries with risk, the average damage award under an accurately applied *ex post* methodology will exceed the average value of the foreclosed opportunity;
2. Paradoxically, under the *ex post* methodology a large number of offenders will pay no damages; and
3. Unless otherwise corrected for bias, an accurately applied *ex post* methodology will systematically overcompensate victims, on average, relative to an accurately applied *ex ante* methodology.[33]

Much of the argument over the *ex post* vs. *ex ante* method seems to have focused on the variance of the *ex post* method relative to the *ex ante* method in individual applications, ignoring entirely the difference in expected values of the two approaches. The two approaches differ in expected value because a large number of the foreclosed activities in a risky industry will prove to be losers by the time of trial. An accurate estimate of damages will thus produce negative damages under the *ex post* standard for these cases. However, if the victim knows he cannot prove damages, he will not sue the violator. Violators cannot, of course, sue their victims to collect such negative damages from the beneficiaries of their offenses. Consequently, the cases of negative *ex post* damages cannot be averaged into the expected value of the damages awarded.

The *ex post* method thus incorporates a basic asymmetry relative to both the *ex ante* method and the foreclosed opportunity. An investor in the foreclosed opportunity will face a distribution of possible outcomes that includes both positive and negative outcomes. A victim will face the same distribution of possible outcomes under the *ex ante* method and should be awarded as damages the expected value or weighted average of all the possible outcomes, both positive and negative. A victim under the *ex post* method, however, will face only the positive outcomes because the negative outcomes are truncated by the absence of negative damage awards.[34] The implication is that the victim is, in some sense, immediately made better off by the violation under an *ex post* method because the method eliminates the possibility of a negative outcome.

Alternatively, it can be argued that if the purpose of awarding damages is to deter illegal behavior, then the potential offender's perceptions about the expected benefits and costs (potential damages) of the alternatives at the time of the offense must be the guidepost for choosing among the alternatives. However, this does not necessarily mean the *ex post* approach should be rejected, because potential offenders will act on their beliefs at the date of a possible offense as to what future damages would be under this methodology if they are informed that it will be applied.

There is another reason, in addition to the truncation of negative damages, to expect the average victim to be better off under an *ex post* method at time of trial. Under the *ex ante* method, the victim is relieved of the risk of the lost opportunity. The victim is awarded an amount as of the date of the violation that is, in principle, independent of the actual course of future events. By discounting expected future cash flows back to the date of the violation at the appropriate risk adjusted rate to estimate the net present value of lost cash flows, the reward to risk taking is implicitly deducted from the damage award.

Under the *ex post* method, the victim, in essence, continues to bear some of the risks of the lost opportunity, at least to the time of trial. Damages are estimated to be the cash flows actually lost in each time period between the time of the violation and the time of trial.[35] These estimated lost cash flows depend on actual events in the marketplace and may differ dramatically from the levels expected as of the time of the violation. Since the plaintiff continues to bear risk under the *ex post* method, it is appropriate that the expected "but-for" cash flows earn a return at a risk-adjusted rate from the time of the violation to the time that the cash flows are realized.[36] All else equal, these differences in discount rates for the two methods will cause the expected values of the *ex ante* and *ex post* award to differ.

Tables 4.5 and 4.6 summarize the advantages and disadvantages of the two approaches. While the *ex ante*, approach clearly has some attractive theoretical properties, the chief complaint about the *ex ante* approach is its susceptibility to overly optimistic projections, which are likely to be exposed in the sober light of actual experience, or put less pejoratively, the lack of hard facts and excessive reliance on speculation. The victim will very likely paint a glowing picture of the but-for world, and the *ex post* methodology may provide the basis for a reality check on these projections.

Table 4.5
Problems With the Ex Post Approach

• An accurate application of the ex post approach on average will yield systematically larger damages than an accurate application of the ex ante approach on average.
• The expected value of damages under the ex post method will be greater than the expected value of opportunity that was taken away.
• Paradoxically, a substantial number of victims would nevertheless receive no damages under an accurately-applied ex post approach in a risky industry.
• The option to select between approaches after the cards are face up makes the problem even worse.

Table 4.6
Problems With the Ex Ante Approach

• Use of actual results in retrospect may give greater realism (less speculation) than ex ante expectations.
• Judges and juries cannot purge hindsight.
• Discovery may not reveal objective data on expectations.
• Difficulty in interpreting historical evidence of expectations.
• It may be burdensome to estimate the entire distribution of possible future outcomes.
• Problems with dealing with continuing offenses.

4.6 Special Consideration of Antitrust Damages

The chief unique factor that must be taken into account in antitrust proceedings is the disallowance of prejudgment interest.[37] This procedure is not as obvious as it looks and provides another opportunity for a possible discrepancy between the expected value of the *ex post* and *ex ante* methods. If trebling is to offset prejudgment interest, it is not exactly clear what is meant by prejudgment interest.

Deleting prejudgment interest from the *ex ante* award would appear relatively simple. Since the procedure produces an estimate of damages at the date of the offense as an intermediate product, the estimation procedure could stop at this point.

Under the *ex post* methodology the approach is not so clear. The usual approach is to calculate the net present value of future damages at the time of trial and simply sum up pretrial damages with no compounding of interest.

An *apparent* prejudgment interest problem is that under the typical *ex post* approach, post-trial lost profits are increasing in expected value to the end of the damage period at the risk-adjusted rate in the foreclosed opportunity.[38] The difference could be considerable. However, this is not actually a matter of prejudgment interest. Rather, it simply reflects the fact that if cash flows happen to equal their initial expected values, the *ex post* value of that outcome will exceed the *ex ante* value.

It does, however, matter how compensation for certain risks, if properly awarded, is to be done. If risks of illiquidity or nonrecovery because of the offender's default are assumed to be either ignored as a matter of law or economics, recovered through trebling, of appropriately part of prejudgment interest, such risks will be excluded from the damage award. But if a decision is made to include these costs in damages (according to a desire to "make the victim whole"), they will not only be included but will be trebled!

4.7 Conclusions

Despite the large financial stakes involved, the economic and legal principles governing the determination of damages in cases involving the loss or diminution in business opportunities are not well established. Conceptual disagreements immediately arise in almost every case as to: (1) appropriate considerations that should be given to future uncertainty in estimating damages; and (2) whether damages should be calculated on the basis of knowledge as of the time of infraction or as of the time of trial (the appropriate role of hindsight). Nevertheless certain general principles seemed to be agreed upon by most experts:

After-tax expected cash flows of damages should be discounted at the appropriate risk-adjusted, after-tax discount rate to obtain the net present value of damages from foreclosed market opportunities;
The relevant values for discounting are those that are expected in the statistical sense;
Opportunity costs (mitigation possibilities) must be accounted for; and
Unrealistic assumptions about market imperfections should not be relied upon.

Less consensus can be found regarding:

Whether the victim should be made indifferent at the time of offense or the time of trial (the appropriate role of hindsight).

All other things being equal, damage awards based on an accurate application of the *ex post* approach (making the victim whole as of the date of award of damages) are on average systematically more than those that would be obtained under an accurate application of the *ex ante* approach (making victims whole as of the date of the offense). Paradoxically, a substantial number of victims would nevertheless receive no damages under an accurately applied *ex post* approach in a highly risky industry. Despite these properties, practical considerations may justify the *ex post* methodology, or at least use of actual result in retrospect to give greater realism to *ex ante* expectations.

Endnotes

1. As economists and financial analysts, and not attorneys, the authors are not writing on the legal issues in damage awards. A version of this article was originally published in 17 RESEARCH IN LAW AND ECONOMICS 83 (1995).

2. This result is confirmed by the authors' literature search in preparing this article. Until recently, most of it addresses standing issues (*e.g.*, *Illinois Brick* and the definition of "antitrust damages") or disputes over legislative changes to treble damages penalties arid optimal enforcement and deterrence. A cursory examination of the American Bar Association syllabus on the subject would also indicate less attention to various theories of damage in the case law. *See* Michael Nachwalter, William J. Blechman & Scott E. Perwin, STANDING AND DAMAGES, SECTION OF ANTITRUST LAW, AMERICAN BAR ASSOCIATION, *Antitrust Fundamentals*: *Course Materials*, 39th Annual Antitrust Spring Meeting, April 10, 1991, Washington, DC. On the other hand, *see* ABA SECTION OF ANTITRUST LAW, PROJECT COMMITTEE ON ANTITRUST DAMAGES, *Proving Antitrust Damages: Legal and Economic Issues* (Chicago: American Bar Association, 1996).

3. For a spirited implicit defense of Texaco's strategy not to sponsor a damage study as a good decision/bad outcome, *see* Richard B. Miller, *The Damages Dilemma in the Bet-the-Company Case*, 17 LITIGATION (Winter 1991), at 12-16, 54-56.

4. While not an antitrust case, it illustrates the issues well. Lost profits" from a foreclosed opportunity, the measure we are *see*king to measure in this article, should not depend on the cause of market foreclosure. For more on the case, *see* Robert H. Mnookin & Robert B. Wilson, *Rational Bargaining and Market Efficiency: Understanding* Pennzoil v. Texaco, 75 VA. L. REV. 295 (1989). *See* also Douglas Laycock, *The Remedies Issues: Compensatory*

Damages, Specific Performance, Punitive Damages, Supersedeas Bonds, and Abstention, 9 REV. LITIGATION 474 (1990).

5. *See* William B. Tye, Stephen H. Kalos & A. Lawrence Kolbe, *How to Value a Lost Opportunity: Defining, Proving and Measuring Damages from Market Foreclosure*, 17 RES. L. & ECON. 83 (1995).

6. We focus on foreclosures and related offenses because they *seem* to raise the most difficult disputes. In the antitrust area, cartelization, price-fixing, etc., raise other issues and are addressed by others such as Jeffrey H. Howard k David Kaserman, *Proof of Damages in Construction Industry Bid-Rigging Cases*, 34 ANTITRUST BULL. 359 (1989); and David C. Hjelmfelt & Channing D. Strother, Jr., *Antitrust Damages for Consumer Welfare Loss*, 35 CLEV. ST. L. REV. 505 (1991).

7. Here our starting point is consistent with almost every other approach to the subject. *See* Note, *Private Treble Damage Antitrust Suits: Measure of Damages for Destruction of All or Part of a Business*, 80 HARV. L. REV. 1566 (1967). *See also* A. MITCHELL POLINSKY & STEVEN SHAVELL, SHOULD LIABILITY BE BASED ON HARM TO THE VICTIM OR GAIN TO THE INJURER? (Stanford Law School, Working Paper No. 109, Dec. 1993).

8. *See* dissent by Judge Easterbrook in *Fishman v. Estate of Wirtz*, 807 F.2d 520, 582-584 (7nd Cir. 1986), for the argument for not excluding prejudgment interest from antitrust damage estimates on the grounds that the victim should be fully identified before trebling.

9. Precedents are not as helpful as they might otherwise appear to be because they usually offer great latitude to a case-by-case approach, with no argument firmly rejected. As the Devil can quote the Scriptures to prove his point, so can legal research provide a precedent for a variety of approaches.

10. For the purpose of this discussion, we assume away issue of measurement methodology. Note, *supra* note 7, at 1574-77 identifies these as (1) "before and after," (2) the "yardstick" test, (3) defendant's profits, and (4) expert testimony. *See also* ALRRED L. PARKER, MEASURING DAMAGES IN FEDERAL TREBLE DAMAGE ACTIONS, 17 ANTITRUST BULL. 497 (1972). *See* John D. Guilfoil, *Damage Determination in Private Antitrust Suits*, 42 NOTRE DAME LAW. 647 (1967), for a survey of various methods approved by the courts. *See* also Elmer J. Schaefer, *Uncertainty and the Law of Damages*, 19 WM. S. MARY L. REV. 719 (1977-1978).

11. It is very important that the damage methodology use the term "expected" in exactly the same way as finance experts do when they define and measure the cost of capital. In this context, "expected" must be used in the statistical sense. *See* 1 WILLIAM L. HAYS & ROBERT L. WINKLER, STATISTICS 136-37 (1970). As with all averages, the probabilities of outcomes on the upside of the expected value exactly offset the probabilities on the downside. In the language of financial analysis, it most definitely does not mean a "hoped for" rate of return or a "threshold" rate of return, as these terms are sometimes used in investment analyses. Nor does it mean the "mostly likely" outcome. Considerable confusion arises if one applies common dictionary meanings of "expected," "to consider probable or certain" or "to consider reasonable, due, or necessary." *See* WEBSTER'S NEW COLLEGIATE DICTIONARY 402 (1976). The term "expectation" in lieu of "expected value" is very much to be avoided because it may mean something very different in the law of damages.

12. For the purpose of illustration, we are assuming that damages are equal to future lost profits. This does not rule out other possible measures of damages. *See* Jeffrey C. Bodington, *Appraising the Profits Lost by a Failed New Venture,* 4 J. FORENSIC ECON. 7 (1990).

13. It is also unwise to create incentives for potential plaintiffs to create a false record of expectations in order to create a paper trail for future litigation.

14. *See* Neil Hamilton & Virginia B. Come, *Mitigation of Antitrust Damages*, 66 OR. L. REV. 339 (1987).

15. *See Fishman v. Estate of Wirtz*, 807 F.2d at 556-57:

The economic concept of "Opportunity cost" has been used in a variety of cases as a loose label for any of a number of adjustments to value involving the idea that for every use of one's resources there is an alternative use, with its own return, foregone.

"...[U]nder facts like the ones in this case, antitrust damages may be offset by a figure that accounts for the fact that the plaintiffs actually had use of money that, but for the violation, would have been tied up in the lost business opportunity. This figure can be labeled the `plaintiffs' opportunity cost, in the context of this case. Under the unique facts here, we think this `plaintiffs' opportunity cost' is, for all practical purposes, equivalent to mitigation and we agree that the tort rules regarding mitigation of damages can have their place in the law of antitrust." [footnotes omitted]

However, it should be noted that the legal concept of mitigation can differ considerably in practice from the economist's concept of opportunity costs. *See* Judge Easterbrook's dissent in *Fishman v. Estate of Wirtz*, 807 F. 2d at 581, where it becomes clear that the cost of capital can provide an area where the economists, concept of the opportunity cost may differ from the legal precedents on mitigation. *See also ALPO Pet Foods, Inc. v. Ralston Purina Company*, 997 F.2d 949, 954 (D.C. Cir. 1993).

The district court erred, however, in refusing to reduce the award to reflect ALPO's alternative use of the funds it did not have to expend on a national rollout. In order to reflect economic reality, damages awarded in order to compensate for loss of a business opportunity should equal the "'plaintiff's opportunity cost,' or the return it could have made on an alternative investment" of the funds not spent on the foregone opportunity. *Fishman v. Estate of Wirtz*, 807 F.2d at 555. *See Hanover Shoe v. United Shoe Machine*, 892 U.S. 481, 503-04 (1968).

16. A perfectly contestable market is one subject to hit-and-run entry. *See* WILLIAM J. BAUMOL, JOHN C. PANZER & ROBERT D. WILLIG, CONTESTABLE MARKETS AND THE THEORY OF INDUSTRY STRUCTURE (1982).

17. Hit-and-run entry is possible in a perfectly contestable market because there are no sunk costs, i.e., investments that would have no salvage value upon exit from the market.

18. Presaging the discussion below on *ex ante* versus *ex post* measurements of damages, there is an issue as to whether the opportunity costs should be measured as the expected results at the time mitigation occurred or as the actual outcome from the mitigation alternative in the light of hindsight. A fortuitously favorable outcome in the mitigation alternative could easily produce negative damages that were unanticipated at the time of the offense. *See* Note, *supra* note 7, at 1578-79; and Jeffrey G. MacIntosh & David C. Frydenlund, *An Investment Approach to a Theory of Contract Mitigation*, 37 U. TORONTO L.J. 113 (1987).

19. The authors are indebted to A. Lawrence Kolbe for proposing this formulation of the theory of damages.

20. We discuss the principles that govern selection of an appropriate interest rate below.

21. However, since sunk costs can be an important form of market imperfection, the consistency of a claim for one form of damages without the other should be checked.

22. *See Pennzoil v. Texaco*, 17 LITIGATION 14 (1991).

23. *See* Richard A Epstein, *The Pirates of Pennzoil*, 9 REGULATION, Nov/Dec 1985, at 18-24, 42.

24. Alternatively, the Getty assets could have been evaluated at Texaco's purchase price, producing damages equal to the difference between the two offers, or $496 million. *See Pennzoil v. Texaco, supra* note 22, at 14. It would obviously be more difficult for Texaco to argue that Getty was worth less at the time of its offer than Texaco's purchase price. Whether the $496 million constitutes damages under this theory, however, depends on Pennzoil's mitigation opportunities.

25. Clearly, the facts in the case cannot be resolved without reliance on some theory of market imperfections. Why would Pennzoil's management spend $10.87 of stockholders' money to acquire another barrel of reserves if each was immediately depreciated to less than $3.40 on the stock exchange? Pennzoil's damage theory and its investment policy were not consistent with shareholders, best interests. If it makes sense to buy somebody else's oil company at a premium over the prior price (but at a discount from replacement cost), it makes even more sense to buy your own by retiring stock rather than to drill for more oil. Pennzoil would not have to achieve the alleged benefits of the merger by acquiring Getty. It could achieve even more benefits for its stockholders by spending the $3.40 billion to repurchase its own stock. Possible scenarios where this would be true involve assumptions that Pennzoil's reserves are similarly undervalued by stockholders, that a sufficiently large number of them would sell their shares at the same premium over prior market prices as Getty's shareholders got, absence of sufficiently large negative tax consequences for the transaction.

26. Ironically, Pennzoil attempted but failed to enjoin Texaco and Getty from the merger! Had Pennzoil succeeded with a permanent injunction, the ultimate result might simply have been restitution.

27. If 43% of Getty produces a windfall of $7.5 billion, 100% produces a windfall of $17,442 billion. Netting out Texaco's higher price ($1.53 billion on 100%) and total damages after the court of appeals remitted $2.0 billion (thereby reducing damages to $8.5 billion) leaves Texaco with a profit of $7,412 billion.

28. Potential investors in Texaco's bond were clearly not willing, to bet their own money based on the jury's view of what Pennzoil was worth. As the capital markets judged, the damages to Pennzoil from being deprived of 43% of Getty exceed the net worth of all of Getty plus all of Texaco. Another relevant factor is that Pennzoil settled for $3 billion. Although this reduced figure undoubtedly reflected litigation risk, it also may have reflected Pennzoil's concurrence with the judgment of the capital markets that the damage award exceeded the combined net worth of Texaco and Getty.

29. According to Pennzoil's damage theory, the joint value of the two firms should have been increased by roughly $15.912 billion by the offense ($8.5 billion for Pennzoil and $7.412 billion for Texaco). However, DAVID M. CUTLER & LAURENCE H. SUMMERS, *The Costs of Conflict Resolution and Financial Distress: Evidence from the Texaco-Pennzoil Litigation*, 19 RAND J. ECON. 157 (1988), found that the litigation reduced the combined market value of Pennzoil and Texaco by $3.4 billion (30% of the joint value of the two firms prior to the breach), and only about two-thirds of the loss was recovered upon settlement. These losses were found not to be the result of litigation costs. Nor could the gap reasonably be explained by the decline in oil prices after the offense (other integrated oil firms without such damages liability did not go bankrupt from the price decline).

30. As a matter of fact, Texaco later announced a charge of $640 million to account for book values of oil properties in excess of market values, including "prize properties acquired during Texaco's purchase of Getty Oil Co. in the mid-1980s..." Allanna Sullivan & Anne Reifenberg, *Texaco To Take Charge Totaling $640 Million*, WALL ST. J., Dec. 11, 1995, at A3.

31. For an excellent discussion of the arguments for the two approaches, *see* the majority opinion in *Fishman v. Estate of Wirtz*, 807 F.2d 520, 550-55 (7th Cir. 1986), endorsing the *ex post* approach, and Judge Easterbrook's dissent 807 F.2d at 578-82, endorsing the *ex ante* approach. For further discussions of the issues raised by the alternatives together with some hypothetical and actual examples, *see* John D. Taurman & Jeffrey C. Bodington, *Measuring Damage to a Firm's Profitability: Ex ante or Ex post*?, 37 ANTITRUST BULL. 57 (1992); Konrad Bonsack, *Damages Assessment, Janis Joplin's Yearbook, and the Pie-Powder Court*, 13 GEO. MASON U.L. REV. 1 (1990); and Franklin M. Fisher & R. Craig Romaine, *Janis Joplin's Yearbook and the Theory of Damages*, 5 J. ACCT., AUDITING & FIN. 145 (1990).

32. *See* R.F. Lanzillotti & A.K. Esquibel, *Measuring Damages in Commercial Litigation: Present Value of Lost Opportunities*, 5 J. ACCT., AUDITING &

FIN. 125 (1990); and James M. Patell, Roman L. Weil & Mark A. Wolfson, *Accumulating Damages in Litigation: The Roles of Uncertainty and Interest Rates*, 11 J. LEGAL STUD. 341 (1982).

33. *See* Tye, Kalos & Kolbe, *supra* note 5, for formal demonstration of these conclusions.

34. The source of the systematic difference is that under the *ex post* award system, the costs of expected losers are paid for by violators while they are netted out of the awards to antitrust victims under the *ex ante* system.

35. Recall that the risk of a cumulative negative outcome has been taken away by the method itself.

36. Assuming, of course, that this component of "prejudgment interest" is left in an antitrust damage award.

37. We assume for the purpose of argument that prejudgment interest is disallowed as a component of antitrust damages, but this is not always the case. For discussion of some legal precedents, *see* Taurman & Bodington, *supra* note 31.

38. *See* Tye, Kalos & Kolbe, *supra* note 5, for demonstration.

Chapter 5

How to Value a Lost Opportunity: Defining and Measuring Damages from Market Foreclosure

William B. Tye, Ph.D. Stephen H. Kalos, Ph.D. and
A. Lawrence Kolbe, Ph.D.

Synopsis

This chapter was first published in and is herein reprinted by permission from Research in Law and Economics, Volume 17, William B. Tye, Stephen H. Kalos and A. Lawrence Kolbe, pages 83-125,

Despite a long history and the large financial stakes involved, the economic and legal principles governing the determination of damages in lawsuits involving market foreclosure are not well established. Conceptual disagreements typically arise as to: (1) the appropriate recognition of future uncertainty in estimating damages; (2) whether damages should be calculated on the basis of knowledge as of the time of infraction or as of the time of trial (the appropriate role of hindsight); and (3) the appropriate interest or discount rates to be used to value cash flows at different times.

All other things being equal, damage awards based on an accurate application of the ex post approach (making the victim whole as of the date of award of damages) are on average systematically more than those that would be obtained under an accurate application of the ex ante approach (making the victim whole as of the date of the offense). Paradoxically, a substantial number of victims of market foreclosure would nevertheless receive no damages under an accurately applied ex post approach in a highly risky industry. If practical considerations nonetheless justify the ex post methodology, it is possible in principle to develop an adjustment to ex post awards that makes the expected adjusted ex post award equal to the ex ante value. However, there are severe practical difficulties in finding the right adjustment.

The appropriate rate for prejudgment interests, if awarded, is not determined by the risk of the foreclosure economic activity. It may depend on whether the ex ante or ex post damage methodology is employed. Consideration of risk in prejudgment interest may also depend on whether any risk actually exists, and if so, whether it may already have been taken into account in the damage estimate itself, through the trebling procedure in an antitrust lawsuit, or disallowed as a matter of public policy.

> *The dramatic increase in commercial litigation in recent years has focused attention on the measurement of damages, if any, to be awarded to plaintiffs. A review of judgments awarded by the courts reveals a hodgepodge of approaches and theories on which awards have been rendered. A striking aspect of the judgments is their lack of consistency in applying basic principles of economics and finance.*
>
> —Lanzillotti and Esquibel 1990, p. 125 (footnote omitted)

> *Discounting and similar mathematical exercises may be the only mechanisms for risk adjustments known in finance theory, but trials are not exercises in applied finance...Only a wholesale revolution in how cases are tried and decided would close the gap between the realities of litiga-*

tion and strict adherence to finance theory. It is doubtful that the gap is worth closing. Despite its acknowledged force in the valuation of business opportunities, finance theory has only a meager claim as the model for resolving disputes about what might have been.

—Taurman and Bodington 1992

5.1 Introduction*

A. Objectives of this [Chapter]

This [chapter] seeks to clarify some of the major debates over damages in cases of market foreclosure. We pose the following objectives for the pages that follow:

1. Evaluate two general approaches, the ex ante and ex post methods, for assessment of damages due to an illegally foreclosed business opportunity, of which an antitrust offense is a special case;
2. Identify the economic properties of the contending methodologies, including why they produce different answers on average;
3. Identify what steps would be required to make them give the same answer; and
4. Address implementation issues for the two alternatives, including calculation of discount and prejudgment interest rates.

As with most such matters, where you end up depends in part on where you start. Therefore, it is important that we state clearly our starting assumptions.

B. Preliminary Ground Rules

The sensible place to start is to ask what the damage award in a civil litigation proceeding is designed to accomplish. Alternative objectives of the award of damages that have been proposed are to:

1. Punish the violator;
2. Deter the potential violator;
3. Compensate the victim[1]
    a. By "making the victim whole" as of the time of the violation; or
    b. By "making the victim whole" as of the time of trial; and
4. Motivate optimal decisions for private litigants to sue and/or settle.

This [chapter] focuses on the third objective,[2] and in particular, on timing issues associated with how to "make the victim whole."[3] Even with this narrowed focus, a number of disputes over appropriate methodology arise because of (1) time gaps between the violation itself and the compensation for the damages arising from the violation, and (2) uncertainty at any point in time as to future costs to the victim of the violation. These methodological issues translate into disputes over (1) the size of the prejudgment interest rate (if any) to be applied to damages between the date of offense and the date of trial, and (2) the appropriate discount rate for future lost profits, and the appropriate role of hindsight in accounting for damages during the period between violation and trial.

In this [chapter], we limit ourselves to damages arising from market foreclosure.[4] This still leaves us with a major question: At what point in time should the victim be made whole, at the time of infraction or at the time of trial? Such a distinction can make a large difference in the amount of damages. To clarify the methodological disputes, we assume initially that a one-time violation occurs and that detection, judgment, and compensation are immediate. We then employ more realistic examples to examine the effect of delays in justice on the appropriate award. Throughout we assume that the victim's recovery of attorney's fees and litigation expenses are not an element of damage, either as a matter of public policy or because they may be recovered through other means in certain circumstances.

We also assume for the purposes of argument that compensation for bearing the risks associated with the uncertainty inherent in the legal system itself (e.g., the outcome of the liability phase of the trial) is not to be recovered through the damage award. This assumption is tantamount to the assumption that (1) plaintiffs bear no risk that justice will not be served, (2) justice is accomplished on average (no systematic bias toward plaintiffs or defendants), or alternatively that (3) the risks of failing to litigate a meritorious claim successfully are either not to be compensated as a matter of public policy or are recovered in other ways (e.g., the trebling factor in the case of antitrust).

Other related risks, such as those inherent in the damage methodology itself and the possible default by a losing defendant, are treated as fair game for argument. Illiquidity resulting from difficulties of assignment of a damage claim by the victim is likewise not excluded automatically.

For the purpose of argument we also assume that damages are paid at the conclusion of the damages phase of the trial. When complaint and trial come well after the alleged offense, we assume that a statute of limitations is not a constraint on the damage period. Difficulties raised by the appeal process and collecting damage awards are then considered. We address only the issue of a legally enforced damage award and do not address settlement possibilities, while recognizing that the former will affect the latter.

For most of the [chapter] we also assume that the contending methods for computing damages are accurately applied and that there is no disagreement as to what result a particular methodology will produce.[5] This encompasses the assumption that adequate data are available to implement all methodologies without undue speculation. Where a methodology produces an inherently uncertain result, we assume initially that there is consensus as to the expected (i.e., average) value of the alternative possible results. Evaluation of the alternative methods is assumed to take place at the time of the offense and without knowing ahead of time the outcome of future uncertain events that will affect the results of the alternative methodologies. These assumptions, too, are then relaxed to consider the likelihood of systematic biases in applying the methodologies, data requirements, and opportunities to "game the system" by use of hindsight to choose the preferred methodology.

Finally, we assume that the analysis is unconstrained by rulings from the bench or controlling precedents (except as identified in the previously-mentioned ground rules).[6]

C. Summary of Conclusions

Based on these assumptions, our analysis demonstrates that the following principles govern the procedures for estimating damages.

1. Future expected after-tax cash flows ("lost profits") should be discounted at the appropriate risk-adjusted after-tax opportunity cost of capital to get the value as of a given date.
2. On average, the ex post method (calculating damages as of the date of the trial) will give a higher value for the damage estimate than the ex ante method (calculating damages as of the date of the offense), for two reasons.
    a. The absence of negative damages means only "winners" will sue under the ex post method; and
    b. Even if negative-value outcomes do not exist, the plaintiff bears the risk of the actual outcome under the ex post method, and therefore can expect on average a higher rate of increase in value of the damage award between the date of the offense and the date of the trial as a result.
3. In principle, the ex post method could be purged of the first of these sources of difference, although in practice it would be very difficult; the second source of difference is economically appropriate and requires no remedy, *providing* the decision to use the ex post approach is not made opportunistically, that is, only after it is known that this approach gives higher results (in that case, an additional adjustment would be needed to purge that source of bias on average).

4. The risk of the investment in the foreclosed activity should not govern the prejudgment interest rate, if any.
5. Instead, the appropriate prejudgment interest rate may equal either the risk-free rate or the risk-free rate plus a default premium. Whether to include a default premium may depend on the damage methodology chosen (i.e., ex ante or ex post) and other issues.

5.2 A Framework for Estimating the Value of Lost Opportunities

This chapter focuses on the use of hindsight in damage calculations. A common starting point requires that we first identify what we believe to be widely accepted principles of damage calculation in a case where the issue of hindsight does not arise.[7]

A. Damages when Hindsight is Irrelevant

Consider the simplest case of damages from market foreclosure. Assume that a one-time offense results in denial of market access (e.g., an illegal market foreclosure) and that a verdict for the plaintiff and compensation immediately follow the offense. Assume also that there are no opportunities for the foreclosed firm to pass on the costs of the foreclosure to its customers,[8] thereby eliminating an *Illinois Brick* issue.[9] Figure 5.1 illustrates that the damage estimation issues in that case are similar to a breach of contract. The offense occurs at Time 0 (T_0), immediately followed by a finding for plaintiff and payment of damages, also at T_0. *Expected* net revenues to the enterprise are reduced from the "but for" levels as shown, but recover fully at T_1, producing expected net revenue losses (damages) in the shaded area.[10] The victim's business is subject to risk, that is, actual net revenues after the offense are uncertain and may turn out to be greater than, equal to, or less than expected actual net revenues in every future period. "But for" net revenues are subject to similar uncertainty or risk. Actual revenues in the "but for" world will never be known, but we assume that expected values of future actual and "but for" net revenues can be estimated. The expected values and relevant risk characteristics of future actual and "but for" net revenues are assumed to be known for every period. Figure 5.1 illustrates that the expected future cash flows, say at T_1, are normally the means (i.e., averages) of an uncertain process; these means are only one outcome of a distribution of possible values.

A basic valuation approach where markets for the opportunity in question do not exist is "net present value" (NPV), based on "discounted cash flow" (DCF) analysis.[11,12] The DCF method calculates the value of a project as the sum of the expected future cash flows it will generate,[13] discounted for the time until each cash flow is to be received and for the risk of each cash flow.[14] *Net* present value is the present value of future investor receipts minus investor outlays. Here we assume that the DCF estimate of NPV is the economically appropriate approach to valuing the lost opportunity.[15] The discount rate in an NPV calculation equals the after-tax "opportunity cost of capital" (hereafter simply "cost of capital").[16] We assume there is no special, nonmarket value of the lost opportunity to the victim (e.g., sentimental value). Any lost transaction costs, except for those associated with the litigation process itself, are assumed to be included separately in the damage calculation. The foreclosed business opportunity thus is simply to be valued in the same manner as any business opportunity, and it would not matter whether the opportunity were degraded in value (as shown in Figure 5.1) or destroyed outright.

In this [chapter] we focus on timing issues; and even in this simple case, a timing issue arises in the choice of a discount rate. The discount rate issue arises in other forms in more realistic cases, as well, so a brief review of the relevant principles is required.

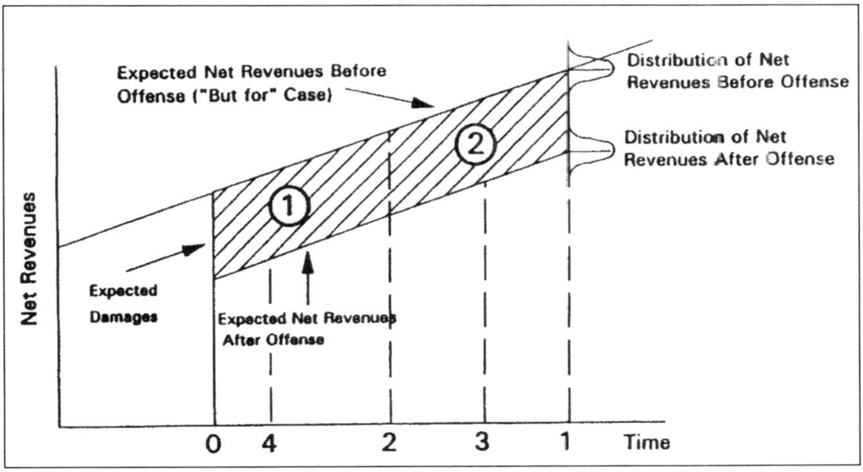

Time O: Beginning of damage period immediately followed by verdict for plaintiff of damages.
Time 1: Cessation of damages.
Time 2: Alternative case (to be considered below) where trial and payment of damages follow offense at Time 2.
Time 3: Example of Post-trial Lost Profits.
Time 4: Example of Pretrial Lost Profits.

Figure 5.1 *Effect of Market Foreclosure on Expected Net Revenues*

To understand the debate over appropriate discount rates, it is important to understand the rationale for the net present value criterion in the theory of financial and consumer economics. The appropriate discount rate to translate future uncertain cash flows to obtain known current asset values is that rate that makes the asset holder indifferent between a sum (S) paid today for sure in cash (the asset value) and an uncertain payment at time (t) in the future.

The *expected* value of the uncertain future payment is S x(1 + r), where r is the opportunity cost of capital for assets of that risk class. The cost of capital is ordinarily assumed to be a fixed number, albeit one that has to be estimated using various methods.[17]

As noted earlier, we assume that the objective of estimating damages is to make the victim indifferent. The cost of capital is determined in capital markets where competition drives expected rates of return to the lowest value compatible with a given level of risk. It represents the market trade-off between present and future cash at that risk level. Thus the NPV is the best estimate of the market value that a non-traded asset would have if it were publicly traded. It is in this sense that a damage award equal to the opportunity's NPV makes the victim indifferent.

An immediate consequence is that the appropriate discount rate is based on the risk class of the asset and not the "source of capital," for example, whether it was financed via debt or equity, or which company is making the investment.[18] Equally irrelevant is the expected rate of return in the particular company's next best investment opportunity. This principle has important implications for issues such as prejudgment interest, as discussed subsequently.

A corollary of these principles occurs when the future cash flow to be discounted is not an uncertain one with a range of possible outcomes, but rather a certain one with only one possible outcome. Here, the appropriate discount rate is the "risk-free" rate, generally equated to the yield on short-term U.S. Treasury securities.

The distinction between *risk-free* future cash values being discounted at the risk-free rate and *expected values* of uncertain future cash values being discounted at the appropriate risk-adjusted rate is critical to the discussion that follows. The risks that are to be taken into account in such discount rates are generally regarded to be risks that cannot be eliminated via portfolio diversification.[19] As usual, accrual of finance charges at the appropriate interest rates as we move forward in time (the expected rate of asset growth over time) is the reverse of the discounting procedure, once adjusted for the risk embodied in each calculation.

B. Damages when Hindsight is Relevant

Even where the appropriate methodology is widely agreed upon,[20] there is considerable room for dispute when applying it in actual cases.[21] There is clearly great room for honest differences of expert opinion over how to measure costs, expected revenues, and the appropriate discount rate. Such differences exist even in competitive capital markets and may sometimes be exaggerated in the context of litigation, particularly where there are opportunities for the use of hindsight.

Moreover, differences in damage estimates can also arise from clear misapplication of the correct methodology. Two of us discuss these issues in [Chapter 4].[22] For most of this [chapter] we ignore such sources of error and assume that the alternative proposed standards are applied accurately. The issue instead is what the goal of the analysis should be *in principle*. We relax this assumption after evaluating the conceptual properties of the alternatives.

We assumed initially that compensation to the plaintiff for injury is instantaneous. In practice, damages will be awarded at some subsequent point (say T_2 in Figure 5.1). A new series of issues now arises that contrasts sharply with the consensus so far as to appropriate theory (even if practice may lag behind).

Recognizing that damages are ordinarily paid well after the offense raises four questions, the answers to which are in serious dispute among the experts:

1. Assuming that the actual cash flows that would have occurred become known at T_2 (information that was not available at T_0), should hindsight be used to employ data based on historical evidence rather than expected values as of the date of offense?
2. Assuming that one has a valid estimate of damages at T_0 and that is the appropriate point in time for making the victim indifferent, how should the fact that payment of damages occurs at a later date be taken into account?
3. If hindsight is used, does this affect the method by which prejudgment interest should be determined?
4. Should we attempt to make the victim whole as of T_2 instead of T_0?

5.3 Consideration of the Lag Between the Offense and Damages: The Role of Hindsight

The award of damages at T_2 introduces a difficult problem: the possible availability of far more information on subsequent developments at T_2 than was available at T_0. Indeed, at T_2 it may even become apparent that the offender performed the foreclosed victim a favor by preventing that firm from investing in a money-losing venture, that is, damages as measured at T_2 may well be negative. What should be done with the information that damages may be perceived differently in light of hindsight?

Different uses of hindsight can produce huge differences in damage awards.[23] *Pennzoil v. Texaco* provides an extreme but realistic example. Plaintiff's damage estimates at trial were based on certain expectations of the state of oil markets at the time of the offense. By the time of trial, oil prices were declining. What did Pennzoil lose: (1) the opportunity it thought it had at the time of the agreement; or (2) the one it actually lost in retrospect?

A contested bidding process for the Chicago Bulls basketball team provides another excellent illustration of the issues arising when the date for calculating damages is disputed.[24] The court in the case ruled that the plaintiffs had suffered antitrust injury because the defendants' "refusal to lease the Chicago Stadium effectively cut off all competition for the acquisition of the Bulls franchise and injured plaintiffs as a result."[25] However, the defendants argued, and Judge Easterbrook's dissenting opinion agreed, that plaintiffs only "lost an opportunity to buy an asset. That imposes loss only if the price of the asset was a bargain."[26] The defendants argued that because the bidding would have been competitive absent the offense, plaintiffs' lost opportunity was worth very little, if anything, and in any event plaintiffs could have mitigated damages by buying another team.[27]

The majority opinion, however, concluded that "we know of no requirement that damages must always be computed as of the time of the injury..."[28] The court concluded that calculation of ex post damages was simply an exercise using the accepted "yardstick" method, where the economic success of the defendants themselves provided the most appropriate measure of a yardstick of plaintiffs' "but for" world.

This case illustrates that under conditions of economic uncertainty, even an accurate and fair estimate of the sum required to compensate the victim as of the time of trial is likely to differ materially from an accurate and fair estimate of the sum necessary to compensate the victim as of the date of the offense. Not surprisingly, contending theories have emerged for and against the use of hindsight. The two chief approaches go by many names, as shown in Table 5.1. Table 5.2 summarizes the chief features of the two methods.

To help illustrate the difference between the two theories, consider the case where there are no sunk costs, that is, the plaintiff had not yet invested when the opportunity was foreclosed, but there is an expectation of returns to the foreclosed activity in excess of opportunity costs. To simplify, assume that all damages consist of post-trial lost profits (area 2 in Figure 5.1) and there are no pretrial lost profits (thus ridding us for the moment of arguments about the prejudgment interest rate on the damages in area 1 in Figure 5.1). Assume further that there is a great deal of uncertainty about the levels of future profits and these expectations will differ by the time of trial from those at the date of the offense. Suppose the distributions of the date of the offense of possible damage values at the time of trial are as shown in Figure 5.2.[29] This distribution of future asset values is a source of uncertainty at T_0, but when trial arrives we know the actual value among the many possible values in the Figure 5.2 distribution, under our initial assumptions.

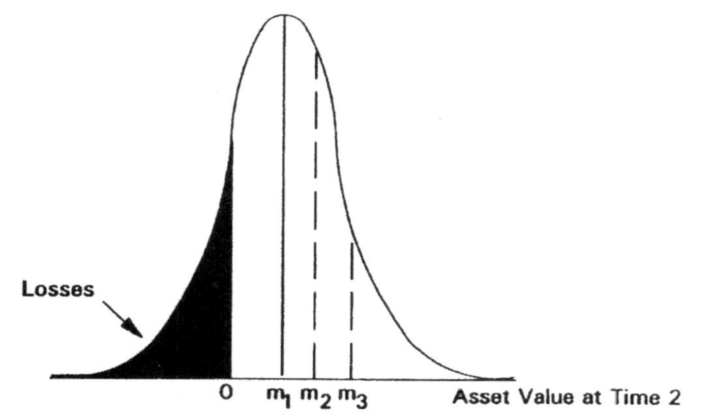

m1 – Mean of the Untruncated Distribution (plus and minus)
m2 – Mean of the Truncated Distribution (plus only)
m3 – Mean of the Distribution where the Plaintiff Chooses the Approach with Greatest Damages at Time of Trial

Figure 5.2 *Distribution of Asset Values at Some Future Point in the Absence of Market Foreclosure*

Table 5.1
Nomenclature of Alternative Estimation Approaches

No hindsight Ex Ante	Use of hindsight Ex Post
Time of offense	Time of trial
Lost going concern value	Lost future profits
Lost expectancy	Lost outcome

Table 5.2
Conceptual Features of the Alternative Approaches

Ex Ante	Ex Post
Uses information available at the time of the violation.	Makes full use of information available at time of trial. (hindsight).
Takes account of full range of possible outcomes	Takes account of subsequent actual events in evaluation of but-for outcome.
Discounts all future damages to time of violation.	Discounts only to time of trial.
Relieves the plaintiff of the risks of the lost opportunity.	Exposes the plaintiff to risks of the lost opportunity to time of trial.
Intended to make victim whole at time of violation.	Intended to make victim whole at time of trial.

Figure 5.2 illustrates the differences between the two methodologies. Under the ex ante method, damages would be estimated by (1) taking the expected cash flow losses in future years, in this example captured by the mean of the distribution, point m_1, in Figure 5.2; (2) discounting them back to T_0 at the risk-adjusted rate;[30] and (3) compounding forward at the rate deemed appropriate for prejudgment interest. The ex post method would simply use whatever random drawing was observed from the distribution in Figure 5.2 at T_2, except that a negative drawing is deemed to constitute zero damages (no negative damages awards).[31] In Figure 5.2, the ex ante number will always be positive, but the ex post number could easily be negative. (The final damage results could also differ because of differences in assumptions regarding prejudgment discount and interest rates, but more on that later.)

Unlike the previously mentioned discussion over valuation methodology, the choice of the appropriate date for establishing the plaintiffs' indifference does not immediately resolve itself either by appeals to legal authority or consensus over economic principles and authority. In the present state of affairs, plaintiffs and defendants may simply perform the calculations and espouse the most attractive result.

Much of the argument over the ex post vs. ex ante method seems to have focused on the variance of the ex post method relative to the ex ante method in individual applications, ignoring entirely the difference in expected values of the two approaches.[32] Figure 5.2 shows the source of these differences: a fraction of the foreclosed activities in a risky industry will prove to be losers by the time of trial. An accurate estimate of damages will thus produce negative damages under the ex post standard for these cases. However, offenders will be unable to collect such negative damages from the beneficiaries of their market foreclosure.

The ex post method thus incorporates a basic asymmetry relative to both the ex ante method and the foreclosed opportunity. An investor in the foreclosed opportunity will face a distribution of possible outcomes that includes both winners and losers (i.e., both the unshaded and shaded areas in Figure 5.2). A victim of an act that wrongly precludes the opportunity to make the same investment will face the same distribution of possible outcomes under the ex ante method and should be awarded the expected value or weighted average of all possible outcomes, positive and negative. A victim of this injury under the ex post method, however, will face only the positive outcomes because the negative outcomes are truncated by the absence of negative damage awards. The implication is that the victim is, in some sense, made immediately better off by the violation under an ex post method, but not under the ex ante method, because the ex post approach eliminates the risk of negative outcomes.[33]

Figure 5.2 also shows the same results in another way: the mean of the untruncated distribution (m_1) is less than the mean of the truncated distribution (m_2), where the latter does not average in the losers. An accurately applied ex ante methodology would produce an average award of m_1, while an accurately applied ex post methodology produces an average award of m_2.[34] Not only do the two methodologies produce different results in a single application; they also produce systematically different results even when averaged over large numbers of cases.[35]

A very important result emerges. The ex post methodology will produce negative damage estimates and zero damage awards in large numbers of cases in risky industries. Paradoxically, this result obtains despite the fact that the average award is higher under the ex post methodology.

Choosing to make the victim indifferent as of the date of trial (the ex post result) can affect the risk of the award as well as the expected value of the award. Assuming a consensus that Figure 5.2 represents the distribution of asset values at trial, all such victims will receive m_1 under an ex ante approach, while individual victims would receive a random drawing from the distribution under the ex post award. Importantly, the risks borne by the victim under the ex post approach more nearly approximate those of the foreclosed opportunity, except for the truncation of adverse outcomes arising from the asymmetry of the litigation process.[36]

This ranking of expected values for the two methods holds for T_0 as well as at T_2. The present value of ex post damages must exceed the value of the foregone opportunity at the time of the infraction because the present value of the shaded are in Figure 5.2 at T_0 must be negative.[37] Thus, if risk-neutral plaintiffs were forced to choose between the ex ante and ex post methods at the time of the violation, as a means of estimating damages at the time of trial, risk-neutral plaintiffs would always select the ex post method. Because plaintiffs usually do not have to select a method until well after the violation, they sometimes choose to use an ex ante method, as Pennzoil did.

The matter gets worse if plaintiffs and defendants are able to pick and choose expediently at the time of trial. Plaintiffs will be arguing for the ex post standard for all cases where it exceeds m_1, while defendants will support ex post results less than m_1. If victims were allowed to choose methodologies, the average award gets even larger (m_3) as the victim gets the better of the two worlds in each individual case.[38]

Figure 5.2 thus reveals that assessing damages under the ex post methodology will have three main consequences as compared with the ex ante approach:

1. In industries with substantial risk, the average damage award under an accurately applied ex post methodology will exceed the value of the foreclosed opportunity;
2. Paradoxically, under the ex post methodology a large number of offenders will pay no damages in a risky industry; and
3. Unless otherwise corrected for bias, an accurately applied ex post methodology will systematically overcompensate victims, on average, relative to an accurately applied ex ante methodology, measured either at time of trial or at time of offense, especially if plaintiffs are allowed to choose which method to employ.

If this were all there was to it, the indemnification principle might clearly support use of the ex ante approach. However, a number of theoretical and conceptual issues must first be considered. The first is the choice of prejudgment interest under the two methods.

5.4 Prejudgment Interest on Post-Trial Lost Profits in the Ex Ante Approach

To clarify the prejudgment interest question, we first consider a pure shift forward in time of the damage award given that a decision is made to use the ex ante approach. Such interest accruals occur under the ex ante approach when the value of the award as determined at T_0 is moved forward to date of trial.

Assume for a moment that a verdict for plaintiff rendered at T_0, and a valid measure of damages at that point is determined, but the offender does not pay immediately. Rather, cash passes to the victim only at T_2. This could arise in a variety of ways, such as the creation of an escrow account or bonding or simply from a delay between the date of judgment and the date of award.[39]

Proposed rates for accrual of prejudgment interest penalties have ranged across the board, as have their rationale, as shown in Table 5.3. In practice, the choice between the available alternatives can have major consequences for the amount of total damages.[40] A lively dispute has evolved, with the participants taking positions supporting one or the other approach while sometimes ignoring some of the basic principles of financial analysis discussed earlier.

This debate arises frequently in cases of commercial damage (e.g., patent infringement), where the prejudgment rate is not fixed by statute.[41] Such arguments over treatment of risk in prejudgment interest with the ex ante method arise for two reasons: first, the appropriate principles of financial economics are not always followed; and second, there is no clear guidance regarding where (1) the costs of being deprived of an asset (cost presumably related to the offense) end, and (2) the costs and risks of recovering its value in court (and thus not part of damages per se) begin. We take these in turn.

Table 5.3
Proposed Rates for Accrual of Prejudgment Interest

Method	Rationale
1. The victim's overall cost of capital.	1. The victim was deprived of the opportunity to earn this expected return.
2. The defendant's overall opportunity cost of capital.	2. The defendant earned this rate of return on the wrongly obtained cash flows.
3. The defendant's borrowing rates.	3. This is the rate at which the defendant is, in effect, borrowing funds from the victim.
4. The victim's borrowing rates.	4. This is the rate at which the victim could borrow to convert the future expected award to immediate cash.
5. The risk-free rate.	5. The damage award is fixed at trial and involves no uncertainty by the time prejudgment interest is calculated.

A. Considerations Based on Principles of Finance

Turning to Table 5.3, critics of the first approach rightly note that the victim is by definition no longer exposed to the risks inherent in the foreclosed enterprise.[42] In their view, this clearly eliminates the first alternative because it may overcompensate or undercompensate the victim.

To illustrate, suppose a victim were foreclosed from a highly risky opportunity (say, trading in a very volatile stock with a correspondingly high expected rate of return). A rational investor would prefer recovery of damages equal to the amount of the investment plus *certain* prejudgment interest at a rate of return equal to the high *expected* returns from the foreclosed activity (but without the risk of losing everything on Black Monday), to having the actual stock with the same expected return and all of the risk still attached.

Modern finance theory shows that the appropriate expected rate of return at which to discount future cash flows or to accrue interest on past cash flows is the *cost of capital*. The cost of capital equals the risk-free rate plus a premium for the (nondiversifiable) risk investors bear *for the investment in question.*[43] If (1) the purpose of the damage award is to make the victim indifferent; and (2) the risk of the victim in recovering damages between offense and trial is likely to be very different from the risk of the foreclosed activity, it becomes clear that (3) the cost of capital for the foreclosed activity cannot automatically be the right answer.[44]

If we have a known magnitude of damages at the time of the offense and propose to accrue interest on that fixed amount, it is inappropriate to reward the victim for risks of investing in the foreclosed enterprise during the time period between offense and trial. Whatever the risks borne by the victim during the time between infraction and payment as a result of the offense, there is no reason to believe that they necessarily coincide with those of the foreclosed activity.

The same argument rules out use of the defendant's overall cost of capital, which depends on the general business risks of the defendant's enterprises. Perhaps less obviously, the same argument also rules out the fourth option in Table 5.3, use of the plaintiff's borrowing rate. The plaintiff's borrowing rate depends on the risk *lenders* face when supplying money to the plaintiff. These risks bear no necessary relation to the risks associated with calculations of prejudgment interest in a trial.

This leaves two candidates in Table 5.3, the defendant's borrowing rate and the risk-free rate. To understand this choice, it is necessary to explore the kinds of risk that prejudgment interest might be intended to address.

B. Considerations Based on Nature of Risk

There are at least three risks or costs that might be candidates for recognition in the prejudgment interest rate with an ex ante damage award:

1. the risk of losing the case;
2. the costs and risks of any illiquidity that the plaintiff might experience as a result of the offense; and
3. the risk that the defendant might go bankrupt before the plaintiff can win the trial.

As noted at the outset, the risk of losing the case ordinarily is ignored as part of the damage calculation. This could be justified by the assumption that the justice system is infallible, so that plaintiffs with meritorious claims never lose and plaintiffs with unsound claims never win. Alternatively, it may be thought that the system picks the "right" winners only on average. Plaintiffs and defendants are then both at risk of "wrongly" losing a lawsuit. Compensation to winning plaintiffs for this risk without equal compensation to winning defendants would create asymmetry that would encourage additional lawsuits.[45]

The risk of losing a lawsuit obviously exists in virtually all cases that actually go to trial. The existence of the second potential factor, costs and risks from illiquidity, will vary from case to case. In an ex ante calculation, the issue is the *expected* costs of illiquidity. An investment that is important enough to the company to create illiquidity problems if the company is foreclosed from making it is also likely to be important enough to create a risk of illiquidity costs even if it goes ahead. That is, stand-alone investment projects typically take more cash than they generate at the outset, and if they turn out badly the result may be much like being deprived of the opportunity at the outset. Nonetheless, it may typically be easier to raise capital against the value of an ongoing project than an ongoing lawsuit. If a plaintiff may run into additional financial distress while awaiting the outcome of the lawsuit and the defendant's actions are judged responsible, the damages associated with the expected cost of that incremental distress are candidates for inclusion in an ex ante award.[46]

For both the first and second factors, then, the issue is thus whether the victim should be compensated for the risks of holding the right to recover damages at some future point, rather than holding the original opportunity.[47] Even if this question is answered affirmatively for either factor, however, *such compensation should not necessarily come in the form of an adjustment to the prejudgment interest rate.*

Clearly, if compensation for these risks is warranted in the prejudgment interest rate, the lawsuit as an asset has risk characteristics different from those underlying all four suggested prejudgment interest rates in Table 5.3. For example, the expected costs of illiquidity need bear no necessary relation to the size of the investment itself, since the costs of illiquidity may be collateral costs that affect other operations of the firm. Thus the "right" increment to the interest rate to compensate for illiquidity would be idiosyncratic to the case at hand. Moreover, and not coincidentally, there are no readily observable interest rates in the economy that could serve as benchmarks to assess just how high a prejudgment interest rate would be compensatory.[48] If these factors are to be considered, it seems more straightforward to estimate the expected consequences directly than to add some "fudge factor" to the prejudgment interest rate.[49]

The third factor, default risk, is one that does naturally fall within the scope of the prejudgment interest rate, but there is again an issue of whether it should be recognized.

The case for use of the defendant's borrowing rate is as follows. If the plaintiff *knows* it has been harmed and brings suit, but does not know when the case will come to trial and the award paid, the plaintiff has effectively lent money to the defendant (in the amount of the upcoming damage award) and deserves the same interest rate the defendant pays to other creditors.[50,51]

Alternatively, some would argue that successful plaintiffs should not be compensated for any risk in the rate of prejudgment interest on the grounds that such risks are, in reality, litigation risks that should be borne by the parties, just like the risk of losing the lawsuit.[52]

Another variant of this argument is that the calculation of prejudgment interest is *intrinsically* an ex post activity, unlike the valuation of investment opportunities ex ante. The problem is that it may be impossible to fully purge the damage calculation process of the knowledge the default did or did not occur. For example, cases that go to trial (rather than settle) will ordinarily have a material dispute either as to the fact of liability or the amount of damages, or both. Ex post, default risk has already been resolved by the date of judgment. The actual calculation of prejudgment interest occurs only after the *fact* of default or its absence is already known. A principle of finance says that the cost of capital depends upon the risk of the investment in question (here, the prejudgment interest on the damage determined to exist as of the date of the computation). Applied here, this implies that the risk-free rate is correct.[53] To give a default premium only to plaintiffs who can collect it compensates them for a risk they did not bear ex post (and is without benefit to plaintiffs who have suffered an actual default by losing defendants).[54]

Whether to include a default premium is the type of issue on which reasonable people can disagree. An interesting point is raised by Stewart C. Myers:[55] inclusion of a default premium means that on average defendants will expect to pay the same rate when "borrowing" by committing intentional wrongful acts as when going to capital markets for cash, which avoids any possibility that such acts could be seen as a source of capital at below-market rates.[56] This raises the issue of willfulness.

The incentive to consider the absence of a default premium to make an illegal act (e.g., a patent infringement) a cheap source of capital would obviously increase as the fair default premium did. *Thus, the need for a default premium will tend to be highest in cases where the wrongful act is intentional (although this is also the case when many winning plaintiffs are unlikely to collect it in the event of actual default).* Moreover, a finding that the act was known to be wrongful in some sense implies that the defendant is knowingly creating a liability at the time of the act, which may persuade even those who feel prejudgment interest is an intrinsically ex post calculation that a default premium is warranted in this type of ex ante damage calculation.

On the other hand, where the act is not willful (i.e., where there is a serious question as to the existence and/or materiality of the liability until the trial is over), retroactive imposition of a default premium after the default risk no longer exists may trouble those who would be inclined to include one for intentionally wrongful acts. This could point the way to a rule of reason on default premiums in ex ante damage calculations, because the issue of intentionality or willfulness sometimes is adjudicated as part of the trial.[57] It seems to us that the case for a default premium in the prejudgment interest rate in an ex ante damage calculation is strongest where a finding of intentional violation is present.[58]

Thus, we cannot rely on economic theory alone to reach a single answer to the correct prejudgment interest rate for an ex ante damage award. The issues of whether the act was willfully wrong or believed to be lawful bear on whether a default premium should be included in the prejudgment interest rate. Even more generally, the issue ultimately cannot be decided without consideration of the four major objectives of damage awards with which we began our [chapter]. These general public policy questions go beyond the calculation of damages in individual cases.[59]

Since we are left with two possibilities, we identify them and move on: we henceforth define a "pure" ex ante methodology as one that uses (1) an ex ante estimate of damages (including, if warranted, any expected illiquidity costs) and (2) a prejudgment interest rate equal to the risk-free rate plus a default premium. We define use of the same damage estimate with a prejudgment interest rate equal to the risk-free rate as a "mixed" ex ante approach. We shall hereafter refer to the rate that emerges from this process as the (pure or mixed) "ex ante prejudgment interest rate."

5.5 Prejudgment Interest on Post-Trial Lost Profits in the Ex Post Method

Many of the same considerations for prejudgment interest arise under the ex post method as under the ex ante method. However, before addressing these issues directly, it is useful to explore an apparent puzzle about the results obtained with the two approaches.

The hypothetical example in Figure 5.2 showed that, other things being equal, a victim on average expects to be better off under the ex post method than under the ex ante method because of the asymmetry of the litigation process (no negative damages). This finding holds whether we are comparing the results of the two methods at the time of infraction or the time of trial.

The processes of discounting and calculating prejudgment interest create another potential source of difference between the two. In particular, the method used for computing prejudgment interest under the ex ante method will generally produce a measurement of damages at T_2 different from that under the ex post methodology even if there is no difference between the expected and actual lost cash flows.[60] Perhaps even more curiously, this difference in expected damage values at T_2 will persist even if the asymmetry problem could be solved to make the ex post and ex ante methods of equivalent expected value at T_0. This might seem to be a sign that one or the other of the methods is being applied incorrectly or must have an inherent flaw; in fact, once the plaintiff's risks under the two methods are properly considered, this difference between the two approaches' results is clearly appropriate.

To explore this issue, and thereby to address the general issue of prejudgment interest in an ex post damage calculation, it is useful to consider discount rate and interest rate issues for post-trial and pretrial lost profits separately.

The source of the difference between the two methodologies is most clearly seen if we return to the example where there are only post-trial lost profits, that is, all damages consist of the area 2 in Figure 5.1, with trial and judgment at Time 2 (T_2). Assume further that the foreclosed activity had only positive outcomes, so that the possibility of negative damages does not arise (imagine that the negative outcomes in Figure 5.2 arise only from hurricanes, and this risk is always insured fully in the foreclosed activity). Again, we continue to assume that the choice of method occurs at the time of the offense and not after the cards are face up at the date of the trial.

Figure 5.3 shows the effect of the difference between awarding the victim prejudgment interest on post-trial profits under the ex ante approach and awarding the victim the expected rate of return in the foreclosed alternative under the ex post method.

First, suppose the entire damage amount consists of a single, uncertain cash flow to be received at a particular future time, say T_3. Suppose also that there happens to have been no change in expectations between times T_0 and T_2. Under the ex ante approach, experts agree that these future damages will be discounted back to T_0 at the risk-adjusted rate and compounded forward to T_2 at the rate explicitly determined for prejudgment interest, a rate likely to be lower than the discount rate used to compute the value of damages as of T_0.[61] The result (Point A in Figure 5.3) will be a value under the ex ante method at T_2 that lies below the direct calculation of the present discounted value of the T_3 cash flow (Point B in Figure 5.3) at T_2.

Now Point B is just the value of the T_3 cash flow under the ex post method, as long as expectations have not changed. Thus even if the expected future cash flows are exactly the same under the ex ante and ex post methods, the ex post value at the time of trial will exceed the ex ante value at the time of trial. We will now argue that this result is entirely appropriate, given the assumptions of the example.

Consider the expected value of the ex post award versus the value of the ex ante award at T_0. They must be the same in this particular example at point C, because they both are the present value of the same expected cash flow discounted at the same rate over the same period of time.

After T_0, however, the expected value of the ex post award grows more rapidly than the ex ante award, *providing* the expected cash flow at T_3 stays the same. That is, the ex post award as of T_0 is expected to grow at the high, risk-adjusted rate used to discount the cash flows in the first place. The ex ante award, in contrast, grows at the (presumably) much lower prejudgment interest rate. Under these assumptions, the ex post approach will be expected to produce a damage award at T_2, significantly above the ex ante damages plus prejudgment interest (pure or mixed).

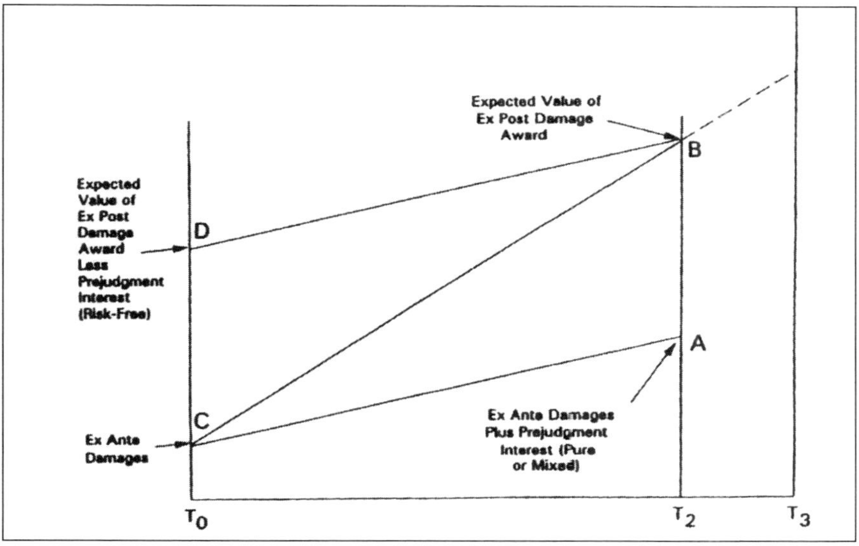

Figure 5.3 *Risk and Return for Post-trial Lost Profits Under the Ex Ante and Ex Post Approaches*

The reason this outcome is appropriate is that the plaintiff bears the risk under the ex post method that the expected cash flow at T_3 may change dramatically in value by the time of trial. Under the ex ante method, the plaintiff gets whatever the discounted expected value was at T_0, plus an appropriate interest rate on that fixed quantity.

Since the plaintiff continues to bear risk under the ex post method, it is appropriate that the *expected* award grow at a risk-adjusted rate. However, the actual award ex post may turn out to be very different from the level at Point B, the amount that would be expected at T_0. The reason is that some of the uncertainty about the cash flows at T_3 will have been resolved by T_2. The higher expected value of the ex post award at T_2 is offset by the greater uncertainty of the award between T_0 and T_2.

We are now in a position to address the question of the implicit prejudgment interest rate on post-trial lost profits. As of the date of trial, the post-judgment damages under the ex post method have a known value, such as Point B in Figure 5.3. Since this value is known as of T_2, if one wanted to know its present value as of T_0, when viewed from T_2, one would discount it *at the risk-free interest rate*. The intuition behind this result is simple: as of T_0, investors would prefer a known value equal to Point B at T_2 to a risky *expected* value equal to Point B at T_2. Therefore, the known value must be more valuable to investors as of T_0. The value of the ex post damage award shown in Figure 5.3 as of T_0 is at Point D, which just discounts the Point B amount back at the risk-free rate.

Figure 5.3 shows that the ex post award will typically have a higher expected value at both T_0 and T_2, when viewed from T_2. This is appropriate because the ex post award methodology incorporates higher risk (i.e., the risk of the foreclosed opportunity) for post-infraction lost profits.

A related issue that sometimes arises is whether the difference at T_2 implies a different implicit rate of prejudgment interest between the ex ante and ex post methods. That is, the different growth rates for the expected payoffs to the two methods (i.e., in terms of Figure 5.3, from Point C to Point A for the ex ante approach and from Point C to Point B for the ex post approach) may seem to correspond to different rates of prejudgment interest. That is incorrect, however, because only the ex ante method has actually calculated prejudgment interest in the example to this point, at least in the ordinary sense of making an annualized cash addition (interest) to the award based on a specified amount of principal and prior interest.

Table 5.4 can now sum up the prejudgment discount and interest rates for post-trial damages under the two methodologies.[62]

Table 5.4
Appropriate Procedures for Discounts and Interest Rate Calculations for Post-trial Lost Profits

Approach	How Done	Rate of Prejudgment Interest
Ex Ante (pure)	Discount to T0 at risk-adjusted rate and compound forward to T2 at ex ante prejudgment interest rate.	Risk-free rate plus a default premium.
Ex Ante (mixed)	Same as Ex Ante (pure).	Risk-free rate.
Ex Post	Discount to T2 at risk-adjusted rate and discount to T0 at risk-free rate; compound forward to T2 at risk-free rate.	Risk-free rate (implicit).

5.6 Prejudgment Interest for Pretrial Lost Profits

We now turn to the treatment of prejudgment interest for pretrial lost profits (Area 1 in Figure 5.1) under the two methodologies. The lost net revenues at Time 4 (T_4) in Figure 5.1 constitute an example of such damages. Possible procedures for prejudgment interest for these damages can readily be derived from the principles already stated, and are shown in Table 5.5.

The ex ante method deals with expected cash flows as of T_0 (see Figure 5.1) by discounting them back to T_0 at the risk-adjusted rate and forward to trial (T_2) at the rate of prejudgment interest on ex ante damages. Table 5.5 shows an intermediate stopping point at T_4 for the purpose of comparing the methods.

Table 5.5 defines the "pure" ex post approach compounding the "actual" cash flow[63] forward to the time of trial at the risk-free rate. This is the pure ex post method in the sense that it uses the absence of actual default to exclude a default premium from the prejudgment interest rate.

Application of the pure ex post method is the clearest case where a risk-free rate is justified for prejudgment interest. Table 5.5 shows, however, that victims will often pursue a mixed approach, arguing for the use of hindsight in establishing the level of pretrial damages, but employing an ex ante approach to pretrial interest.[64] Note that the use of a prejudgment interest rate with a default premium

Table 5.5
Potentially Appropriate Procedures for Prejudgment Interest for Pretrial Lost Profits

Approach	Cash Flow Discounted or Compounded	How Done
Ex Ante (pure)	Expected Cash Flow at T_4	1.Discount back to T_0 at risky rate. 2a. Compound forward to T_4 at risk-free rate plus default premium. 2b. Compound forward from T_4 to T_2 at risk-free rate plus default premium.
Ex Ante (mixed)	Expected Cash Flow at T_4	1. Discount back to T_0 at risky rate. 2a. Compound forward to T_4 at risk-free rate. 2b. Compound forward from T_4 to T_2 at risk-free rate.
Ex Post (pure)	"Actual" Cash Flow at T_4	1. Compound forward from T_4 to T_2 at risk-free rate.
Ex Post (mixed)	"Actual" Cash Flow at T_4	1. Compound forward from T_4 to T_2 at risk-free rate plus default premium.
Legend to Chronology (see Figure 5.1)	T_0 Date of offense T_1 End of damage period	T_2 Date of Trial T_4 Date of lost profits

involves the selective use of hindsight. The analyst is willing to use hindsight in determining the amount of the damage and the fact that the defendant was actually liable as of T_0, yet unwilling to use hindsight to disallow compensation for a nonexistent default by the defendant.

The only principled argument in favor of such a practice that we have been able to conceive would be in the case of a willfully unlawful act, on the grounds that inclusion of a default premium avoids the incentive to treat the act as a source of cheap capital. However, such an incentive-based argument would have to deal explicitly with the bias in the ex post method caused by the truncation of the negative possible outcomes, by reducing the amount of the award *before* prejudgment interest in the fashion described subsequently. Otherwise, it would be selective use of an incentive argument,[65] which has no more principled justification than selective use of hindsight.[66]

Table 5.5 also shows that the level of damages (i.e., the principal) to be compounded forward will typically differ between the two methodologies. It may seem that the ex post method will be compounding forward a riskier cash flow than the ex ante method. Some experts call for use of the risk-adjusted rate in the foreclosed opportunity under the ex post approach, to account for the greater risk of the ex post cash flows.

However, this logic is incorrect for the reasons already given. It is true that if the ex post method were applied consistently and accurately, the victim would be exposed to exactly the same risks as the foreclosed opportunity in recovery of pretrial lost profits (except for cases where negative damages would arise, which are excluded by assumption from this part of the [chapter]). Once any particular cash flow is realized, however – for example, by being identified as occurring at T_4—*that cash flow is no longer subject to the risk of the lost opportunity.* That cash flow becomes a fixed or certain number, just like the value of the lost opportunity at T_0 under the ex ante method. The appropriate interest rate for fixed quantities is the risk-free rate, perhaps plus a default premium in some views of the ex ante damage calculation. These conclusions follow immediately from the definition of the cost of capital as reflecting the risk of the cash flow in question.

5.7 An Integrated Approach to Prejudgment Interest and Damage Methodology

The difference in treatment of prejudgment interest as shown in Figure 5.3 is often cited as evidence condemning either the ex post or ex ante methodology. These arguments are misplaced, assuming that the discount rates have been chosen appropriately under the two methodologies.

Possible differences in prejudgment interest in Figure 5.3 will create a difference in the expected damage award at the date of trial even if the value of the damage award at all times between the violation and trial under the ex post award is exactly the same expected value under the ex ante award.[67] For example, the difference can be perceived as arising from the differences in the rates for compounding interest from T_4 to T_2 under the four methods as shown in Table 5.5.

The difference can also be perceived as arising from the "round-trip" from T_4 to T_0 under the ex ante methodology, which need not occur under the ex post methodology. Note that Table 5.4 also assumes there will be a "round-trip" from T_3 to T_0 and back to T_2. This round-trip is mandatory in the ex ante method, but is optional for the ex post method, since the ex post answer at T_2 will be the same either way. (That is, one can simply compound the "actual" T_4 cash flow forward to T_2 at the risk-free rate under the ex post methodology.) Table 5.5 shows that the ex ante damages are discounted back to T_0 at the risk adjusted rate, but compounded forward to T_4 at the (presumably lower) ex ante rate for prejudgment interest. The extra "round-trip" under the ex ante methodology will generally cause ex ante damages at T_4 to be lower than the average under the ex post approach. This loss of expected value will, of course, also be present after compounding forward to T_2.

This source of systematic difference between the two methods initially may seem arbitrary and provide an offsetting argument in favor of the ex post method. However, if done correctly, it alone is not a defect in either the ex ante or the ex post method. The reason is the difference in discount rates (third column of Table 5.5). The effect of the "round-trip" in the ex ante methodology is to purge the damage award of the expected return to risk-taking for the foreclosed opportunity between T_0 and T_4. But this is appropriate, because the victim did not bear this risk under the ex ante method. By definition, the victim always gets the expected value at T_4 as of T_0 under the ex ante method, which does not change as the risks of the foreclosed opportunity evolve.

We thus come to a conclusion that appears to differ from the literature and practice of awarding prejudgment interest. Much of the current argument over prejudgment interest and the choice of measurement methodology for damages proceeds in a vacuum without accounting for the interdependence between them.[68] In choosing the correct rates for discounting and accruing prejudgment interest, one needs to distinguish carefully among:

1. The risks of the foreclosed activity;
2. The risks of the damage award under the ex ante approach; and
3. The risks of the damage award under the ex post approach.

There is no reason per se for the risks of the three alternatives to be the same, so the appropriate discount/interest rates may vary. If such rates are chosen correctly, the fact that they differ should not by itself be interpreted as grounds for choosing among damage approaches. Nor is one approach to be preferred over the other simply on the grounds of relative risk, assuming that the discount rates have been chosen correctly.[69]

5.8 Should Damages Seek to Make the Victim "Whole" as of the Offense or as of the Trial?

A. Purging the Ex Post Method of Bias

The rub to this conclusion, of course, is that the ex post method in practice does not truly replicate the risks of the foreclosed opportunity. As shown in Figure 5.2, the expected damage award under the ex post method will exceed that under the ex ante applied to the same facts. If this were all there was to it, the ex post method would be difficult to justify. In risky industries, large numbers of offenders would go scot-free even after a long inquiry, yet victims on average would be receiving in excess of their expected damages, even before trebling in the antitrust context. Large uncertainties over eventual awards under the ex post method would greatly complicate the settlement process once differences in expectations and attitudes toward risk were incorporated into the model.

This raises the question of whether it is possible to correct the ex post method by purging it of the bias. Patell, Weil, and Wolfson (1982) propose that this be done by treating the asymmetry from negative damages as a valuable option to the victim to sue whenever ex post results justify. To correct for the bias, they would subtract the value of the option from ex post damages. We are not aware of any cases where this has actually been done, but we endorse the principle (subject to the caveats here).

Unfortunately, the calculation of the appropriate option value turns out to be difficult, and not merely because options can be difficult to value.[70] Consider what the fair value of the option would be ex ante to have the right to sue under the ex post approach. This is equivalent to a standard call option, where the buyer has the right but not the obligation to buy a stock at a future date for a specified price. The option is "exercised" only if it is "in the money": the price of the stock on that future day (read "ex post damage amount at time of trial") exceeds the exercise price specified in the option.

However, unlike the case of a standard call option, the option to sue under the ex post approach is not collected in advance from all foreclosed victims, but rather only from plaintiffs whose ex post damages are sufficiently large to provide something left over after having the value of the option deducted from their damage award. That is, in a typical option market, both winners and losers would have to pay the option's price in advance to insure against downside losses. Under what we shall call ex post *less option price* methodology, the option fee would be paid only by the really big winners who exercise the option to pay the option fee and sue only after the cards are face up.

The kind of difficulty this presents is most clearly illustrated by the limiting case of a zero ex ante damage award (i.e., a case where the present value of the expected cash flow equaled the amount of the initial investment, so the net present value of the investment opportunity was zero). Suppose the option approach were adopted and legal precedent implied that the option value in the case of a zero ex ante damage award would be 100 times the amount of the initial investment, so that very few plaintiffs would find it worthwhile suing ex post (a desirable outcome if indemnification were the only objective, given that there was zero damage ex ante). Still, there could be a few plaintiffs whose actual ex post outcomes justified a suit (say, because the actual outcome turned out to be 101 times the amount of the initial investment). Those few winning plaintiffs would obtain damages even though they were not actually damaged at the time. In the case of a zero net present value investment ex ante, the only ex ante option value big enough to deter all lawsuits by plaintiffs who would have won ex post is one equal to the maximum possible size of the ex post damage amount.[71]

In cases where there is positive damage ex ante, it will be possible in principle to calculate the appropriate ex ante option value to purge the ex post method of bias.[72] However, even if this were done successfully, another perhaps more profound problem remains. Purging the ex post award of biases does not really reestablish the goal of "making the plaintiff whole" as of the date of trial. In fact, no individual victim will be "made whole" by collecting such premiums, even if victims on average can expect to recover their damages.

The problem arises because the major beneficiaries ignored by the ex post approach are the victims who were fortuitously foreclosed from making an investment mistake. There is no way these individuals can be "made whole" except by payment of negative damages to offenders. When the average benefit of these foreclosures is netted from the value of the winners' awards, the "average victim" is made whole, but all winners are made worse off than they would have been with no foreclosures. Thus, no individual victim can be "made whole" while purging the ex post method of its biases.[73]

Even more troubling, whatever advantages the ex post method has with regard to simplicity and economy of data might be lost through the need to conduct an ex ante valuation of the correct premium for the option. Purging the ex post award of the truncation bias thus might require the damage study to implement both methodologies.

B. Difficulties in Accurately Applying the Ex Ante and Ex Post Methods

Until this point in the discussion, we have made a very important assumption. It was assumed that the methods were applied "accurately." This means that the distribution of ex post outcomes that plaintiffs and defendants will observe at trial (Figure 5.2) will not differ systematically from the ex ante expectations at the date of offense (Figure 5.1). That is, the distribution of possible future outcome is correctly perceived at the time of the violation.

It is not difficult to imagine ways in which this assumption will be violated. We have already seen one, the effects of truncation arising from the asymmetry of the litigation process, which biases upward the expected values under the ex post methodology. Sources of bias in the ex ante method are not so obvious, but may well be significant.

Suppose, for example, that the industry from which the victim was foreclosed was a highly risky one, where most entrants fail. Nevertheless, entrants are constantly entering because they misperceive their chances of success (note the existence of a market imperfection because each believes success is likely despite the failure of most). Entrants' expectations, if used to estimate future expected values, could be seriously upward-biased as compared with the actual distribution of successes observed at trial.

The procedure for estimating ex ante damages could also incorporate upward biases in expected damages as compared with an objective distribution of outcomes in the foreclosed opportunity. If a businessperson foreclosed from an opportunity were actually to forecast ex ante "but for" cash flows, such forecasts could be of the "everything goes right" variety. The reason, of course, is that it is often impossible to project the "unknown unknowns" that could go wrong—strikes, lawsuits, environmental disasters, uninsured hurricane damage, and so forth. The difficulty of accounting for such risks in any future projection could be a source of upward bias in the ex ante approach.

C. Opportunism in the Choice of Methodology

Plaintiffs face not only the risks of achieving successful litigation and recovery of damages, illiquidity, and so forth. They (as well as defendants) also face the considerable risk of not knowing what damage methodology will ultimately be applied. And even if the methodology were specified from the bench, there is considerable uncertainty over what results a particular methodology will produce, given the sensitivity of all of the methods to the assumptions employed in the presence of data gaps.

Table 5.6
Problems with the Ex Post Approach

• An accurate application of the ex post approach on average will yield systematically larger damages than an accurate application of the ex ante approach. • The expected value of damages under the ex post method will be greater than the expected value of the opportunity that was taken away. • Correcting the ex post approach of its biases may require a full-blown ex ante analysis. • Paradoxically, a substantial number of victims would nevertheless receive no damages under an accurately-applied ex post approach in a risky industry. • The option to select between approaches after the cards are face up makes the problem even worse.

Table 5.7
Problems with the Ex Ante Approach

• Judges and juries cannot always purge hindsight. • Discovery may not reveal objective data on expectations. • Historical evidence on expectations may be difficult to interpret. • It may be burdensome to estimate the true expected value of possible future outcomes. • Continuing offenses may be difficult to analyze.

D. A Summing Up

Tables 5.6 and 5.7 summarize the problems in implementing the two methodologies. In practical situations, these advantages and disadvantages would have to be weighed.

At the outset, we noted that the purpose of compensatory damages was to compensate the victim, not to punish the offender (which is accomplished by trebling in the antitrust context, and punitive damages in other contexts). Thus, we have expressed concern over methodologies that would consistently make it more profitable to invite foreclosure and become a victim and sue, rather than to pursue risky ventures.[74]

While the ex ante approach clearly has some attractive theoretical properties, the chief complaint about the ex ante approach is its susceptibility to overly optimistic projections, which are likely to be exposed in the sober light of actual experience. The victim may paint a glowing picture of the "but for" world, and the ex post methodology may provide the basis for a reality check on these projections.

The ex post methodology, however, has an intrinsic bias in its expected outcome due to the truncation problem—no negative damages. While it is possible in principle to correct for this problem, it is likely to be extraordinarily hard to do so in practice.

Our actual choices (and those of the decision makers) are not pure ones to be made before the cards are face up. In actual cases, judges and juries may find it hard to let the offender get off entirely just because the offender happened to be lucky that time.[75] Members of juries who serve maybe once in a lifetime may find the notion of "doing justice on average" unattractive.

If judges and juries are going to be fashioning a hybrid of the methods anyway, there may be an argument for the experts' doing so explicitly. Indeed, some experts are already arguing for "mixed" approaches to prejudgment interest. One method would be to use hindsight to purge the ex ante method of excessive optimism and speculation, while still seeking to estimate expected values as of the date of violation. Table 5.8 illustrates a template for balancing such issues in actual cases.

Table 5.8
Issues in Evaluating Alternative Methodologies for Estimating Damages

Issue	Ex Post	Ex Ante
Allocation of risk between offenders and victims		
Equity (fairness)		
Deterrence		
Data requirements		
Garning/Expediency		
Punish violators		
Compensate the victim		
Optimal litigation choices		

5.9 Special Consideration of Antitrust Damages

The chief unique factor that must be taken into account in antitrust proceedings is the disallowance of prejudgment interest.[76] This procedure provides another opportunity for a possible discrepancy between the expected value of the ex post and ex ante methods. If trebling is to offset prejudgment interest, it is not exactly clear what is meant by prejudgment interest.

Deleting prejudgment interest from the ex ante award would appear relatively simple. Since the procedure produces an estimate of damages at T_0 as an intermediate product, the estimation procedure could stop at this point.

Under the ex post methodology the approach is not so clear. The usual approach is to calculate the net present value of future damages at time of trial (Area 2 in Figure 5.1) and simply sum up pretrial damages (Area 1 in Figure 5.1) with no compounding of interest.

An *apparent* prejudgment interest problem is that under the typical ex post approach, post-trial lost profits are increasing in expected value to the end of the damage period at the risk-adjusted rate in the foreclosed opportunity. The difference could be considerable, as shown in Figure 5.3. However, we have shown that this is not actually a matter of prejudgment interest. Rather, it simply reflects the fact that if cash flows happen to equal their initial expected values, the ex post value of that outcome will exceed the ex ante value.

It does, however, matter how compensation for certain risks, if properly awarded, is to be done. If risks of illiquidity or nonrecovery because of the offender's default are assumed to be either ignored as a matter of law or economics, recovered through trebling, or appropriately made part of prejudgment interest, such risks will be excluded from the damage award. But if a decision is made to include these costs in damages (according to a desire to "make the victim whole"), they will not only be included but will be trebled!

5.10 Conclusion

Appropriate methods for calculation of damages from market foreclosures are subject to considerable argument at the present time. This article has attempted to clarify some of the still-controversial issues. The analysis showed that consistent employment of the ex post methodology will bias upward the average damage award because of the asymmetry in the litigation process, that is, no negative damages. The average ex post award will also be higher because the risky expected cash flows will on average equal their expected value, not their lower, risk-adjusted present value as of the date of the trial. However, this is not a *bias* in the ex post method, because it appropriately reflects the risks plaintiffs actually bear under that method (assuming it is not selected opportunistically). Other problems may arise in the ex ante method, however, and practical considerations will govern the choice of approaches in practice. If awarded, the appropriate rate for prejudgment interest may depend upon the damages methodology, especially for the ex post method. In the ex ante method, it may also be influenced by whether the liability could reasonably have been identified at the time of the act, that is, on whether the wrong was "willful." Broader public policy questions than those analyzed explicitly in this article (e.g., the implications of the incentives plaintiffs face when deciding whether to sue, and the implications of a presumption of innocence) may also come into play.

Endnotes

* The introductory paragraphs to this chapter as originally published have been omitted from this publication given their repetitive character with respect to the introductory paragraphs of Chapter 4, supra.

1. Throughout this [chapter], we define "victim" as a party who has been found at trial to have been wronged by another party. Thus the use of the terms "violator" and "victim" flow from the presumption that liability has already been established at trial. Trial on both liability and fact of damage is assumed to have resulted in a verdict in plaintiff's favor, leaving only the issue of the amount of damages.

2. Thus, we assume that trebling in antitrust or patent cases, or punitive damages in other cases take care of the first two goals, and perhaps the fourth as well. Here our starting point is consistent with almost every other approach to the subject. *See* note (1967, pp. 1566-1567).

   The private antitrust suit attempts both to compensate victims of illegal conduct and to deter such conduct. Difficulties arise because determination of what should be done to compensate injured parties is essentially unrelated to, and may conflict with, the consideration of what penalty should attach to violations. Thus, the measure of antitrust damages... cannot properly be analyzed in *vacuo*, because the private suit's public function of enforcing the antitrust laws introduces policy considerations that can affect the setting of the compensatory award.

   In private antitrust suits, damages are measured to achieve the ordinary compensatory results of putting the plaintiff in as good a position as he would have occupied in the absence of the violation. The court then automatically trebles the award, giving the plaintiff a sizeable windfall, to advance more general public purposes.

> It is agreed that Congress meant the prospect of awards of treble damages and attorney's fees to induce private parties to bring costly and uncertain antitrust litigation, thus enlisting the business public as a supplementary enforcement body dealing with violations against with the Government, with its limited enforcement resources, fails to proceed. In addition, the heavy recovery was meant to deter violations by augmenting the relatively light equitable and criminal remedies available to the Government (footnotes omitted).

Any other assumption makes either the trebling factor or the guilty verdict a generalized "fudge factor" capable of blessing any fault in the damage calculation by citing an offsetting correction.

3. In this regard, a special problem arises in the antitrust context. The notion of indemnification of the victim of an antitrust offense is not necessarily achieved under the current rules, even in theory. Traditionally, prejudgment interest is excluded from antitrust damages on the grounds that trebling makes such award unnecessary. Without trebling, such interest would otherwise be included within the damage award if the victim is to be made whole. (*See* dissent by Judge Easterbrook in *Fishman v. Estate of Wirtz,* 807 F.2d 520, 582-84 (7th Cir. 1986), for the argument for not excluding prejudgment interest from antitrust damage estimates on the ground that the victim should be fully indemnified before trebling.) The antitrust victim necessarily will not be made indifferent to the economic consequences of the offense by the award of antitrust damages prior to trebling, if trebling is assumed to include any measure of indemnification to the victim.

4. We focus on foreclosures and related offenses because they seem to raise the most difficult dispute. In the antitrust area, cartelization, price-fixing, and so on, raise other issues and are addressed by other such as Howard and Kaserman (1989), and Hjelmfelt and Strother (1991).

5. This assumption means that, although the methodologies are applied under uncertainty, the value of the damage award is set so that it is equal to the true amount necessary to make the victim whole. Errors of application are thus assumed away initially. It is sometimes said that one should resolve uncertainties in favor of the plaintiff. It is not clear how to do so without creating an upward bias in the process, thereby undercutting the objective of making damages compensatory. Resolving every uncertainty in favor of the victim would clearly make the damage award preferable to the foreclosed opportunity.

6. In actual practice, the appropriate procedures for calculating damages may be affected by such factors. Precedent or differing circumstances might govern the appropriate objective of the damage estimate, the appropriate methodology to achieve a given objective, or appropriate assumptions for a given methodology. For example, the rate for prejudgment interest may already have been established via legal precedent or rulings. (These precedents or rulings should be thoroughly researched by counsel prior to embarking upon any damage study.) In many cases, however, such precedents may not be helpful, and in any case vary considerably across legal jurisdictions. Precedents often seem to offer great latitude for a case-by-case approach, with no argument firmly rejected if sufficient legal research is done. And most fundamentally for our present purposes, these precedents cannot be said always to be based on sound principles of economics and finance.

7. We believe the principles discussed in the next section to be widely accepted in the United States. We understand that this has traditionally been less true in international legal matters. We also understand, however, that some recent cases suggest these principles may be growing more accepted in international law, as well (*see* for example, Lieblich 1990, 1991).

8. Hypotheses about future ownership of the asset can also arise. We are, in effect, assuming that the victim would not pass on any of the benefits or costs to others via sale.

9. Under the *Illinois Brick* doctrine, indirect purchasers may be denied standing in an antitrust case. *See Illinois Brick v. Illinois*, 431 U.S. 720 (1977).

10. These net revenues are cash flows, net of all costs including taxes, not accounting profits, as nearly all experts would agree. *See*, for example, Brealey and Myers (1991, pp. 95-96).

11. For the purpose of illustration, we are assuming that damages are equal to future lost cash flows. This does not rule out other possible measures of damages. *See* Bodington (1990).

12. Where markets do exist (e.g., if traded stocks are to be valued), the actual market prices are used.

13. Such cash flows are sometimes referred to as "lost profits," although in reality they are net cash revenues, measured apart from any reporting of profits to shareholders or tax authorities. As long as the horizon is indefinite, most experts would use this approach. If the horizon is truncated for some reason, some experts would argue for a profit measure to account for accruals that show us as cash flows in later periods. *See* Wagner (1990).

14. The DCF formula for present value is:

$$NPV = CF_0 + \frac{CF_1}{(1+R)} + \frac{CF_2}{(1+r)^2} + \ldots + \frac{CF_N}{(1+r)^N}$$

where:
CF_1 = the expected cash flow to be received at time i;
r = the discount rate, which reflects the cost of time and risk;
N = the last period in which a cash flow is expected.

The initial cash flow, CF_0, is usually negative, representing the initial cost of the investment, and other early cash flows may be negative, also.

15. This will not always be true. For example, the DCF approach is not used to value options. *See* Brealey and Myers (1991, chapters 20 and 21). More generally, in practice a wide variety of approaches could be used to estimate the victim's loss of asset value resulting from the offense and many of these can be interpreted as functional equivalents of the net present value approach. We concentrate on the explicit NPV calculation because it provides valuable insights into the different approaches to use of hindsight, prejudgment interest, and so forth.

16. The correct definition of the opportunity cost of capital should not be in dispute, as virtually all authorities define it in two parallel ways;

    1. The expected rate of return on investments in capital markets on alternative investments of equivalent risk; and
    2. The discount rate for determining the net present value of future uncertain cash flows by discounting their *expected values*.

    These definitions of the cost of capital do not require endorsement of any particular theory of what determines the cost of capital. For a discussion of the definitions, *see,* for example, Brealey and Myers (1991, chapter 7), or Kolbe, Read, and Hall (1984, chapter 2). This is sometimes referred to as the "risk-adjusted cost of capital."

17. *See*, for example, Kolbe, Read, and Hall (1984, chapters 3 and 4), for an evaluation of various techniques used to estimate the cost of capital.

18. In addition to reducing the expected value of future cash flows, a market foreclosure *may* also alter the degree of uncertainty regarding the future

cash flows (Bodington 1990). If so, the appropriate discount rates for the "but for" and actual world's expected future cash flows will differ accordingly. Bodington also suggests that the risk premium on costs (as opposed to revenues or net cash flows) is negative. "[W]hile the present value of a projected revenue declines with risk, the present value or certainty equivalent of a projected cost rises with risk: (Bodington 1992, p. 217). This is incorrect. The risk that matters in determining the appropriate discount rate is the "market risk" of an investment, that is, the risk that cannot be diversified away in large portfolios (*see* note 23). This market risk is determined by the relationship between net cash flows in the project in question and returns to the market as a whole. In order for the risk premium on cost to be negative, it must be true that the costs of a project fall as returns to the market as a whole rise. This clearly cannot be true as a general principle. Costs generally decline as economic activity declines and as market returns fall. The intuitive explanation is that "*risky*" costs are variable costs, while "*safe*" costs are fixed costs, when undiversifiable risk is the measure. Variable costs are less burdensome and so *should* have a smaller net present value.

19. Thus, the appropriate discount rate may be the risk-free rate even for uncertain cash flows, in cases where the uncertainty is uncorrelated with other economic events and so can be diversified away in large portfolios. For example, consider an investment where in one year a coin is tossed, and heads pays you $1,000 and tails pays you nothing. The outcome is uncertain, yet an institutional investor who bought a portfolio of a million such coin tosses could predict the expected value of the portfolio in one year ($500 million) with a very high degree of certainty. Such an investment therefore is a candidate for a discount rate equal to the risk-free rate, despite the uncertainty if only one coin toss is bought. *See*, for example, Brealey and Myers (1991, chapters 7 and 8).

20. This agreement on methodology is found only among financial analysts, not necessarily in legal practice. *See* Schaefer (1977-1978).

21. For example, the assumption that we knew the distribution of net revenues in the actual and "but for" worlds assumes away issues of measurement methodology. Note (1967, pp. 1574-1577), identifies these as (1) "before and after," (2) the "yardstick" test, (3) defendant's profits, and (4) expert testimony. *See also* Parker (1972). *See* Guilfoil (1967) for a survey of various methods approved by the courts.

22. Tye and Kalos (1996).

23. For further discussions of the issues raised by the alternatives together with some hypothetical and actual examples, *see* Taurman and Bodinton (1992); and Bonsack (1990).

24. For a thorough discussion of the arguments for the two approaches, *see* the majority opinion in *Fishman v. Estate of Wirtz*, 807 F.2d 520, 550-555 (7th Cir. 1986), endorsing the ex post approach, and Judge Easterbrook's dissent 807 F.2d 520, 578-582, endorsing the ex ante approach.

25. 807 F.2d 520, 533.

26. 807 F.2d 520, 578.

27. 807 F.2d 578-582.

28. 807 F.2d 552.

29. Note that the data used to prepare damage estimates under either method do not ordinarily include sufficient information to plot the entire distribution, as we have done in Figure 5.2. The example assumes that some such distribution exists for actual ventures and could be plotted in principle. The example also assumes that the distribution is symmetric, but this assumption could be relaxed with no loss of generality.

30. The other mean values in the Figure, m_2 and m_3, are discussed in the following text.

31. The actual ex post value in Figure 5.2 represents the net present value of the future cash flows as of the date of trial, after substantially more information has become available.

32. Patel, Weil, and Wolfson (1982) appear to be the exception, as they provide examples that show the differences in expected value under the two methods.

33. We are indebted to Victor P. Goldberg for noting that the ex post method's superiority to the actual investment is true only when the plaintiff's loss due to litigation costs is expected to be less than the gain due to the avoidance of the investment's negative outcomes. However, as noted at the outset, our chief focus is on the alternative ways of measuring damages, and we see no reason to elieve litigation costs will vary systematically between the ex ante and ex post damage methods. In any case, the optimal way to make a dam-

age award cover litigation costs is to award litigation costs directly, not to make an arbitrarily high award for compensatory damages.

34. The source of the systematic differences is that under the ex post award system, the expected costs of the "losers" are never recovered by offenders, while they are netted out of the awards to victims under the ex ante system.

35. Taurman and Bodington (1992, p. 79), pose the problem of negative damages under the ex post methodology as follows:

While the failure to award negative damages obviously disadvantages defendants, this result hardly seems unfair. Defendants are given the benefit of gains conferred on a plaintiff by wrongful conduct as a vehicle for reducing the plaintiff's recovery; only when the gains produced exceed the losses caused are defendants deprived of any further benefit. At bottom, the question is how much it matters if wrongful conduct that benefits others goes unrewarded. The answer should be that it matters very little (footnote omitted).

If the authors are addressing issues of fairness, we have no economic basis to agree or disagree. However, they may be defining the issue as one of whether negative damages should be instituted to motivate welfare-enhancing restrictions on competition. If so, we must note that no one is proposing to do this, at least in the field of antitrust. Anticompetitive behavior is to be deterred because ex ante it imposes expected costs on society. In the cases where it does not, the benefits to intended victims cannot be identified in advance. When they can, the solution is likely to be antitrust immunity, not award of negative damages. The real issue with negative damages is that they may result in an asymmetry in the litigation process. Taurman and Bodington were clearly aware of the negative damages problem, but apparently were not aware of the bias it creates even if ex post methods are otherwise accurately implemented. Unless accounted for or otherwise offset, this asymmetry inherently biases the ex post result and violates the indifference principle that was the starting point of the analysis.

36. Fisher and Romaine (1990, p. 145), reject ex post methods on the following grounds:

The violation did not merely deprive the plaintiff of the stream of returns that would have accompanied the asset. It also relieved the plaintiff of the uncertainty surrounding that stream. To use hindsight is to ignore the latter effect. As already explained, the way in which both effects can be taken into account is to value the asset as of the time of violation, taking account of uncertainty, and then award the time value of money making no allowance for uncertainty.

...[H]indsight does not change the value that the asset had when it was destroyed. Making the plaintiff whole today means making it whole as of the date of violation plus compensation for the pure time value of money. Giving the plaintiff the lost profits that hindsight suggests does not place it in the position it would have occupied without the violation; it replaces an uncertain world with a particular outcome.

It seems to us that this argument does not address the thrust of the opposing argument for the ex post approach. If done right, the ex post method seeks to put back into the damage award the risk taking that the violation had taken away from the plaintiff. Of course, Figure 5.2 shows that "done right" means that the ex post method must be chosen *before* the realized outcome is known. We have assumed at the outset that evaluation of the competing methods occurs at the time of the offense and not after the cards are face up at the date of the trial. We assume that the method must be selected prior to any chance of opportunism in light of hindsight. But even if opportunism is avoided, the real problem is that the ex post method cannot restore the plaintiff to its no-violation status as long as truncation is at work to impose asymmetry in the damage award, which was not present in the foreclosed opportunity.

37. Note that under the assumptions employed in this hypothetical, the present value of the foreclosed opportunity is simply the sum of the present value of the expected ex post damage award minus the present value of the expected loss if a loss occurs.

38. If the realized outcome is less than m_1, plaintiffs will always choose the ex ante method and receive m_1. If the realized outcome is greater than m_1, they choose the ex post method and receive the realized outcome. This distribution of outcomes is truncated at m_1 and its mean is m_3. Similarly, if defendants were allowed to choose methodologies, the average award would be less than m_1, the average value of the lost opportunity.

39. Thus, in some ways this initial assumption is closer to post-judgment interest, but it provides a useful starting point for the discussion.

40. *See Fishman v. Estate of Wirtz*, 807 F.2d 520, 581, where the differences between methods 1 and 4 in Table 5.3 exceeded the estimate of lost profits before interest! Fisher and Romaine (1990, p. 145), cite another case where, in their view, incorrect treatment of interest amounted to damages being overestimated by 100 percent.

41. One might argue that these arguments are irrelevant in the antitrust context, because prejudgment interest is routinely denied to antitrust victims. However, one cannot be oblivious to the issue even in the antitrust context. It matters how compensation for certain risk-related costs in the damage award is to be treated in an antitrust case: if included as part of prejudgment interest, these costs are ignored entirely, but if treated as part of the damage award itself, they are trebled! Moreover, since it will be seen that prejudgment interest is not necessarily treated identically in the ex ante and ex post methods, the impact can vary with the damage method use.

42. *See,* for example, Lanzillotti and Esquibel (1990, p. 130):

> By making a damage award today for profits that have not yet been lost, a court gives a plaintiff lost profits without requiring that he bear the risk associated with e investment project...However, because the plaintiff no longer has to bear the investment's risk, the plaintiff is not entitled to be compensated for risk factors. In short, the plaintiff's damage award should not include the amount of the risk premium (the excess of the present value of the profits discounting at the risk-free rate over discounting at the cost of capital adjusted to the risk of the project. (footnote omitted),

Fisher and Romaine (1990) make the same argument.

43. Diversification eliminates some risks, and competition in capital markets therefore purges compensation for diversifiable risks from the cost of capital. *See* notes 22 and 23.

44. The example of trading a risky stock illustrates why the discount rate appropriate to the risk of the foreclosed activity cannot be justified as the appropriate rate for prejudgment interest via a generalized "opportunity cost" rationale. Proponents of using the cost of capital for the foreclosed investment would argue that the foreclosed trader was prevented from earning, say, an *expected* 30 percent annually, and would have reinvested all pretrial lost profits at this high expected rate on the damage award. But in the foreclosed activity, the trader could have earned such a high rate of return only by accepting exposure to the possibility of being wiped out on Black Monday. Unless the damage methodology exposed the victim to precisely the same risks, the damage award accruing interest at 30 percent would always be preferred to the foreclosed activity, contrary to the indifference principle (indemnification) in the damage award process. This does not mean, of course, that the victim was not harmed by being precluded from taking the risks of trading and possibly being forced to tie up assets in litigation with different risks. Arguments about how a defendant would have reinvested pretrial lost

profits are generally regarded as speculative, self-serving, and as we shall show, are ultimately irrelevant. *See* Fisher and Romaine (1990).

45. Such a policy is not necessarily undesirable, but it should be a matter of conscious choice rather than being hidden in some ad hoc prejudgment interest rate approach. Trebling, for example, already encourages additional lawsuits in the antitrust context. Also, contingency in Judge William's concurring opinion in *King v. Palmer,* 906 F.2d 762 (D.C. Cir. 1990), the formula for the contingency markup is a tool of social policy that will determine how risky a lawsuit plaintiffs' attorneys are willing to bring, and hence the amount of such litigation.

46. The issue of multiple sources of responsibility for the financial distress would clearly have to be considered, too. For a discussion of the costs of financial distress, *see* Brealey and Myers (1991, pp. 434-444).

47. Patell, Weil, and Wolfson (1982) consider this question, for example, and decide the answer turns on whether the plaintiff's consumption pattern has been changed.

48. Readily observable interest rates are by definition based on liquid, traded securities.

49. Thus, the issue would be whether illiquidity caused by deprivation of the foreclosed activity would be *expected* to do incremental, identifiable harm to the plaintiff in an ex ante calculation, or *actually* did incremental harm in an ex post calculation. For example, illiquidity due to a foreclosed opportunity may delay an unrelated project due to funding constraints. The cost of the delay can be measured as part of the damages estimate.

50. The source of this view is Patell, Weil, and Wolfson (1982). Strictly speaking, however, it goes to far even when a verdict for the plaintiff is established at the time of the offense. The defendant's borrowing rate includes compensation for (1) the pure item value of money (i.e., the risk-free interest rate); (2) the nondiversifiable risk of the defendant's debt, if any; (3) the risk defendant will default; and (4) the legal and related expenses creditors would expect to pay if the defendant did default. The fourth time, however, does not belong in prejudgment interest, since recovery of attorneys' fees and court costs may be the topic of separate consideration in trials. To include this element of compensation in both the prejudgment interest rate and an award of legal costs would be doubling counting, and to include it when legal costs have been denied plaintiff is to grant the compensation by the back door when it has been denied at the front door.

Compensation for nondiversifiable risk, item (2) in the list, generally attaches to longer-term debt. Thus, as long as a short-term rate is sued to compute prejudgment interest, the issue comes down to whether or not a default premium should be added to the risk-free rate.

51. This is the rationale that underlies the ruling in *Oil Spill by the Amoco Cadiz off the Coast of France on March 16, 1978* 1992 U.S.A. LEXIS 833 (7th Cir.), decided January 24, 1992:

   By committing a tort, the wrongdoer creates an involuntary creditor. It may take time for the victim to obtain an enforceable judgment, but once there is a judgment the obligation is dated as of the time of the injury.

   It should be noted that the prejudgment interest rate was set at the prime rate in *Amoco Cadiz* because of the absence of evidence on Amoco's borrowing rate. This is almost certainly too high a rate for company like Amoco, suggesting the need for defendants to introduce evidence on the appropriate default premium. In this regard, *see also* note 54.

52. *See* Fisher and Romaine (1990).

53. Thus, this view would argue that the Court in *Amoco Cadiz* (see note 55) was incorrect to reason that because the Court believed that "once there is a judgment the obligation is dated as of the time of the injury" then the plaintiff is entitled to a default risk premium in addition to the risk-free rate. The backdating of the liability, in this view, is a fiction that ignores the fact that the bankruptcy risk during the trial has *already* been resolved before the liability for prejudgment interest is ever established.

54. We are indebted to Carlos Lapuerta for noting that this view may relate to the legal debate about whether judges make or discover law. In a case where a judge "makes" law, it seems natural to view a finding that liability exists as unknowable until after the trial ends. If judges "discover" law, however, it is less clear to us as non-attorneys whether that fact alone would imply that a finding that liability exists is something that should have been known all along, or whether the particular facts in a given case still might imply that liability was unknowable until the court ruled.

55. Private communication.

56. It also means that plaintiff will expect, at time of infringement, to be made whole.

57. For example, Section 4 of the Clayton Act was amended to permit recovery of prejudgment interest in antitrust cases where the defendant intentionally sought to delay the litigation or otherwise acted in bad faith. We understand that trebling of patent infringement damages may be imposed where the infringement is found to be intentional. Similarly, we understand that the Clean Air Act and Clean Water Act have a provision for additional penalties for intentional or egregious noncompliance. Also, the willfulness of the violation may sometimes be indicated by whether the defendant is required to pay the plaintiff's legal fees.

58. However, we are indebted to Carlos Lapuerta for noting that if the legal standards for a finding of willfulness reach such a conclusion only in the clearest possible cases, the expected default premium an intentionally unlawful act commands may be less than the full default premium, possibly not presenting some defendants with the full expected cost of their acts.

59. We are indebted to Carlos Lapuerta for noting that these issues also are related to a legal debate as to whether the law is determinate (which we understand is the traditional legal ideal) or indeterminate (which may be more realistic in practice). If the law is determinate, legality can be known in advance and willfulness judged accordingly. If there is only a probability that any given act is illegal, the concept of "willfulness" is blurred. If there were no concern over plaintiffs' incentives, the latter view might argue for a default premium in all but the clearest cases of legal "surprise," so that the expected cost of a potentially illegal act would be properly considered by defendants before undertaking a legally uncertain action. However, plaintiffs' incentives in deciding whether to bring questionable lawsuits would also have to be considered before reaching such a conclusion.

60. *See* Taurman and Bodington (1992) who provide hypothetical examples.

61. By the results of the last section, the ex ante prejudgment interest rate should equal either the risk-free rate or the risk-free rate plus a default premium.

62. One potential definition of the implicit rate of prejudgment interest for the ex post method is the internal rate of return which equates the value of the damage award expected at T_2 with the value at T_0, that is, the expected rate of return in the foreclosed opportunity. However, that definition looks forward from T_0 rather than backward from T_2, as we must under the ex post methodology. The value of any outcome known for certain at T_2 must be discounted back at the risk-free rate to determine its value at T_0. In effect, use of a single internal rate of return would ignore the risk difference between the known *value* of the expected T_3 cash flow as of T_2 (which is the ex post

award ordered by the court) and the uncertain amount of the cash flow itself at T_3, which is still in the future as of the date of trial. Since the risk changes at T_2, use of a single rate of return is inappropriate.

63. That is, the difference between the estimated cash flow the plaintiff would have received in the "but for" world using ex post information versus the actual cash flow the plaintiff received.

64. Plaintiffs may also argue for use of the defendant's cost of capital or the plaintiff's borrowing rate, possibilities raised in the ex ante damage context in Table 5.3. However, the reasons those rates are always economically inappropriate hold true for the ex post approach as well, and so are not repeated here.

65. That is, the bias in the ex post method creates economically perverse incentives for plaintiffs, for example, it is better to be wronged than to make the investment.

66. Indeed, one would have to show that the downward bias in ignoring the default premium would more than offset the upward bias in truncating the distribution.

67. *See* Taurman and Bodington (1992, pp. 35-36), who provide examples where the damage values at trial differ considerably even when the assumed cash flows are the same under the two methodologies.

68. Fisher and Romaine (1990) recognize the dependency, and defend the ex ante method as a logical method consistent with their argument for the appropriate discount rate. However, this alone does not explain why it would not be equally consistent to use the ex post methodology to replicate the risks under the foreclosed opportunity and accept the correspondingly higher expected rate of appreciation in the value of the ex post award. As Bonsack (1990) puts it:

F & R's [Fisher and Romaine's] own methodology, rather than the defendant's violation, is what ultimately relieves the plaintiff of the risks associated with the destroyed asset. F & R would have the court award only the asset's value of exchange as of the time of the violation, i.e., the risk-reduced expected future benefits discounted to their present value as of the time of the violation. Such an award makes whole the plaintiff's reasonable expectations at the time of violation., but it does not maximize the likelihood that the plaintiff will be made whole for all time. The use of hindsight is what enables the court to return the asset's riskiness to the plaintiff (pp. 20-21).

Bonsack, however, does not propose to eliminate the asymmetry that frustrates the ability of the ex post damage award to "return the asset's riskiness to the plaintiff."

69. Assuming away the truncation problem for the moment (which we consider explicitly subsequently), it is clear that the ex post method imposes more risk on the victim at time of trial under our assumptions. IF applied accurately and consistently, the risk borne under the ex post method during the time between offense and trial could be exactly the same as in the foreclosed opportunity. Truncation aside, that approach in principle is just as "fair" as the ex ante approach.

70. *See*, for example, Brealey and Myers (1991, chapters 20 and 21).

71. Logically, an alternative in such a case is to adopt an ex post option value as well, which would equal the amount of the ex post damage award. However, this is equivalent to forced use of the ex ante method, and hence not in the spirit of purging the ex post method of bias.

72. Fisher and Romaine (1990) find the ex post method to be inherently biased. This can be overcome in principle, at least. A companion paper (Kolbe, n.d.) illustrates the conditions under which the ex ante and ex post methods of damage calculation can be made to have the same expected value at the time the damaging act occurs. It demonstrates that in principle, courts could choose to employ either the ex ante or ex post methods consistently, *providing* the value of the appropriately calculated option is subtracted in the ex post method. However, this approach is unlikely to be practical. Calculation of the value of the option requires a good deal more information about the project than direct calculation of the ex ante value: information that permits calculation of the *distribution* of possible ex post project values as of the trial date must be known, not just the expected project value ex ante.

73. This feature is, in fact, characteristic of the trial process in general in at least one respect. Specifically, consider that some offenders will become bankrupt and default on their damage claims by time of trial. The average plaintiff will expect lower damage awards in the presence of such default risk, and some offenders will pay no damages (or reduced damages). Even if a decision is made to include default risk in damages, through use of the "pure" ex ante method, for example, defaulted offenders will not pay the premium and their victims will still be shortchanged (the winners will be the victims lucky enough to be harmed by solvent offenders).

74. Note that this discussion addresses the effects of net biases in a particular methodology as a whole as perceived at the time of a potential offense and cannot be used solely as a basis for deciding on the appropriate choice of subcomponent of the methodology. As discussed above, such choices often appeal to the need to offset some bias elsewhere in the methodology.

75. This may be particularly true in bifurcated trials. The damages jury, having few of the facts available to the liability jury, may be loathe to find no or low damages, having been told that their job is to punish an offender.

76. We assume for the purpose of argument that prejudgment interest is disallowed as a component of antitrust damages, but this is not always the case. For discussion of some legal precedents, *see* Taurman and Bodington (1992).

References

Bodington, J.C. (1990) "Appraising the Profits Lost by a Failed New Venture," *Journal of Forensic Economics,* Vol. 4(1), pp. 7-14.

________. (1992) "Discount Rates for Lost Profits," *Journal of Forensic Economics*, Vol. 5(3), pp. 209-219.

Bonsack, K. (1990) "Damages Assessment, Janis Joplin's Yearbook, and the Pie-Powder Court," *George Mason University Law Review*, Vol. 13(1), pp. 1-26.

Brealey, R.A., and S.C. Myers. (1991) *Principals of Corporate Finance* (4th ed.), New York: McGraw-Hill Book Company.

Fisher, F.M., and R.C. Romaine. (1990) "Janis Joplin's Yearbook and the Theory of Damages," *Journal of Accounting, Auditing, and Finance*, Vol. 5, pp. 145-158.

Fishman v. Estate of Wirtz. (1986) 807 F.2d 520 (7th. Cir.).

Guilfoil, J.D. (1967) "Damage Determination in Private Antitrust Suits," *Notre Dame Lawyer*, Vol. 42, pp. 647-679.

Hjelmfelt, D.C., and C.D. Strother, Jr. (1991) "Antitrust Damages for Consumer Welfare Loss," *Cleveland State Law Review*, Vol. 35(4), pp. 505-520.

Howard, J.H., and D. Kaserman. (1989) "Proof of Damages in Construction Industry Bid-rigging Cases," *The Antitrust Bulletin*, Vol. 34, pp. 359-393.

Illinois Brick Co. v. Illinois. (1977) 431 U.S. 720.

King v. Palmer. (1990) 906 F.2d 762 (D.C. Cir.).

Kolbe, A.L. (n.d.) "The Potential Value of the Option to Use the Ex Post Damage Methodology in Lawsuits," working paper in progress.

Kolbe, A.L. and J.A. Read, Jr., with G.R.Hall. (1984) *The Cost of Capital,* Cambridge, MA: The MIT Press.

Lanzillotti, R.F., and A.K. Esquibel. (1990) "Measuring Damages in Commercial Litigation: Present Value of Lost Opportunity," *Journal of Accounting, Auditing, and Finance*, Vol. 5(1), pp. 125-142.

Laycock, D. (1990) "The Remedies Issues: Compensatory Damages, Specific Performance, Punitive Damages, Supercedes Bonds, and Abstentation," *Review of Litigation*, Vol. 9(3), pp. 473-529.

Lieblich, W.C. (1990) "Determinations by International Tribunals of the Economic Value of Expropriated Enterprises," *Journal of International Arbitration*, Vol. 7(1), pp. 37-76.

__________. (1991) "Determining the Economic Value of Expropriated Income-Producing Property in International Arbitration," *Journal of International Arbitration*, Vol. 8(1), pp. 59-80.

Miller, R.B. (1991) "The Damages Dilemma in the Bet-the-Company Case," *Litigation*, Vol. 17(2), pp. 12-16, 54-56.

Mnookin, R.H., and R.B. Wilson. (1989) "Rational Bargaining and Market Efficiency: Understanding *Pennzoil v. Texaco*," *Virginia Law Review*, Vol. 75(2), pp. 295-334.

Nachwalter, M., W.J. Blechman, and S.E. Perwin. (1991) "Standing and Damages," Section of Antitrust Law, American Bar Association, *Antitrust Fundamentals: Course Materials*, 39th Annual Antitrust Spring Meeting, April 10, Washington, DC.

Note. (1967) "Private Treble Damage Antitrust Suits: Measure of Damages for Destruction of All or Part of a Business," *Harvard Law Review*, Vol. 80, pp. 1566-1586.

Oil Spill by the Amoco Cadiz off the Coast of France on March 16, 1978. (1992) U.S. A LEXIS 833 (7th Cir.), decided January 24.

Parker, A.L. (1972) "Measuring Damages in Federal Treble Damage Action," *The Antitrust Bulletin*, Vol. 17, pp. 497-517.

Patell, J.M., R.L. Weil, and M.A. Wolfson. (1982) "Accumulating Damages in Litigation: The Roles of Uncertainty and Interest Rates," *Journal of Legal Studies*, Vol. 11, pp. 341-364.

Project Committee on Antitrust Damages. (1993) *Proving Antitrust Damages: Legal and Economic Issues,* ABA Section of Antitrust Law. Draft, November 15.

Schaefer, E.J. (1977-1978) "Uncertainty and the Law of Damages," *William and Mary Law Review*, Vol. 19, pp. 719-769.

Taurman, J.D., and J.C. Bodington. (1992) "Measuring Damage to a Firm's Profitability: Ex Ante or Ex Post?," *The Antitrust Bulletin*, Vol. 37(1), pp. 57-106.

Tye, W.B., and S.H. Kalos. (1996) "Antitrust Damages from Lost Opportunities," forthcoming in *The Antitrust Bulletin.*

Wagner, M.J. (1990) "How Do You Measure Damages? Lost Income or Lost Cash Flow?," *Journal of Accountancy*, February, pp. 28-32.

Chapter 6

Economic Authority and the Limits of Expertise in Antitrust Cases

John E. Loptka, J.D., L.L.M. and William H. Page, J.D., L.L.M.

Synopsis

6.1 Introduction

The reorientation of antitrust over the past thirty years has increased the importance of expert economic testimony in antitrust litigation.[1] The Supreme Court's narrowing or elimination of per se illegality has led to an expansion of factual inquiries requiring expert testimony by professional economists.[2] Nevertheless, a jury's evaluation of conflicting economic opinions rarely decides cases because federal judges' choices limit the scope and force of expert testimony. Some of these choices occur in the application of the methodological strictures of the *Daubert* trilogy of Supreme Court decisions;[3] others occur in evaluating the sufficiency of expert evidence to support a jury verdict.[4] This much is well known. This [chapter] argues, however, that regardless of the nominal procedural context, these judicial choices rest on economic authority,[5] a body of authoritative economic knowledge adopted by courts—directly or indirectly—from the scholarly literature.[6] Although some have suggested that interdisciplinary approaches have made legal scholarship generally less useful to courts,[7] the use of economics in modern antitrust scholarship has had the opposite effect. Economic authority largely drawn from that scholarship now provides the conceptual basis for many judicial decisions in antitrust cases, including decisions defining the role of expert testimony.

Antitrust law has always implicitly drawn on economic ideas,[8] but over the past three decades, its reliance on them has become overt and sophisticated.[9] Judge Richard Posner has gone so far as to suggest that "antitrust law has become a branch of applied economics."[10] It is critical to recognize, however, that the institutional context of litigation influences how courts receive and apply economic theory.[11] For example, over the past twenty-five years the Supreme Court has frequently relied on Chicago School[12] models in deciding antitrust cases,[13] but largely for institutional reasons it has not adopted Chicago proposals for rules of per se legality.[14] Instead, the Court has used the models to replace rules of per se illegality with rule of reason inquiries and to refocus judicial inquiries in subsidiary decisional contexts at various stages of litigation.[15] This process has led courts to open some domains to expert testimony and to foreclose other domains. Moreover, this process has allowed courts to retain ultimate control over the influence that expert testimony has on the outcome of a case. Courts jealously guard their prerogative both to select and to determine the use of the economic ideas guiding antitrust case outcomes. They are "gatekeepers" not only of the reliability of experts' economic data and methods under *Daubert*, but of the kinds of competing economic theories and policy arguments that matter.

Though related, economic authority and expert testimony, as grounds for decision in antitrust cases, rest on different conceptual foundations. *Daubert's* inquiry into the reliability of expert testimony reflects a positivist view that scientific and technical knowledge is objectively true and that, consequently, the statements of experts should be testable by recognized methods.[16] In contrast, judicial adoption of economic authority implicitly acknowledges a sociological dimension to the acceptance of theory. The Supreme Court, in particular, has chosen among available models based upon their apparent explanatory value, their prevalence among scholars, and their congruence with the courts' institutional constraints.[17] This process of choice recognizes that economic knowledge rests, in large part, on a foundation of shared beliefs and values.[18] By choosing among economic models, the Supreme Court has maintained judicial control over the evolution of antitrust doctrine—sometimes foreclosing the use of expert testimony and sometimes insisting on its consideration.

This [chapter] examines the processes by which courts use economic authority to control experts. [Section 6.2] begins with a brief discussion of the role of conceptual models, including expert models, in judicial decision making generally. [Section 6.3] analyzes the role of economic authority in the judicial development of antitrust law, particularly since the Chicago School's influence began to transform antitrust in 1977. [Section 6.3] also describes how economic authority guides the application of the four screens that courts apply to expert testimony in the antitrust context: the scrutiny of experts' qualifications and of their testimony's relevance, reliability, and sufficiency. [Section 6.4] examines the courts' use of these screens in those evidentiary contexts in which the Supreme Court's structuring of the legal framework has made expert testimony most critical: predatory pricing, market definition and market power, cartels, and damages. The goal of our argument to this point is largely positive: to identify the factors governing how courts choose and implement economic authority, particularly when exercising control over expert testimony. The final [Section, 6.5,] however, examines the legitimacy of assigning such a leading role to economic authority in the application of the screens, focusing on the continuing controversy over the role of post-Chicago economic analysis in antitrust.

6.2 Conceptual Models, Expert Testimony, and the Process of Adjudication

Before examining the role of economic authority in constraining expert testimony in antitrust cases, this [chapter] considers more generally the nature of fact determination and the role of expertise in it. Fact-finders rely on conceptualizations of reality, explicit or implicit, to evaluate evidence. When courts rely on expert testimony, these conceptualizations become more explicit and subject to direct scrutiny by the opposing parties, the jury, and the court. Despite the relative transparency of this process, it holds well-recognized dangers.

A. Models, Evidence, and Adjudication

Although the legal system formally separates questions of law and fact,[19] the role of the fact-finder necessarily has a normative dimension.[20] A party's representation of "what happened" in a case is not simply an arrangement of evidence into a neutral narrative of the events, if such a thing is possible.[21] A party's presentation of its case is an exercise in persuasion[22] aimed at fulfilling a strategy.[23] The presentation is guided not only by the applicable legal standards, which determine the relevance of the evidence, but also by shared conceptualizations of the way the world works.[24] As Clifford Geertz has observed, making a case involves representing facts and framing arguments in light of prevailing ideas of normal and abnormal behavior.[25] These ideas influence how parties frame legal issues and how juries evaluate the presentation of a case.[26] Further, this process requires a party, through evidence and argument, to describe the conduct at issue, as Geertz puts it, in both the "language of specific consequence" and the "language of general coherence."[27] The persuasiveness of the descriptions of what happened and of what happens reinforce each other.[28]

Courts channel the construction and representation of a party's case theory by controlling the domain of the jury[29] through a series of decisions: rulings on the pleadings and the scope of discovery, decisions in limine and at trial on the admissibility of evidence,[30] rulings on motions for summary judgment, and the framing of pretrial orders, among many others.[31] Of course, to function rationally, the courts must be capable of finding facts. The days are long gone when cases were decided by ordeal, battle, compurgation, or other purely irrational means.[32] Nevertheless, since the emergence of trial by jury, courts have also taken measures to prevent factual issues from overwhelming the decisional process.[33] The elaborate English system of pleading at common law, to cite an early example, was designed to force the parties to narrow their disagreement to a single decisive issue of fact or law.[34]

Many aspects of the modern legal system still manifest this "fear of fact"[35] —not a fear of objective reality, but an apprehension that the fact-finding process, especially where it involves juries, may lapse into irrationality and speculation and thus undermine the substantive law. These manifestations include efforts to impose stricter pleading standards in certain types of disputes[36] and to eliminate juries in cases considered too complex for laymen to fathom.[37] Many evidence rules likewise reflect an awareness of juries' limited cognitive capacities.[38] But the most significant constraint on jury fact-finding by far is the courts' ability to adjust the boundaries between fact and law in ways that "do not conform to the theoretical distinction between law and fact."[39] If the courts believe a jury is incapable of determining an issue of fact, they may characterize the issue as one of law[40] or change the law so as to make a more tractable factual issue the relevant one.[41] Moreover, the sufficiency of the evidence needed to support a finding of fact is always a question of law—a principle that allows a trial court to remove questions from the jury through summary judgment or judgment as a matter of law whenever it concludes that no reasonable jury could find a material fact in favor of the party opposing the motion.[42] In some instances, as we will see repeatedly in Part III, standards of sufficiency themselves can be adjusted for policy reasons. In all of these decisions, formally characterized as "legal," the courts' findings of generalized (or "legislative") facts about society and human nature allow courts to recast the adjudicative roles of judge and jury.

B. Expert Testimony and *Daubert*

Expert testimony occupies a special role in the process of proof.[43] Experts are permitted to testify to both fact and opinion because they bring to bear a system of knowledge that is outside the jury's everyday knowledge.[44] The law of evidence requires an expert opinion to be based on a theoretical construct or other specialized knowledge that the expert applies to the evidence.[45] Expert testimony must be stated in the language of general coherence, to use Geertz's term, but that language must rely on formalized models in addition to common sense and other intuitive preconceptions.[46] Juries are supposed to evaluate the testimony based upon their everyday sense of credibility, measuring the witnesses' accounts against their own experience.[47] Thus, juries will often be asked to choose between expert accounts that rest on complex analyses far from the jurors' usual experience.[48]

An expert must, therefore, support statements of opinion in an understandable and plausible way, with reasoning that relies on the relevant theoretical construct. Moreover, the expert must maintain the plausibility of the testimony in the face of challenges by opposing counsel and the adversary's expert witnesses. *Daubert* itself stressed that cross-examination, rebuttal, and jury instructions are normally sufficient to control dubious expert testimony.[49] Nevertheless, the rules governing the admissibility of expert opinions are prime examples of the law's fear of fact.[50] Conceivably, courts might admit all relevant testimony[51] and rely on the parties to avoid introducing implausible testimony and to attack the plausibility of their rivals' testimony. The law of evidence, however, has never entirely trusted juries to sort out probative expert testimony from superficially plausible nonsense.[52] Courts have suggested that expert testimony may be too complex to allow juries to use in resolving issues, may fail to consider relevant factors, or may offer a spurious precision that could mislead jurors.[53] Because of the hired-gun character of expert witnesses, courts are especially wary of tendentious testimony.[54] Although some have advocated the use of neutral, court-appointed experts to mitigate this concern,[55] the most widely used mechanisms to control experts are the special evidentiary standards for admissibility of expert opinion testimony.

The admissibility of expert testimony is governed by the Federal Rules of Evidence, particularly Rule 702, which provides:

> If scientific, technical, or other specialized knowledge will assist the trier of fact to understand the evidence or to determine a fact in issue, a witness qualified as an expert by knowledge, skill, experience, training, or education, may testify thereto in the form of an opinion or otherwise, if (1) the testimony is based upon sufficient facts or data, (2) the testimony is the product of reliable principles and methods, and (3) the witness has applied the principles and methods reliably to the facts of the case.[56]

Daubert interpreted an earlier version of Rule 702, which ended with the words "or otherwise."[57] The list of conditions at the end of the present rule, added in 2000 in response to *Daubert* and later cases, "affirms the trial court's role as gatekeeper and provides some general standards that the trial court must use to assess the reliability and helpfulness of proffered expert testimony."[58]

Rule 702, read alongside *Daubert*, imposes "three distinct substantive restrictions on the admission of expert testimony: qualifications, reliability, and fit."[59] *Daubert* is perhaps best known for (and is sometimes used synonymously with) its controversial requirement of "reliability."[60] *Daubert* read Rule 702's characterization of expert knowledge as "scientific, technical, or...specialized" to mean that the knowledge must be "derived by the scientific method" to assure its reliability.[61] The Court required consideration of whether an expert's methodology is objectively testable, whether it was subject to peer review or publication, whether its rate of error is known, whether it was subject to controls, and whether it is generally accepted in the relevant scientific community.[62] *Kumho Tire*[63] later made clear that these standards apply to any testimony based on specialized knowledge, even if it is not strictly scientific.[64]

Although *Daubert* limited its analysis of reliability to the expert's methodology,[65] the Court observed later in *Joiner*[66] that

> conclusions and methodology are not entirely distinct from one another. Trained experts commonly extrapolate from existing data. But nothing in either *Daubert* or the Federal Rules of Evidence requires a district court to admit opinion evidence that is connected to existing data only by the *ipse dixit* of the expert. A court may conclude that there is simply too great an analytical gap between the data and the opinion proffered.[67]

Thus, a court must scrutinize not only the expert's data and formal analysis, but also the expert's grounds for drawing particular conclusions. The 2000 amendments emphasize this point by requiring the expert's opinion to be "based upon" data and to apply principles properly.[68]

In addition to assuring that there is no analytical gap between the expert's data and opinions, *Daubert* instructs the court to consider whether expert testimony will "assist the trier of fact to understand the evidence or to determine a fact in issue,"[69] as required by Rule 702. This requirement of helpfulness "goes primarily to relevance,"[70] or "fit."[71] Testimony that is either irrelevant to an issue in the case, or relevant but outside the scope of the witness's expertise, will always fail the helpfulness prong of *Daubert*. The relevance standard reiterates Rule 402's requirement that any evidence be relevant,[72] which Rule 401 defines as "having any tendency to make the existence of any fact that is of consequence to the determination of the action more probable or less probable than it would be without the evidence."[73] Irrelevant expert testimony, therefore, might be excluded under either the helpfulness prong of *Daubert* or Rule 402. The redundancy, though sometimes confusing,[74] is harmless so long as courts recognize the distinction between the relevance and reliability inquiries.

The requirement that even relevant expert testimony be within the witness's area of expertise is critical in considering what one scholar has termed "the 'ultimate issue' issue."[75] Rule 704 makes clear that expert testimony "otherwise admissible is not objectionable because it embraces an ultimate issue to be decided by the trier of fact."[76] Thus, if a legal term has professional significance in the relevant area of expertise, it should be admissible and subject to the usual adversarial testing.[77] If, however, the law defines an ultimate issue in terms having no meaning—or a different meaning—in the witness's profession, the witness's testimony on that issue may not be "otherwise admissible."[78]

Even if evidence is admissible because it meets the conditions of qualification, reliability, and relevance, it may still be insufficient to raise a material question of fact for the jury. The Court stressed in *Daubert* that "in the event the trial court concludes that the scintilla of evidence presented supporting a position is insufficient to allow a reasonable juror to conclude that the position more likely than not is true, the court remains free to direct a judgment...and likewise to grant summary judgment."[79] The admissibility and sufficiency screens are related, and have the common consequence of removing testimony from the jury's consideration. But allocating the evaluation of the evidence to the sufficiency inquiry has important procedural consequences on appeal: the district court's evaluation of admissibility of evidence is reviewed only for an abuse of discretion,[80] while its evaluation of sufficiency is reviewed de novo.[81]

6.3 Economic Authority and Expertise in Antitrust Cases

The preceding [Section] examined the interaction between factual inquiries and conceptualizations, expert and otherwise, of normal and abnormal conduct. These interactions have special importance in antitrust litigation. The decline of per se rules over the past thirty years has made certain factual issues, and the expert testimony necessary to resolve them, more important than they were in earlier decades. The consequences of this trend will be the focus of the remainder of this [Chapter]. To understand the special role of expertise in antitrust cases, however, one must recognize that it is subordinate to economic authority—the judicially adopted models and empirical estimates that provide the conceptual basis for legal rules. Courts acquire economic knowledge independently of expert testimony and rely on it to frame rules of liability, standing, and evidentiary sufficiency. These rules are designed to raise issues that courts can practically resolve without deterring benign conduct. This process then determines the qualifications that trial experts must have, the issues about which they may testify, the models upon which they may rely, and the methodologies they may use in formulating their testimony.

A. Economic Authority and Antitrust: Models, Rules, and the Domain of Fact

From the earliest years of the Sherman Act, economic ideas have influenced antitrust law through unstructured judicial adoption.[82] The Supreme Court has approached the formulation of antitrust law as a common law process, finding in the legislative text or history of the statutes few decisive constraints on its rulemaking discretion.[83] In this process the Court recognizes economic authority by accepting theoretical and generalized empirical propositions as its basis for formulating or applying rules of law.[84] The Court adopts this form of authority in much the same way it acquires knowledge of legal precedents: by pragmatically examining the scholarly literature in the context of existing case law and adopting the most persuasive and plausible accounts.[85]

The lower federal courts engage in the same sort of inquiry, constrained to varying degrees by the decisions of the Supreme Court. In many instances, the lower courts have taken the lead in the process of legal change, relying on economic authority in a variety of doctrinal contexts in order to resolve cases in ways that minimize the harmful effects of Supreme Court decisions or that invite Supreme Court correction.[86] Whatever might be said of its validity in other contexts, judicial inquiry into social science research has been integral to the development of antitrust law and has framed the role of expertise in antitrust litigation.

1. Adoption of economic authority

Perhaps the most visible example of courts adopting economic authority in antitrust has been the Supreme Court's acceptance of the Chicago School's economic models of many of the practices that have most concerned antitrust: cartels, vertical price fixing, territorial restraints, tying arrangements, and predatory pricing. As we have explained at greater length elsewhere, the Chicago models show the effects of various practices on individual actors and on overall efficiency, using the standard economic assumption of value-maximizing behavior.[87] From those assumptions, neoclassical economics has constructed the theories of cost and consumer behavior, the firm, competition, monopoly, and dominant firm pricing. Chicago analysts apply the same assumptions in adapting price theory (understood to encompass considerations of transaction and information costs)[88] to the antitrust problem.[89] They assume that firms engage in those practices which enhance profits, either by gaining and exercising monopoly power (through cartels or exclusionary practices), by improving efficiency, or both. The antitrust problem, in Chicago terms, is to identify the likely effects of the practice on efficiency,[90] bearing in mind that rivals, suppliers, and customers will also respond to monopolistic actions with value-maximizing behavior of their own—increasing output, substituting new suppliers or customers, or entering new markets. Using these assumptions, the Chicago analysis sought to refute traditional monopolistic explanations for a host of practices.[91] The Court has referred to the Chicago models in a variety of doctrinal contexts, adopting much of Chicago's analytical framework, including the assumption that firms act rationally to maximize profits and minimize losses.[92]

Courts usually offer at best only citations to legal and economic literature when "explaining" the process by which they choose one model over another. In one important case, however, we have inside information. The Court's decision in *Sylvania*,[93] which overturned the per se rule against vertical, non-price restraints established in *Schwinn*,[94] was driven by Chicago School economics entering the Court's deliberative process directly and indirectly through the legal and economic literature, not through expert testimony.[95] The Court endorsed an essential Chicago insight: that vertical restraints may enhance interbrand competition by allowing manufacturers to limit free riding by their distributors, thus creating incentives for the distributors and retailers to provide costly pre-sale services.[96] As Andrew Gavil has shown, Justice Lewis Powell played the pivotal role in persuading the Court to overrule *Schwinn*, and his advocacy within the Court stemmed from an economic conviction shaped by a Chicago analysis that Powell learned outside of the record and briefs.[97] Powell's law clerk was a former student of William Baxter, a Chicago-oriented scholar at Stanford Law School; the clerk's memorandum to Powell criticizing *Schwinn* highlighted the work of

Baxter, Robert Bork, and Richard Posner.[98] In the margin of his pre-conference notes, Powell wrote three names: "Posner, Baxter, Bork."[99] And in a critique of his clerk's first draft opinion, Powell wrote: "It also is important to demonstrate the economic illiteracy of Schwinn."[100] Powell's final opinion for the Court relied heavily on Chicago scholarship.[101] Professor Gavil concludes,

> [T]he collective imprint of the Chicago School is unmistakable. By creating an accessible body of academic commentary and criticism that presented an alternative, coherent "school of thought," it is arguable that commentators like Bork and Posner, as well as their predecessors, Director, Levi, Telser, and Bowman, facilitated change, providing specific grounds for displacing and discarding the doctrine they criticized.[102]

Justice Powell similarly adopted Chicago models of predatory pricing in his opinion in *Matsushita*.[103] In neither *Sylvania* nor *Matsushita* did he conduct the sort of inquiry into reliability contemplated later by *Daubert*. Of course, Chicago-inspired arguments have not been universally successful in the Court.[104] The crucial point to note at this stage is that unstructured choice among competing models has been an integral part of the development of legal standards in antitrust.

The question remains as to why courts choose one available model over another. One of the grounds, of course, must be the model's explanatory value. Milton Friedman has famously argued that economists, like all scientists, choose theories (or should do so) based on their predictive accuracy, rather than, for example, the realism of their assumptions.[105] To illustrate, Friedman hypothesizes a theory that the leaves on a tree are distributed as if the leaves were trying to expose themselves to the optimal degree of sunlight; Friedman suggests that such a theory would be perfectly valid if empirical testing showed that it accurately predicted the distribution of leaves.[106] Ronald Coase has objected, however, that no such process of testing typically occurs when economists accept or reject theories.[107] Instead, economists adopt theories of market phenomena based upon an intuitive assessment of how well the theory helps them understand the processes at work.[108] Coase presents a number of instances in which the vast majority of economists adopted a newly presented theory without any evidence at all that it made accurate predictions.[109] Economists are likely to adopt a model identifying previously unrecognized causal factors in a market phenomenon. Coase tellingly argues that Friedman's example of a valid theory of leaf distribution would be extraordinarily unsatisfying, regardless its predictive accuracy: it would be "a very poor basis for thinking about leaves" because it tells us nothing about the biological forces at work in the tree.[110]

Courts, like economists, are undoubtedly influenced in their choices by intuitions about each theory's explanatory value. Presumably Justice Powell's adoption of the Chicago model in *Sylvania* was based on his sense that it explained manufacturers' use of restricted distribution better than other available models. He certainly required no formal falsification of the competing models, as Friedman's standard of choice would have required. But what accounts for these intuitions? One factor Coase does not discuss is the role of social visions, or ideologies—which have influenced antitrust law from its inception.[111] Ideologies, unlike theories, are highly abstract conceptions of social causation.[112] Antitrust law has always been torn between relatively laissez-faire and relatively interventionist visions of the proper roles of the state and the market in organizing economic affairs.[113] The Sherman Act itself is a legislative compromise that relies on the undirected market (framed by common law rules of property and contract) to organize production and allocation of goods and services, but also assumes that sporadic judicial intervention will sometimes be necessary to bring monopolies and cartels to a timely end.[114]

The interpretation of the statute over the course of antitrust history has likewise been influenced by whether the interpreter—be it a court or a scholar—adheres to a relatively laissez-faire or a relatively dirigiste ideology. The populist antitrust of the post-War era reflected a perception that markets tend toward monopoly without constant governmental vigilance.[115] The Chicago School's critique of that perception reflected the conviction that the self-correcting forces of the market were powerful and would typically thwart monopolistic practices.[116] Economists associated with the Chicago School are influenced by their market-oriented vision when accepting or rejecting theories. Similar factors undoubtedly influence courts in their choices as well. The Chicago School did not gain widespread judicial acceptance until its underlying free-market ideology became more widely held in the judiciary.[117] The appointment process no doubt played a role in these changes, but even justices not otherwise commonly associated with political conservatism have been influenced by Chicago ideas.[118]

Although this [Chapter] has suggested that courts accept models on largely the same grounds as economists, even economically sophisticated judges must make their choices under institutional circumstances very different from those of professional economists. Judicial recognition of a theory has far broader consequences than recognition of the same theory by a scholar. Thus, a judge may reject a theory as a basis for resolving a legal issue even if the judge accepts the theory as a matter of abstract economics.[119] As the next section explains, institutional concerns strongly influence the kinds of rules in which courts are inclined to embody economic authority.[120] Such considerations have led the Supreme Court, rightly or wrongly, to give special weight to the immediate or obvious effects of practices on consumers. Theoretical arguments purporting to contradict the obvious evidence of a practice's effect thus face greater obstacles to adoption.

In some instances, this preference for obvious effects has led the Court to rely on post-Chicago analyses that detect inefficiencies in a wider range of circumstances than do Chicago models.[121] These post-Chicago victories have occurred mainly in cases in which the practice at issue results in evident and immediate consumer harms that a Chicago analysis suggests are illusory or transitory. In *Aspen*, for example, the leading operator of skiing facilities stopped participating in an all-Aspen ski pass that it had offered jointly for many years with its smaller rival.[122] Under a Chicago analysis, at worst this refusal was competitively benign because it could not have reduced output in the market. Nonetheless, the Court affirmed a jury verdict for plaintiffs, observing that consumers wanted the pass and were immediately harmed by its termination.[123]

Chicago arguments have generally been successful in limiting antitrust liability where the defendant's conduct confers an immediate benefit on consumers.[124] As then-Judge Breyer put it, courts "should be cautious—reluctant to condemn too speedily—an arrangement that, on its face, appears to bring low price benefits to the consumer."[125] For example, in cases which have involved maximum resale price fixing[126] and predatory pricing,[127] the practices at issue immediately resulted in lower prices to consumers, but plaintiffs alleged that the practices should nevertheless be illegal because they might eventually lead to higher prices. The Court has rejected these claims, not because the alleged harm could never occur, but because a rule focusing on an immediate, certain benefit made more sense than one based on possible future harm. In predatory pricing cases, "[e]ven if the ultimate effect of [a price] cut is to induce or reestablish supracompetitive pricing, discouraging a price cut and forcing firms to maintain supracompetitive prices, thus depriving consumers of the benefits of lower prices in the interim, does not constitute sound antitrust policy."[128]

Courts thus adopt theoretical models (and attendant empirical assumptions) from various sources in order both to explain current effects and to predict future effects of practices. They appear to do so on the basis of the theory's explanatory value, its consistency with the court's ideological conception of the relationship between the market and the state, and the special institutional context of antitrust litigation. Section 6.4 examines some of the questions of legitimacy that this process raises. For now, however, it is important only to stress the absence of constraints on reliability analogous to those imposed by *Daubert*. While *Daubert* reflects a belief that scientific and technical knowledge is objectively true and thus should meet criteria of testability, the process of judicial adoption of economic authority implicitly recognizes that economic knowledge may be socially constructed.

2. Implementation of economic authority

We are now in a position to discuss how courts make use of economic authority in formulating and applying antitrust rules. The implications of a theory allow courts to predict that a practice will have monopolistic effects in specified circumstances. Using these predictions, the courts can identify the sorts of factual inquiries necessary to determine whether liability is appropriate. Courts must then formulate rules that define the factual issues on which the outcome of the case depends. At the most general level, courts may choose to adopt a substantive rule of per se illegality or some version of the rule of reason. But there are many other decisional contexts that affect the outcome of litigation, including rules of antitrust injury or standing and rules defining evidentiary sufficiency. All of these rules define the domain of fact and, hence, the role of expert testimony.

The most sweeping use of economic authority occurs in the adoption of per se rules. When economic authority indicates that a practice would "always or almost always" reduce consumer welfare, a court may announce and apply a rule of per se illegality.[129] In such a case, the court uses economic authority to give economic content to the law ex ante, leaving a relatively narrow range of factual issues for trial courts.[130] Per se rules, of course, economize on the direct costs of litigation—no small consideration given the daunting evidentiary challenges in antitrust litigation.[131] These costs might be acceptable if the investment in protracted litigation were likely to yield more accurate results, but antitrust commentators have been skeptical that the "big case" is worth its institutional costs.[132] Apart from the sheer volume of evidence, the issues presented are often technical and remote from the judge's or jury's everyday experiences. Parties must, as in other kinds of cases, rely on narratives that describe the events in ways jurors will recognize as coherent;[133] but the business practices at issue in antitrust cases are not always easily understood in terms of a generalist factfinder's frame of reference.

These concerns at one time led the Supreme Court to justify rules of per se illegality by observing that "courts are of limited utility in examining difficult economic problems. Our inability to weigh, in any meaningful sense, destruction of competition in one sector of the economy against promotion of competition in another sector is one important reason we have formulated per se rules."[134] As this Article will show, the Court has also denied standing to entire classes of injured parties where it doubted the ability of litigation—even with expert witnesses—to measure individual harm accurately.[135] The court stressed that "'in the real economic world rather than an economist's hypothetical model,' the latter's drastic simplifications generally must be abandoned."[136]

Of course, the inability of courts to weigh actual competitive effects of a practice in litigation does not necessarily mean that the practice should be illegal per se. If the relevant economic authority suggests, ex ante, that the practice is unlikely to reduce competition, a rule of per se legality may be appropriate.[137] Some Chicago scholars have argued that there should be a default rule of legality for novel or complex practices because markets generally have a comparative advantage over courts in identifying and destroying monopolies; an erroneous determination that a practice is monopolistic is likely to be long-lasting and costly, while an erroneous determination that the practice is benign will eventually be corrected by market forces.[138] The Supreme Court has increasingly recognized the dangers of "false positives" in defined circumstances.[139]

For institutional reasons, however, the Court has usually implemented Chicago models in less sweeping ways, which leave open avenues for factual refutation.[140] In *Sylvania*[141] and in *Khan*,[142] the only cases in which the Court has expressly abandoned rules of per se illegality, it replaced them with some version of the rule of reason rather than with the suggested rules of per se legality.[143]

More commonly, the Court has used Chicago models to guide subsidiary inquiries, especially characterization, sufficiency of the evidence, and antitrust injury.[144] First, even if a practice, broadly defined, is per se unlawful, courts must characterize particular conduct as within or without the rule.[145] This inquiry involves a facial evaluation of the practice's "obvious" tendencies in light of the policies underlying the rule—policies that necessarily reflect the implications of models by which courts understand the practices.[146] Should courts find the per se rule inapplicable, then some form of the rule of reason applies.

Second, courts must determine whether the evidence presented to prove the occurrence of a particular practice is sufficient to create a jury issue. Because sufficiency is a matter of law, the inquiry incorporates policy considerations, which may be guided by models. The Court has even suggested that the plausibility of a party's theory, viewed in light of the relevant models of rational economic behavior, may influence the burden of production on the party proposing the theory.[147] Finally, courts must determine whether the harm that the plaintiff suffered is compensable—that is, whether it constitutes antitrust injury and whether the plaintiff has antitrust standing.[148] As discussed below, this process requires courts to consider the model of the alleged anticompetitive practice in determining whether the alleged injury bears the necessary relationship to the inefficiency associated with the practice.[149] All of these determinations allow courts, guided by economic authority, to structure the scope of factual inquiry, including the use of expert testimony.

B. Economic Authority and Expert Testimony in Antitrust Cases

To this point, we have shown that antitrust law incorporates economic theory by an unstructured process of judicial adoption. Courts pragmatically select among theories based upon explanatory value, ideology, and the legal process. This process, which establishes economic authority, normally precedes any consideration of expert testimony. The Court in *Khan*,[150] for example, rejected the assertion that it should not overturn the per se illegality of maximum resale price fixing without expert testimony showing that the per se rule had anticompetitive effects.[151] Instead, the Court demanded evidence that the rule had positive effects: "It is the retention of the rule of Albrecht, and not...the rule's elimination, that lacks adequate justification."[152] Notably, the Court referred approvingly to legal and economic scholarship arguing that the adverse effects predicted by Albrecht are either implausible or not anticompetitive.[153] In such instances, the unstructured adoption of economic authority, rather than the structured reception of expert testimony, is the primary mechanism by which antitrust law changes.

Once adopted, economic authority governs factual inquiries, including the use of expert testimony.[154] The pronounced fear of fact that produced the per se rules of antitrust law in pre-Chicago years has continued to manifest itself in the subsidiary decisional contexts we considered in the last section.[155] Courts have since, of course, opened up factual inquires for expert testimony. At the same time, however, they have expressed skepticism about the utility of expert testimony,[156] especially where it appears to be biased.[157] Because of these concerns, courts have not hesitated to use economic authority to define rules which limit the scope of expert testimony and to scrutinize expert testimony directly in those contexts in which the law permits it.

The previous section discussed the screens the Federal Rules of Evidence have established for expert testimony. This [Section] briefly describes how economic authority guides each of these screens in antitrust cases. The [following] section shows how courts have applied them in the particular antitrust contexts in which expert testimony has been most crucial.

1. Qualifications

Before examining the reliability, relevance, and sufficiency of expert testimony, a court must decide whether the proposed witness has sufficient "knowledge, skill, experience, training, or education" to qualify as an expert.[158] This requirement has been interpreted liberally[159] and in most antitrust cases the expert's qualifications are not challenged.[160] Antitrust litigation involves large stakes, and expert testimony is often necessary for success. Consequently, the parties in antitrust cases usually have sufficient means and awareness of the issues to choose a qualified expert. Most disputes over expertise relate to the proposed testimony itself, which may be inadmissible, irrelevant, or insufficient even if the witness is a distinguished economist.[161]

Nevertheless, proposed experts are sometimes disqualified, for example, on grounds of inadequate education, teaching, or scholarship.[162] Disqualification, when it occurs, is a necessary implication of economic authority, because the increased sophistication of the economic theory on which antitrust law is based all but forecloses nonacademic experts, and even otherwise qualified economic experts who are not familiar with antitrust law.[163] Thus, prior testimony in antitrust cases,[164] "general business experience unrelated to antitrust economics,"[165] and training in engineering and experience in market analysis as a business consultant[166] have all been found insufficient qualifications. Even economic expertise in one industry may not qualify a witness to testify concerning a separate industry.[167]

2. Relevance and helpfulness

Economic authority determines the relevance of expert testimony. First, it forecloses expert testimony not directed to the factual issues that the law defines: "Expert testimony which does not relate to any issue in the case is not relevant and, ergo, non-helpful."[168] In *Daubert* terms, courts may make an expert's testimony irrelevant or lacking in fit by adopting or interpreting economic authority. For example, the Court's retention of the per se rule against horizontal price fixing forecloses the use of expert (or other) testimony to show that a naked cartel agreement, if established by direct evidence, did not cause competitive harm in a particular case.[169] Similarly, as this [Chapter] will show in more detail below, the Court's adoption of a test expressed in economic terms, like an incremental cost test for predatory pricing, renders irrelevant any expert's testimony based on any other measure of cost.[170] On the other hand, the Court may adopt a rule that explicitly or implicitly contemplates the use of expert testimony. The Court's rejection of a per se rule, whether per se lawful or unlawful, typically implies the need for expert testimony to show the requisite competitive effect.

Even if expert testimony is relevant to an issue in the case, it may still be unhelpful. For instance, an expert's testimony might be redundant or the issue sufficiently simple to be within the common understanding of lay jurors. The test of "helpfulness" implies an assessment of the marginal benefit of the testimony in informing the trier of fact. In addition, if the issue is not within the witness's expertise, the testimony is unhelpful.[171] For all the influence of economic authority on antitrust law, not all rules of antitrust law are stated in purely economic terms. To the extent that a rule of law incorporates non-economic terms, an economic expert should not be permitted to testify that the rule is or is not satisfied.[172] For example, as discussed later, the Sherman Act does not frame the definition of "agreement" in purely economic terms. Though experts may testify to a number of subsidiary issues relevant to the existence of an agreement, they may not testify to the ultimate issue of whether an agreement exists within the meaning of the statute.

3. Reliability

Most of the *Daubert* opinion dealt with the requirement that an expert's methodology be scientifically reliable. This aspect of *Daubert* has provoked the most discussion in antitrust circles because of its potential effect on the way courts treat expert testimony regarding economics, which some have argued is not a science.[173] Defining the line between science and non-science, however, is less important after *Kumho Tire*,[174] which extended the reliability inquiry to all expert testimony, including economic testimony in antitrust cases.[175] Courts will scrutinize an economist's methodology to ensure that the expert has assembled reliable data, selected reliable principles, and applied the principles in a reliable way.[176] This inquiry is common, as the next Part will show, when expert economists rely on statistical methods such as a multiple regression analysis. In those cases, courts examine the data set itself, in addition to the selection and use of statistical methods.[177]

Reliability differs from relevance. One court erroneously suggested that an expert's "methodology must be guided by the controlling legal principle, and to the extent that the expert ignores that principle, the expert's testimony fails *Daubert's* test of a reliable methodology."[178] This statement confuses *Daubert's* methodological inquiry with its requirement that the testimony be relevant to the issues defined by the law. An economic expert may propose to offer methodologically sound testimony unexceptionable among economists, yet excluded as irrelevant or held insufficient to support a jury verdict, if the fact is not in issue under the appropriate legal standard.

Reliability is nevertheless related to relevance because antitrust law imposes significant constraints on methodology. The economic authority underlying antitrust rules may have methodological implications that displace or overlap with professional criteria of reliability. Most disputes over the reliability of economic testimony in antitrust cases turn on the requirements that the testimony be "based upon sufficient facts or data" and that it rest upon "reliable principles and methods."[179] Courts say that the expert must have "applied the principles and methods reliably to the facts of the case," and that the testimony must "incorporate all aspects of the economic reality of the...market," including "inconvenient" evidence.[180] Moreover, under *Joiner*,[181] even if the methodology is sound, the testimony may still be excluded if "there is simply too great an analytical gap between the data and the opinion proffered."[182]

Antitrust law, however, has also incorporated criteria like these into the framework of liability itself. The determination of issues such as the definition of "relevant market" requires the consideration of both empirical studies and theoretical models. For example, in *Microsoft*,[183] the court of appeals rejected the plaintiff's definition of the market for Internet browsers because there was insufficient evidence in the record to support it.[184] The court could have reached this same result using *Daubert* criteria for reliability.[185] Instead, the court faulted the testimony of the plaintiff's experts on the issue for "uncertainty"[186] because it offered "little more than conclusory statements" rather than concrete evidence.[187] The court's analysis of the fit and reliability of the expert's testimony made no reference to *Daubert*. Instead, the court treated the requirements of certainty and supporting evidence as part of the legal standard for market definition. This characterization of the issue bypassed the *Joiner* rule that trial court rulings on the admissibility of evidence are reviewable only for an abuse of discretion;[188] the legal sufficiency of the evidence is reviewable de novo.

The approach to expert testimony in *Microsoft* illustrates a more general point about the significance of *Daubert* for antitrust. Before *Daubert* purportedly relaxed the standards for admissibility of expert testimony, federal courts evaluated scientific testimony under *Frye v. United States*,[189] which focused on whether the expert's methodology had gained general acceptance in the relevant field.[190] Significantly, courts in antitrust cases never applied the *Frye* test,[191] yet they now routinely apply the *Daubert* trilogy. Thus, while *Daubert* "may create a less stringent evidentiary standard than *Frye*, its standard appears to apply to a greater range of expert testimony."[192] Nevertheless, both judges[193] and mainstream economists[194] have expressed the belief that courts in antitrust cases do not disregard expert testimony much more after *Daubert* than they did in the years immediately before. This should not be surprising. Economic authority is embodied in rules defining the elements of antitrust offenses, the requirements for antitrust injury, and other substantive antitrust rules guiding both the methodology and relevance of economic testimony. Consequently, economic authority pervasively controlled antitrust decision making before *Daubert*, and it continues to do so regardless of the procedural heading under which courts deploy it.

4. Sufficiency

The primacy of economic authority is perhaps most evident in the criteria for the legal sufficiency of evidence. As *Daubert* itself emphasized, expert testimony, even if admissible, may be found insufficient to create an issue of fact for a jury.[195] Thus, a court's finding that evidence meets the threshold standard of reliability does not bar the court from finding the evidence insufficient to raise a jury issue—even on the specific issue the testimony addresses. More importantly, the issues of relevance and helpfulness also necessarily affect sufficiency. A court will grant summary judgment to the defendant if it finds that the plaintiff's expert's testimony is irrelevant because the testimony applies a standard inconsistent with economic authority.[196] The same result could follow if the court allowed expert testimony on subsidiary legal issues, but excluded testimony on the ultimate issue on the ground that such testimony was outside the expert's area of expertise. In such a case, the court would be required to determine whether a jury, based on the expert's evidence, could reasonably infer the existence of the necessary fact from all of the evidence, including the expert's testimony on the subsidiary issues.

In antitrust cases, however, economic authority has a special role in the analysis of the sufficiency of evidence. In some instances, the Court has placed particular weight on certain theoretical propositions about business behavior and its relationship to antitrust policy. Where the Court has determined, based on economic authority, that allegations "make[ ] no economic sense,"[197] it has required more than the usual amount of evidence of the conduct to create a jury issue. In effect, the Court increased the plaintiff's burden of production on the issue. In such circumstances, the Court has approved summary judgment even where expert testimony on the issue was admissible.[198] Once again, economic authority defines the role of expert testimony; the sufficiency inquiry "forces the antitrust judge to get into the expert's discipline itself, rejecting the expert's own substantive conclusions in favor of the judge's own."[199]

6.4 Judicial Control of Expert Testimony in Critical Contexts

Thus far, this [Chapter] has considered the rubrics under which courts decide whether juries will be allowed to consider expert testimony on antitrust issues. A court may disqualify an expert altogether. If the expert is found qualified, the court may still exclude the expert's testimony on a motion in limine on the ground that it is irrelevant, unhelpful, or unreliable. Even if the testimony is not excluded at this stage, the court may consider its consistency with legal standards and its sufficiency to create a jury issue on a motion for summary judgment or on a motion for judgment as a matter of law. Thus, many of the same issues considered on the motion in limine may be considered at various points in the process of adjudication. The procedural context is less important in determining the extent of judicial control than the applicable economic authority.

This [Section] examines how the Supreme Court and the lower federal courts have used economic authority to control expert testimony in the doctrinal contexts in which it has proven most important.[200] In each case, courts have confined expert testimony by formulating rules defining the offense and the scope of liability. Having defined the boundaries of the offense, courts then police the boundaries by evidentiary rulings on either admissibility (usually for relevance) or sufficiency. In some instances, courts have used the *Daubert* inquiry to examine methodologies against the standard of the economics profession. The extent and effect of judicial control vary depending upon the nature of the issue the court must resolve.

A. Predatory Pricing

The subject of predatory pricing has generated more academic heat than any other antitrust issue of the last twenty years.[201] Economists have debated the circumstances in which price-cutting may lead to inefficient results and have proposed a myriad of tests by which the courts should identify predatory pricing.[202] From this spectrum, the Supreme Court has chosen a Chicago School analysis of predation, including both theoretical models and broad empirical estimates of the significance of the practice.[203] Earlier courts had assumed that a dominant firm could use retained earnings or profits from other markets to finance a campaign of low pricing to eliminate existing rivals and deter new entrants. The Chicago critique, however, suggested that certainty of present losses to the dominant firm in such a campaign, combined with the uncertainty of future profits, made the conventional story of predatory pricing dubious.[204] Under this analysis, predation is an implausible explanation for a dominant firm's behavior in a price war because only in rare circumstances would predation be rational, profit-maximizing behavior. Thus, most instances of aggressive price-cutting are beneficial to consumers both initially and in the long run. The policy implication was either that price-cutting should be per se lawful[205] or that the test for its existence should be stringently drawn to avoid overdeterrence. The Court has opted for the latter course, making the claim of predatory pricing difficult—but not impossible—to sustain.[206] The adoption of this view of predatory pricing as economic authority has drastically narrowed the scope of expert testimony in predatory pricing cases.

In *Matsushita*,[207] the Court made perhaps its most explicit use of the Chicago models to affirm a summary judgment. The case alleged a twenty-year conspiracy by Japanese firms to charge predatory prices on sales of electronic products in the United States.[208] The Court discerned a "consensus among commentators that predatory pricing schemes," even by a single firm, "are rarely tried, and even more rarely successful."[209] In *Matsushita* itself, the alleged predation was even less plausible because the defendants would have had to organize and maintain a cartel over many years to put the scheme into effect. Thus, the improbability of either a stable cartel or a successful campaign of predatory pricing combined to make the claim especially implausible. To make matters worse, an erroneous finding of liability would "chill the very conduct the antitrust laws are designed to protect"—in this case price-cutting, which "is the very essence of competition."[210]

The *Matsushita* Court did not, however, adopt a standard of per se legality, as some Chicagoans had proposed. Instead, the Court relied on the theoretical critique to alter the standard for summary judgment: if the defendants "had no rational economic motive to conspire..., and if [defendants'] conduct is consistent with other, equally plausible explanations, the conduct does not give rise to an inference of conspiracy."[211] Where the claim alleges a type of conduct, such as predatory pricing, that is intrinsically implausible in light of the relevant economic authority, the plaintiff must offer more concrete evidence that the conduct is monopolistic. The higher burden on the plaintiff carries with it a higher standard of sufficiency of evidence to create a jury question. In *Matsushita*, the combination of implausibilities justified summary judgment.[212]

The Court dismissed as insignificant the plaintiffs' expert testimony "that petitioners had sold their products in the American market at substantial losses."[213] The district court originally excluded the testimony on the grounds that it was based on assumptions about the defendants' costs that were implausible and inconsistent with the evidence.[214] The court of appeals, however, reversed the district court on this issue.[215] The Supreme Court did not disagree, but nevertheless relied on the substance of the district court's ruling to discount the probative value of the testimony. The Court held that "the expert opinion evidence of below-cost pricing has little probative value in comparison with the economic factors...that suggest that such conduct is irrational."[216] The Court thus explicitly subordinated expert testimony on an issue of fact to the Court's own inferences from models it had adopted as economic authority. The theoretical critique of the predatory pricing doctrine was sufficiently powerful to reduce to insubstantiality admissible expert testimony that the pricing was below cost.

The expert's report, discussed at greater length in Justice White's dissent, portrayed the defendants as participating in a cartel whose aim was to raise prices in the Japanese market but to lower them in the United States.[217] Thus, in Justice White's view, the American manufacturers were injured not only by predatory pricing, but also by the larger illegal cartel agreement, of which predation was only a part. The report "alone creates a genuine factual issue regarding the harm to respondents caused by Japanese cartelization and by agreements restricting competition among petitioners in this country."[218] Justice White caustically observed, "No doubt the Court prefers its own economic theorizing to Dr. DePodwin's, but that is not a reason to deny the factfinder an opportunity to consider Dr. DePodwin's views on how petitioners' alleged collusion harmed respondents."[219] Moreover, Justice White challenged the majority's insistence that the plausibility of the defendants' scheme depends upon a measure of profit maximization rather than growth maximization, which, he said, should have been given to the jury as an issue of fact.[220]

The majority rejected the substance of Justice White's argument by characterizing the higher prices in Japan as irrelevant to the predation claim in the United States.[221] Even if the cartel prices in Japan provided the means to sustain long-term losses, that fact did not supply a motive, without which the alleged scheme remained implausible.[222] The majority did not respond directly to Justice White's argument for the primacy of expert testimony, but it evidently believed that economic authority (what Justice White called the Court's "own economic theorizing") could set limits on the range of acceptable expert opinion.

In *Brooke Group*,[223] the Court refined the standard for predatory pricing into a two-part test. First, the plaintiff must show that defendant's prices are below an appropriate measure of cost.[224] Second, the plaintiff must prove that the defendant "had a reasonable prospect...of recouping its investment in below-cost prices."[225] Both of these requirements have imposed significant constraints on experts. The first requirement excludes all expert opinion that even above-cost pricing may be predatory, regardless of whether that proposition is respected among economists.[226] Then-Judge (now Justice) Breyer had reasoned in an earlier case that, even if above-cost price cutting by dominant firms could be theoretically inefficient, the law should not recognize claims on this basis for institutional reasons associated with the legal process:

> [A] price cut that ends up with a price exceeding total cost—in all likelihood a cut made by a firm with market power—is almost certainly moving price in the "right" direction (towards the level that would be set in a competitive marketplace). The antitrust laws very rarely reject such beneficial "birds in hand" for the sake of more speculative (future low-price) "birds in the bush."[227]

The Supreme Court in *Brooke Group* likewise suggested that "it would be illogical to condemn" an above-cost price cut because to do so would deter price cutting that might undermine a noncompetitive price structure, and, in any event, such a policy would "depriv[e] consumers of the benefits of lower prices in the interim."[228] In effect, above-cost pricing, no matter how destructive to competitors, falls within a "safe harbor"[229] —a form of per se legality.[230]

Thus, the Court acknowledged that above-cost price-cutting might impose social costs, but for institutional reasons rejected any rule imposing liability. In these situations, the immediate and obvious benefit to consumers outweighs as a matter of law the potential social cost, even though the latter may predominate in theory. Thus, even if a plaintiff's expert proposed to testify that prices above average total cost were predatory, the testimony would be insufficient as a matter of law.[231] Even if the testimony were admitted and the expert testified that the defendant's price-cutting drove the plaintiff from the market, and, as a result, prices in the market increased, the plaintiff would still lose as a matter of law.[232]

Brooke Group's definition of a predatory price went still further. The Court referred to "incremental cost" in its adoption of the requirement that prices be below cost.[233] Because the parties had agreed "that the relevant measure of cost is average variable cost," the Court explicitly "decline[d] to resolve the conflict among the lower courts over the appropriate measure of cost."[234] Nevertheless, *Brooke Group* appears to point toward some measure of incremental cost rather than average total cost as the relevant standard. This refinement of the rule imposes still more onerous restrictions on experts who propose to testify that price cuts are predatory.[235]

In *American Airlines*,[236] for example, the government alleged that American strategically added capacity on four core routes from its Dallas hub in order to drive out low-cost carriers and garner monopoly profits, both on those routes and on others where it had established a reputation for predation.[237] Characterizing the charge as predatory pricing,[238] the courts held that the alleged pricing behavior was nonpredatory as a matter of law, even though, as the court of appeals acknowledged, recent post-Chicago theories of predatory pricing justified greater receptiveness to claims of predation.[239] The court scrutinized the government experts' testimony, which purported to show that American priced below the various measures of cost that American itself used in making business decisions.[240] The court concluded that the testimony was insufficient to create a jury issue, holding that marginal cost is the appropriate theoretical standard for judging whether prices are predatory, that any proxy for marginal cost "must be accurate and reliable in the specific circumstances of the case at bar," and that average variable cost is such a proxy.[241] The government's proposed cost tests, however, were not proxies for marginal cost, or its close relative incremental cost. Consequently, those tests were "implicitly ruled out by *Brooke Group's* mention of incremental costs only."[242] The court identified elements of the government expert's proposed measure of cost that "do not vary proportionately with the level of flight activity" but "are allocated arbitrarily to a flight or route."[243] For the court, these elements of cost rendered the government expert's proposed measure non-incremental, and therefore irrelevant.[244]

The second prong of the *Brooke Group* test requires that plaintiffs prove the defendant has a reasonable prospect of recouping its investment in the predatory campaign.[245] This requirement also affects expert testimony because it typically involves proof that the defendant will be able to exercise market power.[246] In *Cargill*,[247] for example, the Court examined market share and other factors bearing on market power to evaluate the plausibility of a claim that a firm was capable of predation.[248] Also, the Court's adoption in *Brooke Group* of an express requirement of recoupment has led lower courts to scrutinize expert testimony regarding the likelihood of recoupment, largely on the grounds of market definition and market power.[249] The skepticism implicit in the governing models of the practice, combined with the fear of overdeterrence, diminishes the deference afforded to expert opinions.

In *Brooke Group* itself, the plaintiff offered a complex argument that recoupment would occur as a result of the restoration of oligopoly pricing after the victims of predation were sufficiently chastened.[250] The Court, however, relied on economic authority to reject the plaintiff's evidence, including its expert testimony. The Court pointed out that, although there was evidence prices were increasing, output was increasing as well—a fact inconsistent with the economic principle that "[s]upracompetitive pricing entails a restriction in output."[251] Moreover, the evidence concerning price increases was questionable because it focused on list prices rather than transaction prices.[252] Given the difficulty of tacitly coordinating prices, the Court found insufficient evidence that the strategy was likely to allow recoupment.[253]

Expert testimony did not change this assessment.[254] According to the Court, "[e]xpert testimony is useful as a guide to interpreting market facts, but it is not a substitute for them."[255] Moreover, "[w]hen an expert opinion is not supported by sufficient facts to validate it in the eyes of the law, or when indisputable record facts contradict or otherwise render the opinion unreasonable, it cannot support a jury's verdict."[256] For example, the expert in *Brooke Group* relied on the defendant's internal documents expressing a desire to slow the growth of the generic cigarette market.[257] Yet the Court found the documents insufficient because the defendant had engaged in a marketing effort to increase demand for generic cigarettes[258] —behavior consistent with the Court's economic authority.[259] The critical point to note here is that economic authority—the theoretical models and related assumptions that the Court adopted—defined the facts and evidence for which the Court searched. Whatever the legitimacy of the expert's testimony as a matter of economics, it did not trump the Court's own economic assumptions.

B. Markets and Market Power

Some form of monopoly power is necessary for any restriction of competition. Historically, however, antitrust's reliance on per se rules often bypassed the requirement that plaintiffs prove that defendants possessed market power.[260] If it appeared that a form of conduct was unlikely to occur in the absence of monopoly power, and if the conduct did not appear to have any redeeming qualities, the courts believed they could safely find a violation based on proof of conduct alone.[261] Where market power was an issue, as in merger cases, market definition was sometimes conducted formalistically in an effort to generate high or low market shares, which were then viewed as all but conclusive proof of market power.[262] Ad hoc notions like "submarkets" contributed to this sort of gerrymandering.[263]

The growing economic sophistication of the courts has changed this pattern radically. First, as we have seen, the Court has abandoned or limited traditional per se rules, recognizing that the practices the rules covered were not inevitably monopolistic. Under the new rules, if anticompetitive effects are proven directly or can be inferred from an accepted theory, and if there is no contrary and plausible explanation for these effects, courts must find that market power exists because market power is a prerequisite for competitive harm. Courts have also become more aware, through the unstructured acquisition of economic authority, of the factors that bear on market definition and their relevance to market power.[264] Courts now recognize that market definition requires the sophisticated use of data and theory—a process that typically requires expert testimony.[265] At the same time, however, the law's incorporation of the economic criteria of market definition now constrains how experts can address the issues. Courts insist on adherence to economic authority in market definition and the inference of market power.

1. Market definition

In recent years, the views of professional economists and the lower federal courts on the criteria for market definition have converged:[266] "[T]he issues of principle that plagued market definition in the early years have receded, and the cases now involve questions of fact within a settled framework of economic theory."[267] Under this new consensus, courts insist on the consideration of all sources of substitution, both in demand and supply, that may affect consumer welfare and thus influence the definition of product or geographic markets.[268] Some courts require experts to perform standard statistical tests before testimony on market definition will be admitted.[269] In effect, widely recognized economic criteria for market definition have become elements of antitrust law. Consequently, many of the same issues arise whether the court considers the admissibility of the evidence on the grounds of reliability or relevance.[270] And the same issues may arise in evaluating the probative value of evidence on a motion for summary judgment or judgment as a matter of law.[271]

Courts thus routinely exclude expert testimony or find it insufficient on the basis of economic authority. For example, Judge Easterbrook recently affirmed summary judgment for the defendant on a claim that the defendant's exclusive contracts for placement of at-shelf coupon dispensers in retail stores unreasonably restrained trade.[272] The plaintiff had submitted expert testimony that at-shelf coupons constitute a market distinct from other forms of promotional devices.[273] Judge Easterbrook, however, found the evidence insufficient to raise a jury issue.[274] According to Judge Easterbrook's reading of the economic authority, products are in the same market if statistical evidence shows that the price or output of one varies with the price of the other. The plaintiff's experts, however, had offered only "a potpourri of survey research and armchair economics."[275] A survey purporting to show that consumers prefer at-shelf coupons to other kinds of coupons was indeed properly excluded under Rule 702 as "unscientific,"[276] but was "economically irrelevant anyway"[277] because substitution in supply or substitution by consumers with no preference among kinds of coupons could still prevent the exercise of market power by producers of at-shelf coupons. Similarly, evidence that the output of at-shelf coupon dispensers rose and that the price paid retailers to accept placement increased during a period of competition was not evidence that the product constituted a market; the evidence failed to show whether the increase was the result of substitution away from other promotional devices. Evidence of a shift toward at-shelf dispensers in response to an effective reduction in price would tend to show that all promotional devices are in the same market.[278] Finally, because the economists had used both list prices instead of transaction prices and an incorrect measure of cost, Judge Easterbrook discounted a study purporting to demonstrate that price/cost margins for at-shelf dispensers had increased as market share increased.[279]

The plaintiff's economists maintain that Judge Easterbrook failed to address tests they did perform, placed too much weight on the absence of a covariance analysis, and erred in his assessment of their price/cost analysis.[280] The crucial point for our purposes, however, is that Judge Easterbrook resolved these questions as a matter of the law of market definition, based on his own interpretation of economic authority. This approach, while more economically assured than that of most judges, is fairly typical.[281]

Despite these strictures, courts recognize that economists must be pragmatic in the process of market definition. Courts do not prevent experts from making simplifying assumptions in the data they collect and analyze, so long as the experts have legitimate grounds for their choices and the choices are consistent with sound econometric practice.[282] For example, one court upheld under *Daubert* an expert's decision to exclude from the market for air travel those cities less than 150 miles from each other because ground travel was assumed to be a viable substitute at those distances.[283]

2. Market power

While legal standards for market definition closely track economic standards, the legal definition of market power differs significantly from its economic counterpart.[284] In economic theory, a firm has market power if it faces a downward-sloping demand curve. A competitive firm faces a horizontal demand curve; it takes the market price as given and sets its output at the point at which the marginal cost of production equals the price. If the firm faces a downward-sloping demand curve, it will recognize that its output decisions affect the price—the definition of market power.[285] The law, however, has long recognized that this definition is far too inclusive to be of any practical legal use.[286]

Consequently, antitrust law has fallen back on a variety of proxies for market power, especially market share.[287] To determine market share, the court must first define the relevant market. At one time, market share figures were all but decisive in determining market power—a phenomenon closely related to the practice of gerrymandering in market definition.[288] Courts now recognize that other factors, especially the absence of barriers to entry, may undermine an inference of market power even from very high market shares.[289]

Nevertheless, it remains a matter of economic authority that market share is relevant to the existence of market power.[290] First, high concentration still creates an inference of market power. In merger cases, for example, the presence of a high Herfindahl-Hirshmann Index (HHI)[291] combined with a significant increase in concentration creates a prima facie case that the merger will lead to anticompetitive effects.[292] Very "high market concentration levels...require, in rebuttal, proof of extraordinary efficiencies."[293] An expert opposing such figures is at a disadvantage. In *Heinz*, for example, the court of appeals reversed the district court's finding that a merger in a market with very high HHI figures and high entry barriers would not increase the risk of tacit collusion, despite expert testimony.[294] Economic authority embodied in scholarly literature and the enforcement agencies' Merger Guidelines made the district court's reliance on expert testimony erroneous as a matter of law. On the other hand, low market shares virtually foreclose the existence of market power. Yet the law continues to impose market share thresholds on findings of market power, and thus forecloses any expert opinion to the contrary.[295] Expert opinions that firms with market shares of under fifty percent have monopoly power have been found insufficient as a matter of law.[296] Likewise, courts frequently reject expert testimony resting on unorthodox proxies for market power.[297]

In some instances, courts have allowed plaintiffs to bypass the market share inquiry (and therefore the market definition inquiry) by permitting "direct" proof of market power—for instance, by showing that the defendant in fact exercised market power by reducing output and increasing price.[298] The FTC has successfully argued, for example, that a merger of close competitors in a broader market of differentiated products may result in unilateral anticompetitive effects.[299] Traditionally, antitrust law evaluates mergers by estimating the risk that the increased concentration will facilitate price coordination. This "unilateral effects" approach attempts to identify mergers in which the surviving firm, even if lacking a large share of a conventionally defined market, may be able to increase the price of an item without diverting sufficient sales to competitors to make the increase unprofitable.[300] Economists using price data from a range of geographic markets are able to provide a firm basis for predicting the effects of a merger by showing the effects of competition between close competitors.

3. Aftermarkets

The Supreme Court's decision in *Eastman Kodak*,[301] and its aftermath in the lower federal courts, illustrates the interaction of economic authority and expertise in resolving a critical issue of market definition and market power. The Supreme Court in *Kodak* rejected an argument that economic theory foreclosed any inquiry, by expert testimony or otherwise, into the existence of monopoly power in so-called aftermarkets—the "markets" for a single firm's parts and repair services.[302] The decision predictably led to a flood of lawsuits by the rivals of large firms in their downstream parts and service markets. The lower courts stemmed the tide, however, by identifying in the facts of *Kodak* conditions for liability that firms could avoid in structuring their aftermarket programs.[303]

In *Kodak*, independent service organizations that provided parts and maintenance for Kodak copiers and micrographic equipment[304] were driven from the market by Kodak's sale of replacement parts only to purchasers of Kodak equipment who either used Kodak's repair service or who repaired their own equipment.[305] The Court held that there was sufficient evidence to create a jury issue that *Kodak* had economic power in the tying (parts) market to restrain trade in the tied (service) market.[306] *Kodak* argued that if it attempted to charge supracompetitive prices in the aftermarkets for parts and services, consumers would simply switch to competitors' equipment in their initial purchases.[307] Consumers would include the price of parts and service over the useful life of the equipment as part of the real price.[308] Consequently, as a matter of economic authority, the sort of market power a firm has over aftermarkets in parts and service did not permit the firm to restrain trade; "basic economic reality" dictates that when a defendant lacks market power in the primary market for equipment, it lacks power in aftermarkets to charge supracompetitive prices.[309] If consumers were injured, it would not be because of the exercise of market power, but because of an opportunistic exploitation of a long-term commitment. As Justice Scalia argued in his dissent:

> Leverage, in the form of circumstantial power, plays a role in each of these relationships; but in none of them is the leverage attributable to the dominant party's market power in any relevant sense. Though that power can plainly work to the injury of certain consumers, it produces only "a brief perturbation in competitive conditions—not the sort of thing the antitrust laws do or should worry about."[310]

In a result widely viewed as a rebuff to the Chicago School,[311] the Court rejected this argument, noting that under Kodak's new policy prices to its customers rose, but sales of equipment did not decline.[312] Instead of the Chicago argument, the Court accepted plaintiffs' economic argument that significant information and switching costs could prevent customers from protecting themselves from rising prices in the aftermarkets.[313] In an unorthodox move, *Image Technical's* brief informed the Court that its argument had "been developed with the assistance of Professor Steven C. Salop, Professor of Economics and Law at Georgetown University Law School. Professor Salop is a recognized expert in the fields of industrial organization, competition, and antitrust. He is cited with approval by Kodak."[314] Apparently impressed, the Court cited three articles by Professor Salop to support its rejection of Kodak's theory.[315] The Court reasoned that consumers required a substantial amount of data and a "sophisticated analysis" to calculate their expected parts and service costs over the life of the Kodak equipment.[316] Indeed, according to the Court, some consumers were unable to take lifecycle prices into account at the time of initial purchase.[317] Further, consumers who had already purchased Kodak equipment would tolerate some increase in aftermarket prices because once "locked in" customers faced prohibitively high costs in switching to a competitors' equipment.[318]

Unlike the alleged predatory pricing in *Matsushita*, "[t]he alleged conduct—higher service prices and market foreclosure—is facially anticompetitive and exactly the harm that antitrust laws aim to prevent."[319] This passage echoed the argument of an amicus curiae that *Kodak* was "precisely the opposite [of *Matsushita*]: conduct that produces direct and immediate harm to consumers—higher (service) prices, which antitrust law generally aims to prevent—is being defended on the speculative theory that such conduct is from a broader perspective, actually beneficial to consumers."[320] Thus, *Kodak's* assertion of economic authority was insufficient to establish as a matter of law that, "despite evidence of increased prices and excluded competition, an inference of market power is unreasonable."[321] In circumstances where there is immediate, facial harm to consumers, "[l]egal presumptions that rest on formalistic distinctions rather than actual market realities are generally disfavored in antitrust law. This Court has preferred to resolve antitrust claims on a case-by-case basis, focusing on the 'particular facts disclosed by the record.'"[322] In this context, "formalistic distinctions" meant theoretical predictions of necessary effects enshrined as economic authority; "actual market realities" and the "particular facts disclosed by the record" implied the prospect of expert testimony. In the litigation on remand, the case predictably turned on factual questions raised by expert testimony.[323]

Interestingly, however, *Kodak* has not markedly expanded the influence of expert testimony in litigation. Instead, it has refocused the application of economic authority in the terms of the *Kodak* majority's reasoning. In one ensuing decision, the district court admitted expert testimony for both sides[324] but ultimately granted judgment as a matter of law to the defendant.[325] A manufacturer of merchandise security tags alleged that its competitor had attempted to monopolize the market. The plaintiff's expert testified that the market was limited to the type of tag manufactured by the parties because, as in *Kodak*, it was costly for their customers to switch to other types.[326] Unlike in *Kodak*, however, information costs were trivial: the defendant provided its "sophisticated" customers with detailed projections of future tag costs,[327] which customers could readily use to negotiate reduced prices.[328] The plaintiff's expert's testimony that the relevant market was limited to one type of tag thus could not support a jury's verdict.[329] The *Kodak* rationale for rejection of a rule of per se legality became the basis for close scrutiny of the record, ultimately rendering the expert's testimony insufficient on the undisputed facts.

C. Cartels

Although the Chicago School's influence has diminished the scope of rules of per se illegality, the per se rule prohibiting naked cartels remains in place. Chicago scholars generally have supported the rule, arguing that it should be the primary, if not exclusive, focus of antitrust.[330] Economic theory predicts that cartels will restrict output and increase prices. Some have argued that a legal prohibition is unnecessary because entry of competitors and cheating among the cartel participants will eventually destroy any cartel,[331] and others have argued that cartels may in some instances be efficient.[332] Nevertheless, the Supreme Court has from the earliest years of the Sherman Act foreclosed any testimony that cartels are necessary to prevent "ruinous competition" or that they are justified by some other social policy.[333] Courts continue to enforce the per se rule against naked cartels.[334]

The per se illegality of price fixing does not mean expert testimony is unnecessary in price-fixing cases. The prosecution in a criminal case might prove the offense using only the direct testimony of participants in a naked cartel.[335] But if the existence of a cartel agreement must be inferred from circumstantial evidence, an expert is almost always necessary.[336] Still, the peculiar nature of the law's definition of "agreement" may preclude expert testimony on some issues and limit the probative value of the testimony on others. Before turning to the proof of agreement, however, we examine an issue that is perhaps more basic: what sorts of admitted agreements are per se unlawful cartels? Expert testimony may be appropriate—or even necessary—in answering this question as well.

1. Characterization

Historically, antitrust law has divided practices into those governed by a per se rule and those judged under an open-ended rule of reason.[337] More recently, however, the Court has suggested that there is no bright line distinction between practices "that give rise to an intuitively obvious inference of anticompetitive effect and those that call for more detailed treatment."[338] The Court must make

> an enquiry meet for the case, looking to the circumstances, details, and logic of a restraint. The object is to see whether the experience of the market has been so clear, or necessarily will be, that a confident conclusion about the principal tendency of a restriction will follow from a quick (or at least quicker) look, in place of a more sedulous one.[339]

The Court thus mandates first a facial examination of the practice, and then an appropriately detailed "empirical" evaluation. The more obvious the harm to consumers, the more circumscribed will be the evidence necessary to establish liability—and by necessary implication, the narrower the scope for expert testimony.

The facial evaluation of practices occurs primarily at the level of economic authority. In *Broadcast Music*,[340] for example, the Court refused to apply a rule of per se illegality to a blanket licensing arrangement by which organizations with market power fixed the prices of performance rights for copyrighted musical works.[341] The question, according to the Court, was whether the practice facially appears to restrict output or to enhance efficiency.[342] Because the activities of performing rights societies evidently reduce transaction costs and make some desirable transactions possible without foreclosing others, they should be judged under the rule of reason.[343] Similarly, in *Sharp*,[344] the Court relied on the Chicago School models of resale price maintenance and cartels to exclude from the per se category those vertical agreements that merely limit price-cutting.[345] Accepting the view that resale price maintenance was per se illegal only because it might facilitate cartelization,[346] the Court reasoned that only vertical agreements setting a price or price level could be effective to police retail or manufacturing cartels.[347]

In some instances, expert testimony—or the lack of it—may influence the court's characterization decision. In *California Dental*,[348] the Court examined a dental association's ban on certain price and quality advertising and concluded that the association's suggested justifications were plausible enough to warrant more exacting scrutiny than a "quick look."[349] The FTC had rested its case in part on published studies of the effect of advertising restrictions on consumer welfare in markets other than dental services[350]—in effect a claim that economic authority was sufficiently conclusive to justify a truncated rule of reason inquiry. The Supreme Court, however, credited a different body of economic authority, one that identifies a form of market failure known as "the lemon effect":[351]

> In a market for professional services, in which advertising is relatively rare and the comparability of service packages not easily established, the difficulty for customers or potential competitors to get and verify information about the price and availability of services magnifies the dangers to competition associated with misleading advertising.[352]

The Court quoted the seminal article by George Akerlof for the proposition that in a market characterized by informational asymmetries, "dishonest dealings tend to drive honest dealings out of the market."[353]

On remand, the Ninth Circuit read the Supreme Court's decision to require that the record contain "some relevant data from the precise market at issue in the litigation."[354] The FTC's counsel had not thought it "necessary to supplement the existing economic literature cited by the FTC with the testimony of an expert economist witness."[355] The Ninth Circuit concluded, however, that "the social science evidence cited by the FTC does not constitute substantial evidence of the anticompetitive nature of the California Dental Association's advertising restrictions."[356] The California Dental Association, in contrast, offered an expert who testified that the restrictions in the dental services market prevent "buyers from getting mistaken impressions about information contained in advertisements, and therefore arms them with more accurate and verifiable information; makes them better able to search for their particular value."[357] The court of appeals reasoned on this basis that, by standardizing the form of price advertising,

> the restrictions create a kind of network externality by mandating a common language to be used by those CDA members who advertise discounts. As a result, a consumer's costs of searching for the less expensive service would be reduced...We are therefore persuaded that CDA's restrictions do mitigate some of the informational asymmetries that exist in the market for dental services.[358]

The court found all of the factual claims of the association to be "well-supported by expert testimony and anecdotal evidence from individual dentists practicing in California."[359] Thus, a remand to the agency was unnecessary.[360] Whatever the merits of this assessment,[361] the decisions of the Supreme Court and the Ninth Circuit make clear that judicial choices on matters of economic authority dictate the role of expert testimony in the characterization inquiry.

2. "Contract, Combination..., or Conspiracy"

The concept of collusion in economics is related to, but distinct from, the concept of collusion in antitrust law. In evaluating market behavior, economists consider whether firms are cooperating. Game theory, for instance, distinguishes between cooperative games, which involve coalitions of players formed through communication and trustworthy promises, and noncooperative games, in which players act independently for their own welfare.[362] Similarly, the theory of cartel behavior assumes complete cooperation among the cartel members,[363] and various models of oligopoly predict "noncompetitive" outcomes based on rivals' mutual awareness of the circumstances of the market.[364] Economics has also identified practices that might facilitate cooperation and thus foster some forms of interaction that lead to noncompetitive outcomes.[365]

Like the economist's idea of cooperation, antitrust law's concept of agreement is an effort to distinguish noncompetitive from competitive behavior. Because of the institutional characteristics of the legal system, however, antitrust must consider other factors in shaping the legal categories within which courts determine the existence of an agreement.[366] The distinctive features of the law's concept of agreement are not apparent in its abstract definitions. Section 1 of the Sherman Act condemns every "contract, combination…, or conspiracy, in restraint of trade."[367] The courts have said that an illegal agreement requires "a unity of purpose," "a common design and understanding," or "a meeting of the minds in an unlawful arrangement."[368] The general definitions pose little difficulty where the case involves evaluating direct evidence of an express, though clandestine, agreement to fix prices[369] or the competitive effects of an explicit agreement to engage in practices that almost certainly facilitate noncompetitive outcomes.[370]

The issue becomes crucial, however, when the case requires the inference of an agreement from circumstantial evidence of parallel conduct by rivals. Game theory suggests that competitors may be able to raise prices to supra-competitive levels without overt communication or explicit agreement simply by taking each other's anticipated reactions into account in setting their own prices.[371] This phenomenon is variously labeled interdependent pricing, oligopolistic interdependence, tacit collusion, and conscious parallelism.[372] Economists also have identified a variety of practices that might facilitate the coordination of prices or the detection of cheating among cartel participants.[373] An economist might characterize firms' behavior in an oligopoly as noncompetitive or even collusive, particularly in the presence of these facilitating practices.

The courts, however, have been unwilling to allow juries to infer the existence of unlawful agreements solely on the basis of parallel behavior.[374] The legal challenge of applying Section 1 to consciously parallel behavior was the focus of a debate between Donald Turner and Richard Posner.[375] Both scholars sought to formulate a rule that embodied the economic theory of oligopoly in a way that took account of the institutional strictures of the legal system. Turner argued that when oligopolists simply take into account the probable reactions of competitors in setting their basic prices, there is either no agreement at all or, at most, no unlawful agreement.[376] He reasoned that an oligopolist acts rationally, just as a competitive firm does, except that the oligopolist "takes one more factor into account—the reactions of his competitors to any price change he makes."[377] Turner thus implicitly suggests that it would be unjust to punish firms for acting rationally.[378] More importantly, he noted that there is no practical remedy against such interdependent behavior; an injunction would be "hopelessly vague,"[379] demand "irrational behavior,"[380] or result in something akin to undesirable "public-utility regulation."[381] Turner did, however, willingly condemn parallel adoption of certain facilitating practices, such as basing-point price systems,[382] because in those cases an injunction would effectively promote price competition.[383]

Posner first responded to Turner thirty-five years ago, but has recently updated his arguments. He agrees with Turner that "tacit collusion" is "a form of concerted action," but he argues that it may be unlawful as well.[384] Because "[t]acit collusion is not an unconscious state," an injunction against it would not "tell[ ] oligopolists to behave irrationally."[385] Courts might infer the existence of unlawful collusion from certain types of parallel facilitating conduct, such as the use of a basing-point system,[386] then award damages[387] and an injunction against the facilitating practices.[388] Thus, the practical difference between Turner and Posner is that, in the case of pure pricing interdependence—a case both believe will be unusual[389]—Turner would find no unlawful agreement, whereas Posner would impose damages.

The Turner-Posner debate is echoed in the judicial evaluation of parallel conduct. Posner's analysis has influenced what is recognized as economic circumstantial evidence of agreement. This influence first appeared in enforcement agencies' efforts in the 1970s and early 1980s to challenge "shared monopolies" by using economic evidence of market structure, predisposing characteristics, and facilitating practices.[390] Litigants and courts continue to classify and discuss evidence of "tacit collusion" in Posner's terms. Nevertheless, courts have maintained barriers to the inference of agreement from this kind of evidence.[391] Courts have required evidence of certain "plus factors,"[392] defined tautologically[393] as activity that "tend[s] to exclude the possibility that the defendants merely were engaged in lawful conscious parallelism."[394] Courts have suggested that "plus factors may include evidence demonstrating that the defendants: (1) acted contrary to their [individual] economic interests, and (2) were motivated to enter into a price fixing conspiracy,"[395] though neither of these conditions alone is sufficient.[396] Courts thus require evidence that justifies the inference of an actual agreement, rather than simply noncompetitive market behavior.[397]

Consequently, the focus is on whether the defendant's actions are rational choices for a firm acting in its individual self-interest. In other words, the court will ask whether the action would make sense for a firm acting independently but taking account of the past and anticipated actions of its rivals. If the evidence shows only the sort of action supporting an affirmative answer, then no jury question of collusion is created.[398] Moreover, if the plaintiff introduces evidence tending to show a plus factor, the defendant must have the opportunity to offer an independent business justification for the practice.[399] If the competing justifications are equally plausible, then, again, no jury question is created.[400] One implication of this approach is that a plus factor must involve behavior that increases the probability of supra-competitive pricing. Predisposing market conditions, such as high concentration, hospitable to interdependent pricing are insufficient because the presence of such conditions cannot exclude the possibility of independent action.[401] Courts justify this approach—in ways reminiscent of Turner—by pointing to the dangers of overdeterrence. If it were rational for oligopolists to act interdependently, then penalizing them for doing so would deter socially beneficial conduct. This consideration is magnified when the alleged practices involve price-cutting, which the Supreme Court has accorded special protection from erroneous findings of liability.

The Posner-Turner debate frames the role of economic experts. Experts are typically necessary to identify and analyze practices and conditions conducive to tacit understandings.[402] But to be admissible under *Daubert*, their testimony must be reliable, relevant to the existence of an agreement, and helpful to the jury; moreover, to avoid summary judgment, the evidence must be sufficient to create a jury issue.[403] Reliability depends largely on the empirical and theoretical standards of the economics profession. Courts occasionally exclude portions of expert testimony on this ground in cases alleging the inference of price fixing. The Eleventh Circuit, for example, relied on *Daubert* to exclude testimony based in part on sales data from a state outside of the area of the alleged conspiracy.[404] The inclusion of the data "skew[ed] any cumulative measurements, such as percentages and frequencies, that depend upon the size and characteristics of the database as a whole and that are intended to describe the alleged conspiracy."[405] Consequently, where the expert could not easily segregate the extraneous data, his testimony based on those data was inadmissible.[406]

Courts also occasionally exclude as irrelevant expert testimony on the issue of collusion. Facilitating practices, for example, are not necessarily plus factors.[407] To incur liability, the facilitating practices, viewed in light of the market structure and their competitive effects, must tend to exclude the possibility of independent action by making it more plausible that the defendants' conduct emanated from collusion than from unilateral conduct in the defendant's own self-interest.[408] Expert testimony that the defendant's conduct is collusive in some sense other than the one the law defines is irrelevant.[409]

Some courts go further and exclude expert testimony that the defendant's conduct is collusive within the law's definition.[410] Identifying unlawful collusion is outside the domain of economic expertise because the legal definition of collusion differs from the related economic concept.[411] Thus, the expert should testify only to the nature of the practice and its likely motivations.[412] For example, an expert might testify that a particular course of action was contrary to the self-interest of the defendants.[413]

Two decisions of the Eleventh Circuit illustrate these points. In *City of Tuscaloosa v. Harcros Chemicals, Inc.*,[414] the district court had excluded expert testimony that the circumstantial evidence in the case justified a finding of price-fixing. The lower court reasoned that, because the expert failed to distinguish between an illegal agreement and consciously parallel behavior, his testimony failed *Daubert's* criteria for reliability.[415] Based on the evidentiary ruling, the court granted summary judgment for the defendants.[416] The Eleventh Circuit held, however, that the district court erred in requiring the expert, as a condition of admissibility under *Daubert*, to "show a successful conspiracy."[417] Experts' opinions "need not prove the plaintiffs' case by themselves; they must merely constitute one piece of the puzzle that the plaintiffs endeavor to assemble before the jury."[418] Summary judgment was inappropriate because the expert's evidence of parallel behavior tended to show a plus factor sufficient to distinguish conscious parallelism from unlawful collusion.[419] The court of appeals did agree with the exclusion of the expert's opinion concerning the ultimate issue of whether a conspiracy existed, however, because a jury is "entirely capable of determining whether or not to draw such conclusions without any technical assistance from [experts]."[420] The rules of evidence permit experts to testify to an ultimate issue, but only if the testimony would assist the jury. Because the legal definition of agreement differed from economic concepts of collusion or cooperation, the issue was outside of the expert's domain.

The distinction between economic and legal concepts of agreement was also crucial in *Philip Morris*,[421] where the plaintiffs tried to prove by circumstantial evidence[422] that cigarette manufacturers had fixed prices.[423] The district court granted summary judgment in an extended opinion stressing the failure of the plaintiffs' expert to distinguish between facilitating practices and plus factors.[424] The plaintiffs identified, for example, "signaling" of intended price changes in press conferences and analyst reports, monitoring of competitive behavior by reports to a central organization, reducing the number of tiers in defendants' price structure, and engaging in prior conspiracies to limit health-based marketing of cigarettes and to fix prices.[425] The court examined each of these practices and found that they either had legal justifications or did not tend to exclude the possibility of independent action, even though they may have facilitated collusion.[426]

Plaintiffs' expert submitted an affidavit stating:

> I characterize the behavior that I have observed in the cigarette industry during the relevant period as a "collusive oligopoly" or a "loose cartel." I believe that the cigarette companies have engaged in activities beyond mere conscious parallelism, and indeed have participated in various facilitating practices that are anticompetitive in purpose and effect.[427]

According to the court, the expert was "positing a new theory where certain aspects of conscious parallelism should be found to be anticompetitive."[428] The court continued: "The failure of Plaintiff's expert to distinguish conscious parallelism from cartel behavior makes his subsequent opinion inadmissible as he finds inferences of collusion where the law finds none."[429] The expert failed to explain how the facilitating practices excluded the possibility of independent action, and his "allegations of 'anticompetitive' conduct [were] broad and could be read to include lawful activity."[430] Consequently, "his flawed view of the law" rendered his testimony inadmissible.[431] The court of appeals agreed that because the witness

> defined collusion to include conscious parallelism...he did not differentiate between legal and illegal pricing behavior, and instead simply grouped both of these phenomena under the umbrella of illegal, collusive price fixing. This testimony could not have aided a finder of fact to determine whether appellees' behavior was or was not legal, and the district court properly excluded it.[432]

D. Damages

This [chapter] has shown that the process of formulating antitrust law requires the adoption of economic authority and the integration of its insights with institutional considerations. This process is equally evident in the rules governing the proof of antitrust damages. Section 4 of the Clayton Act[433] authorizes those injured by antitrust violations to recover treble damages, but courts qualified this right by formulating a system of rules linking damages to the purposes of the antitrust laws in ways the courts can administer. Courts rely on economic authority to structure the process of proof so that damages reflect not only the net harm to the plaintiff, but also the net social harm.[434] First, using the doctrines of antitrust injury and standing, courts define the measure of compensable harms to reflect the social harm flowing from the unlawful practice so that damage awards will not deter efficient conduct. As this Article shows below, courts must look to economic authority to identify the inefficiencies to which each practice is directed. Second, rules governing proof of harm assure that actual damages are measured by the difference between the plaintiff's actual condition as a result of the offense and its hypothetical condition but for the offense. Proof of this amount requires the construction of a theoretically sound damage model that accurately projects the "but for" world. Expert testimony is almost always essential to this process. Because the process depends largely on statistical methods that transcend the antitrust context, courts typically evaluate those methods using *Daubert's* reliability inquiry, incorporating the standards of the economics profession.

1. Antitrust injury and standing

Despite the general language of Section 4 of the Clayton Act, the law does not permit all those who suffer injury from an antitrust violation to recover. The Supreme Court has limited recovery to prevent antitrust law from deterring efficient conduct and to assure that the appropriate deterrent penalty be imposed efficiently.[435] The Court's vehicles in this task have been the antitrust injury and standing doctrines, both of which are shaped by economic authority and, in turn, determine the appropriate role of expert testimony. The antitrust injury doctrine requires a plaintiff to have suffered a harm caused by the anticompetitive aspect of a practice.[436] It is not enough for the plaintiff to prove that a violation inflicted harm; the harm must be one causally connected to the inefficiency for which the practice is prohibited. Proper application of the doctrine requires a court to determine, in light of the relevant economic authority, whether the alleged harm bears the requisite causal relationship to the inefficiency associated with the practice.[437] The effect of such an inquiry on expert testimony is apparent in *Brunswick*,[438] which first articulated the antitrust injury doctrine.[439]

Brunswick, a manufacturer of bowling equipment, acquired and began operating some of its customers' bowling centers in financial difficulty. The competitors of those centers sued, alleging that the acquisitions violated Section 7 of the Clayton Act and that the plaintiffs were injured by the preservation of the failing centers.[440] The plaintiffs offered the testimony of qualified experts concerning the "profits which the plaintiff bowling centers would have made but for defendant's violations of law."[441] The Court's adoption of the requirement of antitrust injury,[442] however, rendered the testimony irrelevant. Even if the acquisitions were unlawful, the plaintiffs' lost profits should not have been allowed as a measure of damages because they were unrelated to the reason for the prohibition of the merger.[443] This requirement imposes important constraints on experts. Instead of showing simply that the defendant's conduct injured the plaintiff, an expert must show that the harm stems from the inefficient aspect of the practice.[444] Thus, the measures of cost that determine whether the defendant's price-cutting is predatory also determine whether the harm to its rival from the price-cutting constitutes antitrust injury.[445]

In addition to the requirement of antitrust injury, the Supreme Court has imposed antitrust standing restrictions limiting the right to sue to the classes of actors who would be the most efficient plaintiffs.[446] One example of these restrictions is the rule of *Illinois Brick*.[447] A decade earlier, the Supreme Court had already held that those who purchase directly from antitrust offenders may sue for the entire overcharge, even if they passed on a portion of it to others in the chain of distribution.[448] In *Illinois Brick*, the Court extended the logic of that holding by denying the right to sue for damages to indirect purchasers who pay an overcharge as a result of an antitrust violation.[449] Explaining the rule, the Court emphasized the limitations of expert testimony in resolving factual issues in complex markets. It noted the

> serious problem of measuring the relevant elasticities—the percentage change in the quantities of the passer's product demanded and supplied in response to a one percent change in price. In view of the difficulties that have been encountered, even in informal adversary proceedings, with the statistical techniques used to estimate these concepts...it is unrealistic to think that elasticity studies introduced by expert witnesses will resolve the pass-on issue.[450]

The Court observed that the "economist's hypothetical model"[451] of the incidence of an overcharge among actors in a chain of distribution cannot reliably capture the real-world complexities of identifying the degree of passing on. The "sound laws of economics" actually "heighten[ed] the awareness of the difficulties and uncertainties involved in determining how the relevant market variables would have behaved had there been no overcharge."[452] The *Illinois Brick* rule means that expert testimony concerning the overcharge to indirect purchasers, which is routinely offered in state court indirect purchaser class actions,[453] is categorically inadmissible in federal court because the Supreme Court has determined, as a matter of economic authority, that it would be unduly costly or unreliable.[454]

2. Proof of damages

The antitrust injury and standing doctrines identify which measures of harm are consistent with the public goals of the antitrust laws. The plaintiffs must then prove that the defined harm occurred—typically with an expert's model that compares the plaintiffs' actual condition, measured by the appropriate index, with their but-for condition.[455] Again, economic authority controls the process; the law of damages, much like the law of market definition, has grown to embody accepted economic criteria for assessing the net harm attributable to a practice.

The models courts use to determine the existence of the practice and its likely effects on competition also guide any inquiry into the effects of the practice on the plaintiff.[456] The antitrust injury inquiry assures that the alleged harm bears the necessary causal link to the inefficiency associated with the practice. That causal link forms the basis for any damage model.

Ideally, the damage model would isolate the antitrust offense as the single causal factor accounting for the difference between its actual condition and the but-for condition.[457] Thus, the model must account for other major causal factors that may have affected the index during the relevant period.[458] To do this, an expert typically must (1) gather the necessary data; (2) identify a benchmark, or normative, period that was free from illegal conduct, but was otherwise comparable to the damage period; and (3) project the but-for world using an appropriate theoretical model of firm behavior[459] and appropriate statistical methods, usually multiple regression analysis. Courts should scrutinize each of these steps to assure that the expert's model is reliable and consistent with economic authority.[460]

In addition, the expert first must ensure that the data used in the model are accurate. For example, an expert attempting to show that the defendant's actions delayed the production of the plaintiff's product, thus reducing the plaintiff's profits, may not simply accept without verification the plaintiff's projections of its likely production volumes and sales.[461] The expert must verify the accuracy of the data.[462] Although errors in an expert's selection of a sample from a verified data set generally "bear on the weight of the testimony, not its admissibility,"[463] in some instances, errors may reduce the weight of the evidence sufficiently to warrant summary judgment.[464] Courts also scrutinize the normative period on which the expert bases the projection of the but-for world. The normative period should be a reasonable proxy for the market as it would have been absent the illegal conduct. Selection of a period in which the plaintiff's fortunes were unusually good is improper, because it would exaggerate the difference between the plaintiff's normal condition and its condition during the damage period.[465] Courts now require experts to conduct standard statistical tests to reinforce the reliability of their selection of a normative period.[466]

Courts also insist that experts use appropriate statistical techniques in projecting the but-for world. In some instances, this has led to a requirement that the expert conduct a multiple regression analysis, by which the expert can calculate the effect that a change in an independent or explanatory variable has on the dependent variable, the variable that the model seeks to "explain."[467] In antitrust actions, the dependent variables are some critical elements of a damage model, such as profit, sales, or price. A simple weighted average of the critical variable during a normative period does not provide a basis for projecting what the competitive price would have been but for the violation because it assumes that the only difference between the normative and damage periods is the violation.[468] Consequently, a regression analysis is necessary to isolate the effects of other variables.[469]

Of course, regression analyses themselves are subject to challenge. It is not enough that regression is a legitimate technique for estimating damages; the expert's use of it must be reliable and consistent with economic authority.[470] The considerations of the profession and those of the legal system in evaluating regressions are similar, but not necessarily identical.[471] One common ground for challenge is the failure to include appropriate variables in the regression model.[472] This issue is as much a matter of economic authority as one of reliability. Independent variables must have a theoretical influence on the dependent variable,[473] and the relevant theoretical models of challenged practices are inevitably elements of economic authority.[474] Cost theoretically affects price, so if price is the dependent variable, cost must normally be included as an independent variable. Failure to include an important independent variable may lead to biased results[475] or reduce the explanatory power of the model.[476] Similarly, including too many independent variables may lead to spurious results.[477] Adding variables that are correlated with each other can diminish the effect of individual variables.[478]

Challenges on these grounds have had mixed results,[479] however, in part because of the Supreme Court's decision in *Bazemore v. Friday*,[480] which predates *Daubert*. In *Bazemore*, the lower courts in an employment discrimination case had excluded a regression analysis on the ground that it failed to include "'all measurable variables thought to have an effect on salary level.'"[481] The Supreme Court reversed, stating:

> While the omission of variables from a regression analysis may render the analysis less probative than it otherwise might be, it can hardly be said, absent some other infirmity, that an analysis which accounts for the major factors must be considered unacceptable as evidence of discrimination. Normally the failure to include variables will affect the analysis' probativeness, not its admissibility.[482]

Although this language suggests that failure to include all relevant variables affects only the weight to be accorded a regression analysis,[483] the Court did note that "[t]here may, of course, be some regressions so incomplete as to be inadmissible as irrelevant."[484]

In some instances, the relative lenience of *Bazemore* has led to a kind of burden shifting. Some courts have required a party to support with evidence any contention that the omission of particular variables renders a regression unreliable,[485] and the party offering the regression may then be required to rebut.[486] One basis for evaluation is a high R^2 figure for the regression. This may suggest that the independent variables in the model are good at accounting for the factors affecting the dependent variable and that the addition of more independent variables would not significantly alter the model's predictive power.[487]

The *Polypropylene Carpet* litigation illustrates the complexities confronting courts in analyzing experts' use of regression in antitrust cases.[488] The plaintiffs' damages expert used a multiple regression analysis to estimate what the prices would have been during the damage period but for the alleged conspiracy[489] by using manufacturing style, selling style, shipping point, and order quantity as the independent variables.[490] The expert did not use total manufacturing cost as an independent variable,[491] instead using the ratio of the price of carpet to fiber costs as the dependent variable.[492] Defendants challenged the expert's treatment of the cost variable[493] and asserted that his failure to consider variables for demand, changes in income, interest rates, business cycle characteristics, capacity utilization, the entry of competition, and growing buying power rendered the expert's model unreliable.[494]

The plaintiff's expert explained the decision not to use manufacturing cost as a variable by arguing that sufficient data to estimate properly the effect cost had on price in the benchmark period were unavailable;[495] that differences in the measures of fiber costs between the benchmark and conspiracy period may cause extrapolation error[496] from the use of an unrepresentative sample;[497] and that the price of carpet might affect cost, thus raising problems of endogeneity or simultaneity.[498] The defendants did not challenge the expert's extrapolation error and endogeneity concerns, but argued instead that there were sufficient data to measure the coefficient of cost to price.[499] The defendants observed that the expert had run a *Chow* test[500] to determine if the coefficients of the independent variables remained constant in the benchmark and damage periods.[501] The court, however, concluded that the sufficiency of the data in performing a *Chow* test did not mean that the data were sufficient to estimate a coefficient.[502] Thus, the expert's justifications for not using cost as a variable stood unrebutted.[503]

6.5 Evaluating the Primacy of Economic Authority Over Expertise

So far this [Chapter] has argued that economic authority, which appellate courts—especially the Supreme Court—adopt from the legal and economic literature, dictates the role of expert testimony in antitrust cases. This [Section] considers the possible justifications for such an arrangement and how the legitimacy of this process might be reinforced. First, it examines the institutional characteristics of the two mechanisms for gathering economic knowledge. Although both have shortcomings, the informal process of economic authority has decisive advantages within the antitrust system. Nevertheless, it is subject to abuses that appellate courts should acknowledge and address. Second, as an illustration, this [Section] examines the proper treatment of post-Chicago economics. Even though some have argued that post-Chicago methodologies, when used by experts, fail *Daubert's* criteria for admissibility,[504] this [Chapter] argues that such a categorical approach is inappropriate. Instead, the confrontation between Chicago School and post-Chicago School economics should occur at both the level of economic authority and the level of expert testimony, using criteria appropriate to each.

A. Comparing Institutional Characteristics

As we have seen, economic authority can render expert testimony irrelevant or unreliable. Even if expert testimony clears these obstacles to admission, courts may still dismiss the testimony as insufficient to create a jury issue. Is such an arrangement defensible? One might argue that it conflicts with *Daubert's* admonition that courts should avoid taking on the role of super-experts and instead limit themselves to a neutral gatekeeping function that preserves the fact-finding role of the jury.[505] All would concede that economics is necessary for antitrust decision making. At first glance, though, it may not be obvious that the economics appellate courts learn by examining the merits of competing economic ideas should take precedence over expert testimony in the particular case. If courts' only concern is how to gain the economic knowledge necessary to decide a particular case, a presentation of the competing views of retained experts to the trier of fact might seem preferable.

This approach has some superficial appeal. Expert testimony occurs in a structured pretrial and trial process that assures that the credentials, sources, data, and reasoning of the opposing experts are laid bare for comparison. A jury endorses one expert's opinion only after a full opportunity for argument and rebuttal on both sides. In contrast, appellate courts absorb economic teaching and adopt economic authority by reading the briefs of the parties and amici curiae and by conducting an ad hoc, non-adversarial search of the legal and economic literature. These latter techniques are clear and flexible,[506] but they also ignore *Daubert's* list of criteria for the reliability of expert testimony. Nevertheless, the priority of economic authority is a necessary product of the institutional characteristics of the antitrust process. First, and most obviously, antitrust must be a body of law that integrates economics into its rules over time so that the rules can provide an efficient system of incentives for businesses. Unlike areas of law that look to expertise to resolve occasional issues of fact, antitrust must incorporate economics into every substantive and evidentiary rule and standard, while remaining open to incremental change. A series of choices made by various juries between competing experts is unlikely to create a coherent system of law, embodying both economic and institutional considerations, to guide business conduct and future cases.

Although no formal rules traditionally constrain the judicial notice of legislative, as opposed to adjudicative, facts,[507] courts do not have unbounded discretion. The legitimacy of the process of adopting of social science research rests on the same basis as any common law process: courts must draw upon the record and external sources of knowledge while deciding cases according to law, and they must articulate the reasons for their decisions. In enacting the antitrust laws, Congress fully anticipated that courts would give meaning to the general language of the antitrust laws using this common law process.[508]

The selection of theories in formulating rules to govern practices at the most general level is part and parcel of the process of legal change, which always requires courts to generalize about economic behavior. Whatever method by which courts adopt theories—be it from an independent review of the literature, from briefs, or from expert testimony—their choice is subject to evaluation on the same grounds as their adoption of available precedent. In each case, the criteria include applicability, plausibility, and generality of acceptance. Such an approach acknowledges not only objective factors, like coherence, but also subjective factors like ideology, because some propositions of economic theory are more likely to gain wide acceptance in favorable ideological climates. This dependence on social visions is unavoidable because antitrust embodies a compromise between competing conceptions of the proper roles of the state and the market. The courts' receptivity to theories necessary to the resolution of antitrust issues has predictably followed the fortunes of the competing ideologies in the larger culture.

Though appellate adoption of economic authority is necessary and legitimate, it does involve risks of abuse by courts and litigants. To curb any potential for abuse, courts should take steps to help ensure the legitimacy of their decisions. First, the reliance on economic authority should be as transparent as possible. Where a court has surveyed the literature in a contentious area, it should acknowledge the controversy and justify its reliance on one viewpoint.[509] Where a court formulates a rule or standard, it should identify not only the economic theory on which it relies, but also the institutional considerations that affect its decision. The Supreme Court has recognized "the necessity, particularly great in the quasi-common-law realm of antitrust, that courts explain the logic of their conclusions" in order to allow scholarly criticism.[510] This observation has particular force because Congress has so rarely interfered with the "quasi-common-law" evolution of the field.[511] Second, courts should be alert to the strategic use of scholarship to influence the creation of economic authority. Both government and private litigants may produce scholarly literature in briefs in order to reinforce the positions they wish to take.[512] Although funded scholarship may be of high quality, courts should be conscious of its partisan origins and view it with some degree of skepticism, just as they take note of hired-gun expert testimony.

The most conclusive uses of theory—rules of per se legality or illegality—require the most justification. For example, courts have not used Chicago School models systematically to replace rules of per se illegality with explicit rules of per se legality. Instead, they have acknowledged the contingency of theory by using the models to limit the application of rules by imposing substantive and remedial preconditions. This method is consistent with congressional intent that the Sherman Act be "experimental,"[513] with the testing to occur in litigation. The Supreme Court has often claimed that judicial experience in evaluating a practice allows a surer basis for the formulation of rules to govern it.[514] Similarly, it has been suggested that experience under a rule—and scholarly criticism of it—can expose the rule's flaws.[515] Exacting studies of the records of antitrust cases have been crucial to the development of the law.[516] As receptive as they have been to Chicago models, members of the modern Court have been influenced also by the Legal Process school of jurisprudence, which emphasizes the role of institutional competence, and the "allocation of institutional responsibilities."[517] Just as courts may be receptive to the viewpoint that markets have important advantages over courts in eroding monopolistic practices, they also recognize the institutional demands of precedent and the fact-finding process.

The preference for experimentation and the assumption that antitrust knowledge can grow in the process has guided courts' use of economic authority to both enhance and confine expert testimony. Where economic authority is most robust, it can foreclose factual inquiries and identify the preconditions for anticompetitive effects. Thus, economic authority can be used to formulate subsidiary rules that focus factual inquiry on indicia that the practice is efficient or inefficient. It may also be used to limit "the permissible inferences"[518] a jury may make from evidence of parallel conduct, or to increase the burden on a party seeking to establish an anticompetitive effect from alleged predatory pricing. This approach acknowledges the role of the jury in resolving the empirical issues, and thus defines the domain for expert testimony. It also recognizes the role of these institutional actors in the process of accumulation of knowledge. Expert testimony is an essential but volatile ingredient in this process. Deference to experts without a proper policy framework would be a prescription for uncertainty. Properly confined, however, expert testimony can be central to the development of the law. As the courts' confidence in the economics profession's ability to resolve difficult factual issues grows, courts will be more likely to design legal tests dependent on economic evidence submitted in trial courts by expert witnesses.

B. Implications for the Confrontation Between Chicago and Post-Chicago Economics

This [chapter] has used the example of the Supreme Court's adoption and use of Chicago School models to illustrate the role of economic authority in shaping antitrust analysis, particularly in expanding and refocusing the role of expert testimony. In each doctrinal context, the Court has crafted legal categories that foreclose certain economic inquiries and require others. Through restrictions on expert testimony, the Court thus gives economic content to rules ex ante, while preserving a domain for acquiring economic content ex post. In essence, where the theory is insufficiently determinate to justify a per se rule, the Court frames rules in such a way that subsequent cases provide the most reliable possible tests of the practice's competitive effects.

One continuing dimension of this process in recent years has been the role of Post-Chicago Economics (PCE). Some have argued that PCE is unsuited to the formulation of legal rules[519] or that it fails *Daubert's* standards of reliability. Our account suggests that the confrontation between the Chicago and post-Chicago schools cannot be resolved so categorically. Judicial choice of theory depends upon the relationship of the theory to a range of institutional factors. Just as there was no ratchet in antitrust law to prevent contraction of liability in response to Chicago analyses,[520] there is none to prevent expansion of liability in response to post-Chicago analyses.

Nevertheless, the characteristics of PCE influence its suitability as economic authority or as expert testimony. Much of PCE is based on game theoretic mathematical modeling of strategies firms might adopt to maximize their profits, taking into account the strategies of other players.[521] Given only a limited set of facts, this sort of model is likely to have multiple equilibria, or outcomes. While one of these outcomes may be anticompetitive, neither the model itself nor empirical testing can show its likelihood. If, on the other hand, the model incorporates more assumptions to make it more determinate, it becomes difficult to apply in litigation.

Because of these characteristics, critics have challenged game theory's usefulness to antitrust. Franklin Fisher argues, for example, that game theory offered too few determinate, robust predictions to form the basis for policy.[522] Bruce Kobayashi, writing before *Joiner* and *Kumho Tire*, argued that game theoretic models of industrial organization should be excluded under the reliability prong of *Daubert*.[523] Specifically, he focused on the language in *Daubert* that, to be reliable, scientific testimony "must be derived by the scientific method."[524] Because these almost purely theoretical economic models "have not been empirically verified in a meaningful sense,"[525] and because conclusions drawn from them "tend to be very sensitive to the way problems are defined and the assumptions that follow,"[526] testimony based on them is not "arrived at through the scientific method."[527] Malcolm Coate and Jeffrey Fischer argue that PCE testimony should be excluded for failure to satisfy the helpfulness prong of *Daubert*.[528] Their central argument is that, at best, PCE models demonstrate only what could happen, and an expert who cannot testify as to what did happen or even what probably happened does not assist the trier of fact in the dispute resolution process.[529]

These critiques, while telling, do not foreclose the use of PCE in antitrust. True, PCE models cannot support new rules of per se illegality, because they do not identify a limited set of observable facts that predictably imply anticompetitive harm.[530] PCE models may, however, suggest avenues for empirical identification of anticompetitive effects in circumstances that established antitrust law might miss. One success in this regard has been the proof of unilateral anticompetitive effects in merger cases using sophisticated econometric methods.[531] Unilateral effects analysis goes beyond traditional conceptions of market definition and market power. Nevertheless, it rests on sound theoretical and empirical grounds and is viewed by some as a more secure basis for predicting the competitive effects of a merger than conventional coordinated effects analysis alone.[532]

PCE models may also be used to challenge rules of per se legality, as they were in *Kodak* to defeat the proposed rule that firms lacking market power in an equipment market can never exercise market power in aftermarkets for parts and service.[533] Post-Chicago scholarship has also challenged the established rule that above-cost prices are never predatory[534] and the Chicago argument that tying arrangements can never be anticompetitive.[535] To be sure, these examples suggest the challenge facing those who propose the adoption of PCE as economic authority: the *Kodak* experiment has failed, and PCE challenges have had little effect on predatory pricing and tying doctrine thus far, evidently because of problems in estimating the costs of false positives.[536] Nevertheless, these difficulties may be surmountable.

More importantly, the inconclusiveness and intractability that make PCE difficult to use in the formulation of rules do not pose as substantial an obstacle to its use in expert testimony. PCE does not categorically fail the reliability inquiry. Certainly, where PCE relies on sophisticated statistical methods, it will be admissible under accepted standards of reliability. In *Kumho Tire*, the Court extended the *Daubert* inquiry to testimony based on "technical" and "other specialized" knowledge, explaining that the purpose of the inquiry "is to make sure that an expert...employs in the courtroom the same level of intellectual rigor that characterizes the practice of an expert in the relevant field."[537] Without question, reliance on game theoretic models is common in the economics profession, and an expert who bases his testimony on such models is employing the same level of rigor that characterizes the professional study of economics.[538]

As this [chapter] has shown, the relevance, helpfulness, and sufficiency of economic testimony depend upon the substantive law and its attendant economic authority. When PCE testimony conflicts with a rule adopted by the Court through economic authority, it is irrelevant and therefore unhelpful. For some offenses, however, evidence that an anticompetitive outcome could have occurred satisfies the traditional test of relevance by making "the existence of any fact that is of consequence to the determination of the action more probable or less probable than it would be without the evidence."[539] For example, game theory may help a court understand pricing strategies in a predatory pricing case.[540] And game theoretic demonstration that certain types of facilitating practices might make price coordination more likely is relevant in a price-fixing case.[541] Conversely, in one striking instance, expert testimony based on game theory showed that a pattern of bidding might not have been collusive by revealing that a key competitor had an independent justification for its actions.[542]

Thus, testimony based on PCE is not categorically inadmissible or insufficient. Instead, it should be measured against the requirements of economic authority to determine its relevance and against the requirements of Rule 403 to determine if its "probative value is substantially outweighed by the danger of...confusion."[543] If admissible, it can be tested by "[v]igorous cross-examination, presentation of contrary evidence, and careful instruction on the burden of proof."[544] Finally, a court could ultimately conclude that PCE testimony fails to create a jury issue.[545]

6.6 Conclusion

In interpreting and applying the antitrust laws, courts pragmatically gather economic knowledge that functions as authority in the formulation and application of antitrust rules. Their criteria for adoption include both those used by economists and those recognizing the institutional characteristics of the legal system. Thus, whether courts adopt an economic idea and in what legal context they employ that idea hinge in part on the courts' sense of juries' fact-finding capabilities. Economic expert testimony is a critical element in this analysis. Though courts can rely on economic authority to adopt per se rules foreclosing most significant factual issues, the availability of economic expertise allows courts to frame rules that allow the ex post acquisition of the information necessary to identify competitive effects. At the same time, however, relying on ex post expertise carries the danger of significant direct and indirect costs. Consequently, courts have shaped antitrust rules to raise factual issues they believe expert testimony can help resolve, but have maintained control over the specifics of expert testimony offered on the issues. Although these controls come under several headings—relevance, sufficiency, or reliability—they ultimately depend on economic authority.

Endnotes

1. *See, e.g.*, HERBERT HOVENKAMP, *Economic Experts in Antitrust Cases*, *in* 3 MODERN SCIENTIFIC EVIDENCE: THE LAW AND SCIENCE OF EXPERT TESTIMONY 111, 112 (David L. Faigman et al. eds., 2002); Andrew I. Gavil, *After Daubert: Discerning the Increasingly Fine Line Between the Admissibility and Sufficiency of Expert Testimony in Antitrust Litigation,* 65 ANTITRUST L.J. 663, 663 (1997). For concise, nontechnical discussions of the role of economic expertise in recent antitrust cases, *see* THE ANTITRUST REVOLUTION: ECONOMICS, COMPETITION, AND POLICY (John E. Kwoka, Jr. & Lawrence J. White eds., 4th ed. 2004) [hereinafter THE ANTITRUST REVOLUTION].

2. *See*, e.g., *Cal. Dental Ass'n v. FTC,* 526 U.S. 756 (1999) (requiring a more extensive factual inquiry into a dental association's rules restricting certain types of price and quality advertising); *State Oil Co. v. Khan*, 522 U.S. 3 (1997) (overruling the per se illegality of vertical maximum price fixing in favor of the rule of reason); *Cont'l T.V., Inc. v. GTE Sylvania Inc.*, 433 U.S. 36 (1977) (overruling the per se illegality of vertical territorial restraints in favor of the rule of reason).

3. See *Kumho Tire Co. v. Carmichael*, 526 U.S. 137 (1999) (holding that *Daubert* applies to testimony by engineers and other non-scientist expert witnesses); *Gen. Elec. Co. v. Joiner,* 522 U.S. 136 (1997) (holding that the district court's decision on admissibility under *Daubert* should be reviewed under an abuse-of-discretion standard); *Daubert v. Merrell Dow Pharms., Inc.*, 509 U.S. 579 (1993) (holding that the Federal Rules of Evidence supply the test for admissibility of expert testimony); *see* also Roger D. Blair & Jill Boylston Herndon, *The Implications of Daubert for Economic Evidence in Antitrust Cases, 57* WASH. & LEE L. REV. 801, 802 (2000) ("*Daubert* challenges to the admissibility of the economic expert's testimony already are becoming routine in antitrust cases."); Gavil, *supra* note 1, at 669-88 (detailing the ways in which *Daubert* affects the presentation and acceptance of expert testimony in antitrust cases).

4. *See* Gavil, *supra* note 1, at 664-67, 688-98.

5. Our use of this term is an homage to John Monahan and Laurens Walker's concept of "social authority." *See* John Monahan & Laurens Walker, *Social Authority: Obtaining, Evaluating, and Establishing Social Science in Law,* 134 U. PA. L. REV. 477 (1986). We do not argue, however, that antitrust courts always engage in the sort of screening of economic ideas that those authors propose for social science research generally. *See id.* at 499-509.

6. *See* Richard A. Posner, *The Law and Economics of the Economic Expert Witness*, 13 J. ECON. PERSP., Spring 1999, at 91, 92 ("The considerations, including the economic considerations, that go to shape legal doctrine...are not considered questions to be decided by taking testimony and testing its accuracy by cross-examination, but by reference to general questions of law and policy.").

7. *See*, e.g., Richard A. Posner, *Legal Scholarship Today*, 115 HARV. L. REV. 1314, 1324 (2002) (arguing that "interdisciplinary legal scholarship is intended to be read by professors...rather than by practitioners (including judges)"). In that article, Judge Posner cites Judge Harry T. Edwards, who complains that many interdisciplinary articles are impractical and useless to courts, Harry T. Edwards, *The Growing Disjunction Between Legal Education and the Legal Profession,* 91 MICH. L. REV. 34 (1992), and Michael McClintock, who finds "a 47.35% decline in the use of legal scholarship by courts over the past two decades, the most notable decline occurring in the past ten years," Michael D. McClintock, *The Declining Use of Legal Scholarship by Courts: An Empirical Study,* 51 OKLA. L. REV. 659, 660 (1998). *See* Posner, *supra*, at 1324 & n.25; *see* also Louis J. Sirico, Jr., *The Citing of Law Reviews by the Supreme Court: 1971-1999,* 75 IND. L.J. 1009, 1009-10 (2000) (finding a decline in citation of legal scholarship by the Supreme Court); cf. *Seminole Tribe v. Florida,* 517 U.S. 44, 68 (1996) (criticizing the dissent for "disregard[ing] our case law in favor of a theory cobbled together from law review articles and its own version of historical events").

8. *See* HERBERT HOVENKAMP, *The Reckoning of Post-Chicago Antitrust*, *in* POST-CHICAGO DEVELOPMENTS IN ANTITRUST LAW 1, 1-3 (Antonio Cucinotta et al. eds., 2002) [hereinafter Hovenkamp, Reckoning] (arguing that courts relied on, but did not cite, prevailing economic theory before 1980). *See* generally Herbert Hovenkamp, *Fact, Value and Theory in Antitrust Adjudication,* 1987 DUKE L.J. 897 (detailing various economic theories that have significantly influenced the development of antitrust doctrine).

9. *See generally* William H. Page, The *Chicago School and the Evolution of Antitrust: Characterization, Antitrust Injury, and Evidentiary Sufficiency*, 75 VA. L. REV. 1221 (1989) (describing the Supreme Court's explicit reliance on economic literature since 1977); Ronald J. Allen & Ross M. Rosenberg, *Legal Phenomena, Knowledge, and Theory: A Cautionary Tale of Hedgehogs and Foxes,* 77 CHI.-KENT L. REV. 683 (2002) (showing that microeconomic theory has influenced jury instructions far more in antitrust cases than in negligence cases).

10. RICHARD A. POSNER, THE PROBLEMATICS OF MORAL AND LEGAL THEORY 229 (1999).

11. As then-Judge Breyer famously wrote:

    [W]hile technical economic discussion helps to inform the antitrust laws, those laws cannot precisely replicate the economists' (sometimes conflicting) views. For, unlike economics, law is an administrative system the effects of which depend upon the content of rules and precedents only as they are applied by judges and juries in courts and by lawyers advising their clients. Rules that *see*k to embody every economic complexity and qualification may well, through the vagaries of administration, prove counter-productive, undercutting the very economic ends they *see*k to serve.

    Barry Wright Corp. v. ITT Grinnell Corp., 724 F.2d 227, 234 (1st Cir. 1983); *see also* William H. Page, *Legal Realism and the Shaping of Modern Antitrust,* 44 EMORY L.J. 1, 49-53 (1995) (arguing that legal process considerations guide the use of theory in antitrust decisionmaking).

12. *See infra* Part II.A.1. The Chicago School is a tradition of antitrust scholarship based upon a shared set of positive economic models of practices (like cartels, tying arrangements, and predatory pricing) and empirical estimates of the frequency and effects of those practices. The Chicago School is also associated with a set of normative prescriptions for antitrust law. Both the models and the policy program reflect, in general, a confidence in the market's ability to prevent or remedy monopolistic practices (despite asserted "imperfections") and a skepticism about courts' ability to do so. For a description of the Chicago School's principal characteristics, *see* Page, *supra* note 9, at 1228-43. Virtually all Chicago scholars trace the origins of central ideas and methods of the school to the late Aaron Director. *Id.* at 1229-30 n.44.

13. Page, *supra* note 9, at 1255 ("The Court has taken account of the normative implications of the models by reinterpreting existing doctrine.").

14. *Id.* at 1253-57.

15. *Id.* at 1257-94 (describing use of models in the contexts of characterization, antitrust injury, and evidentiary sufficiency).

16. *See, e.g.*, Christopher Slobogin, *The Structure of Expertise in Criminal Cases,* 34 SETON HALL L. REV. 105, 105 (2003) (arguing that *Daubert* and its progeny "push the criminal justice system away from the notion that knowledge is socially constructed and toward a positivist epistemology that assumes we can know things objectively"); *see also id.* at 106 n.8 (responding to the

view that *Daubert* and *Kumho Tire* reflect a "realist-constructivist view of science").

17. *See infra* Part II.A.1.

18. *See* Page, *supra* note 9, at 1297 (arguing that judicial adoption of a widely held theory "implicitly recognizes the relationship between theory and the prevailing intellectual climate, since a theory will be more widely held and more persuasive to the extent that it is consistent with the dominant intellectual system"); *see also* ROBERT H. NELSON, ECONOMICS AS RELIGION: FROM SAMUELSON TO CHICAGO AND BEYOND 229 (2001) (arguing that all economics involves "value assumptions" that "shape the form of analysis" and assert the "special merit" of these assumptions as descriptions of "the human condition").

19. *See*, e.g., Ronald J. Allen & Michael S. Pardo, *The Myth of the Law-Fact Distinction,* 97 NW. L. REV. 1769, 1778 (2003) ("Under the conventional view, legal issues concern the applicable rules and standards; factual issues involve the underlying transaction or events, in other words, 'who did what, where, when, how, why, with what motive or intent.'"(internal citation omitted)); Lynn M. LoPucki & Walter O. Weyrauch, *A Theory of Legal Strategy,* 49 DUKE L.J. 1405, 1407 (2000) ("In the...legal process, courts define facts and then apply law to those facts to generate outcomes.").

20. As Holmes observed:

> Legal, like natural divisions, however clear in their general outline, will be found on exact scrutiny to end in a penumbra or debatable land. This is the region of the jury, and only cases falling on this doubtful border are likely to be carried far in court. Still, the tendency of the law must be to narrow the field of uncertainty.

OLIVER WENDELL HOLMES, JR., THE COMMON LAW 101 (Mark DeWolfe Howe ed., Harvard Univ. Press 1963) (1881).

21. *See, e.g.,* WILLIAM TWINING, RETHINKING EVIDENCE: EXPLORATORY ESSAYS107-08 (1990) (arguing that fact determinations are not "value-free"); Catharine Wells, *Situated Decisionmaking*, 63 S. CAL. L. REV. 1728, 1743 (1990) ("What we *see* and hear is filtered and interpreted within a cognitive framework that is constructed largely from our own individual temperament and prior experience."); *cf.* David L. Faigman, *"Normative Constitutional Fact-Finding": Exploring the Empirical Component of Constitutional Interpretation*, 139 U. PA. L. REV. 541, 544 (1991) (critically examining how "[t]he [Supreme] Court interprets facts," manipulating social "facts" in constitutional interpretation).

22. *See* Edward D. Ohlbaum, *Basic Instinct: Case Theory and Courtroom Performance,* 66 TEMPLE L. REV. 1, 24-25 (1993). Ohlbaum observes:

> The facts are the circumstances of a case—the states of events and of mind— that constitute the universe of components that make up the model of what happened. Fact extraction requires the advocate to evaluate the facts fully and exhaustively, not merely by mulling them over and hypothesizing how they fit or clash with the theory, but by placing the facts in the context of the examinations and arguments in which they will ultimately be featured. Those facts that remain incompatible with the theory must be analyzed and explained, consistent with the principles of persuasion. The advocate must select from among the facts those that strategically may be presented and reinforced most persuasively.

Id. For a recent elaboration on this idea, *see* generally Binny Miller, *Teaching Case Theory*, 9 CLINICAL L. REV. 295 (2002) (arguing that, over time, case theory has moved more toward a model of "persuasive storytelling").

23. LoPucki & Weyrauch, *supra* note 19, at 1409-10 ("Lawyers devote substantial time and energy to the development of legal strategies and regard them as capable of determining outcomes across a wide spectrum of cases.").

24. *See* Reid Hastie & Nancy Pennington, *The O.J. Simpson Stories: Behavioral Scientists' Reflections on The People of the State of California v. Orenthal James Simpson,* 67 U. COLO. L. REV. 957, 959-61 (1996) (arguing that "jurors begin their decision-making process by constructing a narrative to explain the available facts they have heard at trial" and that the "story...will consist of some subset of the events and causal relationships referred to in the presentation of evidence, as well as additional events and causal relationships inferred by the juror"); Paul F. Kirgis, *The Problem of the Expert Juror,* 75 TEMPLE L. REV. 493, 493-94 (2002) ("[W]e expect jurors to possess and rely on a large body of general knowledge about the world, and we allow the parties, in determining what evidence to present, to assume that the jurors have such a body of knowledge."). *See generally* Anthony J. Bocchino & Samuel H. Solomon, *What Juries Want to Hear: Methods for Developing Persuasive Case Theory*, 67 TENN. L. REV. 543 (2000) (distinguishing the processes of formulating a legal theory, a factual theory, and a persuasive theory of a case).

25. CLIFFORD GEERTZ, LOCAL KNOWLEDGE 167-75 (1983). Geertz argues that making a case "comes to describing a particular course of events and an overall conception of life in such a way that the credibility of each reinforces the credibility of the other." I*d.* at 175.

26. These ideas may include certain nonrational biases. *See, e.g.,* Robert A. Prentice & Jonathan J. Koehler, *A Normality Bias in Legal Decision Making,* 88 CORNELL L. REV. 583 (2003) (discussing the effects of omission and normality biases in legal decisionmaking).

27. Geertz, *supra* note 25, at 175. Geertz continues, "Any legal system that hopes to be viable must contrive to connect the if-then structure of existence, as locally imagined, and the as-therefore course of experience, as locally perceived, so that they *see*m but depth and surface versions of the same thing." *Id.*; *see also* Hastie & Pennington, *supra* note 24, at 961 (arguing that the jurors' confidence in a narrative explanation of an event depends on the narrative's "coverage of the evidence" and its "coherence," which hinges in part on its "plausibility"—that is, the "extent [to which] it corresponds to the decision maker's knowledge about what typically happens in the world").

28. *See* Mark P. Denbeaux & D. Michael Risinger, *Kumho Tire and Expert Reliability: How the Question You Ask Gives the Answer You Get*, 34 SETON HALL L. REV. 15, 24 (2003)

> [A]s to fact witness testimony, and various forms of documentary, physical, or circumstantial proof, the assumption is that average people have developed, through the process of living in society, sufficient knowledge about the world of humans and its workings that they have a fair chance to evaluate and accurately weigh and discount information coming from such familiar sources.

29. For an illuminating history of procedural controls on federal juries, *see* Ann Woolhandler & Michael G. Collins, *The Article III Jury,* 87 VA. L. REV. 587 (2001).

30. *See generally* Matthew S. Rosengart, *The Motion In Limine: The Hidden Arrow in the Federal Litigator's Quiver*, 48 FED. LAW., June 2001, at 24 (discussing effective utilization and strategic advantages of motions made in limine).

31. *Cf.* Lars Noah, *Civil Jury Nullification*, 86 IOWA L. REV. 1601, 1653-57 (2001) (analyzing devices used to focus civil juries on applicable legal standards).

32. 2 FREDERICK POLLOCK & FREDERIC WILLIAM MAITLAND, THE HISTORY OF EENGLISH LAW BEFORE THE TIME OF EDWARD I 632-44 (2d ed. 1968) (describing various common law institutions supplanted by the trial by jury); *see also* George Fisher, *The Jury's Rise as Lie Detector,* 107 YALE L.J. 575, 585-602 (2001) (describing the way in which criminal juries came to replace the trial by ordeal).

33. *See* GEERTZ, *supra* note 25, at 172 ("The judge's job in admissibility questions is to decide...when 'the trial [will be] better off without the evidence.'" (internal citations omitted)).

34. *See* Stephen N. Subrin, *How Equity Conquered Common Law: The Federal Rules of Civil Procedure in Historical Perspective*, 135 U. PA. L. REV. 909, 916 (1987) ("Under single issue pleading, the parties pleaded back and forth until one side either demurred, resulting in a legal issue, or traversed, resulting in a factual issue.").

35. GEERTZ, *supra* note 25, at 171.

36. *See generally* Christopher M. Fairman, *Heightened Pleading*, 81 TEX. L. REV. 551 (2002) (surveying judicial and congressional efforts to impose pleading requirements stricter than the notice requirements of Rule 8 of the Federal Rules of Civil Procedure).

37. *See, e.g.,* In re Japanese Elec. Prods. Antitrust Litig., 631 F.2d 1069, 1080 (3rd Cir. 1980) (reading Supreme Court precedent to leave "open the possibility that the 'practical abilities and limitation of juries' may limit the range of suits subject to the seventh amendment").

38. *See generally* Ronald J. Allen & Craig R. Callen, *The Juridical Management of Factual Uncertainty*, 7 INT'L J. EVIDENCE & PROOF 1 (2003) (analyzing the various evidentiary tools used to limit factual uncertainty in civil cases); Craig R. Callen, *Adjudication and the Appearance of Statistical Evidence*, 65 TUL. L. REV. 457, 475-96 (1991) (discussing the use of summary judgment and burdens of proof to remove some questions from the deliberations of the jury); Craig R. Callen, *Hearsay and Informal Reasoning*, 47 VAND. L. REV. 43, 55-78 (1994) (discussing the use of hearsay rules to place limits on fact-finders).

39. Adrian A.S. Zuckerman, *Law, Fact or Justice?*, 66 B.U. L. REV. 487, 488 (1986). Zuckerman notes that "questions of law—namely, questions which are not concerned with the existence of facts outside the law—are frequently treated as questions of fact" and that "questions concerned with the process of ascertaining the facts sometimes receive the kind of treatment usually accorded to questions of law." *Id.* For an interesting example of this process at work, see *United States v. Microsoft Corp.,* 84 F. Supp. 2d 9 (D.D.C. 1999), in which Judge Jackson issued "findings of fact" without accompanying conclusions of law. Because the findings were couched in terms made relevant by the law, it was possible to predict the legal conclusions. Judge Jackson told a reporter, "What I want to do is confront the Court of Appeals

with an established factual record which is a fait accompli," because "I take mild offense at their reversal of my preliminary injunction in the consent-decree case, where they went ahead and made up about ninety percent of the facts on their own." KEN AULETTA, WORLD WAR 3.0: MICROSOFT AND ITS ENEMIES 230 (2001). The court of appeals responded:

Whether the District Judge takes offense, mild or severe, is beside the point. Appellate decisions command compliance, not agreement. We do not view the District Judge's remarks as anything other than his expression of disagreement with this court's decision, and his desire to provide extensive factual findings in this case, which he did.

United States v. Microsoft Corp., 253 F.3d 34, 118 (D.C. Cir. 2001).

40. Allen & Pardo, *supra* note 19, at 1782 (arguing that "law" and "fact" are "the labels [that] are applied after the pragmatic allocative decision is made").

41. *See, e.g.*, Woolhandler & Collins, *supra* note 29, at 631-36 (describing the ways in which nineteenth century judges used jury instructions to specify legal standards, which allowed judges to control the juries' fact-finding).

42. *See generally* Fleming James, Jr., *Sufficiency of the Evidence and Jury-Control Devices Available Before Verdict*, 47 VA. L. REV. 218 (1961) (discussing "the concept of sufficiency of the evidence and...closely related mechanisms" as ways of controlling juries before verdict).

43. For a discussion of the evolution of expert evidence, *see* Learned Hand, *Historical and Practical Considerations Regarding Expert Testimony*, 15 HARV. L. REV. 40 (1901).

44. *See* CHRISTOPHER B. MUELLER & LAIRD C. KIRKPATRICK, EVIDENCE 723-25 (1995) (cataloging a range of issues to which experts can, and often do, testify in civil and criminal cases).

45. Hand, *supra* note 43, at 51-52 (arguing that an expert supplies "general propositions" that, if believed, take the place of the "common knowledge" by which jurors normally evaluate evidence).

46. *See* Eileen A. Scallen & William E. Wiethoff, *The Ethos of Expert Witnesses: Confusing the Admissibility, Sufficiency and Credibility of Expert Testimony,* 49 HASTINGS L.J. 1143 (1998). Scallen & Wiethoff argue that "[e]xpert testimony, even that based on natural or social science, is argumentation" rather than simply evidence. *Id.* at 1144; *see also* Posner, *supra* note 6, at 95-96 (arguing that concerns about the intelligibility of expert testimony are mitigated by the fact that jurors find clarity more persuasive

than credentials and by the fact that "lawyer's [have an] incentive to call persuasive witnesses").

47. For data on jurors' assessments of expert credibility, *see* Sanja Kutnjak Ivkovic & Valerie P. Hans, *Jurors' Evaluations of Expert Testimony: Judging the Messenger and the Message*, 28 LAW & SOC. INQUIRY 441 (2003).

48. Hand, *supra* note 43, at 54-55 ("What hope have the jury...of rational decision between two such conflicting statements each based on [expert] experience.").

49. *Daubert v. Merrell Dow Pharms., Inc.*, 509 U.S. 579, 596 (1993). The exclusion of expert testimony is supposed to be exceptional: "[T]he trial court's role as gatekeeper is not intended to serve as a replacement for the adversary system." FED. R. EVID. 702 advisory committee's note. Confronted by the argument that relaxed standards of admissibility "will result in a 'free-for-all' in which befuddled juries are confounded by absurd and irrational pseudoscientific assertions," *Daubert*, 509 U.S. at 595-96, the Court responded that "[v]igorous cross-examination, presentation of contrary evidence, and careful instruction on the burden of proof are the traditional and appropriate means of attacking shaky but admissible evidence." *Id.* at 596.

50. We exclude from our discussion certain non-evidentiary rules that may result in exclusion of expert witnesses. *See, e.g.*, Kendall Coffey, *Inherent Judicial Authority and the Expert Disqualification Doctrine*, 56 FLA. L. REV. 195 (2004) (discussing judicial doctrines allowing disqualification of experts for conflicts of interest).

51. Slobogin, *supra* note 16, at 106.

52. *See* Denbeaux & Risinger, *supra* note 28, at 24 ("The commonsense fear is that factfinders will defer to the unreliable expert and treat the unreliable expert's testimony as reliable.").

53. See, e.g., *E. Auto Distribs., Inc. v. Peugeot Motors of Am., Inc.*, 795 F.2d 329, 338 (4th Cir. 1986) ("Scrutiny of expert testimony is especially proper where it consists of 'an array of figures conveying a delusive impression of exactness in an area where a jury's common sense is less available than usual to protect it.'").

54. *See* Posner, *supra* note 6, at 93-94 (observing that the "expert has both motive and means of slanting the truth in favor of the client," but further noting that reputational considerations tend to limit such incentives); *see also*

William L. Foster, *Expert Testimony—Prevalent Complaints and Proposed Remedies*, 11 HARV. L. REV. 169, 170-71 (1897) (quoting an earlier commentator's observation that experts do not "wilfully misrepresent what they think, but their judgment becomes so warped by regarding the subject in one point of view that even when conscientiously disposed, they are incapable of expressing a candid opinion"). For an argument that present controls on the dishonesty of partisan experts are insufficient, *see* Jeffrey L. Harrison, *Reconceptualizing the Expert Witness: Social Costs, Current Controls and Proposed Responses*, 18 YALE J. ON REG. 253 (2001).

55. *See*, e.g., RICHARD A. POSNER, ANTITRUST LAW 277-78 (2d ed. 2001) (suggesting the use of a neutral expert agreed upon by each party's expert); Posner, *supra* note 6, at 96 (suggesting replacement of each party's expert with a single, jointly agreed-upon expert); *see also* Hand, *supra* note 43, at 56 (arguing for "a board of experts or a single expert, not called by either side, who shall advise the jury of the general propositions applicable to the case which lie within his province"); cf. In re High Fructose Corn Syrup Antitrust Litig., 295 F.3d 651, 665 (7th Cir. 2002) (Posner, J., majority) (recommending that the district court use the powers granted to it by Rule 706 of the Federal Rules of Evidence to appoint its own neutral expert).

56. FED. R. EVID. 702.

57. *Daubert v. Merrell Dow Pharms., Inc.,* 509 U.S. 579, 588 (1993).

58. FED. R. EVID. 702 advisory committee's note.

59. *Elcock v. Kmart Corp.,* 233 F.3d 734, 741 (3d Cir. 2000).

60. *See Daubert*, 509 U.S. at 590 & n.9.

61. *Id.* at 590.

62. *Id.* at 593-94. On remand, Judge Kozinski read *Daubert* to require courts "to resolve disputes among respected, well-credentialed scientists about matters squarely within their expertise, in areas where there is no scientific consensus as to what is and what is not 'good science,' and occasionally to reject such expert testimony because it was not 'derived by the scientific method.'" *Daubert*, 43 F.3d at 1316.

63. *Kumho Tire v. Carmichael,* 526 U.S. 137 (1999).

64. *Id.* at 147.

65. *Daubert*, 509 U.S. at 595 (noting that the focus "must be solely on principles and methodology, not on the conclusions that they generate").

66. *Gen. Elec. Co. v. Joiner*, 522 U.S. 136 (1997).

67. *Id.* at 146.

68. FED. R. EVID. 702 advisory committee's note ("[W]hen an expert purports to apply principles and methods in accordance with professional standards, and yet reaches a conclusion that other experts in the field would not reach, the trial court may fairly suspect that the principles and methods have not been faithfully applied.").

69. *Daubert*, 509 U.S. at 588 (quoting Federal Rule of Evidence 702).

70. *Id.* at 591 (emphasis added).

71. *Id.* (crediting Judge Becker in *United States v. Downing*, 753 F.2d 1224, 1242 (3d Cir. 1985), for use of the term "fit").

72. FED. R. EVID. 402.

73. FED. R. EVID. 401.

74. *See, e.g.*, In re Brand Name Prescription Drugs Antitrust Litig., 186 F.3d 781, 786 (7th Cir. 1999) (finding that the objection to expert economic evidence "actually had nothing to do with *Daubert*; it was that the evidence mainly concerned a matter not in issue"). This *see*ms to suggest, incorrectly, that *Daubert* does not itself impose a requirement of relevancy.

75. Christopher Slobogin, *The "Ultimate Issue" Issue*, 7 BEHAV. SCI. & L. 259 (1989).

76. FED. R. EVID. 704(a) (emphasis added).

77. *See* Slobogin, *supra* note 75, at 261-62.

78. *Id.* at 263.

79. *Daubert v. Merrell Dow Pharms., Inc.*, 509 U.S. 579, 596 (1993).

80. *Gen. Elec. Co. v. Joiner*, 522 U.S. 136, 141-43 (1997). But *cf. United States v. Call,* 129 F.3d 1402, 1405 (10th Cir. 1997) (holding that the court will

"review de novo whether the district court properly followed the framework set forth in *Daubert*," but "once we determine that the district court correctly applied the *Daubert* standards, we may reverse the district court only if the exclusion of the expert testimony constituted an abuse of discretion").

81. *Williamson Oil Co. v. Philip Morris USA,* 346 F.3d 1287, 1298 (11th Cir. 2003).

82. *See* HERBERT HOVENKAMP, EENTERPRISE AND AMERICAN LAW 1836-1937, at 268-69 (1991) ("Antitrust policy has been forged by economic ideology since its inception."); Hovenkamp, Reckoning, *supra* note 8, at 1-3; Joseph F. Brodley, *Oligopoly Power Under the Sherman and Clayton Acts—From Economic Theory to Legal Policy*, 19 STAN. L. REV. 285, 298 (1967) ("The extent to which the basic economic theory of oligopoly has become explicit in the Court's recent decisions is striking."); James May, *Antitrust in the Formative Era: Political and Economic Theory in Constitutional and Antitrust Analysis*, 1880-1918, 50 OHIO ST. L.J. 257, 300-09 (1989) (describing judges' use of prevailing economic and political theories in early interpretation of the Sherman Act).

83. See, e.g., *Bus. Elecs. Corp. v. Sharp Elecs. Corp.,* 485 U.S. 717, 731-32 (1988) (reasoning that the Sherman Act's use of common law terminology carries with it the dynamic common law process of legal change); Frank H. Easterbrook, *Workable Antitrust Policy*, 84 MICH. L. REV. 1696, 1705 (1986) (observing that "[t]he Sherman Act set up a common law system in antitrust" and that "[t]he statute and its legislative history authorize the ongoing transition to an efficiency-oriented approach"). For criticism of the Supreme Court's approach, *see* Thomas C. Arthur, *Farewell to the Sea of Doubt: Jettisoning the Constitutional Sherman Act*, 74 CAL. L. REV. 263 (1986), proposing an interpretation of the Sherman Act which is predicated on Congress's basic policy choices, and David F. Shores, *Antitrust Decisions and Legislative Intent,* 66 MO. L. REV. 725 (2001), criticizing the modern Supreme Court's failure to rely on legislative intent when interpreting the Sherman Act.

84. Page, *supra* note 9, at 1295-98 (describing the process of judicial selection of theories).

85. *See* Robert E. Keeton, *Legislative Facts and Similar Things: Deciding Disputed Premise Facts*, 73 MINN. L. REV. 1 (1988) (describing judicial adoption of facts as premises for formulation of a legal rule); *cf.* Monahan & Walker, *supra* note 5, at 488-95 (arguing that the adoption of social science research should be treated like the adoption of legal precedent).

86. For example, in *Khan v. State Oil Co.*, 93 F.3d 1358 (7th Cir. 1996), Judge Posner held that a dealer suffered antitrust injury from vertical maximum price fixing, but the court expressed "considerable sympathy with the argument that *Albrecht v. Herald Company*, 390 U.S. 145 (1968), which made the practice per se unlawful,] is inconsistent with the cases that establish the requirement of proving antitrust injury." *Id.* at 1363. The court stated: "In fact, we think the argument is right and that it may well portend the doom of Albrecht." *Id.* The Supreme Court accepted the invitation, overruling Albrecht and reversing Judge Posner's decision. *State Oil Co. v. Khan*, 522 U.S. 3, 22 (1997); *see also* Fred S. McChesney, *Talking 'Bout My Antitrust Generation: Competition For and In the Field of Competition Law*, 52 EMORY L.J. 1401, 1408-11 (2003) (discussing the various ways that lower courts have of minimizing the effect of harmful Supreme Court precedent).

87. *See* Page, *supra* note 9, at 1231-37.

88. *See* Alan J. Meese, *Price Theory, Competition, and the Rule of Reason*, 2003 U. ILL. L. REV. 77, 138 n.328.

89. Page, *supra* note 9, at 1237-43.

90. *See id.* at 1239.

91. *See id.* at 1235-37.

92. As Herbert Hovenkamp has pointed out, even though economists now question the universal assumption of rationality, the law has largely adopted it as both a positive and normative starting point. Hovenkamp, *supra* note 1, at 120 (observing that a "rational actor hypothesis is part of the law of predatory pricing").

93. *Cont'l T.V., Inc. v. GTE Sylvania Inc.*, 433 U.S. 36 (1977).

94. *United States v. Arnold, Schwinn & Co.*, 388 U.S. 365 (1967).

95. *Sylvania*, 433 U.S. at 54-55 ("Economists have identified a number of ways in which manufacturers can use such restrictions to compete more effectively against other manufacturers.").

96. *See Sylvania*, 433 U.S. at 55. The article that introduced this economic theory is Lester G. Telser, *Why Should Manufacturers Want Fair Trade?*, 3 J.L. & ECON. 86 (1960). In recognizing the free rider effect, the Court cited Richard A. Posner, Antitrust *Policy and the Supreme Court: An Analysis of the*

Restricted Distribution, Horizontal Merger and Potential Competition Decisions, 75 COLUM. L. REV. 282, 285 (1975). Posner relies on Telser. *Id.* at 283 n.6.

97. *See* Andrew I. Gavil, *A First Look at the Powell Papers: Sylvania and the Process of Change in the Supreme Court*, ANTITRUST, Fall 2002, at 8, 9-11.

98. *Id.* at 11.

99. *Id.*

100. *Id.* at 10.

101. *See Sylvania*, 433 U.S. at 48 n.13, 55-58 nn.24, 26, 29 (citing articles).

102. Gavil, *supra* note 97, at 11.

103. *Matsushita Elec. Indus. Co. v. Zenith Radio Corp.*, 475 U.S. 574 (1986); *see infra* Part III.A.

104. *See infra* Part III.

105. MILTON FRIEDMAN, *The Methodology of Positive Economics*, *in* ESSAYS IN POSITIVE ECONOMICS 3, 15 (1953) (observing that whether or not the assumptions of a theory are valid depends not on whether they are "descriptively 'realistic,'" but on whether the theory "yields sufficiently accurate predictions").

106. *Id.* at 19-20.

107. R.H. COASE, *How Should Economists Choose?*, *in* ESSAYS ON ECONOMICS AND ECONOMISTS 15, 16-18 (1994) (arguing that a theory "serves as a base for thinking" and "helps us to understand what is going on by enabling us to organise our thoughts").

108. *Id.*

109. *Id.* at 19-23.

110. *Id.* at 17.

111. *See generally* William H. Page, *Ideological Conflict and the Origins of Antitrust Policy*, 66 TUL. L. REV. 1 (1991) (discussing the place of various ide-

ologies in the development of national antitrust policy). This Article, as in the article cited above, uses "ideology" and "social vision" in the essentially neutral sense developed by Thomas Sowell. *See* THOMAS SOWELL, A CONFLICT OF VISIONS 14 (1987) (arguing that "visions" are mental constructs that supply "what we sense or feel *before* we have constructed any systematic reasoning that could be called a theory, much less deduced any specific consequences as hypotheses to be tested against evidence"); *see also* J.M. BALKIN, CULTURAL SOFTWARE: A THEORY OF IDEOLOGY 3 (1998) (proposing an "ambivalent conception of ideology," which recognizes that "cognitive mechanisms" can be "useful in certain contexts, but in others...can mislead and help produce or sustain unjust conditions").

112. *See* Page, *supra* note 11, at 9-10.

113. *See id.* at 9-23, 40-44.

114. *See id.* at 35-39.

115. *See id.* at 18-23.

116. *Id.* at 43-47.

117. Page, *supra* note 9, at 1300; *cf.* William E. Kovacic, *Judicial Appointments and the Future of Antitrust Policy*, ANTITRUST, Spring 1993, at 8, 9 (concluding, based on an empirical study, that "the Reagan/Bush strategy of nominating conservative academics has exerted an importan[t] qualitative influence by fostering acceptance of analytical approaches that discourage judicial intervention"); Keith E. Whittington, *Extrajudicial Constitutional Interpretation: Three Objections and Responses*, 80 N.C. L. REV. 773, 816 (2002) (arguing that political affiliations heavily influence judicial outcomes). Since 1976, judges have also heard about Chicago-oriented economics at institutes sponsored by Henry Manne's Law & Economics Center. *See*, e.g., William E. Kovacic, *The Antitrust Paradox Revisited: Robert Bork and the Transformation of Antitrust Policy*, 36 WAYNE L. REV. 1413, 1434 (1990).

118. See, e.g., *Atl. Richfield Co. v. USA Petroleum Co.,* 495 U.S. 328 (1990) (Brennan, J.) (holding that "a firm does not suffer an 'antitrust injury'... when it loses sales to a competitor charging nonpredatory prices pursuant to a vertical, maximum-price-fixing scheme").

119. In Thomas Cotter's terms, the courts use economic theory pragmatically. *See* Thomas F. Cotter, *Legal Pragmatism and the Law and Economics Movement*, 84 GEO. L.J. 2071, 2139-40 (1996) (arguing that "the pragmatist

accepts the insights of economic analysis for what they are worth," avoiding "brilliant, but acontextual, policy recommendations" in favor of "a more skeptical, neoinstitutionalist approach in considering policy alternatives").

120. *See infra* Part II.A.2.

121. For a survey of post-Chicago successes and failures, *see* Herbert Hovenkamp, *Post-Chicago Antitrust: A Review and Critique*, 2001 COLUM. BUS. L. REV. 257.

122. *Aspen Skiing Co. v. Aspen Highlands Skiing Corp.,* 472 U.S. 585 (1985).

123. *See id.* at 606; *see* also John E. Lopatka & William H. Page, *Monopolization, Innovation, and Consumer Welfare*, 69 GEO. WASH. L. REV. 367, 379-83 (2001) (noting that, although the Aspen Court arguably should have required a showing that total output declined, the Court "undeniably examined other evidence of consumer harm").

124. *See* John E. Lopatka & William H. Page, *'Obvious' Consumer Harm in Antitrust Policy: The Chicago School, the Post-Chicago School and the Courts, in* POST-CHICAGO DEVELOPMENTS IN ANTITRUST LAW, *supra* note 8, at 129-30.

125. *Kartell v. Blue Shield of Mass., Inc.,* 749 F.2d 922, 931 (1st Cir. 1984).

126. E.g., *State Oil Co. v. Khan*, 522 U.S. 3 (1997).

127. *See infra* Part III.A.

128. *Brooke Group, Ltd. v. Brown & Williamson Tobacco Corp.,* 509 U.S. 209, 224 (1993); see also *Concord Boat Corp. v. Brunswick Corp.,* 207 F.3d 1039, 1061-62 (8th Cir. 2000) (holding that Brunswick's market share discounts were simply price cutting and, therefore, protected by the rule of *Brooke Group*).

129. *Broad. Music, Inc. v. CBS,* 441 U.S. 1, 19-20 (1979).

130. For a fuller discussion of how rules determine in advance what conduct is permissible, leaving only factual issues for courts, *see* generally Louis Kaplow, *Rules Versus Standards: An Economic Analysis*, 42 DUKE L.J. 557, 559-60 (1992).

131. MANUAL FOR COMPLEX LITIGATION § 33.1, at 300 (3d ed. 1995).

132. *See*, e.g., Andrew I. Gavil, *The End of Antitrust Trench Warfare?: An Analysis of Some Procedural Aspects of The Microsoft Trial*, ANTITRUST, Summer 1999, at 7 (considering procedural expedients in the Microsoft trial aimed at avoiding the costly and protracted proceedings typical of prior monopolization cases).

133. *See* Joshua A. Newberg, *The Narrative Construction of Antitrust*, 12 S. CAL. INTERDISC. L.J. 181 (2003) (analyzing the competing narratives presented by the parties to the Microsoft litigation); Richard G. Parker, *Simplifying Antitrust Cases*, SH045 ALI-ABA 19 (Westlaw JLR Database) (2002) (describing the importance of presenting an antitrust case in a way that it is consistent with common sense and involves a "simple theme or two around which to organize the evidence").

134. *United States v. Topco Assocs., Inc.*, 405 U.S. 596, 609-10 (1972) (citations omitted).

135. *See infra* Part III.D.1.

136. See *Ill. Brick Co. v. Illinois,* 431 U.S. 720, 742 (1977) (quoting *Hanover Shoe, Inc. v. United Shoe Mach. Corp.*, 392 U.S. 481, 493 (1968)).

137. *See* Richard A. Posner, *The Next Step in the Antitrust Treatment of Restricted Distribution: Per Se Legality*, 48 U. CHI. L. REV. 6, 23 (1981) ("The same considerations of judicial economy and legal certainty that justify the use of per se rules of illegality in some cases justify the use of rules of per se legality in others.").

138. *See* Frank H. Easterbrook, *Comparative Advantage and Antitrust Law*, 75 CAL. L. REV. 983 (1987); *see* also Frank H. Easterbrook, *Information and Antitrust*, 2000 U. CHI. LEGAL F. 1, 18.

> Per se rules conserve on information and on the costs of litigation. They hold down the sum of excusing conduct that is harmful, condemning conduct that is beneficial, and inducing firms to steer clear of potentially beneficial practices that create risks of condemnation (or costly litigation). We apply per se rules of illegality to cartels and mergers to monopoly. We apply per se rules of legality in fact if not in name to the introduction of new products (although that may destroy desirable substitutes), to the redesign of old products (same potential effects), to price competition (provided price exceeds cost of manufacture), to charging what the traffic will bear (although that may extract monopoly profits), to expanding capacity (even though new plants may discour-

age entry), and to non-price vertical restraints. All of this we do on a categorical basis, for to examine the practice at hand in any detail is to abandon per se treatment.).

139. See, e.g., *Verizon Communications Inc. v. Law Offices of Curtis V. Trinko*, 540 U.S. 398, 414 (2004) ("The cost of false positives counsels against an undue expansion of § 2 liability.").

140. *See* Page, *supra* note 11, at 49-53 (arguing that the Court's hesitance to adopt rules of per se legality shows the influence of legal process jurisprudence); *see* also Richard A. Posner, *Reply: The Institutional Dimension of Statutory and Constitutional Interpretation*, 101 MICH. L. REV. 952, 958 (2003) ("Being a judge...brings institutional issues to the forefront of consciousness.").

141. *Cont'l T.V., Inc. v. GTE Sylvania Inc.,* 433 U.S. 36 (1977).

142. *State Oil Co. v. Khan*, 522 U.S. 3 (1997) (overruling the per se illegality of vertical maximum price fixing).

143. *Id.* at 15-19; *Sylvania*, 433 U.S. at 55-59.

144. Page, *supra* note 11, at 50-51.

145. Page, *supra* note 9, at 1257-62.

146. *See* infra Part III.C.1.

147. Page, *supra* note 9, at 1287-90.

148. *Id.* at 1268-78.

149. *See infra* Part III.D.1.

150. *State Oil Co. v. Khan,* 522 U.S. 3 (1997).

151. *Id.* at 19.

152. *Id.*

153. *Id.* at 15. The Court observed: "Thus, our reconsideration of Albrecht's continuing validity is informed by several of our decisions, as well as a considerable body of scholarship discussing the effects of vertical restraints." *Id.*; *see also* Roger D. Blair & John E. Lopatka, *The Albrecht Rule After Khan:*

Death Becomes Her, 74 NOTRE DAME L. REV. 123, 146-50 (1998) (describing the way the Supreme Court used economic authority to overrule the per se rule against vertical maximum price fixing).

154. *See, e.g.*, Posner, *supra* note 6, at 92 ("The expert will not be permitted to testify that antitrust law should not forbid price fixing, but will be permitted to testify that the defendants' pricing behavior is inconsistent with their having agreed to fix prices...").

155. See *Cal. Dental Ass'n v. FTC*, 224 F.3d 942, 959 (9th Cir. 2000) [The FTC's] complaint counsel made a tactical decision not to call a previously designated expert economist to counter the testimony of CDA's expert economist. Rather, complaint counsel focused on winning the case under per se or abbreviated rule of reason, evidently assuming that the economic literature would suffice to win the case under full-blown rule of reason if the Ninth Circuit or Supreme Court required a more onerous level of analysis.); *see also* In re Compact Disc Minimum Advertised Price Antitrust Litig., 216 F.R.D. 197, 212 (D. Me. 2003) (stating that the application of the rule of reason "will require expert testimony defining the market (geographically and by product) and will give the defendants the opportunity to assert business justifications").

156. See, e.g., *Brooke Group Ltd. v. Brown & Williamson Tobacco Corp.*, 509 U.S. 209, 242 (1993) ("Expert testimony is useful as a guide to interpreting market facts, but it is not a substitute for them.").

157. See, e.g., *Lantec, Inc. v. Novell, Inc.*, 146 F. Supp. 2d 1140, 1154 (D. Utah 2001) ("[The witness] is clearly a hired gun and any semblance of objectivity is lacking. His opinions lack all indicia of reliability and as such can only confuse and mislead the jury."); In re Brand Name Prescription Drugs Antitrust Litig., No. 94 C 897, MDL 997, 1999 WL 33889, at *11 (N.D. Ill. Jan. 19, 1999) (asserting that the expert "abdicated entirely the concept of the independence of expert witnesses and simply became the sponsor for the Class Plaintiffs' theory of the case"), rev'd on other grounds, 186 F.3d 781 (7th Cir. 1999); In re Aluminum Phosphide Antitrust Litig., 893 F. Supp. 1497, 1499-500, 1506-07 (D. Kan. 1995) (describing expert as "an expert for hire ...driven by a desire to enhance the measure of plaintiffs' damages, even at the expense of well-accepted scientific principles and methodology").

158. FED. R. EVID. 702.

159. *See, e.g.,* In re Paoli R.R. Yard PCB Litig., 35 F.3d 717, 741 (3d Cir. 1994) ("Rule 702's liberal policy of admissibility extends to the substantive as well

as the formal qualification of experts."); *Berlyn, Inc. v. Gazette Newspapers, Inc.,* 214 F. Supp. 2d 530, 534 (D. Md. 2002); *ID Sec. Sys. Can., Inc. v. Checkpoint Sys., Inc.,* 198 F. Supp. 2d 598, 602 (E.D. Pa. 2002).

160. See, e.g., *Sanner v. Bd. of Trade of Chicago,* No. 89 C 8467, 2001 WL 1155277, at *3 (N.D. Ill. Sept. 28, 2001); In re Polypropylene Carpet Antitrust Litig., 93 F. Supp. 2d 1348, 1353 (N.D. Ga. 2000).

161. See, e.g., *Concord Boat Corp. v. Brunswick Corp.,* 207 F.3d 1039, 1046, 1057 (8th Cir. 2000) (holding that testimony of Stanford economist should have been excluded); Brand Name Prescription Drugs Antitrust Litig., 1999 WL 33889, at *10-11 (excluding the testimony of Nobel Prize economist).

162. See, e.g., *Thomas J. Kline, Inc. v. Lorillard, Inc.,* 878 F.2d 791, 799-800 (4th Cir. 1989) ("[T]his witness cannot satisfy even the minimal requirements of FED. R. EVID. 702."); *Berlyn, Inc. v. Gazette Newspapers, Inc.,* 214 F. Supp. 2d 530, 533-36 (D. Md. 2002); *Bailey v. Allgas, Inc.,* 148 F. Supp. 2d 1222, 1237 (N.D. Ala. 2000) (finding expert's lack of expertise "staggering"), *aff'd,* 284 F.3d 1237 (11th Cir. 2002).

163. See *W. Parcel Exp. v. United Parcel Serv. of Am., Inc.,* 65 F. Supp. 2d 1052, 1060 (N.D. Cal. 1998) (granting summary judgment for failure to establish the relevant market, and noting that "neither [of plaintiff's experts] has a background in antitrust economics, both disclaimed expertise in antitrust law in their depositions, and neither has offered an opinion on the definition of relevant markets in antitrust litigation"), *aff'd,* 190 F.3d 974 (9th Cir. 1999).

164. *See Thomas J. Kline,* 878 F.2d at 800 ("[I]t would be absurd to conclude that one can become an expert simply by accumulating experience in testifying.").

165. *Id.* (reversing district court on admissibility issue for abuse of discretion); *see Berlyn,* 214 F. Supp. 2d at 536. But see *Conwood Co. v. U.S. Tobacco Co.,* 290 F.3d 768, 793 (6th Cir. 2002) (finding that a damage award was supported in part by the testimony of plaintiff's CEO that, but for defendant's conduct, plaintiff "would have had a national market share of approximately 22 to 23 percent").

166. See *Virginia Vermiculite, Ltd. v. W.R. Grace & Co.,* 98 F. Supp. 2d 729, 732 (W.D. Va. 2000). The proposed witness had no apparent understanding of basic economic concepts, such as elasticity of demand. *Id.* at 734-35.

167. See *Lantec, Inc. v. Novell, Inc.,* 306 F.3d 1003, 1025 (10th Cir. 2002) (agreeing with district court that economics expert did not understand computers or the computer market); In re Baby Food Antitrust Litig., 166 F.3d 112, 134 (3d Cir. 1999) (faulting the expert for knowing nothing about the baby food industry). Although certain qualifications are necessary, multiplication of "credentials" does not necessarily make a witness more credible, and may mislead jurors. Jeffrey Harrison argues that courts should constrain appeals to "institutional authority" where credentials are duplicative or irrelevant to the question of competence. *See* Harrison, *supra* note 54, at 294-301.

168. *Daubert v. Merrell Dow Pharms., Inc.,* 509 U.S. 579, 591 (1993) (quoting 3 JACK B. WEINSTEIN & MARGARET A. BERGER, WEINSTEIN'S EVIDENCE P 702[02], at 702-18 (1988)).

169. *Arizona v. Maricopa County Med. Soc'y,* 457 U.S. 332, 351 (1982) ("The anticompetitive potential inherent in all price-fixing agreements justifies their facial invalidation even if procompetitive justifications are offered for some.").

170. *See infra* Part III.A.

171. *City of Tuscaloosa v. Harcros Chems., Inc.,* 158 F.3d 548, 567 n.27 (11th Cir. 1998) (noting in dicta that the expert's "opinions regarding the legal standards applicable to the case are outside of his competence as an economist (and are erroneous) and should be excluded").

172. *See infra* Part III.C.2 (discussing expert testimony on the issue of collusion).

173. Many have questioned whether economics is truly a "science," given the difficulty of testing the implications of economic models by the scientific method. *See* Gavil, *supra* note 1, at 675 (arguing that "the testability and rate of error factors from *Daubert* did not contemplate economics, or any other social science for that matter"); *see also Brooks Fiber Communications of Tucson, Inc. v. GST Tucson Lightwave, Inc.,* 992 F. Supp. 1124, 1132 (D. Ariz 1997) (holding that *Daubert* did not apply to expert economist testimony using "basic economic modeling principles regarding price and cross-elasticity"); *Bell Atl. Bus. Sys. Servs., Inc. v. Hitachi Data Sys. Corp.,* 1995-2 Trade Cas. (CCH) P 71,259, at 76,130-31 (N.D. Cal. 1995) (holding that Daubert was not applicable to expert's testimony concerning whether and how consumers perform total cost of ownership analysis).

174. *Kumho Tire Co. v. Carmichael*, 526 U.S. 137 (1999).

175. *See Coastal Fuels, Inc. v. Caribbean Petroleum Corp.,* 175 F.3d 18, 34 n.12 (1st Cir. 1999) ("The district court's gatekeeping function extends to all expert evidence, including economic analysis, not merely to evidence involving scientific conclusions." (citing *Kumho Tire*, 526 U.S. at 138)); *see* also Hovenkamp, *supra* note 1, at 121 (discussing pre-Kumho Tire precedent).

176. *See Coastal Fuels*, 175 F.3d at 34 (stating that "*Daubert* requires 'that the proponent of the evidence show that the expert's conclusion has been arrived at in a scientifically sound and methodologically reliable fashion"' (quoting *Ruiz-Troche v. Pepsi Cola Bottling Co.*, 161 F.3d 77, 85 (1st Cir. 1998))).

177. *See*, e.g., *Conwood Co. v. U.S. Tobacco Co.,* 290 F.3d 768, 793 (6th Cir. 2002); *Concord Boat Corp. v. Brunswick Corp.,* 207 F.3d 1039, 1056-58 (8th Cir. 2000); *Blomkest Fertilizer, Inc. v. Potash Corp.,* 203 F.3d 1028, 1038 (8th Cir. 2000); *Blue Dane Simmental Corp. v. Am. Simmental Ass'n,* 178 F.3d 1035, 1040-41 (8th Cir. 1999); In re Polypropylene Carpet Antitrust Litig., 93 F. Supp. 2d 1348, 1358 (N.D. Ga. 2000); In re Aluminum Phosphide Antitrust Litig., 893 F. Supp. 1497, 1504 (D. Kan. 1995).

178. *ID Sec. Sys. Can., Inc. v. Checkpoint Sys., Inc.,* 198 F. Supp. 2d 598, 607 (E.D. Pa. 2002).

179. FED. R. EVID. 702.

180. *Concord Boat*, 207 F.3d at 1056-57.

181. *Gen. Elec. Co. v. Joiner,* 522 U.S. 136 (1997).

182. *Id.* at 146.

183. *United States v. Microsoft Corp.*, 253 F.3d 34 (D.C. Cir. 2001).

184. *Id.* at 82-83.

185. For an example, *see Worldwide Basketball and Sports Tours, Inc. v. NCAA,* 273 F. Supp. 2d 933, 944 (S.D. Ohio 2003), in which the court excluded, on *Daubert* grounds, expert testimony that pre- and post-season college basketball tournaments are a submarket of the market for Division I college basketball. The court noted that the expert "fail[ed] to offer a basis from which to conclude that this [was] an appropriate definition," and instead "testified in conclusory fashion as to the definition and parameters of this submarket." *Id.* The court concluded that the "testimony as to tournament

games submarket lacks a sufficient indicia of reliability to be admissible for purposes of Rule 702." *Id.*

186. *Microsoft*, 253 F.3d at 83.

187. *Id.* "Simply invoking the phrase 'network effects' without pointing to more evidence does not suffice to carry plaintiffs' burden in this respect." *Id.* at 84.

188. It is fairly rare to find explicit appellate applications of the Joiner rule to expert testimony in antitrust cases, though such examples do exist. *See, e.g., Williamson Oil Co. v. Philip Morris USA*, 346 F.3d 1287, 1323 (11th Cir. 2003) (affirming exclusion); *Conwood Co. v. U.S. Tobacco Co.*, 290 F.3d 768, 781, 792-95 (6th Cir. 2002) (affirming refusal to exclude); *Coastal Fuels, Inc. v. Caribbean Petroleum Corp.*, 175 F.3d 18, 33-34 (1st Cir. 1999) (affirming refusal to exclude); *City of Tuscaloosa v. Harcros Chems., Inc.*, 158 F.3d 548, 562-65 (11th Cir. 1998) (reversing some exclusions and affirming others).

189. 293 F. 1013 (D.C. Cir. 1923).

190. *Id.* at 47.

191. *See* Christopher B. Hockett & Frank M. Hinman, *Admissibility of Expert Testimony in Antitrust Cases: Does Daubert Raise a New Barrier to Entry for Economists?*, ANTITRUST, Summer 1996, at 40, 42.

192. *Id.*

193. *See Interview with Judge Kathryn Vratil*, ANTITRUST, Spring 2003, at 19, 20-21 (stating that while *Daubert* motions are burdensome and frequently unsuccessful, they are often nonetheless useful because they facilitate an early evaluation of the economic issues in the case).

194. *See Economists' Roundtable*, ANTITRUST, Spring 2003, at 8, 14

195. *See Daubert v. Merrell Dow Pharms., Inc.*, 509 U.S. 579, 596 (1993).

196. *See infra* Part III.

197. *Matsushita Elec. Indus. Co. v. Zenith Radio Corp.*, 475 U.S. 574, 587 (1986)

198. *Id.* at 598.

199. Hovenkamp, *supra* note 1, at 137.

200. Our concern is with the mechanisms for judicial deployment of economic authority. The substance of the legal and economic ideas at issue is incidental to this discussion, and we have not, for obvious practical reasons, attempted a comprehensive survey of the economic ideas relevant to antitrust decisionmaking.

201. For a survey of the early literature, *see* Joseph F. Brodley & George A. Hay, *Predatory Pricing: Competing Economic Theories and the Evolution of Legal Standards*, 66 CORNELL L. REV. 738 (1981). For more recent treatments, *see* Aaron S. Edlin, *Stopping Above-Cost Predatory Pricing*, 111 YALE L.J. 941 (2002) and Einer Elhauge, *Why Above-Cost Price Cuts to Drive Out Entrants Are Not Predatory—and the Implications for Defining Costs and Market Power*, 112 YALE L.J. 681 (2003).

202. *See, e.g.*, John S. McGee, *Predatory Pricing Revisited*, 23 J.L. & ECON. 289, 304-26 (1980).

203. *See* Page, *supra* note 9, at 1287-90 (discussing the Court's analysis in *Matsushita Elec. Indus. Co. v. Zenith Radio Corp.*, 475 U.S. 547 (1986), and the extension of that analysis in *Ind. Grocery, Inc. v. Super Valu Stores, Inc.*, 864 F.2d 1409, 1415-16 (7th Cir. 1989)).

204. *See* Robert H. Bork, *The Antitrust Paradox* 149-54 (1978); McGee, *supra* note 202, at 294-300. But *see* Richard A. Posner, *The Chicago School of Antitrust Analysis*, 127 U. PA. L. REV. 925, 939-44 (1979) (criticizing McGee's and Bork's orthodox Chicago theory that predatory pricing is irrational, and in the long run improbable, merely because of the ill effects on the predator's short run profits).

205. *See* generally Bork, *supra* note 204, at 144-54 (discussing and critiquing the theory and techniques of predation).

206. *See*, e.g., *Beech Nut Nutrition Corp. v. Gerber Prods. Co.,* 69 Fed. Appx. 350, 352-53 (9th Cir. 2003) (upholding the sufficiency of plaintiff's predatory pricing claim).

207. *Matsushita Elec. Indus. Co. v. Zenith Radio Corp.,* 475 U.S. 574 (1986).

208. *Id.* at 574-78.

209. *Id.* at 588.

210. *Id.* at 594.

211. *Id.* at 596-97.

212. *Id.* at 579. 580, 598.

213. *Id.* at 594 n. 19.

214. *Zenith Radio Corp. v. Matsushita Electric Indus. Co.,* 505 F. Supp. 1313, 1356-63 (E.D. Pa. 1980).

215. Unlike the district court, the court of appeals thought the expert's testimony was helpful to the jury:

> What the court in effect did was to eliminate all parts of the report in which the expert economist, after describing the conditions in the respective markets, the opportunities for collusion, the evidence pointing to collusion, the terms of certain undisputed agreements, and the market behavior, expressed the opinion that there was concert of action consistent with plaintiffs' conspiracy theory. Considering the complexity of the economic issues involved, it simply cannot be said that such an opinion would not help the trier of fact to understand the evidence or determine that fact in issue.

In re Japanese Elec. Prods. Antitrust Litig., 723 F.2d 238, 280 (3d Cir. 1983), rev'g, *Matsushita*, 505 F. Supp. at 1342-46.

216. *Matsushita Elec. Indus. Co. v. Zenith Radio Corp.,* 475 U.S. 574, 594 n.19 (1986).

217. *Id.* at 602 n.2 (White, J., dissenting).

218. *Id.* at 603 (White, J., dissenting).

219. *Id.* (White, J., dissenting).

220. *Id.* at 604 (White, J., dissenting) (The Court, in discussing the unlikelihood of a predatory conspiracy, also consistently assumes that petitioners valued profit-maximization over growth...In light of the evidence that petitioners sold their goods in this country at substantial losses over a long period of time,...I believe that this is an assumption that should be argued to the fact-finder, not decided by the Court.

221. *Id.* at 593 ("[T]here is nothing to suggest any relationship between petitioners' profits in Japan and the amount petitioners could expect to gain from a conspiracy to monopolize the American market.").

222. *See id.*

223. *Brooke Group Ltd. v. Brown & Williamson Tobacco Corp.*, 509 U.S. 209 (1993).

224. *Id.* at 223.

225. *Id.* at 224.

226. *See, e.g.*, Edlin, *supra* note 201, at 941 (arguing that "there is no compelling reason to restrict predation cases to below-cost pricing, as above-cost pricing can also hurt consumers by limiting competition"); *see* also Hovenkamp, *supra* note 1, at 138 (suggesting that the requirement of below-cost predatory pricing "has little to do with economic theories of limit pricing" and everything to do with "perceived limitations in the fact finding process").

227. *Barry Wright Corp. v. ITT Grinnell Corp.*, 724 F.2d 227, 233-34 (1st Cir. 1983); *see also Matsushita*, 475 U.S. at 594 (placing a special evidentiary burden on predatory pricing claims because outlawing a practice that brings lower prices to consumers is "especially costly" since "cutting prices in order to increase business often is the very essence of competition").

228. *Brooke Group*, 509 U.S. at 223-24; *see also Concord Boat Corp. v. Brunswick Corp.*, 207 F.3d 1039, 1060-63 (8th Cir. 2000) (holding that Brunswick's market share discounts were simply price cutting and, therefore, protected by Brooke Group). But *cf. LePage's, Inc. v. 3M*, 324 F.3d 141, 162-63 (3d Cir. 2003) (holding that bundled rebates covering multiple product lines, combined with exclusive dealing arrangements, were illegally exclusionary even if above cost).

229. 3 PHILLIP E. AREEDA & HERBERT HOVENKAMP, ANTITRUST LAW, P 735, at 318 (rev. ed. 1996).

230. The Court also noted that "[a]lthough unsuccessful predatory pricing may encourage some inefficient substitution toward the product being sold at less than its cost, unsuccessful predation is in general a boon to consumers." *Brooke Group*, 509 U.S. at 224.

231. *See Virgin Atl. Airways Ltd. v. British Airways PLC*, 257 F.3d 256, 268-69 (2d Cir. 2001) (affirming summary judgment where the plaintiff, despite its expert's testimony, "failed in its burden to show below cost pricing").

232. *See Rebel Oil Co. v. Atl. Richfield Co.,* 51 F.3d 1421, 1444 (9th Cir. 1995). Consequently, the losses suffered by competitors during this period "are not the stuff of antitrust injury. It would be incongruous to award damages to plaintiffs for actions that in general benefit consumer welfare." *Id.*

233. *Brooke Group*, 509 U.S. at 223 (observing that, although earlier cases had reserved the question of whether a predatory price could be "above some measure of incremental cost," those cases' reasoning implied that "only below-cost prices should suffice" (citations omitted)).

234. *Id.* at 222 n.1.

235. *Cf. Stearns Airport Equip. Co. v. FMC Corp.,* 170 F.3d 518, 533 n.14 (5th Cir. 1999) (affirming summary judgment where the expert erroneously assumed that the law "allowed a finding of predation when prices are above a firm's variable costs but below a 'short-run profit maximizing price'"); *Rebel Oil Co. v. Atl. Richfield Co.,* 146 F.3d 1088, 1095 (9th Cir. 1998) (finding the expert's use of opportunity cost in predatory-pricing scheme as the measure of defendant's cost was improper as a matter of law).

236. *United States v. AMR Corp.*, 335 F.3d 1109 (10th Cir. 2003), *aff'g* 140 F. Supp. 2d 1141 (D. Kan. 2001).

237. *Id.* at 1111.

238. *AMR*, 140 F. Supp. 2d at 1193 ("The anti-competitive conduct alleged…is predatory pricing: that American, in the face of low fare carrier competition, shifted from its traditional strategy and adopted competitive tools which combined price reductions and capacity increases, and that the cost of these tools was greater than the revenue obtained."), *aff'd*, 335 F.3d 1109, 1115 n.6 ("While the specific behavior complained of in the instant case is an increase in output or frequency, these actions must be analyzed in terms of their effect on price and cost.").

For a criticism of the court's characterization of American's practices as predatory pricing, *see* Gregory J. Werden, *The American Airlines Decision: Not with a Bang but a Whimper*, ANTITRUST, Fall 2003, at 32, 33 (arguing that the government was essentially challenging American Airline's strategy of flying empty seats in excess of those needed for available passengers as a means of drawing passengers away from low-cost entrant).

239. *See AMR*, 335 F.3d at 1115 ("Although this court approaches the matter with caution, we do not do so with the incredulity that once prevailed.").

240. *See id.*

241. *See id.* at 1116.

242. *Id.* at 1117.

243. *Id.* at 1119; *see* also Werden, *supra* note 238, at 34 (suggesting that the court "must have spent months combing the record for even the slightest indication that the Department's experts had overstated true incremental cost").

244. *AMR*, 335 F.3d at 1120. Werden observes that:

> The court did not even mention the Department's proffered expert opinion that avoidable cost had been estimated conservatively. Assuming the court did not just fail to notice this critical testimony, it must have implicitly held that the testimony lacked a sufficient factual basis, or improperly decided a disputed issue of material fact.

Werden, *supra* note 238, at 35; *see* also Aaron S. Edlin & Joseph Farrell, *The American Airlines Case: A Chance to Clarify Predation Policy* (2001), in THE ANTITRUST REVOLUTION, *supra* note 1, at 502 (describing the various measures of cost advanced as the standard of "sacrifice" necessary to establish predation).

245. *Brooke Group Ltd. v. Brown & Williamson Tobacco Corp.*, 509 U.S. 209, 224 (1993).

246. *See id.* at 225.

247. *Cargill, Inc. v. Monfort of Colo., Inc.*, 479 U.S. 104 (1986).

248. *Id.* at 119 n. 15.

249. The district court in American Airlines granted summary judgment on the recoupment issue, because "the uncontroverted evidence establishe[d] that DFW routes are not structurally susceptible to the *supra*-competitive prices which is a prerequisite to a successful predatory pricing scheme." *AMR*, 140 F. Supp. 2d at 1209. The court of appeals did not reach the recoupment issue

because it concluded that the government had failed to establish below-cost pricing. *AMR*, 335 F.3d at 1120-21.

250. *Brook Group*, 509 U.S. at 233.

251. *Id.* at 233-34; *see also id.* at 237 ("Where, as here, output is expanding at the same time prices are increasing, rising prices are equally consistent with growing product demand.").

252. *Id.* at 235-36. ("[I]n an oligopoly setting, in which price competition is most likely to take place through less observable and less regulable means than list prices, it would be unreasonable to draw conclusions about the existence of tacit coordination or *supra*competitive pricing from data that reflect only list prices.").

253. *Id.* at 238-39.

254. *Id.* at 242

255. *Id.*

256. *Id.* But cf. *Metronet Servs. Corp. v. U.S. West Communications*, 329 F.3d 986, 1004-05 (9th Cir. 2003) (reversing the district court's disregard of experts' testimony in the absence of a "reasoned analysis of how their opinions" were inconsistent with the record).

257. *Brooke Group*, 509 U.S. at 241.

258. *Id.* at 241-42.

259. *Id.* at 241-43.

260. *See*, e.g., *Fortner Enters., Inc. v. U.S. Steel Corp.*, 394 U.S. 495. 502 (1969) ("The standard of 'sufficient economic power' does not...require that the defendant have a monopoly or even a dominant position throughout the market for the tying product."); *United States v. Socony-Vacuum Oil Co.*, 310 U.S. 150, 224 n.59 (1940) ("[A] conspiracy to fix prices violates § 1 of the [Sherman] Act...[,] though it is not established that the conspirators had the means available for accomplishment of their objective...").

261. *See N. Pac. Ry. v. United States*, 356 U.S. 1, 5 (1958) ("[T]here are certain agreements or practices which because of their pernicious effect on competition and lack of any redeeming virtue are conclusively presumed to be

unreasonable and therefore illegal without elaborate inquiry as to the precise harm they have caused or the business excuse for their use.").

262. *See, e.g.,* Robert Pitofsky, *New Definitions of Relevant Market and the Assault on Antitrust*, 90 COLUM. L. REV. 1805, 1808 (1990) (observing that early approaches to market definition produced "excessively, and sometimes ludicrously, narrow market definitions").

263. *See* Jonathan B. Baker, *Stepping Out In An Old Brown Shoe: In Qualified Praise Of Submarkets*, 68 ANTITRUST L.J. 203, 206 (2000) ("Blind application [of the submarket concept] allowed courts to define inappropriately narrow submarkets within the outer bounds of markets properly defined with reference to substitution possibilities.").

264. Gregory J. Werden, *The History of Antitrust Market Delineation*, 76 MARQ. L. REV. 123, 125 (1992) ("Much of the intellectual development of the concepts relating to antitrust market delineation took place in classrooms and seminar halls at law schools and economics departments, in judges' chambers, and in the offices of enforcement agencies, law firms, and economic consultants." (citations omitted)).

265. *See, e.g., Am. Key Corp. v. Cole Nat'l Corp.*, 762 F.2d 1569, 1579 (11th Cir. 1985) (holding that "[c]onstruction of a relevant economic market or a showing of monopoly power in that market cannot...be based upon lay opinion testimony"); *Va. Vermiculite, Ltd. v. W.R. Grace & Co.,* 108 F. Supp. 2d 549, 576 n.16 (W.D. Va. 2000) (holding expert testimony practically necessary for market definition); *Drs. Steuer & Latham, P.A. v. Nat'l Med. Enters., Inc.,* 672 F. Supp. 1489, 1512 n.25 (D.S.C. 1987) ("Failure to adduce expert testimony on competitive issues such as market definition augurs strongly in favor of granting summary judgment against an antitrust plaintiff."), *aff'd*, 846 F.2d 70 (4th Cir. 1988) (Table). Although the court in *Anti-Monopoly, Inc. v. Hasbro*, Inc., 958 F. Supp. 895 (S.D.N.Y.), *aff'd*, 130 F.3d 1101 (2d Cir. 1997), stated that "experts are not always essential to defining the relevant market," *id.* at 904, it cited for this proposition *United States v. Pabst Brewing Co.,* 384 U.S. 546, 549 (1966), which dates from an era in which market definition was not conducted on economic grounds.

266. *See* Posner, *supra* note 55, at 156 (arguing that the Supreme Court has left development of the law of market definition to the lower courts, which have, in turn, followed the enforcement agencies' Merger Guidelines in developing a new consensus).

267. *Id.*

268. *See, e.g., United States v. VISA U.S.A.,* Inc., 344 F.3d 229, 239 (2d Cir. 2003) (affirming the definition of a market for "general purpose credit cards" based on expert testimony concerning consumer preferences in forms of payment).

269. *See, e.g., Berlyn, Inc. v. Gazette Newspapers, Inc.,* 214 F. Supp. 2d 530, 539 (D. Md. 2002) (excluding an expert's opinion because his methods were not shown to be "of the type that other experts would use to determine the relevant markets in an antitrust case"); *Vermiculite*, 108 F. Supp. 2d at 736 (excluding expert testimony for, among other things, failure to test alternative hypotheses or to use an Elzinga-Hogarty test).

270. *See, e.g., Bailey v. Allgas, Inc.,* 284 F.3d 1237, 1246-47 (11th Cir. 2002) (granting summary judgment where the plaintiff's expert ignored Eleventh Circuit precedent on market definition); *City of Tuscaloosa v. Harcros Chem., Inc.,* 158 F.3d 548, 567 n.27 (11th Cir. 1998) (stating in dicta that expert's assertion that the relevant market is the "largest market for which data are available" was contrary to law); *FTC v. Swedish Match*, 131 F. Supp. 2d 151, 160 (D.D.C. 2000) (finding plaintiff's expert's estimate was not credible because it was based on untested assumptions that carried only an eighty-five percent confidence level); *City of Chanute v. Williams Natural Gas Co.,* 743 F. Supp. 1437, 1457 (D. Kan. 1990) (excluding relevant evidence on market definition because it ignored precedent requiring focus on products consumers view as reasonably interchangeable).

271. *See Bailey*, 284 F.3d at 1246-47.

272. *Menasha Corp. v. News Am. Mktg. In-Store, Inc.*, 354 F.3d 661 (7th Cir. 2004).

273. *Id.* at 665.

274. *Id.*

275. *Id.*

276. *Id.*

277. *Id.*

278. *Id.*

279. *Id.* at 666.

280. In a recent communication, one of the plaintiff's economists wrote:

Judge Easterbrook's decision did not address many of the analyses done by the experts engaged by Menasha. For example, Dr. Langenfeld (who the judge characterized as a "marketing" expert) performed a critical loss analysis to determine if at-shelf coupon dispensers was a relevant product market. Dr. Langenfeld's analysis adjusted for cellophane fallacy issues, and supported his approach with several refereed articles. The judge faulted Dr. Warren-Boulton for not performing a statistical covariance analysis similar to that suggested by Stigler and Sherwin in their 1985 article. Although such analyses can be useful in offering support for market definition, the substantial literature since that article has explained the limits of such analyses and, under any condition, the defendant in this case did not provide sufficient information in discovery to perform the detailed statistical analysis of prices over time that Judge Easterbrook favored. Instead, among other analyses, both Dr. Warren-Boulton and Dr. Langenfeld offered evidence (including statistical regression analysis by Dr. Warren-Boulton) of a "natural experiment" that would shed light on the relevant market. NAMIS purchased its main competitor, ActMedia, a few years before the case, and both experts found NAMIS's margins increased as a result of that merger. There was a factual dispute over whether this increase was due to reduced competition, but the evidence was consistent with an at-shelf coupon dispensing market and NAMIS having a dominant position in that market.

E-mail from James Langenfeld to William H. Page (Oct. 18, 2004) (on file with authors).

281. A Ninth Circuit panel, echoing *Brooke Group*, 509 U.S. 209 (1993), wrote that "if there are undisputed facts about the structure of the market that render the inference economically unreasonable, the expert opinion is insufficient to support a jury verdict." *Rebel Oil Co. v. Atl. Richfield Co.,* 51 F.3d 1421, 1435-36 (9th Cir. 1995). The court found insufficient an expert's testimony that full service and self-service gasoline distribution were in different markets, because the expert had failed to consider supply substitution—i.e., that full service pumps can be converted into self-service pumps at virtually no cost. *Id.* at 1436-37.

Another court found insufficient expert testimony that the product market was limited to natural gas sold for residential use, where the record showed that gas sold for other uses was identical, and that other energy sources for home heat were available. *Bailey v. Allgas, Inc.,* 284 F.3d 1237, 1246-47 (11th Cir. 2002). The court also rejected the expert's testimony that the geographic market was limited to a twenty-mile radius around the plaintiffs' distributorship, where the expert failed to consider prices and locations of other distributors or consumer customer preferences. *Id.* at 1248; *see also FTC v. Tenet Healthcare Corp.*, 186 F.3d 1045 (8th Cir. 1999) (holding that the district court erred in defining a geographic market for hospitals in which, expert testimony showed, twenty-two percent of residents use services at hospitals outside of the putative market).

282. *See* In re Polypropylene Carpet Antitrust Litig., 93 F. Supp. 2d 1348, 1365-67 (N.D. Ga. 2000) (finding that the "[e]xclusion of outliers is a common practice in statistical analysis" and that the expert's use of data filters did not alter his analysis).

283. In re Northwest Airlines Corp. Antitrust Litig., 197 F. Supp. 2d 908, 916, 919 (E.D. Mich. 2002). The court also found the expert's testimony admissible even though it excluded city-pairs in which the defendants held fifty percent or less of the market. The court rejected defense arguments that the expert was assuming market power wherever Northwest had more than a fifty percent market share, noting that the expert made the exclusion not to define the market, but to "streamline" the analysis by identifying markets with characteristics that were consistent with market power. *Id.*

284. Paul L. Joskow, *Transaction Cost Economics, Antitrust Rules, and Remedies*, 18 J.L. ECON. & ORG. 95, 100 (2002).

285. Where demand is horizontal, the price (average revenue) is equal to marginal revenue because the firm captures the full revenue from the sale of each additional unit. If demand is downward-sloping, marginal revenue falls below average revenue because the sale of each additional unit drives down the market price, and this applies to all of the intramarginal units. Thus, the firm maximizes profit by setting its marginal cost equal to marginal revenue, not price.

286. *See* Posner, *supra* note 55, at 22 (arguing that "to infer that every seller who faces a downward-sloping demand curve has monopoly power in a sense interesting to antitrust law would be a profound mistake"); cf. Benjamin Klein, *Market Power in Antitrust: Economic Analysis after Kodak*, 3 SUP. CT. ECON. REV. 43, 72-74 (1993) (observing that most economists distinguish among degrees of market power for policy purposes, but advocating instead a distinction between a firm's individual pricing discretion and market power).

287. 2 JOSEPH P. BAUER & WILLIAM H. PAGE, KINTNER'S FEDERAL ANTITRUST LAW 332 (2002).

288. *See* Thomas C. Arthur, *The Costly Quest for Perfect Competition: Kodak and Nonstructural Market Power*, 69 N.Y.U. L. REV. 1, 22 n.90 (1994) (arguing that the Warren Court erred in "setting its market power criteria too low and relying exclusively on market shares, especially in gerrymandered markets…to determine power"); George J. Stigler, *The Economists and the Problem of Monopoly*, 72 AM. ECON. REV. 1, 9 (1982) ("The typical antitrust case is an almost impudent exercise in economic gerrymandering.").

289. *See* Bauer & Page, *supra* note 287, at 333.

290. *See id.* at 334

291. The HHI is a measure of market concentration and is defined as the sum of the squares of the market shares of all of the firms in the market.

292. *See, e.g., FTC v. H.J. Heinz Co.*, 246 F.3d 708, 716 (D.C. Cir. 2001) ("Sufficiently large HHI figures establish the FTC's prima facie case that a merger is anti-competitive.").

293. *Id.* at 720.

294. *Id.* at 724 ("[T]he district court made no finding that any of these 'cartel problems' are so much greater in the baby food industry than in other industries that they rebut the normal presumption [arising from a high HHI]."). For a discussion of Heinz by the defense expert, *see* Jonathan B. Baker, *Efficiencies and High Concentration: Heinz Proposes to Acquire Beech-Nut* (2001), in THE ANTITRUST REVOLUTION, *supra* note 1, at 150.

295. Bauer & Page, *supra* note 287, at 335-37.

296. *See, e.g., Bailey v. Allgas, Inc.*, 284 F.3d 1237, 1250, 1253 (11th Cir. 2002) (holding that market share of fifty percent or less is inadequate as a matter of law to establish market power and that expert's use of return on investment to measure market power had not been accepted by any other circuit).

297. *See, e.g., Bailey v. Allgas, Inc.*, 148 F. Supp. 2d 1222, 1245 (N.D. Ala. 2000) (finding that expert's opinion that the "true test of market power is concentration ratios or other indices, not market share" and use of return on investment to show market power was contrary to law (internal quotation marks omitted)); *Va. Vermiculite, Ltd. v. W.R. Grace & Co.*, 98 F. Supp. 2d 729, 739 (W.D. Va. 2000) (finding that expert's contention that monopolist is a seller that increases prices without reducing output was wrong as a matter of law because monopolists decrease output while increasing price).

298. In NCAA, the collegiate athletic association argued that it had no market power in the sale of rights to televise football games. *NCAA v. Bd. of Regents of Univ. of Okla.,* 468 U.S. 85, 109 (1984). The Court rejected the argument on both legal and factual grounds. *Id.* As to the factual refutation, the Court relied on lower court findings that no good substitutes existed for televised college football games. *Id.* at 111. But it might have simply repeated its earlier conclusion that "[t]he anticompetitive consequences of this arrangement are apparent...Price is higher and output is lower than they otherwise would be." *Id.* at 106-07. Even though the Court's conclusion may have been wrong, its logic compelled the further conclusion that the NCAA had market power.

299. The court in *FTC v. Staples, Inc.*, 970 F. Supp. 1066, 1082-83 (D.D.C. 1997) issued a preliminary injunction against the merger of two office superstores based in part on the FTC's econometric studies showing that markets with a single superstore had significantly higher prices than those in which there were competing superstores. For a discussion of the economic data in the case, *see* Serdar Dalkir & Frederick R. Warren-Boulton, Prices, *Market Definition, and the Effects of Merger: Staples-Office Depot* (1997), in THE ANTITRUST REVOLUTION, *supra* note 1, at 52; *see also* Posner, *supra* note 55, at 157-58.

300. *See generally* Carl Shapiro, *Mergers with Differentiated Products*, ANTITRUST, Spring 1996, at 23 (discussing the unilateral competitive effects test used in policing horizontal mergers).

301. *Eastman Kodak Co. v. Image Technical Servs., Inc.,* 504 U.S. 451 (1992).

302. *Id.* at 486.

303. *See* David A.J. Goldfine & Kenneth M. Vorasi, *The Fall of the Kodak Aftermarket Doctrine: Dying a Slow Death in the Lower Courts*, 72 ANTITRUST L.J. 209 (2004).

304. *Eastman Kodak*, 504 U.S. at 454.

305. *Id.* at 458-60.

306. *Id.* at 462-64.

307. *Id.* at 465.

308. *Id.* at 495 (Scalia, J., dissenting) ("[A] rational consumer considering the purchase of Kodak equipment will inevitably factor into his purchasing decision the expected cost of aftermarket support.").

309. *Id.* at 465-71 (Scalia, J., dissenting); *see also Petitioners' Brief on the Merits* at 26, *Eastman Kodak* (No. 90-1029) ("Overcharging for service is an especially implausible strategy for Kodak, since demand for Kodak service is itself ultimately dependent on new equipment sales.").

310. *Eastman Kodak*, 504 U.S. at 498 (quoting *Parts & Elec. Motors, Inc. v. Sterling Elec., Inc.,* 866 F.2d 228, 236 (7th Cir. 1988) (Posner, J., dissenting)).

311. *See, e.g.,* Robert H. Lande, *Chicago Takes It on the Chin: Imperfect Information Could Play a Crucial Role in the Post-Kodak World*, 62 ANTITRUST L.J. 193 (1993). Even Chicagoan Robert Bork lamented in 1993 that the "Kodak decision may suggest that forward movement [toward a new economic sophistication for antitrust] has stopped or is about to go into reverse." Robert H. Bork, THE ANTITRUST PARADOX 436 (rev. ed. 1993).

312. *Eastman Kodak*, 504 U.S. at 472.

313. *Id.* at 472.

314. Brief for Respondent at 20 n.13, *Eastman Kodak* (No. 90-1029) (quoted in Stephen Calkins, SUPREME COURT ANTITRUST 1991-92: *The Revenge of the Amici*, 61 ANTITRUST L.J. 269, 306 (1993)); *see also* Lisa Meckfessel Judson, Note, *Kodak v. Image Technical Services: The Taming of Matsushita and the Chicago Schoo*l, 1993 WIS. L. REV. 1633, 1671 n.230 (1993) (observing that "the parties' briefs can be *see*n as pitting one school of thought against another").

315. *Eastman Kodak*, 504 U.S. at 473 n.19, 476 n.22.

316. *Id.* at 473.

317. *Id.* at 473, 475.

318. *Id.* at 476.

319. *Id.* at 478 (emphasis added).

320. Brief of Bell Atlantic in Support of Respondent at 14, *Eastman Kodak* (No. 90-1029) (quoted in Ronald S. Katz, *The Kodak Case: Setting the Antitrust Agenda for the Nineties*, C695 ALI-ABA 15, 28-29 (Dec. 12, 1991)).

321. Eastman Kodak, 504 U.S. at 469.

322. *Id.* at 466.

323. *See Image Technical Servs., Inc. v. Eastman Kodak Co.*, 125 F.3d 1195 (9th Cir. 1997). For a discussion of the plaintiffs' theories by one of their experts in the case on remand, *see* Jeffrey K. MacKie-Mason & John Metzler, *Links between Markets and Aftermarkets: Kodak* (1997), in THE ANTITRUST REVOLUTION, *supra* note 1, at 428.

324. *ID Sec. Sys. Can., Inc. v. Checkpoint Sys., Inc.*, 198 F. Supp. 2d 598, 628 (E.D. Pa. 2002).

325. *ID Sec. Sys. Can., Inc. v. Checkpoint Sys., Inc.*, 249 F. Supp. 2d 622, 698 (E.D. Pa. 2003).

326. *Id.* at 643.

327. *Id.* at 643-44.

328. *Id.*

329. *Id.* at 694.

330. *See* Bork, *supra* note 311, at 263; Richard A. Posner, *A Program for the Antitrust Division*, 38 U. CHI. L. REV. 500, 528-29 (1971); *see also* John E. Lopatka & William H. Page, *Posner's Program for the Antitrust Division: A Twenty-Five Year Perspective*, 48 SMU L. REV. 1713 (1995) (reviewing Posner's statement that consensus among economists and efficiency concerns was reason enough for a strong anti-cartel enforcement program).

331. *See, e.g.*, Posner, *supra* note 330, at 529. For discussion of strategies cartels use to foster stability, *see* Christopher R. Leslie, *Trust, Distrust, and Antitrust*, 82 TEX. L. REV. 515 (2004).

332. *See, e.g.*, Lester G. Telser, *The Theory of Efficient Cooperation and Competition* (1987); Donald Dewey, *Information, Entry, and Welfare: The Case for Collusion*, 69 AM. ECON. REV. 587 (1979); cf. George Bittlingmayer, *Price-Fixing and the Addyston Pipe Case*, in 5 Res. in L. & ECON. 57 (1983) (discussing the near impossibility of reaching competitive equilibrium in many market scenarios).

333. One could argue that the ban on competitive bidding in *National Society of Professional Engineers v. United States,* 435 U.S. 679 (1978), was efficient because it reduced search costs, so that consumers who wanted high-qual-

ity services were able to find them. That is, the price paid might have been higher, but the quality was better. Absent a low-cost method of identifying high-quality suppliers, the "lemon effect" could result in high-quality suppliers being squeezed out of the market, which would injure consumers who wanted high-quality service. *See* George A. Akerlof, *The Market for "Lemons": Quality Uncertainty and the Market Mechanism*, 84 Q.J. ECON. 488, 495-96 (1970); John E. Lopatka, *Antitrust and Professional Rules: A Framework for Analysis*, 28 SAN DIEGO L. REV. 301, 365-70 (1991). Nevertheless, the Court was unwilling to trade lower prices for possibly higher quality, concluding that the antitrust laws rested on the premise that "ultimately competition will produce not only lower prices, but also better goods and services." *Prof'l Eng'rs*, 435 U.S. at 695.

334. *See, e.g., FTC v. Ind. Fed'n of Dentists,* 476 U.S. 447 (1986); *Catalano, Inc. v. Target Sales, Inc.*, 446 U.S. 643 (1980); cf. *Cal. Dental Ass'n v. FTC*, 526 U.S. 756, 778 (1999) (refusing to apply a truncated rule of liability to a dental association's rules limiting advertising, even though the rule prevented members from engaging in certain forms of price advertising and making claims of quality—information generally valuable to consumers). The association rule was not a garden-variety cartel because it did not prevent full and detailed price advertising. *See Cal. Dental Ass'n v. FTC,* 224 F.3d 942, 952 (9th Cir. 2000).

335. *See, e.g., United States v. MMR Corp.*, 907 F.2d 489, 495 (5th Cir. 1990) (affirming a conviction for bid rigging where the evidence showed "a deal was struck...in the men's room that MMR, in exchange for a lucrative subcontract, would become part of the conspiracy").

336. *See infra* Part III.C.

337. *See Bd. of Trade of Chicago v. United States*, 246 U.S. 231, 238 (1918). In such cases, the Court has preferred to govern by "standard," allowing "consideration of all or at least most facts that are relevant to the standard's rationale," rather than by "rule." *See MindGames, Inc. v. W. Publ'g Co.,* 218 F.3d 652, 657 (7th Cir. 2000).

338. *Cal. Dental*, 526 U.S. at 780-81; *see also id.* at 779 ("[O]ur categories of analysis of anticompetitive effect are less fixed than terms like 'per se,' 'quick look,' and 'rule of reason' tend to make them appear.").

339. *Id.* at 781. For the sorts of advertising restrictions at issue in the case, the Court concluded, "[t]he obvious anticompetitive effect that triggers abbreviated analysis has not been shown." *Id.* at 778; *see* also William J. Kolasky,

California Dental Association: The New Antitrust Empiricism, 14 ANTITRUST L.J. 68, 70 (1999) (concluding that "courts must apply a sliding scale, in which the amount of proof demanded of the plaintiff depends both on how obvious the anticompetitive effects are and how strong or weak the proffered justifications are").

340. *Broad. Music, Inc. v. CBS*, 441 U.S. 1 (1979).

341. *Id.* at 24.

342. *Id.* at 19-20.

343. *Id.* at 14-16.

344. *Bus. Elecs. Corp. v. Sharp Elecs. Corp.*, 485 U.S. 717 (1988).

345. Page, *supra* note 9, at 1262.

346. *Sharp*, 485 U.S. at 724-25.

347. *Id.* at 726-27.

348. *Cal. Dental Ass'n v. FTC,* 526 U.S. 759 (1999).

349. *See id.* at 778 ("[T]he plausibility of competing claims about the effects of the professional advertising restrictions rules out the indulgently abbreviated review to which the Commission's order was treated. The obvious anticompetitive effect that triggers abbreviated analysis has not been shown.").

350. *See Cal. Dental Ass'n v. FTC*, 224 F.3d 942, 950 (9th Cir. 2000) (noting that the FTC relied on Carolyn Cox & Susan Foster, Bureau of Economics, Federal Trade Commission, *The Costs and Benefits of Occupational Regulation* (1990)); Lee Benham, *The Effect of Advertising on the Price of Eyeglasses*, 15 J.L. & ECON. 337 (1972); James A. Langenfeld & John R. Morris, *Analyzing Agreements Among Competitors: What Does the Future Hold?*, 36 ANTITRUST BULL. 651 (1991); Phillip Nelson, *Advertising as Information*, 82 J. POL. ECON. 729 (1974); and John R. Schroeter et al., *Advertising and Competition in Routine Legal Service Markets: An Empirical Investigation*, 36 J. INDUS. ECON. 49 (1987)). Though Cox and Foster do discuss dental advertising, the study "cites no empirical evidence concerning dental advertising restrictions substantially similar to those enacted by CDA." *Cal. Dental*, 224 F.3d at 951.

351. *See supra* note 333.

352. *Cal. Dental*, 526 U.S. at 772; *see id.* at 771-73 (citing also Jack Carr & Frank Mathewson, *The Economics of Law Firms: A Study in the Legal Organization of the Firm*, 33 J. LAW & ECON. 307, 309 (1990); Robert G. Evans, *Professionals and the Production Function: Can Competition Policy Improve Efficiency in the Licensed Professions?,* in OCCUPATIONAL LICENSURE & REGULATION 225 (Simon Rottenberg ed., 1980); Hayne E. Leland, *Quacks, Lemons, and Licensing: A Theory of Minimum Quality Standards*, 87 J. POL. ECON. 1328, 1330 (1979)).

353. *Id.* at 775 (quoting Akerlof, *supra* note 333, at 495).

354. *Cal. Dental*, 224 F.3d at 952.

355. *Id.* at 958.

356. *Id.* at 952.

357. *Id.*

358. *Id.* at 952-53.

359. *Id.* at 957.

360. *Id.*

361. For the Federal Trade Commission's most recent attempt to embody the teaching of California Dental in an analytical paradigm, *see* In re PolyGram Holdings, Inc., Dkt. No. 9298 (July 24, 2003) (Muris, Chairman), available at http://www.ftc.gov/os/2003/07/polygramopinion.pdf (last visited Jan. 1, 2005).

362. David M. Kreps, *Game Theory and Economic Modelling* 9 (1990); Martin Shubik, *Game Theory in the Social Sciences* 217 (1982).

363. Roger D. Blair & David L. Kaserman, *Antitrust Economics* 136 n.3 (1985).

364. *Id.* at 192-201.

365. DENNIS W. CARLTON & JEFFREY M. PERLOFF, MODERN INDUSTRIAL ORGANIZATION, 126-36 (3d ed. 2000).

366. As one court has noted:

> [T]he Supreme Court has applied a gloss to the term "concerted action" when using it in the antitrust context. And, accordingly, courts must treat this phrase as a term of art in the context of the Sherman Act; it cannot be understood as it might be in ordinary parlance, to reach any and all forms of joint activity by two or more persons. It must be defined consonant with its role in the antitrust analysis, as the basis for determining the unlawfulness of conduct prohibited by section 1.

Va. Vermiculite, Ltd. v. Historic Green Springs, Inc., 307 F.3d 277, 281-82 (4th Cir. 2002), cert. denied, 598 U.S. 998 (2003).

367. Courts have not distinguished among the three statutory terms, treating all three as denoting the same concept of concerted action. *See*, e.g., *In re Baby Food Antitrust Litig.*, 166 F.3d 112, 117 n.3 (3d Cir. 1999); Posner, *supra* note 55, at 262 ("[T]he courts sensibly have not worried about whether the terms 'contract,' 'combination,' and 'conspiracy,' in section 1, have non-overlapping meanings.").

368. *Am. Tobacco Co. v. United States,* 328 U.S. 781, 810 (1946).

369. *See, e.g., United States v. MMR Corp.*, 907 F.2d 489, 495 (5th Cir. 1990) (affirming a conviction for bid rigging where the evidence showed an express agreement to participate in return for a subcontract).

370. *See, e.g.*, In re Brand Name Prescription Drugs Antitrust Litig., 288 F.3d 1028, 1033 (7th Cir. 2002) ("There is authority for prohibiting as a violation of the Sherman Act or section 5 of the Federal Trade Commission Act an agreement that facilitates collusive activity..."); *FTC v. Cement Inst.*, 333 U.S. 683, 696-700, 709-17 (1948) (condemning agreements among competitors to use a basing-point pricing system); *see* also Posner, *supra* note 55, at 91-93; George J. Stigler, *A Theory of Delivered Price Systems*, in The Organization of Industry 147, 148-51 (1968) (discussing various kinds of delivered price systems); Dennis Carlton, *A Reexamination of Delivered Pricing Systems*, 23 J.L. & ECON. 51 (1983); David D. Haddock, *Basing-Point Pricing: Competitive vs. Collusive Theories,* 72 AM. ECON. REV. 289 (1982) (discussing basing-point pricing systems and the legal reaction to the practice).

Explicit agreements to engage in practices that may not facilitate collusion, however, cannot be condemned summarily. *See, e.g., United States v. U.S. Gypsum Co.,* 438 U.S. 422, 441 n.16 (1978) ("[E]xchanges of [price data and other] information do not constitute a per se violation of the Sherman Act."); *Todd v. Exxon Corp.*, 275 F.3d 191, 198 (2d Cir.

2001) (stating that an agreement to exchange price information "is not illegal per se, but can be found unlawful under a rule of reason analysis" (citations omitted)); *see also* Dennis W. Carlton et al., *Communication Among Competitors: Game Theory and Antitrust,* 5 GEO. MASON L. REV. 423, 424 (1997) (arguing that "in the absence of direct evidence to form a 'naked' cartel to restrict output or to raise price, the appropriate standard to judge the flow of information among competitors is the rule of reason").

371. *See* Carlton & Perloff, *supra* note 365, ch. 6 (presenting game theoretic models of noncooperative oligopoly); Blair & Herndon, *supra* note 3, at 818-20 (summarizing theories of shared monopoly).

372. Conscious parallelism is the "process, not itself unlawful, by which firms in a concentrated market might in effect share monopoly power, setting their prices at a profit-maximizing, *supra*competitive level by recognizing their shared economic interests and their interdependence with respect to price and output decisions." *Brooke Group Ltd. v. Brown & Williamson Tobacco Corp.,* 509 U.S. 209, 227 (1993).

373. *See*, *e.g.,* Carlton & Perloff, *supra* note 365, at 139-41.

374. *See* In re Citric Acid Litig., 191 F.3d 1090, 1102 (9th Cir. 1999); *City of Tuscaloosa v. Harcros Chems., Inc.,* 158 F.3d 548, 570 (11th Cir. 1998); *Wallace v. Bank of Bartlett,* 55 F.3d 1166, 1168 (6th Cir. 1995); *Holiday Wholesale Grocery Co. v. Philip Morris, Inc.,* 231 F. Supp. 2d 1253, 1269 (N.D. Ga. 2002), *aff'd sub nom. Williamson Oil Co. v. Philip Morris USA*, 346 F.3d 1287 (11th Cir. 2003). One court summarized the state of the law as follows:

> Courts...have almost uniformly held, at least in the pricing area, that such individual pricing decisions (even when each firm rests its decision upon its belief that competitors will do the same) do not constitute an unlawful agreement under section 1 of the Sherman Act...That is not because such pricing is desirable (it is not), but because it is close to impossible to devise a judicially enforceable remedy for "interdependent" pricing.
>
> *Clamp-All Corp. v. Cast Iron Soil Pipe Inst.,* 851 F.2d 478, 484 (1st Cir. 1988).

375. *See generally* John E. Lopatka, *Solving the Oligopoly Problem: Turner's Try*, 41 ANTITRUST BULL. 843 (1996) (describing both Turner's approach to the problem of oligopoly pricing and Posner's critique of that approach).

376. Donald F. Turner, *The Definition of Agreement Under the Sherman Act: Conscious Parallelism and Refusals to Deal*, 75 HARV. L. REV. 655, 671 (1962).

377. *Id.* at 665.

378. *See id.* This interpretation is bolstered by Turner's further argument that the oligopolists are much like the lawful monopolist that merely charges a monopoly price. *Id.* at 667-68.

379. *Id.* at 669.

380. *Id.*

381. *Id.* at 670.

382. *Id.* at 675-76.

383. *Id.* at 676 ("Finally, in sharp contrast to the basic-price case, here a perfectly understandable, plausible, and readily enforceable injunction can be written which would have excellent prospects, in most cases, of making price behavior substantially more competitive.").

384. Posner, *supra* note 55, at 94. Posner's original reply to Turner was in Richard A. Posner, *Oligopoly and the Antitrust Laws: A Suggested Approach*, 21 STAN. L. REV. 1562 (1969) [hereinafter Posner, Oligopoly]. His position was refined slightly in the first edition of his book on antitrust law. *See* RICHARD A. POSNER, ANTITRUST LAW: AN ECONOMIC PERSPECTIVE 42-77 (1976).

385. Posner, *supra* note 55, at 97, 98.

386. *Id.* at 92 (arguing that evidence that the sellers agreed to establish a basing-point system should be "unnecessary to establish a violation of the Sherman Act").

387. Posner would prefer an action for damages brought by the Justice Department on behalf of the victims of antitrust violations—a form of suit that would require a statutory change—to a private treble-damages action. *Id.* at 99. But he is apparently willing to accept the private damages suit as a second-best alternative.

388. *Id.* at 98-99. This conception of an appropriate Section 1 remedy marks a slight change in thinking. Posner earlier advocated "a relatively simple

and general injunction against express or tacit price-fixing," together with a damages sanction. Posner, *Oligopoly*, *supra* note 384, at 1591 n.76.

389. *See* Posner, *supra* note 55, at 97 ("[T]here probably are few cases of purely tacit collusion."); Turner, *supra* note 376, at 662 ("It may well be that in reality a stable and firm pattern of noncompetitive prices is rarely achieved without some kind of agreement.").

390. *See* generally Lopatka & Page, *supra* note 330, at 1717-20 (discussing the Antitrust Department's adoption of the Chicago School theory of "tacit collusion").

391. One court recently emphasized that "[t]he most important evidence will generally be non-economic evidence 'that there was an actual, manifest agreement not to compete." In re Flat Glass Antitrust Litig., 385 F.3d 350, 361 (3d Cir. 2004) (citations omitted).

392. *See, e.g., Todd v. Exxon Corp.*, 275 F.3d 191, 198 (2d Cir. 2001) (noting that a price fixing agreement "may be inferred on the basis of conscious parallelism, when such interdependent conduct is accompanied by circumstantial evidence and plus factors such as defendants' use of facilitating practices"); *Blomkest Fertilizer, Inc. v. Potash Corp. of Sask.*, 203 F.3d 1028, 1033-34 (8th Cir. 2000) (finding insufficient evidence of "plus factors" to support an inference of agreement in a case based on a theory of conscious parallelism); In re Baby Food Antitrust Litig., 166 F.3d 112, 122 (3d Cir. 1999) (noting that courts "require that evidence of a defendant's parallel pricing be supplemented with 'plus factors'" in order for a court to infer a conspiracy from circumstantial evidence); PHILLIP AREEDA & HERBERT HOVENKAMP, ANTITRUST LAW P 1434a (2d ed. 2002).

393. To say that plus factors "tend to exclude the possibility that the defendants acted independently" merely restates the issue. *Petruzzi's IGA Supermarkets, Inc. v. Darling-Delaware Co.*, 998 F.2d 1224, 1232-33 (3d Cir. 1993). Similarly unhelpful is the explanation that "[t]he simple term 'plus factors' refers to 'the additional facts or factors required to be proved as a prerequisite to finding that parallel action amounts to conspiracy.'" *Baby Food*, 166 F.3d at 122 (quoting AREEDA, ANTITRUST LAW §1433(e) (1986)).

394. *City of Tuscaloosa v. Harcros Chems., Inc.*, 158 F.3d 548, 572 (11th Cir. 1998); *see also Laurel Sand & Gravel, Inc. v. CSX Transp., Inc.*, 924 F.2d 539, 543 (4th Cir. 1991) (holding that to avoid summary judgment, plaintiffs must show that defendants "had a conscious commitment to a common scheme designed to achieve an unlawful objective" and offer "evidence that

excludes the possibility that the alleged coconspirators acted independently or based upon a legitimate business purpose" (internal quotation marks and citations omitted)).

395. *Baby Food*, 166 F.3d at 122; *see also Flat Glass*, 385 F.3d at 360 (using the same test); *Petruzzi's IGA*, 998 F.2d at 1242 (same); *Wallace v. Bank of Bartlett*, 55 F.3d 1166, 1168 ("Examples ofthese 'plus factors' include actions contrary to a defendant's economic self-interest, product uniformity, exchange of price information and opportunity to meet, and a common motive to conspire or a large number of communications." (citations omitted)).

396. *See, e.g., Baby Food*, 166 F.3d at 122; *Coleman v. Cannon Oil Co.*, 849 F. Supp. 1458, 1467 (N.D. Ala. 1993).

397. *Flat Glass,* 385 F.3d at 360 ("[Plus] factors serve as proxies for direct evidence of an agreement.").

398. *See* Bauer & Page, *supra* note 287, at 66-67 ("[E]quipoise is not enough to take the case to the jury.").

399. *See Williamson Oil Co. v. Philip Morris USA,* 346 F.3d 1287, 1301 (11th Cir. 2003).

400. *See id.* at 1310.

401. *See id.* at 1317-18; *see also E.I. Du Pont de Nemours & Co. v. FTC*, 729 F.2d 128, 139 (2d Cir. 1984) (holding that the "mere existence of an oligopolistic market structure in which a small group of manufacturers engage in consciously parallel pricing of an identical product" is lawful because it is merely "a condition, not a 'method;' indeed it could be consistent with intense competition").

402. *See* Robert H. Porter & J. Douglas Zona, *Bidding, Bid Rigging, and School Milk Prices: Ohio v. Trauth* (1994), in THE ANTITRUST REVOLUTION, *supra* note 1, at 211, 216-17 (listing eleven "factors facilitating collusion" in Ohio milk markets identified by economists retained by the state).

403. For an illustration of the relationship among these devices, *see Hall v. United Air Lines, Inc.*, 296 F. Supp. 2d 652 (E.D.N.C. 2003). The court granted summary judgment on the ground that plaintiffs' evidence of plus factors, particularly various forms of "signaling," in an alleged conspiracy by airlines to depress ticket agent commission rates, did not exclude the pos-

sibility of independent action. The court rejected a set of asserted "structural plus factors" as "unfounded under antitrust law." *Id.* at 674. These included concentration on the airlines' side of the market, fragmentation on the ticket agencies' side, entry barriers, "an upward sloping supply curve," and a fungible service. *Id.* The court held that mere participation in an oligopoly is not unlawful, and that price uniformity was to be expected for homogeneous products. *Id.* It denied as moot the defendant's motions to exclude the reports and testimony of the plaintiffs' experts. *Id.* at 681.

404. *See City of Tuscaloosa v. Harcros Chems., Inc.,* 158 F.3d 548, 566 (11th Cir. 1998).

405. *Id.* at 567.

406. *Id.* The court did allow the analysis of Florida data to be used for corroborative purposes. *Id.* at 566-67.

407. *See Holiday Wholesale Grocery Co. v. Philip Morris, Inc.*, 231 F. Supp. 2d 1253, 1274-75 (N.D. Ga. 2002), *aff'd sub nom. Williamson Oil Co. v. Philip Morris USA,* 346 F.3d 1287 (11th Cir. 2003).

408. As one court explained, a plaintiff relying on circumstantial economic evidence to prove an agreement must "present economic evidence that would show that the hypothesis of collusive action was more plausible than that of individual action." In re Brand Name Prescription Drugs Antitrust Litig., 186 F.3d 781, 787 (7th Cir. 1999) (citations omitted). The court pointed out that the plaintiffs did not, "as the defendant manufacturers rather absurdly argue, have to exclude all possibility" that the defendants' parallel conduct "was unilateral rather than collusive." *Id.* And the plaintiffs were "equally wide of the mark... when they argue[d] that proof" of parallel conduct that is equally consistent with individual and collusive behavior "shifts to the defendants the burden of proving that the [conduct] was unilateral rather than collusive." *Id.*

409. *Williamson Oil,* 346 F.3d at 1322-23.

410. *See* Robert A. Milne & Jack E. *Pace III, Conspiratologists at the Gate: The Scope of Expert Testimony on the Subject of Conspiracy in a Sherman Act Case*, ANTITRUST, Spring 2003, at 36, 39-40 (summarizing cases disallowing expert testimony on the existence of a "conspiracy" under Section 1 of the Sherman Act).

411. *See* George J. Stigler, *What Does an Economist Know?*, 33 J. LEGAL EDUC. 311, 312 (1983) ("There is no established economic content to words such

as 'collusion', 'conspiracy', or 'concerted action'."); *see* also Jonathan B. Baker, *Two Sherman Act Section 1 Dilemmas: Parallel Pricing, the Oligopoly Problem, and Contemporary Economic Theory*, 38 ANTITRUST BULL. 143 (1993) (discussing the difficulties of and the strategies for proving collusive behavior from circumstantial evidence of collusion conducive business environments); Malcolm B. Coate & Jeffrey H. Fischer, *Can Post-Chicago Economics Survive Daubert?*, 34 AKRON L. REV. 795, 828 n.131 (2001) (While performance evidence can show an anticompetitive effect, neither a Chicago nor a PCE [Post-Chicago Economics] economist should expect to survive a *Daubert* hearing in an oligopolistic industry because the poor performance may be caused by unilateral pricing behavior, and not by a price-fixing agreement. The problem is particularly acute for the PCE economist as the formal model of unilateral oligopoly pricing may match the cartel outcome.).

412. *See* Milne & Pace, *supra* note 410, at 42 (concluding that expert testimony should be limited to "such relatively objective factors as whether there is an economic motive to conspire, whether the market structure is conducive to collusion, whether defendants' conduct is consistent with their non-interdependent business interests and the like"). Some commentators have suggested that experts should be permitted to testify that the defendant's conduct is collusive in economic terms, leaving the ultimate issue of the legality of the conduct to the jury. *See, e.g.,* Hovenkamp, *supra* note 1, at 141 (stating that an expert should be permitted to testify that "a fact inference of agreement is warranted" by the economic evidence); Robert F. Lanzillotti & James T. McClave, *Comment: Meeting the "Ambiguity" Test Under Daubert*, ANTITRUST, Spring 2003, at 44, 45 (stating that an expert should be permitted to testify to the Bayesian "likelihood ratio" of collusion because they can tell "whether the evidence was more likely to have been generated in a collusive than in a non-collusive market"); Stigler, *supra* note 411, at 311-12. These scholars are all quoted and criticized in Milne & Pace, *supra* note 410, at 37-39. All of these assertions assume that an economist's definition of the "fact" of a "cartel," an "agreement," or "collusion" has a well-understood relationship to the legal definition of a Sherman Act agreement and, thus, that hearing the economist's opinion on the issue would assist the jury. But the jury's almost-certain assumption would be that the two definitions are the same. For this reason, the court in *Williamson Oil Co. v. Philip Morris USA*, 346 F.3d 1287 (11th Cir. 2003), discussed infra, held that this sort of testimony is irrelevant. But cf. In re Brand Name Prescription Drugs Antitrust Litig., No. 94 C 897, MDL 997, 1999 WL 33889 (N.D. Ill. Jan. 19, 1999), *aff'd* in part, *vacated* in part, 186 F.3d 781 (7th Cir. 1999). The trial court, having "instructed the jury that there is...a qualitative difference between the word 'collusion' as he has used it in the conspiracy charge in this

case and what the jury has to find" allowed the expert to testify to collusion so long as his opinion did not "equat[e] collusion in an economic sense and conspiracy in a legal sense." Milne & Pace, *supra* note 410, at 41. Milne and Pace observe that "it is difficult to see how the testimony that was allowed did not convey to the jury that [the expert] believed an explicit conspiracy existed." *Id.*

413. But *cf. Cleveland v. Viacom, Inc.*, 73 FED. APPX. 736 (5th Cir. 2003) (affirming the exclusion of conclusory testimony of plaintiffs' expert that the defendant movie studios' parallel refusals to deal with the plaintiffs on the same terms as with the plaintiffs' dominant rival was contrary to the studios' self interest).

414. 158 F.3d 548, 564 (11th Cir. 1998).

415. *See id.* at 564-65.

416. AREEDA & HOVENKAMP, *supra* note 392, P 322.1 (citing *City of Tuscaloosa v. Harcros Chem., Inc.*, 877 F. Supp. 1504 (N.D. Ala. 1995), *rev'd,* 158 F.3d 548 (11th Cir. 1998)).

417. *City of Tuscaloosa*, 158 F.3d at 564.

418. *Id.* at 565 (citations omitted).

419. *Id.* at 570-73. The necessary plus factor was evidence of incumbency rates that measured the percentage of times the incumbent bidder won subsequent bids on the same account. *Id.* at 572-73. This was evidence that defendants had agreed not to compete on each other's existing accounts. *Id.*

420. *Id.* at 565; *see also Ohio ex rel. Montgomery v. Louis Trauth Dairy, Inc.*, 925 F. Supp. 1247, 1254 (S.D. Ohio 1996) ("[E]xperts may not express an opinion in the form of a legal conclusion regarding the existence of an illegal conspiracy."). But cf. *Petruzzi's IGA Supermarkets, Inc. v. Darling-Delaware Co.*, 998 F.2d 1224, 1240-41 (3d Cir. 1993) (holding that the trial court erred in excluding at the pretrial stage expert testimony that the defendants' conduct was collusive).

421. *Holiday Wholesale Grocery Co. v. Philip Morris Co.*, 231 F. Supp. 2d 1253, 1321 (N.D. Ga. 2002), *aff'd* sub nom. *Williamson Oil Co. v. Philip Morris USA,* 346 F.3d 1287 (11th Cir. 2003).

422. *Id.* at 1274.

423. *Id.* at 1263.

424. *Id.* at 1274-75. Significantly, the court correctly implied that facilitating practices can constitute plus factors; it said simply that they do not necessarily do so. *Id.* Thus, the court observed that "'facilitating devices' are not necessarily sufficient under the law to constitute a 'plus factor.'" *Id.* In *Todd v. Exxon Corp.*, 275 F.3d 191 (2d Cir. 2001), the court *see*med to imply that facilitating practices always constitute plus factors: "[A] horizontal price-fixing agreement may be inferred on the basis of conscious parallelism, when such interdependent conduct is accompanied by circumstantial evidence and plus factors such as defendants' use of facilitating practices." *Id.* at 198 (alteration in original). The suggestion that any facilitating practice is a plus factor was likely inadvertent.

425. *Holiday Wholesale*, 231 F. Supp. 2d at 1274-1310.

426. *Id.* at 1274-1314 (noting that expert's testimony focused on "how certain practices in the cigarette industry would have facilitated an agreement...[, but did] not tend to exclude the possibility that defendants were engaged in lawful competitive conduct").

427. *Id.* at 1322.

428. *Id.* at 1321.

429. *Id.*

430. *Id.* at 1322.

431. *Id.*

432. *Williamson Oil Co. v. Philip Morris USA*, 346 F.3d 1287, 1323 (11th Cir. 2003).

433. 15 U.S.C. § 15 (2000).

434. *See* Roger D. Blair & William H. Page, *"Speculative" Antitrust Damages*, 70 WASH. L. REV. 423, 428-35 (1995).

435. *See* generally William H. Page, *The Scope of Liability for Antitrust Violations*, 37 STAN. L. REV. 1445 (1985) (discussing the relationship between standing and antitrust injury in determining optimal deterrence).

436. *Atl. Richfield Co. v. USA Petroleum Co.,* 495 U.S. 328, 334 (1990).

437. *See generally* Roger D. Blair & William H. Page, *The Role of Economics in the Definition of Antitrust Injury*, 17 MANAGERIAL AND DECISION ECON. 127 (1996) (discussing the economic analysis used by courts in determining standing and antitrust injury).

438. *Brunswick Corp. v. Pueblo Bowl-O-Mat,* 523 U.S. 477, 488-89 (1977).

439. *See generally* John E. Lopatka & William H. Page, *Brunswick* at 25: *Antitrust Injury and the Evolution of Antitrust Law*, ANTITRUST, Fall 2002, at 20 (discussing the Brunswick case and the effect that that case had on substantive antitrust law).

440. *See Brunswick*, 449 U.S. at 486-88.

441. *NBO Indus. Treadway Cos. v. Brunswick Corp.*, 523 F.2d 262, 276 (3d Cir. 1975), *vacated* sub nom. *Brunswick Corp. v. Pueblo Bowl-O-Mat, Inc.,* 449 U.S. 477 (1977).

442. *Brunswick*, 449 U.S. at 489.

443. *Id.* at 488 (holding that it "is inimical to the purposes of these laws to award damages" measured by the "profits [plaintiffs] would have realized had competition been reduced").

444. There are limits to this principle, which are illustrated by *State Oil v. Khan. See* 522 U.S. 3 (1997). Under a strictly economic interpretation, a dealer who suffers lost profits as a result of vertical maximum price fixing does not suffer antitrust injury because the practice itself creates no inefficiency. *See* Page, *supra* note 435, at 1469-70; Blair & Lopatka, *supra* note 153, at 139-46. Under such an interpretation, any expert testimony showing that the dealer had suffered lost profits would be irrelevant. In the court of appeals decision in Khan, however, Judge Posner rejected this conclusion, reasoning that the interpretation voided Albrecht's per se rule: someone must be able to suffer antitrust injury from a per se illegal practice for the rule to have "some domain of application." *Khan v. State Oil Co.,* 93 F.3d 1358, 1364 (7th Cir. 1996), *vacated* on other grounds, 522 U.S. 3 (1997). The rule could only be based on a non-economic rationale, such as protecting trader freedom. Even if there is no inefficiency from vertical maximum price fixing, Judge Posner wrote, the Supreme Court "may also think that interfering with the freedom of a dealer to raise prices may cause antitrust injury." *Id.* Thus, it was possible that "the injury to a dealer like Khan from not being able to

raise his price because of a restriction imposed by his supplier is antitrust injury." *Id.* The expert's report was sufficiently probative to show injury in fact under such a measure. *Id.* at 1366. The Supreme Court reversed, overruling Albrecht's per se rule. *Khan*, 522 U.S. at 22. Thus, the antitrust injury inquiry forced the Court to confront directly the economic absurdity of Albrecht, and this led directly to the demise of the per se rule. *See* Lopatka & Page, *supra* note 439, at 23.

445. *Pool Water Prods. v. Olin Corp.,* 258 F.3d 1024, 1036 (9th Cir. 2001) (holding that where the plaintiff failed to allege pricing below the appropriate measure of cost, its "reduced profits attributable to defendants' decrease in prices [was] not an antitrust injury").

446. *See* Page, *supra* note 435, at 1483-98. Antitrust standing, of course, is distinct from standing in the constitutional sense, "which requires only injury in fact plus redressability." *U.S. Gypsum Co. v. Ind. Gas Co.,* 350 F.3d 623, 627 (7th Cir. 2003).

447. *Ill. Brick Co. v. Illinois,* 431 U.S. 720 (1977).

448. *Hanover Shoe, Inc. v. United Shoe Mach. Corp.,* 392 U.S. 481, 89-94 (1968).

449. *Ill. Brick*, 431 U.S. at 744.

450. *Id.* at 742.

451. *Id.* In using this phrase, the Court echoed its observation in *Hanover Shoe*, 392 U.S. at 493, that it is "difficult to determine, in the real economic world rather than an economist's hypothetical model...what effect a change in a company's price will have on its total sales." *Id.* at 726 n.3.

452. *Ill. Brick*, 431 U.S. at 743 (citation omitted).

453. *See* generally John E. Lopatka & William H. Page, *Indirect Purchaser Suits and the Consumer Interest*, 48 ANTITRUST BULL. 531 (2003) (summarizing the Illinois Brick rule and discussing the failure of state indirect purchaser suits to properly redress harm to consumers).

454. *See Drug Mart Pharmacy Corp. v. Am. Home Prods. Corp.,* NO. 93-CV-5148 (ILG), 2002 WL 31528625, at *10 (E.D.N.Y. Aug 21, 2002) (excluding evidence of lost profits damages on the ground that they were barred by Illinois Brick).

455. Blair & Page, *supra* note 434, 436-38; *see* 2 PHILLIP E. AREEDA ET AL., ANTITRUST LAW PP 390-97 (2d ed. 2000).

456. Blair & Page, *supra* note 434, at 438 (arguing that "the plaintiff must rely on a theoretical model of the illegal practice" and that "[t]he model's assumptions and causal implications will provide the basis for both the measure of damages and the projection of the plaintiff's but-for experience").

457. *See U.S. Tobacco Co. v. Conwood Co.,* 537 U.S. 1148 (2003) (denying certiorari); Brief of Washington Legal Foundation, Stephen E. Fienberg, Franklin M. Fisher, Daniel L. McFadden, and Daniel L. Rubinfeld as Amici Curiae in Support of Petitioners at 10, U.S. Tabacco (No. 02-603) ("An appropriate economic analysis of damages would identify the wrongful acts and devise a scientific test to measure their impact as opposed to those of lawful competitive actions."); D.H. Kaye, *Adversarial Econometrics in United States Tobacco Co. v. Conwood Co.*, 43 JURIMETRICS J. 343, 347 (2003) ("If one could quantify the effects of all the possibly confounding variables, then one could ascertain whether there is any 'left over' effect that should be attributed to the illegal conduct.").

458. *See, e.g.,* In re Brand Name Prescription Drugs Antitrust Litig., 186 F.3d 781, 786 (7th Cir. 1999) (noting that "to obtain damages the plaintiffs would have to separate the price effects of collusion from the price effects of the defendants' lawful market power"); *Image Technical Servs., Inc. v. Eastman Kodak Co.,* 125 F.3d 1195, 1224 (9th Cir. 1997) (holding that the plaintiffs were required to "segregate damages attributable to lawful competition from damages attributable to [defendant's] monopolizing conduct").

459. *See, e.g., Concord Boat Corp. v. Brunswick Corp.,* 207 F.3d 1039, 1055 (8th Cir. 2000), *rev'g* 21 F. Supp. 2d 923 (W.D. Ark. 2000). The expert in Concord Boat relied on a Cournot model of oligopoly, which predicts that in a two-firm market, equally efficient firms producing identical products would have equal market shares. *Concord Boat*, 21 F. Supp. 2d at 926. Based on this model, the expert testified that Brunswick's seventy percent market share must be attributable to exclusionary conduct. *Id.* The district court accepted the testimony because the Cournot model "is an appropriate method for predicting equilibrium price formation in oligopolistic markets." *Id.* at 934. But, as Herbert Hovenkamp has noted, the Cournot model was inapplicable to a market with differentiated products, in which the principal rival had been forced to recall all of its engines. *See* Hovenkamp, *supra* note 1, at 126-29; *see also Heary Bros. Lightning Prot. Co. v. Lightning Prot. Inst.,* 287 F. Supp. 2d 1038, 1066-68 (D. Ariz. 2003) (excluding expert testimony basing damages on Cournot duopoly model, where the expert's assumptions

contradicted the Cournot model's implications concerning the relationship of a firm's marginal cost to its market share).

460. *See, e.g., Am. Booksellers Ass'n v. Barnes & Noble, Inc.*, 135 F. Supp. 2d 1031, 1041 (N.D. Cal. 2001) ("The Fisher model contains entirely too many assumptions and simplifications that are not supported by real-world evidence.").

461. *ID Sec. Sys. Can., Inc. v. Checkpoint Sys., Inc.*, 249 F. Supp. 2d 622, 696 (E.D. Pa. 2003) (Given Dr. Kursh's reliance on [plaintiff's] projections against the background of only generalized research into the EAS systems market..., the court concludes that Dr. Kursh's testimony as to future lost Laserfuse profits should not have been admitted at the *Daubert* stage of these proceedings, nor should it have been placed before the jury at trial, even if the arithmetic model used accurately predicts future lost profits in the typical case.).

462. *Heary Bros.*, 287 F. Supp. 2d at 1065-66 (excluding expert testimony on damages based on the assumption that there were only two sellers of lightning protection equipment before the alleged offense, where the evidence showed that there were other rivals).

463. *Ohio v. Louis Trauth Dairy, Inc.*, 925 F. Supp. 1247, 1253 (S.D. Ohio 1996).

464. In *Petruzzi's IGA Supermarkets, Inc. v. Darling-Delaware Co.*, 998 F.2d 1224, 1241 (3d Cir. 1993), plaintiff's data sample contained only one year of information concerning a particular defendant. The court wrote:

While this data problem is not enough to exclude the price study generally, it does serve to limit the inferences that can be drawn from it as it relates to [the defendant]. Therefore, because this is the only evidence implicating [the defendant], this evidence standing alone is not sufficient to defeat summary judgment. *Id.*

465. In re Aluminum Phosphide Antitrust Litig., 893 F. Supp. 1497, 1504 (D. Kan. 1995). In *Aluminum Phosphide*, the plaintiffs' expert selected the ten-month period after the alleged conspiracy had ended as the normative period, ignoring data from the period before the alleged conspiracy, when prices were higher. *Id.* at 1501-02. The court concluded that the expert's "analysis is driven by a desire to enhance the measure of plaintiffs' damages, even at the expense of well-accepted scientific principles and methodology." *Id.* at 1506-07.

466. *Id.* at 1503 (holding expert should have performed a regression analysis on pricing patterns in the proposed normative period, using a dummy variable for the effect of the conspiracy in order to assure that the conspiracy was not still affecting the market during that time); *see also Blue Dane Simmental Corp. v. Am. Simmental Ass'n,* 178 F.3d 1035, 1040-41(8th Cir. 1999) (affirming the district court's exclusion of expert because expert had not identified and examined independent variables as other economists would have and finding that "before and after" tests are "not typically used to make statements regarding causation without considering all independent variables that could affect the conclusion"); *Sanner v. Bd. of Trade of Chicago*, No. 89 C 8467, 2001 WL 1155277, at *7 (N.D. Ill. Sept. 28, 2001) (excluding expert testimony because expert failed to conduct tests to substantiate his opinion and failed to gather scientific evidence according to accepted methods); In re Brand Name Prescription Drugs Antitrust Litig., No. 94 C 897, MDL 997, 1999 WL 33889, at *12 (N.D. Ill. Jan. 19, 1999) (excluding expert for failure to conduct study of demand elasticities), *rev'd* on other grounds, 186 F.3d 781 (7th Cir. 1999); *Law v. NCAA*, No. 94-2053-KHV, 1998 U.S. Dist. LEXIS 6640, at *12-35 (D. Kan. Apr. 23, 1998) (admitting expert over challenges for failure to perform regression analysis and other standard methodology).

467. *See* ABA SECTION OF ANTITRUST LAW, PROVING ANTITRUST DAMAGES: LEGAL AND ECONOMIC ISSUES 145 (William H. Page ed., 1996) [hereinafter Proving Antitrust Damages].

468. *Id.* at 149.

469. *Aluminum Phosphide*, 893 F. Supp. at 1503-04.

470. *See* Kaye, *supra* note 457, at 346 (noting that to say a study employed regression analysis "is a bit like saying that it used arithmetic or algebra").

471. *See* Posner, *supra* note 6, at 94-95 (arguing that courts should not necessarily adopt statisticians' standards of statistical significance).

472. *See Conwood Co. v. U.S. Tobacco Co.,* 290 F.3d 768, 794 (6th Cir. 2002). For criticism of Conwood's analysis of regressions, *see* Kaye, *supra* note 457, at 350 and D.H. Kaye, *The Dynamics of Daubert: Methodology, Conclusions, and Fit in Statistical and Econometric Studies*, 87 VA. L. REV. 1933, 1988-2010 (2001) (discussing the expert testimony in Conwood). For other cases on the issue, *see Concord Boat Corp. v. Brunswick Corp.*, 207 F.3d 1039, 1056-58 (8th Cir. 2000); *Blomkest Fertilizer, Inc. v. Potash Corp. of Sask.,* 203 F.3d 1028, 1038 (8th Cir. 2000), *cert. denied*, 531 U.S. 815

(2000); *Blue Dane Simmental Corp. v. Am. Simmental Ass'n,* 178 F.3d 1035, 1040-41 (8th Cir. 1999); In re Polypropylene Carpet Antitrust Litig., 93 F. Supp. 2d 1348, 1358 (N.D. Ga. 2000); In re Indus. Silicon Antitrust Litig., No. 95-2104, 1998 WL 1031507, at *3 (W.D. Pa. Oct. 13, 1998); *Law v. NCAA*, No. 94-2053-KHV, 1998 U.S. Dist. LEXIS 6640, at *26 (D. Kan. Apr. 23, 1998); In re Aluminum Phosphide Antitrust Litig., 893 F. Supp. 1497, 1504 (D. Kan. 1995).

473. DANIEL L. RUBINFELD, REFERENCE GUIDE ON MULTIPLE REGRESSION, in REFERENCE MANUAL ON SCIENTIFIC EVIDENCE 181 (2d ed. 2000); PROVING ANTITRUST DAMAGES, *supra* note 467, at 146; *see also* Kaye, *supra* note 457, at 347 ("Deciding which variables might affect sales and how they could be related requires substantive economic theory.").

474. *See* Kevin A. Kordana & Terrance O'Reilly, *Daubert and Litigation-Driven Econometrics*, 87 VA L. REV. 2019, 2022 (2001) (suggesting that it may be "unnecessary to worry about finding the right statistical technique to test [the Conwood expert's] theory, since the underlying model itself does not seem to be drawn from an established theory of market behavior").

475. PROVING ANTITRUST DAMAGES, *supra* note 467, at 162-63; Daniel L. Rubinfeld, *Econometrics in the Courtroom*, 85 COLUM. L. REV. 1048, 1072 (1985); Daniel L. Rubinfeld & Peter O. Steiner, *Quantitative Methods in Antitrust Litigation*, 46 LAW & CONTEMP. PROBS., Autumn 1983, at 69, 90.

476. *See* Rubinfeld & Steiner, *supra* note 475, at 90-91. The R2 figure provides a measurement of the explanatory power of the model. If important variables are omitted, their effect falls into the error term, and the R2 is lower. Rubinfeld, *supra* note 473, at 215.

477. Franklin M. Fisher, *Multiple Regression in Legal Proceedings*, 80 COLUM. L. REV. 702, 715 (1980).

478. *See, e.g.,* In re High Fructose Corn Syrup Antitrust Litig., 295 F.3d 651, 660 (7th Cir. 2002) (discussing the problem of multicollinearity).

479. *See Conwood Co. v. U.S. Tobacco Co.,* 290 F.3d 768, 793 (6th Cir. 2002) (finding that expert ruled out other factors); *Concord Boat Corp. v. Brunswick Corp.,* 207 F.3d 1039, 1047, 1056-57 (8th Cir. 2000) (concluding that Cournot model using only market share as variable failed to account for other events in the market affecting price and should have been excluded); *Blomkest Fertilizer, Inc. v. Potash Corp. of Sask.,* 203 F.3d 1028, 1038 (8th Cir. 2000) (finding expert's econometric model unreliable—although not

striking it under *Daubert*—for failure to consider events that would have increased prices absent a conspiracy); *Callahan v. A.E.V., Inc.*, 182 F.3d 237, 254-60 (3d Cir. 1999) (finding expert's "but for" model sufficient to create factual question despite alleged failure to consider other variables); *Blue Dane Simmental Corp. v. Am. Simmental Ass'n,* 178 F.3d 1035, 1040-41 (8th Cir. 1999) (finding expert's "before and after" model was unreliable because it failed to take into account other independent variables); *Rossi v. Standard Roofing, Inc.*, 156 F.3d 452, 483-87 (3d Cir. 1998) (same); In re Indus. Silicon Antitrust Litig., No. 95-2104, 1998 WL 1031507, at *3 (W.D. Pa. Oct. 13, 1998) (observing that defendants cannot simply point to excluded variables but must support contention that the variables should have been included); *Law v. NCAA*, No. 94-2053-KHV, 1998 U.S. Dist. LEXIS 6640, at *13-16 (D. Kan. Apr. 23, 1998) (refusing to exclude, on a motion in limine, statistical estimates of the amount of damages from an NCAA salary cap); In re Aluminum Phosphide Antitrust Litig., 893 F. Supp. 1497, 1503-05 (D. Kan. 1995) (finding expert's "before and after" model unreliable for failure to account for several factors); *Colorado v. Goodell Bros.*, Civ. A. No. 84-A-803, 1987 WL 6771, at *4 (D. Colo. Feb. 17, 1987) (concluding that expert's failure to take into account an engineer's estimate of construction project cost indicated that expert's method was unreliable).

480. 478 U.S. 385 (1986).

481. *Id.* at 399-400 (quoting Court of Appeals).

482. *Id.* at 400 (internal quotation marks and citations omitted); *see* also *Conwood,* 290 F.3d at 794 (relying on Bazemore to uphold regression evidence).

483. *See, e.g., Sanner v. Bd. of Trade of Chicago,* No. 89 C 8467, 2001 WL 1155277, at *5 (N.D. Ill. Sept. 28, 2001) (holding that objection to "power" of model is better left for jury to decide); *Law v. NCAA*, No. 94-2053-KHV, 1998 U.S. Dist. LEXIS 6640, at *29 (D. Kan. Apr. 23, 1998) (holding that expert's treatment of "other factors" had a logical basis and "any weakness in the underpinnings of his analysis go to the weight and not the admissibility of his testimony").

484. *Bazemore*, 478 U.S. at 400 n.10; *see* also Kaye, *supra* note 457, at 347 ("*Daubert* requires the expert to take reasonable steps to eliminate [confounding unmeasured variables] and thus confine the estimated damages to the result of the allegedly illegal conduct.").

485. *See, e.g.,* In re Polypropylene Carpet Antitrust Litig., 93 F. Supp. 2d 1348, 1365 (N.D. Ga. 2000) (observing that "defendants do not offer a statisti-

cal analysis of demand and price of polypropylene carpet to explain why exclusion of a variable for demand establishes the unreliability of [the expert's] model"); *In re Indus. Silicon Antitrust Litig.*, No. 95-2104, 1998 WL 1031507, at *3 (W.D. Pa. Oct. 13, 1998) ("[A] party cannot successfully challenge the admissibility of a regression analysis by simply pointing to a laundry list of possible independent variables that were not included in the study."); In re Domestic Air Transp. Antitrust Litig., 137 F.R.D. 677, 690 (N.D. Ga. 1991) (class certification stage) (holding that "it is incumbent upon defendants to substantiate" challenges to statistical models).

486. *See Polypropylene Carpet*, 93 F. Supp. 2d at 1366 (accepting expert's justification for omitting a demand variable because of lack of data and risk of extrapolation error); *Law v. NCAA*, No. 94-2053-KHV, 1998 U.S. Dist. LEXIS 6640, at *29 (D. Kan. Apr. 23, 1998) (finding that expert's treatment of "other factors" had a logical basis and "any weakness in the underpinnings of his analysis go to the weight and not the admissibility of his testimony").

487. *See* In re Polypropylene Carpet Antitrust Litig., No. 1075, 2000 WL 863456, at *3 n.1 (N.D. Ga. Apr. 27, 2000) (noting that the expert's model had an R2 between eighty-six and ninety-six percent and, thus, including a variable for demand would not have increased the model's predictive power).

488. *Polypropylene Carpet*, 93 F. Supp. 2d at 1366.

489. *Id.* at 1359.

490. *Id.* at 1360.

491. *Id.*

492. *Id.*

493. *Id.* at 1360-63.

494. *Id.* at 1364-66.

495. *Id.* at 1361.

496. *Id.*

497. The court provided the somewhat less useful example of "a model that attempts to predict the growth rate in the height of a seventy-year old person

by looking at data from when the person was thirteen years old." *Id.* at 1361 n.10.

498. *Id.* at 1361. Simultaneity occurs when the dependent and independent variables affect each other. *See* RUBINFELD, *supra* note 473, at 195 n.44. If simultaneity exists, then spurious correlation may result. *Id.* at 195. Rubinfeld warns that simultaneity may result in price-fixing cases because if price-fixing occurred, the defendant may have affected the values of the independent variables and biased the results. *Id.* at 195 n.45.

499. *Polypropylene Carpet*, 93 F. Supp. 2d at 1361.

500. The Chow test is a "test of the equality of two independent sets of regression coefficients under the assumption of normally distributed errors." B.S. Everitt, THE CAMBRIDGE DICTIONARY OF STATISTICS 61 (2002).

501. *Polypropylene Carpet*, 93 F. Supp. 2d at 1361.

502. *Id.*

503. Defendants also argued that the expert's failure to include an independent variable for demand in his model rendered the model unreliable by failing to account for the effects of changes in the popularity of carpet and substitute products. *Id.* at 1364-65. The expert again cited a lack of data and the risk of extrapolation error as justifications for his choice, and added that when he had tested the relationship between price and the available measures of demand he had found that the results were contrary to the basic economic theory that increases in demand result in increases in price. *Id.* at 1365. The court accepted the expert's justifications, noting that excluding the demand variable was actually beneficial to defendants since the available data suggested that demand was increasing. *Id.*

504. *See* Coate & Fischer, *supra* note 411; Bruce H. Kobayashi, *Game Theory and Antitrust: A Post-Mortem*, 5 GEO. MASON L. REV. 411, 413 n.18 (1997).

505. *See Daubert v. Merrell Dow Pharms., Inc.*, 509 U.S. 579, 596 (1993) ("Vigorous cross-examination, presentation of contradictory evidence, and careful instruction on the burden of proof are the traditional means of attacking shaky but admissible evidence.").

506. *See* Monohan & Walker, *supra* note 5, at 499-500.

507. Kenneth Culp Davis argued:

> [J]udge-made law would stop growing if judges, in thinking about questions of law and policy, were forbidden to take into account the facts they believe, as distinguished from facts which are "clearly...within the domain of the indisputable." Facts most needed in thinking about difficult problems of law and policy have a way of being outside the domain of the clearly indisputable.

Kenneth Culp Davis, *A System of Judicial Notice Based on Fairness and Convenience*, in PERSPECTIVES OF LAW 82 (1964).

508. *See* Page, *supra* note 9, at 1302-03. *See generally* Andrew N. Kleit, *Common Law, Statute Law, and the Theory of Legislative Choice: An Inquiry Into the Goal of the Sherman Act*, 31 ECON. INQUIRY 647 (1993) (arguing that the Sherman Act and the common law have similar goals of maximizing efficiency).

509. Herbert Hovenkamp has argued that, until the ascendancy of the Chicago School, courts routinely relied on economics, but without citing authority. *See* Hovenkamp, Reckoning, *supra* note 8, at 2-3.

510. *Cal. Dental Ass'n v. FTC*, 526 U.S. 756, 780 (1999) (citing PHILLIP AREEDA, ANTITRUST LAW P 1500, at 364 (1986)).

511. One federal appellate judge, although recognizing that the Chicago School's "economic assumptions are being integrated throughout the courts," has expressed the view that "rather than abdicating the decision of what the antitrust goals should be, Congress...should determine the goals of the antitrust laws and set forth the rules and standards by which the goals shall be obtained." Carol Los Mansmann, *Impact of GTE Sylvania on Third Circuit Jurisprudence*, 60 ANTITRUST L.J. 83, 92 (1991). Congress, however, has shown no inclination to do so.

512. *See, e.g.*, Theodore Eisenberg, *Damage Awards in Perspective: Behind the Headline-Grabbing Awards in Exxon Valdez and Engle*, 36 WAKE FOREST L. REV. 1129, 1147-48 (2001) (summarizing and criticizing studies Exxon funded to support its legal opposition to punitive damage awards in the litigation growing out of the Exxon Valdez oil spill); Richard Lempert, *Juries, Hindsight, and Punitive Damage Awards: Failures of a Social Science Case for Change*, 48 DEPAUL L. REV. 867 (1999) (discussing an Exxon-funded article by W. Kip Viscusi and Reid Hastie on jury bias); Richard Lippitt, Note, *Intellectual Honesty, Industry and Interest Sponsored Professorial Works, and Full Disclosure: Is the Viewpoint Earning the Money, or Is the Money Earning the Viewpoint?*, 47 WAYNE L. REV. 1075 (2001) (proposing

greater disclosure for funded research); *see also United States v. Conn. Nat'l Bank,* 418 U.S. 656, 668-70 (1974) (arguing that Exxon-funded studies of punitive damages are legitimate, but should be scrutinized). In *United States v. Marine Bancorporation, Inc.*, 418 U.S. 602 (1974), the court rejected as without evidentiary support the government's theory that bank mergers would reduce competition by creating a statewide linkage of oligopolies. *Id.* at 622. The theory rested primarily on an article written by an economist associated with the Antitrust Division. *Id.*

513. WILLIAM LETWIN, LAW AND ECONOMIC POLICY IN AMERICA: THE EVOLUTION OF THE SHERMAN ANITRUST ACT 95 (1965).

514. *See, e.g., NCAA v. Bd. of Regents of Univ. of Okla.,* 468 U.S. 85, 100 n.21 (1984) ("[J]udicial inexperience with a particular arrangement counsels against extending the reach of per se rules."); *Arizona v. Maricopa County Med. Soc'y,* 457 U.S. 332, 344 (1982) (suggesting that per se illegality is appropriate "[o]nce experience with a particular kind of restraint enables the Court to predict with confidence that the rule of reason will condemn it"); *White Motor Co. v. United States*, 372 U.S. 253, 261 (1963) (refusing to hold vertical territorial restraints per se illegal because of a dearth of experience). Of course, the Court did not always follow this approach—as Schwinn illustrates. *See United States v. Arnold, Schwinn & Co.,* 388 U.S. 365 (1967) (establishing a per se rule against vertical, non-price restraints).

515. *See, e.g., State Oil Co. v. Khan*, 522 U.S. 3, 13-19 (1997) (reviewing decisions and scholarly criticisms that undermined the per se illegality of vertical maximum price fixing); *see also* Easterbrook, Information and Antitrust, *supra* note 138, at 16-17 (arguing that subsequent economic study of an antitrust case provides greater understanding of a practice); Lopatka & Page, *supra* note 439, at 20 (describing the role of the antitrust injury doctrine in focusing judicial attention on the inefficiencies of substantive rules).

516. Perhaps the most influential study is John S. McGee, *Predatory Price Cutting: The Standard Oil (N.J.) Case*, 1 J.L. & ECON. 137 (1958). Other such studies are F. Jay Cummings & Wayne E. Ruhter, *The Northern Pacific Case*, 22 J.L. & ECON. 329 (1979); Kenneth G. Elzinga & Thomas F. Hogarty, *Utah Pie and the Consequences of Robinson Patman*, 21 J.L. & ECON. 427 (1978); Elizabeth Granitz & Benjamin Klein, *Monopolization by "Raising Rivals's Costs": The Standard Oil Case*, 39 J.L. & ECON. 1 (1996); John E. Lopatka & Paul E. Godek, *Another Look at Alcoa: Raising Rivals' Costs Does Not Improve the View*, 35 J.L. & ECON. 311 (1992); Scott E. Masten & Edward Snyder, *United States versus United Shoe Machinery Corporation: On the Merits*, 36 J.L. & ECON. 33 (1993); John L. Peterman, *The Brown*

Shoe Case, 18 J.L. & ECON. 81 (1975); John L. Peterman, *The International Salt Case*, 22 J.L. & ECON. 351 (1979); David Reiffen & Andrew N. Kleit, *Terminal Railroad Revisited: Foreclosure of an Essential Facility or Simple Horizontal Monopoly?*, 33 J.L. & ECON. 419, 437 (1990).

517. *See* Howard Latin, *Legal and Economic Considerations in the Decisions of Judge Breyer*, 50 LAW & CONTEMP. PROBS. 57, 59-61 (1987). *See generally* ALBERT M. SACKS, JR. & HENRY M. HART, THE LEGAL PROCESS: BASIC PROBLEMS IN THE MAKING AND APPLICATION OF LAW 4 (William N. Eskridge, Jr. & Philip P. Frickey eds., Foundation Press 1994) (1958) (arguing that "every modern society differentiates among social questions, accepting one mode of decision for one kind and other modes for others").

518. *See Matsushita Elec. Indus. Co., Ltd. v. Zenith Radio Corp.*, 475 U.S. 574, 588 (1986) ("[A]ntitrust law limits the range of permissible inferences from ambiguous evidence in a § 1 case.").

519. *See, e.g.*, Timothy J. Brennan, *Do Easy Cases Make Bad Law? Antitrust Innovations or Missed Opportunities in United States v. Microsoft*, 69 GEO. WASH. L. REV. 1042 (2001); Franklin M. Fisher, *Games Economists Play: A Noncooperative View*, 20 RAND J. ECON. 113 (1989).

520. Frank H. Easterbrook, *Is There a Ratchet in Antitrust Law?*, 60 TEX. L. REV. 705 (1982).

521. As two authors explain, the PCE school of thought "generally focuses on the strategic behavior of firms. Instead of focusing on the basic competitive interactions of the market, these models show how firms can enhance or protect their market power by incorporating specific strategies—and the reactions of their rivals—into a complex equilibrium analysis." Coate & Fischer, *supra* note 411, at 812.

522. Fisher, *supra* note 519, at 117-23 (distinguishing generalizing and exemplifying theories); *see also* Keith N. Hylton & Michael Salinger, *Tying Law And Policy: A Decision-Theoretic Approach*, 69 ANTITRUST L.J. 469, 497 (2001) ("The post-Chicago models indicate that tying can be anticompetitive, not that it must be anticompetitive or that it is likely to be anticompetitive.").

523. *See Kobayashi*, *supra* note 504, at 412, 413 n.18.

524. *Daubert v. Merrell Dow Pharms., Inc.*, 509 U.S. 579, 590 (1993); *see Kobayashi*, *supra* note 504, at 413 n.18.

525. *Kobaayshi*, *supra* note 504, at 412.

526. *Id.*

527. *Id.* at 413 n.18.

528. Coate & Fischer, *supra* note 411, at 827-28.

529. *See id.*

530. *See* Hylton & Salinger, *supra* note 522, at 513 (concluding that "each of the four tied-market conditions...emphasized by the post-Chicago literature—entry barriers, complementary goods, network effects, and technologically advancing markets—would be insufficient to justify a per se prohibition even if coupled with the existing requirements for the per se rule").

531. *See FTC v. Staples, Inc.*, 970 F. Supp. 1066, 1082-83 (D.D.C. 1997).

532. *See* Posner, *supra* note 55, at 157-58 (arguing that "[e]conomic analysis of mergers [came] of age" in the FTC's use of statistical methods in Staples); Hovenkamp, Reckoning, *supra* note 8, at 19-21.

533. *See supra* notes 301-23 (discussing the *Kodak* case).

534. *See supra* note 314 and accompanying text.

535. *See generally* Hylton & Salinger, *supra* note 522 (summarizing the post-Chicago challenges).

536. *Id.* at 526 (noting that for the courts to incorporate post-Chicago insights into legal rules "the courts need to make a judgment about the relative frequencies of harmful tying under a lax legal standard on the one hand and the beneficial tying that will not occur under a stricter standard," all while recognizing "that tying is so pervasive even in competitive markets that there is ample evidence that procompetitive tying is a common occurrence").

537. *Kumho Tire Co. v. Carmichael,* 526 U.S. 137, 152 (1999).

538. *See* Coate & Fischer, *supra* note 411, at 824 n.110 ("While Kobayashi's scientific concerns are certainly reasonable, the Supreme Court's algorithm for evaluating scientific testimony may allow a court to admit PCE models as science."); *id.* at 827 ("While the PCE theorists certainly have problems with scientific verification of their theories, the *Daubert* standard itself is

probably flexible enough to accept the characterization of the model as science.").

539. FED. R. EVID. 401.

540. *See United States v. AMR Corp.,* 140 F. Supp. 2d 1141 (D. Kan. 2001) (observing that evidence showed that airlines used game theory in formulating entry strategies), *aff'd*, 335 F.3d 1109 (10th Cir. 2003).

541. *See Re/Max Int'l, Inc. v. Realty One, Inc.,* 173 F.3d 995, 1009-11 (6th Cir. 1999) (holding that an expert's "deposition and report establish a genuine issue of material fact whether unilateral imposition of adverse splits would have been economically rational for the defendants").

542. *See FTC v. Abbott Labs.*, 853 F. Supp. 526, 534-35 (D.D.C. 1994) (crediting testimony based on game theory that "it was in Abbott's unilateral and independent self interest to submit the 'no bid' for the sole source on the second round" of a government bid letting for purchase of infant formula).

543. FED. R. EVID. 403.

544. *Daubert v. Merrell Dow Pharms., Inc.*, 509 U.S. 579, 596 (1993).

545. *See id.*

Chapter 7

The Tension Between Jurisprudential Economics and Microeconomics

Kevin S. Marshall, J.D., M.P.A., Ph.D.

Synopsis

7.1 Introduction

[This chapter specifically illustrates the ongoing tension between what I have termed *jurisprudential economics* and the technical field of microeconomics. Jurisprudential economics simply refers to the judicial application of economic theory within an institutional environment driven by *stare decisis*. As Professors Loptka and Page observed in the previous chapter, it is the "economic authority, which appellate courts—especially the Supreme Court—adopt from the

 A version of this chapter was originally published under the title "Product Disparagement Under the Sherman Act, Its Nurturing and Injurious Effects to Competition, and the Tension Between Jurisprudential Economics and Microeconomics" and is herein reprinted by permission from 46 Santa Clara Law Review 231–254.

legal and economic literature, [that] dictates the role of the expert testimony in antitrust cases." (See Chapter 6, § 6.5, supra.) This chapter demonstrates this observed tension by addressing and analyzing market conduct involving the disparagement of a rival or its product.]

Such conduct may have one of two polar opposite effects on the competitive marketplace. To the extent that the disparagement is truthful and informative, it nurtures and fosters an environment within which competition may thrive. To the extent such disparagement is intentionally false and deceptive, it desecrates the hallowed efficiencies for which competition is so highly touted.

The purpose of this [chapter] is to illustrate and discuss these polar opposite effects from a purely microeconomic perspective.[1] To meet these ends, this [chapter] first cites and explains the United States Supreme Court's definition of "antitrust injury."[2] Next, this [chapter] explains and applies microeconomics to anticompetitive conduct.[3] Then, the [chapter] illustrates the clash between anticompetitive conduct, as defined within a microeconomic framework, and anticompetitive conduct defined by jurisprudential economics.[4] This [chapter] also explains the term jurisprudential economics, which refers to the judicial application of economic theory within an analytical framework driven by stare decisis, as exemplified by Judge Easterbrook's recent opinion in *Sanderson v. Culligan International Co.*,[5] in which he postulates that product disparagement "is not actionable under the antitrust laws."[6] Finally, this [chapter] concludes that the intentionally false disparagement of a rival's goods or services is injurious to competition and constitutes unlawful activity under either § 1 (when in combination with others), § 2, or both, of the Sherman Antitrust Act.[7]

7.2 Antitrust Injury

Antitrust injury is an "injury of the type the antitrust laws were intended to prevent and that flows from that which makes [the] defendants' acts unlawful."[8] It is regarded as synonymous with "injury to competition"[9] and is frequently understood to result in curtailed output and higher prices.[10] To understand "injury to competition," it is necessary to understand the fundamental underpinnings of microeconomics' theoretical model of competition. Although the term "antitrust injury" may be characterized as an action that results in curtailed output and higher prices, the following analysis demonstrates that the term is much richer. It illustrates that whenever market conduct impairs one or more of the requisite antecedent conditions of the perfectly competitive economic model,[11] competition is thereby injured.

In *Brunswick Corp. v. Pueblo Bowl-O-Mat, Inc.*,[12] the United States Supreme Court "christened"[13] the following prima facie element of any antitrust damages claim: "Plaintiffs must prove *antitrust injury*, which is to say injury of the type the antitrust laws were intended to prevent that flows from that which makes defendants' acts unlawful. The injury should reflect the anticompetitive effect either of the violation or of anticompetitive acts made possible by the violation."[14] The Supreme Court clarified that an antitrust plaintiff not only has the burden of establishing an injury-in-fact, but also of proving an antitrust injury—an injury to competition.[15]

Approximately nine years after *Brunswick*, in *Cargill, Inc. v. Monfort of Colorado, Inc.*,[16] the Supreme Court reiterated that a private plaintiff seeking antitrust relief must show a threat of antitrust injury. Supplementing its holding in *Brunswick,* the *Cargill* Court provided that "a showing of loss or damage due merely to increased competition does not constitute such injury."[17] By citing and restating its reasoning in *Brunswick*, the Court made clear that antitrust injury was now a permanent fixture upon the antitrust jurisprudential landscape:[18]

> *Brunswick* holds that the antitrust laws do not require the courts to protect small businesses from the loss of profits due to continued competition, but only against the loss of profits from practices forbidden by the antitrust laws. The kind of competition that Monfort alleges here, competition for increased market share, is not activity forbidden by the antitrust laws. It is simply, as petitioners claim, vigorous competition. To hold that the antitrust laws protect competitors from the loss of profits due to such price competition would, in effect, render illegal any decision by a firm to cut prices in order to increase market share. The antitrust laws require no such perverse result, for 'it is in the interest of competition to permit dominant firms to engage in vigorous competition, including price competition.' The logic of *Brunswick* compels the conclusion that the threat of loss of profits due to possible price competition following a merger does not constitute a threat of antitrust injury.[19]

Brunswick and Cargill clearly established that an antitrust injury is a required element of proof in most, if not all, private federal antitrust lawsuits.[20] Both define an antitrust injury as an injury of the type the antitrust laws were intended to prevent.[21] Thus, since the Supreme Court had previously held that "the antitrust laws...were enacted for the protection of competition,"[22] it logically follows that the "injury should reflect the anticompetitive effect"[23] resulting from a violation of the antitrust laws.

7.3 Microeconomic Analysis of Conduct Injurious to Competition

A. The Perfectly Competitive Model—A Paradigm for Identifying Conduct Injurious to Competition

Instruction on the requisite antecedent conditions[24] underlying the perfectly competitive model not only dramatically simplifies the task of understanding antitrust precedent, but also provides an analytical framework for identifying anticompetitive conduct independent of precedential constraint. Once the requisite antecedent conditions for competition to thrive are identified and understood, the jurist, the antitrust practitioner, and the economic analyst are in a superior position from which to analyze anticompetitive conduct that may trigger statutory liability.

The requisite antecedent conditions of the perfectly competitive model[25] consist essentially of the following:

1. The existence of numerous buyers and sellers,[26] each acting independently[27] and rationally;[28]
2. Each buyer and seller consumes or produces such a negligible amount of the total output that no one buyer or seller can influence price by the amount they either consume or produce;[29]
3. There are no barriers to entry or exit with respect to consumer or producer markets;[30]
4. All market participants (i.e., all buyers and sellers) are fully informed of all relevant economic and technological data;[31]
5. All products are homogeneous, or rather, constitute interchangeable substitutes for each other;[32] and
6. The forces of supply and demand are free to determine the quantity of output in a relevant market, as well as to determine a market-clearing, competitive price with respect to the same.[33]

Microeconomic theory teaches that if these conditions are met, the perfectly competitive model will create efficiencies in consumption, production, and allocation.[34] Further, it is through the creation of such efficiencies that a perfectly competitive market promises the greatest social opportunity for wealth creation.[35] In antitrust parlance, it promises greater output at lower prices.

If the above conditions must be met for the perfectly competitive market to thrive, then, from a purely economic perspective, it follows that any market conduct or activity that impairs, threatens, suppresses, or jeopardizes any one or more of such underlying conditions must be discouraged as a matter of public policy. It is in this context that the underlying conditions provide a powerful analytical paradigm for identifying market conduct or activity that may likely constitute an unreasonable restraint of trade, an unfair method of competition, and a competitive injury.

B. Perfect Competition and Its Assumption of Rationality

Economic theory has long acknowledged that the given environment within which society functions is constrained by scarcity and that such scarcity is the fundamental source of social and political conflict.[36] Given such scarcity, all societies are confronted with the problem of determining (1) what, and how much, to produce, (2) how to produce, and (3) for whom to produce.[37] The field of microeconomics has demonstrated that the adoption of the perfectly competitive model provides a remarkable social mechanism with which to address the social problems generated by scarcity.[38] The perfectly competitive model ultimately nurtures, if not ensures, efficiencies in the allocation, production, and distribution of scarce resources.[39] Central to the perfectly competitive model is the assumption that all market participants are rational, with rational action being defined by the principle of utility/profit maximization.[40] Any act of consumption or production that fails to maximize the utility or profit of an individual or firm is considered to be irrational economic behavior. Economic rationality necessarily requires that all costs and benefits be considered when exercising economic choices. Consequently, in order to act rationally, all market participants must be fully informed of all costs and benefits associated with their respective economic activities.[41] Once informed of all activity costs and benefits, an economically rational actor will weigh his or her costs and benefits, and if the benefits exceed or equal the costs, he or she will engage in such activity.[42] To the extent that all such costs and benefits are not considered—that is, they are external to the rational decision-making process—non-utility/profit-maximizing choices will be made, resulting in unacceptable market inefficiencies.[43]

C. Perfect Competition and Its Information Requirements

In short, rationality requires that market participants be fully informed of all relevant economic and technological data.[44] In fact, as noted above, fully informed market participants are an essential operational condition of the perfectly competitive model. Without full information, distortions in output and price will result.

D. Product Disparagement and Its Nurturing and Injurious Effects

1. Effect on access to information

Product disparagement, if truthful and accurate, is welcome information in the competitive marketplace. To the extent that a disparagement practice might inform a consumer of the differences between two competing products, such a practice nurtures a vigorous competitive environment. As long as the disparagement practice contributes to the information available to market participants, it lubricates the operational efficiencies of the perfectly competitive model. The more information available to market participants, the more rational their choices; the more rational their choices, the more efficient the model is in determining a welfare-maximizing equilibrium.

Conversely, product disparagement that is false and inaccurate is an iniquity that strikes at the very heart of a competitive marketplace and cannot be tolerated. False information impairs rational action on both the demand side and the supply side of the market. For example, conduct falsely disparaging a rival or a rival's goods or services interferes with the consumer's ability to identify all benefits and/or costs associated with the purchase of the rival's goods or services. Most importantly, it distorts the environment within which market participants are expected to effectuate rational choice. In addition, the distorting effect of false and inaccurate information often results in the underproduction of the disparaged product or service and/or the overproduction of the disparager's product or service. In short, the intentional false disparagement of rival goods and services creates disequilibrium with respect to output and price.

As one economist observed:

> Real-world markets often involve deception, cheating, and inaccurate information. For example, car dealers know about defects in the cars they sell but do not always reveal those defects to consumers. Another example is when consumers who want health insurance do not reveal their health problems to the insurance company. In both cases, it is in the interest of the knowledgeable person not to reveal information that the other person or firm would need to know to make an informed decision about the transaction. Hence imperfect information can be a cause of market failure.[45]

Figure 7.1 illustrates the distortions that might result from deceptive and false disparagement practices.[46] The demand function for Firm *A*'s product is a statement of the relation between the quantity demanded, *Q*, and all factors that affect that quantity. These factors include the price of the good or service under analysis, the price of other goods,[47] the number of buyers in the market, the relative income of consumers, consumer tastes and preferences, general marketplace expectations, and other possible influences.[48] To the extent the disparagement distorts the price[49] of the product or negatively influences the taste and preferences of the consumer with respect to Firm *A*'s product, the demand for the product or service may likely shift to the left, from *d* to *d'*, curtailing output of Firm *A*'s product or service from Q^* to Q'.[50]

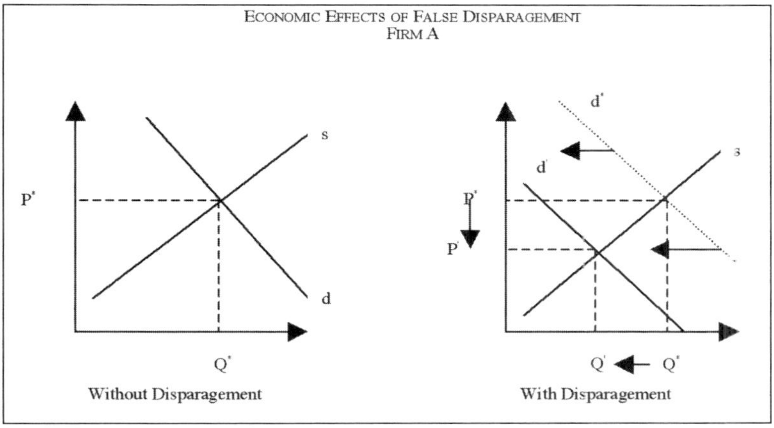

Figure 7.1

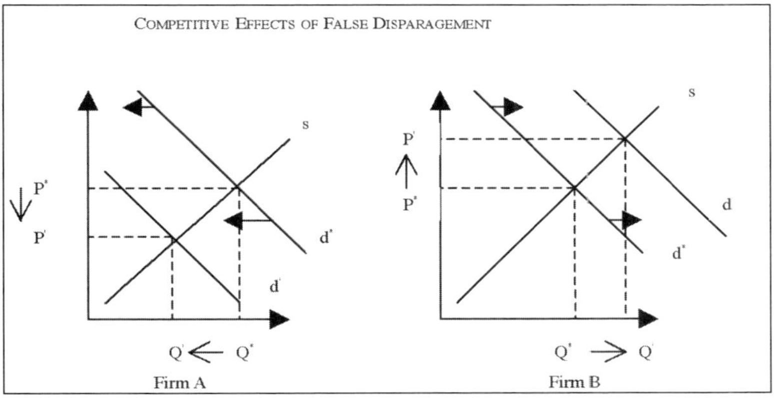

Figure 7.2

Additionally, the disparagement practice may not only distort the market for the disparaged product, but it may also distort the market for product substitutes. For example, in Figure 7.2, Firm *B*, by and through its disparaging practices, may capture market share from Firm *A*, resulting in an increase in Firm *B*'s output from Q^* to Q' as consumers substitute Firm *B*'s products or services for Firm *A*'s.

Successful disparagement also results in a type of market failure commonly referred to in economics as adverse selection.[51] Adverse selection occurs "when buyers and sellers have different amounts of information about the good for sale,"[52] or "when products of different qualities are sold at a single price because buyers or sellers are not sufficiently informed to determine the true quality at the time of purchase."[53] False disparagement practices restrain the rational action necessary for efficient exchange and, therefore, restrain trade. False disparagement vitiates the conditional environment within which competition thrives. Consequently, to the extent the false disparagement of a rival's products creates information asymmetries, it injures competition.

It merits noting that such practices have been held to constitute an unfair method of competition under Section 5 of the Federal Trade Commission Act.[54] In *Carter Products, Inc. v. FTC*,[55] the Fifth Circuit Court of Appeals upheld the Commission's finding that the manufacturer of a popular aerosol shaving cream had engaged in unfair methods of competition when it disseminated information that was misleading, unfair, and damaging to a competing product.[56] The court reasoned that under Section 5(a) [of the Federal Trade Commission Act] the law is clear that an advertisement is illegal if it contains a false claim inducing the purchase of a product inferior to the product the consumer bargained for. The false claim may be a quality, an ingredient, or effectiveness the advertised product does not have. *Or the advertisement may disparage competing products by attributing to them inferiorities they do not possess.*[57]

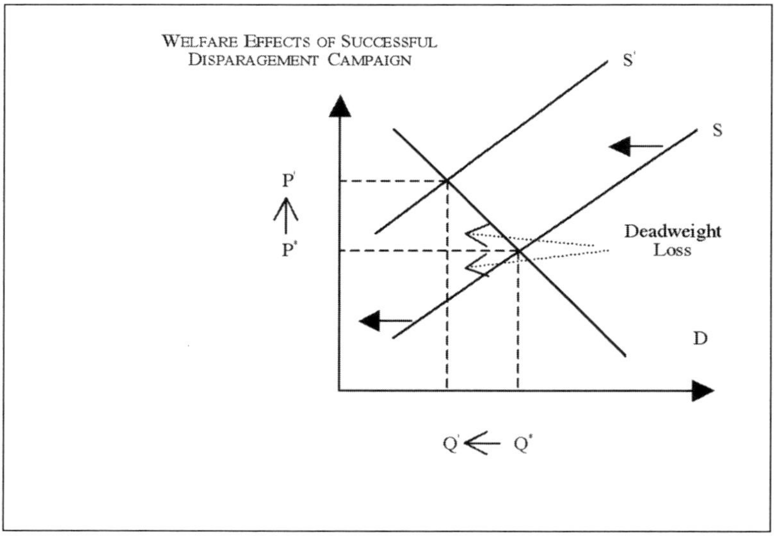

Figure 7.3

2. Effect on other conditions

A successful campaign of disparagement may also jeopardize and threaten other conditions necessary for competition to thrive. It can create entry barriers, lead to capricious market exit, create artificial market equilibrium, or even lead to oligopolies and monopolies. A firm injures competition if it falsely disparages its competitors and their respective products for the purpose of forcing them to exit the market, or to create a barrier to their entry or re-entry into the market. Such practices will certainly drive up prices by curtailing output, as demonstrated in Figure 7.3.

The market supply function, *S*, for a given product is a statement of the relation between the quantity supplied and all factors affecting that quantity. Such factors include the price of the good in question, the price of a supplier's related goods, the number of sellers producing the good, input prices, the current state of technology, and general market expectations.[58] As rival firms are driven from the market as a result of false disparagement, the market supply curve, S, shifts to S', thereby resulting in a curtailment of output (Q^* decreases to Q') and an increase in price (P^* increases to P'). As a result, there is a deadweight loss[59] to society.

7.4 Microeconomics vs. Jurisprudential Economics
A. Antitrust Analysis and the Tension Between Microeconomics and Jurisprudential Economics

The artful application of antitrust law generally depends on the jurist's ability to synthesize an historical morass of evolving common law doctrine, as well as his or her ability to access, understand, and relate fundamental microeconomic theory. The integration of economics is essential in the study and application of antitrust law. Such integration, however, is often problematic given the breadth and depth of both the legal and economics fields, as well as their respective institutional constraints. Although the statutory origins of U.S. antitrust law include a political component,[60] antitrust scholars, academicians, and practitioners tend to orient their analysis exclusively upon economic theory. While economists find clarity in their theories and models, the legal profession's application of such models is often colored with the law's institutional biases, driven by the value it attaches to stare decisis.[61] Consequently, the clarity of microeconomics is often compromised, contorted, and even ignored by jurisprudential economics in an attempt to reconcile economic theory with the factual precedent of past antitrust decisions.

For example, in the recently decided case *Sanderson v. Culligan International Co.*,[62] Judge Frank Easterbrook affirmed the dismissal of the plaintiff's antitrust claims, holding that neither § 1 nor § 2 of the Sherman Act reached the defendant's alleged false and disparaging statements made during a trade show about plaintiff's products.[63] In the Chicago School tradition,[64] Judge Easterbrook, citing precedent, stated:

> Antitrust law condemns practices that drive up prices by curtailing output. False statements about a rival's goods do not curtail output in either the short run or the long run. They just set the stage for competition in a different venue: the advertising market.[65]

Indeed, microeconomic theory maintains that conduct that artificially drives up prices or curtails output obstructs the efficiencies emanating from a competitive market structure.[66] Judge Easterbrook's assertion that "false statements about a rival's goods" do not create similar inefficiencies is simply incorrect and illustrates the enervated nature of jurisprudential economics. As demonstrated above, microeconomic theory abhors false, misleading, and incomplete information because it obstructs the operation of the perfectly competitive model and can result in inefficiencies characterized by reduced demand, curtailed output, higher prices, and economic waste. By making such an absolute statement, Judge Easterbrook compromises and contorts, if not ignores, requisite core economic principles in an attempt to reconcile their application with historical, factual precedent.[67]

B. *Sanderson v. Culligan International Co.*—Judge Easterbrook's Flawed Jurisprudential Economics

Charles Sanderson, an inventor and manufacturer of a number of magnetic devices used to improve certain water qualities, filed suit against Indiana Soft Water Services, Inc. and Culligan International for allegedly publishing and distributing false information that disparaged his products.[68] Sanderson asserted claims under both the Lanham Act and the Sherman Antitrust Act. The trial court dismissed his antitrust claims and granted summary judgment with respect to his Lanham Act claims.[69] At the core of his complaint, Sanderson "allege[d] a widespread conspiracy in the worldwide market beginning in the 1970s 'to discredit and malign magnetic water treatments.'"[70] The Water Quality Association, a trade association, was alleged to be at the center of this conspiracy.[71] Sanderson specifically alleged that the Water Quality Association conspired with others to restrain trade by means including:

> 1. Improper use of various studies and reports derogatory to magnetic water treatment and devices, including interstate and international publication and sale of the studies with knowledge that the information contained therein was not accurate, and acting with reckless

disregard of the truth or accuracy of the conclusions reached in the studies.

2. Distribution of negative position papers and policy statements regarding magnetic water treatment.
3. Banning the display of magnetic treatment devices at the trade shows sponsored by Water Quality Association.
4. The instigation of investigations by various public officials, including various state attorneys general, the Federal Trade Commission, and the Better Business Bureau, with such investigations being prompted by an improper motive, to-wit, the restraint of trade and harassment of a competitor.
5. Placement of letters and other articles of misinformation in the trade press.
6. Direct contact with customers and potential customers of Plaintiff to discredit Plaintiff's products and processes.
7. Appearances at trade shows and other public forums to distribute information negative to magnetic water treatment.[72]

Applying conventional microeconomic theory to the facts in *Sanderson*, if Culligan and others, namely the Water Quality Association, disseminated truthful and accurate information about Sanderson's product, such conduct accommodates competition. Competitors who disseminate accurate and truthful information should be applauded for being exemplar economic citizens. On the other hand, if Culligan combined with others for the express purpose of disseminating false and inaccurate information, such conduct is antithetical to the perfectly competitive model. Such conduct would be anticompetitive and should be condemned as such.

Unfortunately, the parties will never know whether such conduct was nurturing or injurious to the fundamental tenets of the perfectly competitive model. The district court dismissed Sanderson's case for failing to state a claim upon which relief could be granted pursuant to Federal Rule of Civil Procedure 12(b)(6).[73] According to the district court, Sanderson's antitrust claim was built upon allegations that the defendants and others engaged in a deliberate campaign to falsely disparage Sanderson's product.[74] Constrained by precedent,[75] the district court ruled that "Sanderson's antitrust claim fails at the pleading stage for failure to identify any conduct that could be actionable as a restraint of trade."[76] In reaching its summary conclusion, the district court quoted Judge Easterbrook in *Schachar v. American Academy of Ophthalmology, Inc.*: "Warfare among suppliers and their different products *is* competition. Antitrust law does not compel your competitor to praise your product or sponsor your work. To require cooperation or friendliness among rivals is to undercut the intellectual foundations of antitrust law."[77] According to the district court, *Schachar* made it clear that the antitrust laws are not a source of relief for Sanderson's claim that the defendants were making deliberately false or misleading statements about his products.[78] The district court held that "joint criticism," even if proven to be false, is not enough to establish an antitrust violation.[79]

C. Judge Easterbrook's Analysis

On appeal, Judge Easterbrook reiterated the ill-conceived precedential rule of law that the Sherman Act does not reach conduct consisting of the intentional false disparagement of a rival's goods.[80] According to Easterbrook, "[a]ntitrust law condemns practices that drive up prices by curtailing output. False statements about a rival's goods do not curtail output in either the short or the long run. They just set the stage for competition in a different venue; the advertising market."[81]

Judge Easterbrook is right to suggest that competition is "warfare," and therefore "criticism," or rather "product disparagement," alone may constitute a proper and welcomed method of competitive engagement. Product disparagement, if true, provides important information to market participants necessary for competition to thrive. As stated above, one of the critical assumptions of the perfectly competitive model is that "[a]ll market participants, that is all buyers and sellers, are fully informed of all relevant economic and technological data."[82] Information is sacrosanct to competition. Access to information on both the demand and supply side of the equilibrium equation fosters and nurtures vigorous competition. Without accurate information, rationality is impaired and economic waste results.[83]

Judge Easterbrook is wrong, however, to suggest that the intentional, false disparagement of a rival's products cannot rise to the level of a Sherman Act violation. While antitrust law does not compel a competitor to praise a rival's product or sponsor its work,[84] antitrust law does compel a competitor to refrain from anticompetitive conduct that either restrains or attempts to restrain trade, or in fact, may effectuate a monopoly. The antitrust law is the statutory guardian angel of the perfectly competitive model. To reiterate, "antitrust injury" is synonymous with "injury to competition."[85] False information impairs a fundamental operational condition of the perfectly competitive model and, therefore, is injurious to competition. Intentional dissemination of false information about a rival's product restrains trade in that it restrains rational action in the marketplace.

Additionally, a conspiracy engaged in the false disparagement of a rival's product hinders product substitution. It may not only cause firms to exit the marketplace irrationally, but may also create barriers to entry and re-entry. To the extent that such intentional conduct forces suppliers to leave the marketplace, economic theory demonstrates that the supply function is apt to shift to the left, thereby curtailing output and increasing price.[86] Moreover, the antitrust implications of such conduct are accentuated in an already concentrated market, or a dominant firm market. When such conduct forces marketplace exit, it nurtures an environment susceptible to single-firm market power with respect to output and price.

D. Intentional False Disparagement Is Per Se Unreasonable

Information is an essential and necessary condition of the perfectly competitive market. Conduct that intentionally skews, taints, twists, distorts, biases, or contorts information should perhaps be relegated per se unlawful under the Sherman Act. After all, the Supreme Court has held price-fixing to be per se unlawful, regardless of whether the price ultimately fixed might be reasonable.[87] As Justice Douglas observed in *United States v. Socony-Vacuum Oil Co.*:[88]

> [F]or over forty years [the Supreme Court] has consistently and without deviation adhered to the principle that price-fixing agreements are unlawful per se under the Sherman Act and that no showing of so-called competitive abuses or evils which those agreements were designed to eliminate or alleviate may be interposed as a defense.[89]

As with price fixing, combinations, agreements, or conspiracies to engage in the intentional, false disparagement of a rival firm's products or services "may or may not be aimed at complete elimination of...competition,"[90] however, "[w]hatever economic justification [such] particular...agreements may be thought to have, the law [should] not permit an inquiry into [its] reasonableness."[91] Given the fundamental importance of truthful and accurate information in the marketplace, such agreements should "all be banned because of their actual threat to the central nervous system of the economy."[92]

Judge Easterbrook's analysis in *Sanderson v. Culligan International Co.* exemplifies what this article refers to as jurisprudential economics. Constrained by precedent largely established himself, Judge Easterbrook's analysis contorts and twists fundamental microeconomic principles to find a result consistent with that precedent. Although he might be correct to state that "[t]here can be no restraint of trade without a restraint,"[93] he is short-sighted to conclude that the intentional dissemination of false information about a rival's product does not constitute a restraint of trade. Such conduct restrains the autonomous forces of supply and demand, and is therefore injurious to competition. Similarly, it restrains rational action necessary for efficient trade and is therefore a restraint of trade.

7.5 Conclusion

Product disparagement, depending on its motivating origins, can either nurture or spoil a competitive environment. Disparagement motivated by a rivalry grounded in truthful, accurate information is welcome competitive conduct and should be encouraged as a matter of public policy. To the extent such disparagement reveals accurate distinctions with respect to product characteristics and qualities, it cultivates a vigorous, competitive environment. However, product disparagement fueled by a rivalry driven by deception and misinformation is unacceptable and should be discouraged as a matter of public policy. The dissemination of false, deceptive, and inaccurate information desecrates the hallowed efficiencies for which competition is so highly touted. Contrary to the flawed jurisprudential economics applied by Judge Easterbrook in *Sanderson v. Culligan International Co.*, microeconomics instructs that fully informed market participants are a required condition of the perfectly competitive model. If the antitrust laws are intended to protect competition from conduct that is ultimately injurious to its operational foundation, then such laws are relevant and applicable in situations involving the intentional false disparagement of a rival's products. Intentional false disparagement of a rival's product is an unacceptable form of economic warfare, and Judge Easterbrook is amiss to suggest otherwise. Such conduct imperils the operational efficiencies of perfect competition and is proscribed as a matter of microeconomic theory. Accordingly, the Seventh Circuit's summary conclusion that §§ 1 and 2 of the Sherman Act fail to reach such conduct is economically ill-conceived. It defies conventionally accepted economic constructs and, most importantly, it essentially legislates a statutory exception with respect to conduct that threatens the very heart of the perfectly competitive model.

Endnotes

1. ROBERT S. PINDYCK & DANIEL L. RUBINFELD, MICROECONOMICS 3-4 (5th ed. 2001) ("Microeconomics deals with the behavior of individual economic units...More precisely, it is about the allocation of scarce resources. For example, microeconomics explains how consumers can best allocate their limited incomes to the various goods and services available to purchase. It explains how workers can best allocate their time to labor instead of leisure, or to one job instead of another. And it explains how firms can best allocate limited financial resources to hiring additional workers versus buying new machinery, and to producing one set of products versus another.").

2. *See infra* Part II.

3. *See infra* Part III.

4. *See infra* Part IV.

5. Sanderson v. Culligan Int'l Co., 415 F.3d 620 (7th Cir. 2005).

6. *Id.* at 624.

7. *See infra* Part V. Section 1 of the Sherman Act states:

> Every contract, combination in the form of trust or otherwise, or conspiracy, in restraint of trade or commerce among the several States, or with foreign nations, is hereby declared to be illegal. Every person who shall make any contract or engage in any combination or conspiracy hereby declared to be illegal shall be deemed guilty of a felony, and, on conviction thereof, shall be punished by fine not exceeding $100,000,000 if a corporation, or, if any other person, $1,000,000, or by imprisonment not exceeding 10 years, or by both said punishments, in the discretion of the court.

15 U.S.C. § 1 (2000).

Section 2 states:

> Every person who shall monopolize, or attempt to monopolize, or combine or conspire with any other person or persons, to monopolize any part of the trade or commerce among the several States, or with foreign nations, shall be deemed guilty of a felony, and, on conviction thereof, shall be punished by fine not exceeding $100,000,000 if a corporation, or, if any other person, $1,000,000, or by imprisonment not exceeding 10 years, or by both said punishments, in the discretion of the court.

Id. § 2.

8. *Brunswick Corp. v. Pueblo Bowl-O-Mat, Inc.*, 429 U.S. 477, 489 (1977).

9. *Healow v. Anesthesia Partners,* No. 95-35241, 1996 WL 442524, at *5 (9th Cir. Aug. 5, 1996) (unpublished) (holding that an anesthesiologist had no antitrust injury because the underlying market structure did not support any inference of injury to competition).

10. *Culligan*, 415 F.3d at 623; see also *NCAA v. Univ. of Okla.,* 468 U.S. 85, 103-07 (1984); *Broad. Music, Inc. v. CBS, Inc.* 441 U.S. 1, 19-20 (1984); William H. Page, *The Chicago School and the Evolution of Antitrust: Characterization, Antitrust Injury, and Evidentiary Sufficiency*, 75 VA. L. REV. 1221, 1268-73 & n.253 (1989).

11. *See infra* Parts III.A, D.

12. *Brunswick Corp. v. Pueblo Bowl-O-Mat, Inc.,* 429 U.S. 477 (1977).

13. 1 PHILLIP E. AREEDA & HERBERT HOVENKAMP, FUNDAMENTALS OF ANTITRUST LAW § 3.03, at 81 (2002) ("Although the *Brunswick* christened this requirement 'antitrust injury,' the concept is older. It is reflected in criticism of the lower court decision in *Brunswick* itself, as well as in some applications of the 'target area' test for standing." (footnote omitted)). *See also id.* § 3.03, at 81 n.15 ("While the antitrust injury test is not the same as the older 'target area' test, it developed largely through earlier target area cases. In those cases, plaintiffs were ruled ineligible for § 4 damages despite injury caused by the defendant's action, on the ground that they were outside the 'target area' meant to be protected by the antitrust laws. For example, in *Reilbert* [sic] *v. Atlantic Richfield Co.*, 471 F.2d 727 (10th Cir.), *cert. denied*, 411 U.S. 938 (1973), employees of a merged firm were denied damages when they were fired following reorganization resulting from an allegedly illegal merger. Despite the fact that the firings would not have occurred without the merger, the court held that the employee's interest was not one 'which the prohibition of [certain mergers] was clearly intended to protect...If there has been a wrong, appellant cannot show that it results from the lessening of competition. Termination of employment will often occur whether a merger is legal or illegal.' *Id.* at 731. *Accord Carlson Cos. v. Sperry & Hutchinson Co.*, 507 F.2d 959, 962 (8th Cir. 1974) ('[A]ny acquisition is likely to create some injury. But it is only anti-competitive injury which § 7 was intended to eliminate...'); *Billy Baxter v. Coca-Cola Co.,* 431 F.2d 183, 187 (2d Cir. 1970), *cert. denied*, 401 U.S. 923 (1971)").

14. *Brunswick Corp.*, 429 U.S. at 489 (emphasis added).

15. Id.; see also 1 Areeda & Hovenkamp, supra note xiii, § 3.03, at 77.

16. *Cargill, Inc. v. Monfort of Colo., Inc.,* 479 U.S. 104 (1986).

17. *Id.* at 122.

18. Subsequent to the Court's decision in *Brunswick* and prior to its decision in *Cargill*, the Supreme Court confirmed the importance of showing antitrust injury under § 4 of the Clayton Act. In *Blue Shield of Virginia v. McCready*, 457 U.S. 465 (1982), the Court found that "a health-plan subscriber suffered antitrust injury as a result of the plan's 'purposefully *anticompetitive scheme*' to reduce competition for psychotherapeutic services by reimbursing subscribers for services provided by psychiatrists but not for services

provided by psychologists." *Id.* at 483. The Court further noted that antitrust injury "as analyzed in *Brunswick*, is one factor to be considered in determining the redressability of a particular form of injury under § 4." *Id.* at 483 n.19. Similarly, in *Associated General Contractors of California, Inc. v. California State Council of Carpenters*, 459 U.S. 519 (1983), the Court applied the *Brunswick* test. *Id.* at 539-40.

19. *Cargill, Inc.*, 479 U.S. at 116-17.

20. *See* 1 AREEDA & HOVENKAMP, *supra* note xiii, §3.03, at 77-87.

21. *See supra* notes xii-xiv and accompanying text.

22. *Brunswick Corp. v. Pueblo Bowl-O-Mat, Inc.*, 429 U.S. 477, 488 (1977).

23. *Id.* at 489.

24. The requisite antecedent conditions may also be referred to as fundamental assumptions or underlying assumptions.

25. *See* DAVID C. COLANDER, MICROECONOMICS 242 (5th ed. 2004) (outlining the "necessary conditions for perfect competition" to thrive).

26. *See* EDWIN MANSFIELD & GARY YOHE, MICROECONOMICS 356-57 (11th ed. 2004) ("The firm in a perfectly competitive market has so many rivals that competition becomes impersonal in the extreme...A competitive firm faces so little of the market demand curve that its effective demand curve is horizontal at whatever price the market will bear. A competitive firm can only decide the output that it would like to supply to the market at a given price."); PINDYCK & RUBINFELD, *supra* note i, at 328 ("In a perfectly competitive market, the large number of sellers and buyers of a good ensures that no single seller or buyer can affect its price. The market forces of supply and demand determine price.").

27. *See* MANSFIELD & YOHE, *supra* note xxvi, at 426, 433-34 ("Unlike the case of monopolistic competition, the supply side of an oligopoly market is composed of a few firms...Conditions in oligopolistic industries tend to promote collusion, since the number of firms is small and the firms recognize their interdependence. The advantages to the firms of collusion seem obvious; increased profits, decreased uncertainty, and a better opportunity to prevent other's entry."); PINDYCK & RUBINFELD, *supra* note i, at 430 ("In [competitive] markets, each firm could take price or market demand as given and largely ignore its competitors. In an oligopolistic market, however, a

firm sets price or output based partly on strategic considerations regarding the behavior price or output based on strategic considerations regarding the behavior of its competitors.").

28. STEVEN E. LANDSBURG, PRICE THEORY AND APPLICATIONS 634 (6th ed. 2005) ("[T]he economist assumes that people are *rational*."); *see also infra* note xl (discussing rational choice as an equimarginal principle).

29. *See* MANSFIELD & YOHE, *supra* note xxvi, at 290 ("[P]erfect competition requires that *each participant in the market, whether a buyer or a seller, be so small in relation to the entire market that he or she cannot affect the product's price*."); PINDYCK & RUBINFELD, *supra* note i, at 252 ("Because *each individual firm sells a sufficiently small proportion of total market output, its decisions have no impact on market price*...The assumption of price taking applies to *consumers* as well as firms.").

30. *See* MANSFIELD & YOHE, *supra* note xxvi, at 290 ("Perfect competition also requires that *all resources be completely mobile*. Each resource must, in other words, be able to enter or leave the market with ease and to switch from one use to another without fuss or bother."); PINDYCK & RUBINFELD, *supra* note i, at 253 ("[F]ree entry (exit), means that there are no special costs that make it difficult for a new firm either to enter an industry and produce or to exit if it cannot make a profit. *As a result, buyers can easily switch from one supplier to another, and suppliers can easily enter or exit a market*.").

31. *See* MANSFIELD & YOHE, *supra* note xxvi, at 290-91 ("[P]erfect competition requires that consumers, firms, and resource owners have *perfect knowledge of the relevant economic and technological data*. Consumers must be aware of all prices. Laborers and owners of capital must be aware of how much their resources will bring in all possible uses. Firms must know the prices of all inputs and the characteristics of all relevant technologies. And in its purest sense, perfect competition requires that all of these economic decision-making units have an accurate knowledge of the past, the present, *and the future*."); PINDYCK & RUBINFELD, *supra* note i, at 595 ("[W]e have assumed that consumers and producers have complete information about the economic variables that are relevant for the choices they face.").

32. *See* MANSFIELD & YOHE, *supra* note xxvi, at 405 (noting that in perfectly competitive situations the goods sold are "completely homogeneous from one seller to another"); PINDYCK & RUBINFELD, *supra* note i, at 252-53 ("Price-taking behavior typically occurs in markets where firms produce identical, or nearly identical, products. When *the products of all of the firms in a market are perfectly substitutable with one another*—that is, when they

are *homogeneous*—no firm can raise the price of its product above the price of other firms without losing most or all of its business.").

33. *See* MANSFIELD & YOHE, *supra* note xxvi, at 347-48 ("We have seen that a perfectly competitive economy maximizes the total net gain of consumers and producers. We then showed...how deadweight losses—reductions in economic efficiency—result if the government [obstructs the forces of supply and demand by imposing] a price ceiling[,]...a price floor[,]...a tariff, a quota, or an excise tax."); PINDYCK & RUBINFELD, *supra* note i, at 55 n.2 ("The market mechanism is the tendency for supply and demand to equilibrate (i.e., for price to move to the market-clearing level), so that there is neither excess demand nor excess supply.").

34. *See* PINDYCK & RUBINFELD, *supra* note i, at 575-85, 590-91.

35. *See id.*

36. *See* COLANDER, *supra* note xxv, at 5, 9.

37. *Id.* at 5.

38. *Id.* at 9.

39. *See supra* note xxxiii and accompanying text.

40. *See* COLANDER, *supra* note xxv, at 6-8, 239 (noting that "firms are profit-maximizing entrepreneurial firms"); *id.* at 181 ("The analysis of rational choice is the analysis of how individuals choose goods within their budget in order to maximize total utility, and how maximizing total utility can be accomplished by considering marginal utility. The analysis begins with the premise that rational individuals want as much satisfaction as they can get from their available resources. The term *rational* in economics means, specifically, that people prefer more to less and will make choices that give them as much satisfaction as possible."); LANDSBURG, *supra* note xxviii, at 634 ("The economist assumes that people act according to the principle of equimarginality. This is often expressed by saying that the economist assumes that people are *rational.* Indeed, it has been said that a student becomes a true economist on the day when he fully understands and accepts the principle that people equate costs and benefits at the margin."); EDWIN MANSFIELD, MICROECONOMICS: THEORY AND APPLICATIONS 55 (6th ed. 1988) ("Given the consumer's tastes, we assume that he or she is rational, in the sense that he or she tries to *maximize utility.*"); STEPHEN A. MATHIS & JANET KOSCIANSKI, MICROECONOMIC THEORY: AN INTEGRATED APPROACH

2 (2002) ("[M]aking rational choices is a matter of choosing the amount(s) of some decision, or independent, variable(s) such that the extra benefit received from the last unit chosen is just equal to its extra cost. In economics, the process of measuring and comparing the extra benefits and extra costs associated with a rational decision is known as marginal analysis."); PINDYCK & RUBINFELD, *supra* note i, at 254 ("The assumption of *profit maximization* is frequently used in microeconomics because it predicts business behavior reasonably accurately and avoid unnecessary analytical complications.").

41. *See* MANSFIELD & YOHE, *supra* note XXVI, at 290-91 ("[P]erfect competition requires that consumers, firms, and resource owners have *perfect knowledge of the relevant economic and technological data*...Firms must know the prices of all inputs and the characteristics of all relevant technologies. And in its purest sense, perfect competition requires that all of these economic decision-making units have an accurate knowledge of the past, the present, *and the future*.").

42. *See* ANTHONY E. BOARDMAN ET AL., COST-BENEFIT ANALYSIS CONCEPTS AND PRACTICE 31 (3d ed. 2006) ("Choose the combination of [goods and/or inputs] that maximizes net benefits.").

43. MANSFIELD, *supra* note xl, at 675 ("[P]roducers act in ways that cause harm to others without paying the full cost of the damage. In these and other, similar cases, the pursuit of private gain will not necessarily promote the social welfare").

44. *See supra* note xli and accompanying text; PINDYCK & RUBINFELD, *supra* note i, at 595 ("[W]e have assumed that consumers and producers have complete information about the economic variables that are relevant for the choices they face.").

45. COLANDER, *supra* note XXV, at 417; *see also* PINDYCK & RUBINFELD, *supra* note i, at 596-97 ("Market failure can also occur when consumers lack information about the quality or nature of a product and so cannot make utility-maximizing purchasing decisions.").

46. *See infra* Fig.1.

47. Other goods include, namely, compliments and substitutes.

48. MARK HIRSCHEY, MANAGERIAL ECONOMICS 67-68 (10th ed. 2003) ("In functional form, a demand function may be expressed as Quantity of Product *X* Demanded = $Q_x = f$ (Price of *X*, Prices of Related Goods, Expectations

of Price Changes, Consumer Incomes, Tastes and Preferences, Advertising Expenditures, and so on).").

49. Price distortions will necessarily result from the consumer's under-evaluation of the benefits provided by the product, or from the over-evaluation of the costs associated with the product.

50. In this illustration and those that follow in this subsection, the disparagement conduct is exhibited in a highly competitive monopolistic market characterized and driven by product differentiation. *See* PINDYCK & RUBINFELD, *supra* note i, at 424 ("A monopolistically competitive market has two key characteristics: 1. Firms compete by selling differentiated products that are highly substitutable for one another but not perfect substitutes...2. There is *free entry and exit*: it is relatively easy for new firms to enter the market with their own brands and for existing firms to leave if their products become unprofitable.").

51. PINDYCK & RUBINFELD, *supra* note i, at 598; *see also* COLANDER, *supra* note XXV, at 417 ("Such a market failure is called an adverse selection problem—*a problem that occurs when buyers and sellers have different amounts of information about the good for sale.*"); LANDSBURG, *supra* note XXVIII, at 313-15 ("Adverse selection: The problem that arises when people know more about their own risk characteristics than others do.").

52. COLANDER, *supra* note XXV, at 417.

53. PINDYCK & RUBINFELD, *supra* note i, at 598.

54. Section 5(a)(1), the pertinent provision of the Federal Trade Commission Act, states: "Unfair methods of competition in or affecting commerce, and unfair or deceptive acts or practices in or affecting commerce, are herby declared unlawful." 15 U.S.C. § 45(a)(1) (2000).

55. *Carter Prods., Inc. v. FTC,* 323 F.2d 523 (5th Cir. 1963).

56. *Id.* at 530-31.

57. *Id.* at 528 (footnotes omitted) (emphasis added). *Accord Perma-Maid Co. v. FTC,* 121 F.2d 282, 284-85 (6th Cir. 1941) (wherein manufacturers of steel cookware were enjoined from making "representations that food prepared or kept in aluminum utensils was detrimental to health and caused formation of poisons and that the consumption of such food would cause ulcers, cancers, cancerous growths and other ailments, afflictions and diseases"). *But see*

FED. TRADE COMM'N, STATEMENT OF POLICY REGARDING COMPARATIVE ADVERTISING (Aug. 13, 1979), available *at* http://www.ftc.gov/bcp/policystmt/ad-compare.html (last visited March 7, 2006) ("Comparative advertising, when truthful and non-deceptive, is a source of important information to consumers and assists them in making rational purchase decisions. Comparative advertising encourages product improvement and innovation, and can lead to lower prices in the marketplace...[However, s]ome industry codes which prohibit practices such as 'disparagement,' 'disparagement of competitors,' 'improper disparagement,' 'unfairly attacking,' 'discrediting,' may operate as a restriction on comparative advertising. The Commission has previously held that disparaging advertising is permitted so long as it is truthful and not deceptive.").

58. HIRSCHEY, *supra* note xlviii, at 74 ("In functional form, a supply function can be expressed as Quantity of Product *X* Supplied = Q = *f* (Price of *X*, Prices of Related Goods, Current State of Technology, Input Prices, Weather, and so on).").

59. *See* COLANDER, *supra* note xxv, at 272 (defining deadweight loss as "the net cost to society from the existence of monopoly").

60. *See* David Millon, *The Sherman Act and the Balance of Power*, 61 S. CAL. L. REV. 1219, 1223-24 (1988) (concluding "that the language of the Sherman Act meant something far different to those who approved it than it does under Bork's [adoption of the Chicago School theory of consumer welfare] analysis. Congress reacted to a particular problem: pervasive public outrage over the great trusts, and popular demand for the restoration of a balance of economic power in American society."). Professor Millon explains:

> Congress and the American public viewed the great trusts in light of a traditional conception of the connection between individual liberty and economic organization. Liberty was the freedom to pursue one's self-defined goals to the greatest extent consistent with the liberty of others. Trusts threatened this liberty in two ways. First, they possessed the economic power to exclude people from opportunities to *see*k material success through competition in the market. Second, the trusts' immense wealth provided the ability to corrupt the legislative process so as to benefit their owners at the expense of the rest of society. Liberty therefore depended on the decentralization of economic power; the possibility that concentration may have been more efficient in some circumstances could not justify its evils.

Id. at 1224.

61. *Black's Law Dictionary* defines stare decisis as "[t]he doctrine of precedent, under which it is necessary for a court to follow earlier judicial decisions when the same points arise again in litigation." BLACK'S LAW DICTIONARY 1443 (8th ed. 2004).

It merits observing that the Supreme Court's compulsion to conclude that the injury complained of in *Cargill* did not constitute a threat of an antitrust injury was driven by its precedent established in *Brunswick*. *See supra* note xix and accompanying text. And yet, regardless of the factual and legal precedent of *Brunswick*, the economist would have reached the same conclusion in *Cargill* with the aid of microeconomic theory and its models.

62. *Sanderson v. Culligan Int'l Co.*, 415 F.3d 620 (7th Cir. 2005).

63. *Id.* at 622.

64. *See* Herbert Hovenkamp, *Antitrust Policy After Chicago*, 84 MICH. L. REV. 213, 215 (1985) ("The Chicago School model of antitrust policy dictates that allocative efficiency as defined by the market should be the only goal of the antitrust laws.").

65. *Id.* at 623 (citations omitted).

66. PINDYCK & RUBINFELD, *supra* note i, at 347 ("Because monopoly power results in higher prices and lower quantities produced, we would expect it to make consumers worse off and the firm better off.").

67. In rendering his opinion, Judge Easterbrook referenced his previous opinion in *Schachar v. American Academy of Ophthalmology, Inc.*, 870 F.2d. 397 (7th Cir. 1989), involving a supposed commercial falsehood, wherein he explicitly asserted that "[i]f such statements should be false or misleading or incomplete or just plain mistaken, the remedy is not antitrust litigation but more speech—the marketplace of ideas." *Id.* at 400.

68. *Sanderson v. Ind. Soft Water Servs., Inc.*, No. IP00-0459-CHK, 2004 WL 1784755, at *1 (S.D. Ind. July 23, 2004)). It merits noting that after the parties' pre-trial conference, Sanderson stipulated to the dismissal of all claims against Indiana Soft Water Services, leaving Culligan International as the only defendant. *Id.* at 1 n.1.

69. *Id.*; see also *Sanderson v. Culligan Int'l Co.*, 415 F.3d 620, 621-22 (7th Cir. 2005).

70. *Sanderson v. Brugman,* No. IP00-459-C-H/G, 2001 WL 699876, at *1 (S.D. Ind. May 29, 2001).

71. *Id.*

72. *Id.* (citing Sanderson's First Amended Complaint at ¶ 40).

73. *Id.*

74. *Id.* at *2.

75. *See Schachar v. Am. Acad. of Opthalmology, Inc.,* 870 F.2d 397 (7th Cir. 1989).

76. *Brugman*, 2001 WL 699876, at *2-3 (citing *Schachar*, 870 F.2d at 397) ("[T]he Seventh Circuit explained the governing principles here. In *Schachar*, several ophthalmologists sued a professional association and some of its members alleging a conspiracy to restrain trade by labeling a surgical technique (radial keratotomy) as 'experimental,' with the effect of depressing demand for plaintiffs' services in providing the surgery. The Seventh Circuit affirmed a jury verdict in favor of the defendants, but its opinion stated in no uncertain terms that the case should never have been allowed to go to trial because there was no evidence of any restraint of trade...Similarly here, Sanderson has not alleged that defendants imposed any restraints of trade, such as boycotts or other coercive measures, that prevented customers or others from dealing with him or prevented him from selling his products to any willing buyer.").

77. *Id.* at *3. *Accord Schachar*, 870 F.2d at 399; *Ind. Grocery, Inc. v. Super Valu Stores, Inc.,* 864 F.2d 1409, 1413-14 (7th Cir. 1986) ("A firm that reduces costs and expands sales injures rivals—sometimes fatally. The firm that slashes costs the most captures the greatest sales and inflicts the greatest injury. The deeper the injury to rivals, the greater the potential benefit. These injuries to rivals are byproducts of vigorous competition, and the antitrust laws are not balm from rival's wounds."); *Ball Mem'l Hosp., Inc. v. Mut. Hosp. Ins., Inc.,* 784 F.2d 1325, 1338-39 (7th Cir. 1986) ("Competition is a ruthless process...The antitrust laws are for the benefit of competition, not competitors.")

78. *Brugman*, 2001 WL 699876, at *3.

79. *Id.* (interpreting Judge Easterbrook's holding in *Schachar*).

80. See *Sanderson v. Culligan Int'l Co.*, 415 F.3d 620, 623-24 (7th Cir. 2005).

81. *Id.* at 623 (citations omitted).

82. MANSFIELD & YOHE, *supra* note xxvi, at 290-91; *see also supra* note xxxi and accompanying text.

83. *See* discussion *supra* Part III.B.

84. *See Culligan*, 415 F.3d at 623 (quoting *Schachar v. Am. Acad. of Opthalmology, Inc.*, 870 F.2d 397, 399 (7th Cir. 1989)).

85. *See supra* notes viii-x and accompanying text.

86. *See supra* fig.3.

87. See *United States v. Trenton Potteries Co.*, 273 U.S. 392, 397-98 (1927) ("The aim and result of every price-fixing agreement, if effective, is the elimination of one form of competition. The power to fix prices, whether reasonably exercised or not, involves power to control the market and to fix arbitrary and unreasonable prices. The reasonable price fixed today may through economic and business changes become the unreasonable price of tomorrow. Once established, it may be maintained unchanged because of the absence of competition secured by the agreement for a price reasonable when fixed. Agreements which create such potential power may well be held to be in themselves unreasonable or unlawful restraints, without the necessity of minute inquiry whether a particular price is reasonable or unreasonable as fixed and without placing on the government in enforcing the Sherman Law the burden of ascertaining from day to day whether it has become unreasonable though the mere variation of economic conditions. Moreover, in the absence of express legislation requiring it, we should hesitate to adopt a construction making the difference between legal and illegal conduct in the field of business relations depend upon so uncertain a test as whether prices are reasonable—a determination which can be satisfactorily made only after a complete survey of our economic organization and a choice between rival philosophies.").

88. *United States v. Socony-Vacuum Oil Co.*, 310 U.S. 150 (1940).

89. *Id.* at 218.

90. *FTC v. Superior Court Trial Lawyers Ass'n,* 493 U.S. 411, 435 (1990) (citing *Socony-Vacuum*, 310 U.S. at 225-26 n.59).

91. *Id.* (citing *Socony-Vacuum*, 310 U.S. at 225-26 n.59).

92. *Id.* (citing *Socony-Vacuum*, 310 U.S. at 225-26 n.59).

93. *Sanderson v. Culligan Int'l Co.*, 415 F.3d 620, 624 (7th Cir. 2005).

References

Books

ABA Section Of Antitrust Law. 2005. *Market Power Handbook*. Chicago: ABA.

American Bar Association. Section Of Antitrust Law. 1996. *Proving Antitrust Damages: Legal And Economic Issues*. Chicago: American Bar Association.

Areeda, Phillip E., and Herbert Hovenkamp. 2006. *Fundamentals of Antitrust Law § 3.03(b)*. 3rd ed. New York: Aspen Publishers.

Auletta, Ken. 2001. *World War 3.0: Microsoft And Its Enemies*. New York: Random House.

Balkin, J.M. 1998. Cultural Software: A Theory Of Ideology. New Haven, CT: Yale University Press.

Bauer, Joseph P. and William H. Page. 2002. *Kintner's Federal Antitrust Law: Practice Prohibited by the Sherman Act*. Cincinnati, OH: Anderson Pub.

Baumol, William J., John C. Panzer and Robert D. Willig. 1982. *Contestable Markets And The Theory Of Industry Structure*. New York: Harcourt.

Blair, Roger D., and David L. Kaserman. 1985. Antitrust Economics. Homewood, IL: Richard D. Irwin.

Boardman, Anthony E. et al. 2005. *Cost-Benefit Analysis: Concepts And Practice*. 3rd ed. Upper Saddle River, NJ: Prentice Hall.

Bork, Robert. 1978. *The Antitrust Paradox*. New York: Basic Books, Inc.

Bork, Robert. 1993. *The Antitrust Paradox: A Policy At War With Itself*. New York: Basic Books, Inc.

Breyer, Stephen. 1982. *Regulation and Its Reform.* Cambridge, MA: Harvard University Press.

Carlton, Dennis W. and Jeffrey M. Perloff. 2000. *Modern Industrial Organization.* 3rd ed. Reading, MA: Addison Wesley Longman, Inc.

Coase, R. H. 1994. How Should Economists Choose? In *Essays on Economics and Economists.* Chicago: University of Chicago Press.

Colander, David C. 2004. *Microeconomics.* 5th ed. New York: Irwin/McGraw-Hill.

Friedman, Milton. 1953. The Methodology Of Positive Economics. In *Essays In Positive Economics.* Chicago: University of Chicago Press.

Geertz, Clifford. 1983. *Local Knowledge.* New York: Basic Books, Inc.

Hahn, Robert W., ed. 2003. *High-Stakes Antitrust: The Last Hurrah?* Washington, D.C.: American Enterprise Institute Press.

Hays, William L., and Robert L. Winkler. 1970. *Statistics.* New York: Holt, Rinehart, and Winston.

Hirschey, Mark. 2003. *Managerial Economics.* 10th ed. Mason, OH: Thomson/South-Western.

Holmes, Jr., Oliver Wendell. 1963. *The Common Law.* Edited by Mark Dewolfe Howe. Cambridge, MA: Harvard University Press.

Hovenkamp, Herbert. 2002. The Reckoning Of Post-Chicago Antitrust. In *Post-Chicago Developments in Antitrust Law.* Edited by Antonio Cucinotta et al. Northampton, MA: Edward Elgar Publishing.

Hovenkamp, Herbert. 2005. *Federal Antitrust Policy: The Law Of Competition And Its Practice.* 3rd ed. St. Paul, MN: West Group Publishing.

Hylton, Keith N. 2003. *Antitrust Law: Economic Theory And Common Law Evolution.* New York: Cambridge University Press.

Kreps, David M. 1990. *Game Theory and Economic Modelling.* New York: Oxford University Press.

Kwoka, John E., and Lawrence J. White, ed. 2004. *The Antitrust Revolution: Economics, Competition, and Policy*. 4th ed. New York: Oxford University Press.

Landsburg, Steven E. 2005. *Price Theory & Applications*. 6th ed. Mason, OH: Thomson/South-Western.

Letwin, William. 1965. *Law And Economic Policy In America: The Evolution Of The Sherman Anitrust Act*. Chicago: University of Chicago Press.

Lopatka, John E. and William H. Page. 2002. 'Obvious' Consumer Harm in Antitrust Policy: The Chicago School, the Post-Chicago School and the Courts. In *Post-Chicago Developments In Antitrust Law*. Edited by Antonio Cucinotta et al. Northampton, MA: Edward Elgar Publishing.

Mansfield, Edwin, and Gary Yohe. 2003. *Microeconomics: Theory/Application*. 11th ed. New York: Norton.

Mas-Colell, Andreu, Michael D. Whinston, and Jerry R. Green. 1995. *Microeconomic Theory*. Oxford: Oxford University Press.

Mathis, Stephen A., and Janet Koscianski. 2002. *Microeconomics Theory: An Integrated Approach*. Upper Saddle Creek, NJ: Prentice Hall.

Mueller, Christopher B. and Laird C. Kirkpatrick. 1995. *Evidence*. London: Little, Brown & Co.

Nelson, Robert H. 2001. *Economics as Religion: From Samuelson to Chicago and Beyond*. University Park, PA: Pennsylvania State University Press.

Nicholson, Walter. 2005. *Microeconomic Theory: Basic Principles And Extensions*. 9th ed. Mason, OH: Thomson/South-Western.

Page, William H., ed. 1996. American Bar Association Section of Antitrust Law. *Proving Antitrust Damages: Legal And Economic Issues*. Chicago: ABA.

Pindyck, Robert S., and Daniel L. Rubinfeld. 2001. *Microeconomics*. 5th ed. Upper Saddle Creek, NJ: Prentice Hall.

Pollock, Frederick, and Frederic William Maitland. 1968. *The History Of English Law Before The Time Of Edward I*. 2nd ed. London: Cambridge University.

Porter, Robert H., and J. Douglas Zona. 2004. Bidding, Bid Rigging, And School Milk Prices: *Ohio v. Trauth*. In *The Antitrust Revolution*. Edited by John E. Kwoka and Lawrence J. White. New York: Oxford University Press.

Posner, Richard A. 1999. *The Problematics of Moral and Legal Theory*. Cambridge, MA: Belknap Press.

Samuelson, Paul A. and William D. Nordhaus. 2001. *Economics*. 17th ed. New York: Irwin/McGraw-Hill.

Shubik, Martin. 1982. *Game Theory in the Social Sciences,* at 217. Cambridge, MA: MIT Press.

Sowell, Thomas.1987. *A Conflict Of Visions*. New York: William Morrow & Co., Inc.

Stigler, George J. 1970. *The Organization Of Industry*. Homewood, IL: Richard D. Irwin, Inc.

Sullivan, E. Thomas, and Herbert Hovenkamp. Supp. 2005. *Antitrust Law, Policy And Procedure: Cases, Materials, and Problems*. 5th ed. Newark: Lexis Nexis.

Sullivan, Lawrence A., and Warren Grimes. 2006. *Hornbook on The Law Of Antitrust: An Integrated Handbook*. 2nd ed. St. Paul, MN: Thomson West.

Twining, William. 2006. *Rethinking Evidence: Exploratory Essays*. New York: Cambridge University Press.

Viscusi, W. Kip, Joseph E. Harrington, Jr., and John M. Vernon. 2005. *Economics Of Regulation And Antitrust*. 4th ed. Cambridge, MA: MIT Press.

Webster's New Collegiate Dictionary. 1976.

Wetzstein, Michael E. 2004. Microeconomic Theory: Concepts & Connections. Mason, OH: Thomson/South-Western.

Periodicals

Allen, Ronald J., and Craig R. Callen "The Juridical Management of Factual Uncertainty," *International Journal of Evidence and Proof* 7 (2003): 1.

Allen, Ronald J., and Michael S. Pardo "The Myth of the Law-Fact Distinction," *Northwestern Law Review* 97 (2003): 1769.

Allen, Ronald J., and Ross M. Rosenberg "Legal Phenomena, Knowledge, and Theory: A Cautionary Tale of Hedgehogs and Foxes," *Chicago-Kent Law Review* 77 (2002): 683.

Arthur, Thomas C. "Farewell to the Sea of Doubt: Jettisoning the Constitutional Sherman Act," *California Law Review* 74 (1986): 263.

Arthur, Thomas C. "The Costly Quest for Perfect Competition: Kodak and Non-structural Market Power," *New York University Law Review* 69 (1994): 1

Baker, Jonathan B. "Two Sherman Act Section 1 Dilemmas: Parallel Pricing, the Oligopoly Problem, and Contemporary Economic Theory," *Antitrust Bulletin* 38 (1993): 143.

Baker, Jonathan B. "Stepping Out In An Old Brown Shoe: In Qualified Praise Of Submarkets," *Antitrust Law Journal* 68 (2000): 203.

Bittlingmayer, George. "Price-Fixing and the Addyston Pipe Case," *Research in Law and Economics* 5 (1983): 57.

Blair, Roger D., and Jill Boylston Herndon "The Implications of Daubert for Economic Evidence in Antitrust Cases," *Washington and Lee Law Review* 57 (2000): 801.

Blair, Roger D., and John E. Lopatka "The Albrecht Rule After Khan: Death Becomes Her," *Notre Dame Law Review* 74 (1998): 123.

Blair, Roger D., and William H. Page "'Speculative' Antitrust Damages," *Washington Law Review* 70 (1995): 423.

Blecher, Maxwell M., and James Robert Noblin "The Confluence of Muddied Waters: Antitrust Consequential Damages and the Interplay of Proximate Cause, Antitrust Injury, Standing and Disaggregation," *St. John's Journal of Legal Commentary* 13 (1998): 145.

Bocchino, Anthony J., and Samuel H. Solomon, "What Juries Want to Hear: Methods for Developing Persuasive Case Theory," *Tennessee Law Review* 67 (2000): 543.

Bodington, Jeffrey C. "Appraising the Profits Lost by a Failed New Venture," *Journal Of Forensic Economics* 4, no. 1 (1990): 7–14.

Bonsack, Konrad "Damages Assessment, Janis Joplin's Yearbook, and the Pie-Powder Court," *George Mason University Law Review* 13, no. 1 (1990): 1.

Brennan, Timothy J. "Do Easy Cases Make Bad Law? Antitrust Innovations or Missed Opportunities in United States v. Microsoft," *George Washington Law Review* 69 (2001): 1042.

Brodley, Joseph F. "Oligopoly Power Under the Sherman and Clayton Acts--From Economic Theory to Legal Policy," *Stanford Law Review* 19 (1967): 285.

Brodley, Joseph F. "Antitrust Standing In Private Merger Cases: Reconciling Private Incentives And Public Enforcement Goals," *Michigan Law Review* 94 (1995): 1.

Brodley, Joseph F., and George A. Hay "Predatory Pricing: Competing Economic Theories and the Evolution of Legal Standards," *Cornell Law Review* 66 (1981): 738.

Brunet, Edward "Improving Class Action Efficiency by Expanded Use of Parens Patriae Suits and Intervention," *Tulane Law Review* 74 (2000): 1919.

Callen, Craig R. "Adjudication and the Appearance of Statistical Evidence," *Tulane Law Review* 65 (1991): 457.

Callen, Craig R. "Hearsay and Informal Reasoning," *Vanderbilt Law Review* 47 (1994): 43.

Carlton, Dennis, "A Reexamination of Delivered Pricing Systems," *Journal of Law & Economics* 23 (1983): 51.

Carlton, Dennis W., et al. "Communication Among Competitors: Game Theory and Antitrust," *George Mason Law Review* 5 (1997): 423.

Carr, Jack, and Frank Mathewson "The Economics of Law Firms: A Study in the Legal Organization of the Firm," *Journal of Law & Economics* 33 (1990): 307.

Cavanagh, Edward D. "Detrebling Antitrust Damages: An Idea Whose Time Has Come?," *Tulane Law Review* 61 (1987): 777.

Coate, B., and Jeffrey H. Fischer, "Can Post-Chicago Economics Survive Daubert?," *Akron Law Review* 34, no. 4 (2001): 795.

Coffey, Kendall "Inherent Judicial Authority and the Expert Disqualification Doctrine," *Florida Law Review* 56 (2004): 195.

Cotter, Thomas F. "Legal Pragmatism and the Law and Economics Movement," *Georgetown Law Journal* 84 (1996): 2071.

Cox, Carolyn, and Susan Foster, "The Costs and Benefits of Occupational Regulation" Bureau Of Economics, FTC, October 1990.

Cummings, F. Jay, and Wayne E. Ruhter "The Northern Pacific Case," *Journal of Law & Economics* 22 (1979): 329.

Cutler, David M., and Laurence H. Summers "The Costs of Conflict Resolution and Financial Distress: Evidence from the Texaco-Pennzoil Litigation," *RAND Journal of Economics* 19 (1988): 157.

Dalkir, Serdar, and Frederick R. Warren-Boulton. 1997. Prices, Market Definition, and the Effects of Merger: Staples-Office Depot. In *The Antitrust Revolution,* edited by John E. Kwoka, Jr. and Lawrence J. White. New York: Oxford.

Davis, Kenneth Culp "A System of Judicial Notice Based on Fairness and Convenience *Perspectives Of Law* 82 (1964).

Delvin, Alan. "A Neo-Chicago Perspective on the Law of Product Tying," *American Business Law Journal* 44, no. 3 (2007): 521–570.

Denbeaux, Mark P., and D. Michael Risinger "Kumho Tire and Expert Reliability: How the Question You Ask Gives the Answer You Get," *Seton Hall Law Review* 34 (2003): 15.

Dewey, Donald "Information, Entry, and Welfare: The Case for Collusion," *American Economic Review* 69 (1979): 587.

Dorman, Roderick G. "The Case for Compensation: Why Compensatory Components are Required for Efficient Antitrust Enforcement," *Georgetown Law Journal* 68 (1980): 1113.

Easterbrook, Frank H. "Is There a Ratchet in Antitrust Law?," *Texas Law Review* 60 (1982): 705.

Easterbrook, Frank H. "Detrebling Antitrust Damages," *Journal of Law & Economics* 28 (1985): 445, 450.

Easterbrook, Frank H. "Workable Antitrust Policy," *Michigan Law Review* 84 (1986): 1696, 1705.

Easterbrook, Frank H. "Comparative Advantage and Antitrust Law," *California Law Review* 75 (1987): 983.

Easterbrook, Frank H. "Information and Antitrust," *University of Chicago Legal Forum* 1 (2000): 18.

Edlin, Aaron S. "Stopping Above-Cost Predatory Pricing," *Yale Law Journal* 111, no. 4 (2002): 941–991.

Edwards, Harry T. "The Growing Disjunction Between Legal Education and the Legal Profession," *Michigan Law Review* 91 (1992): 34.

Eisenberg, Theodore "Damage Awards in Perspective: Behind the Headline-Grabbing Awards in Exxon Valdez and Engle," *Wake Forest Law Review* 36 (2001): 1129.

Elhauge, Einer "Why Above-Cost Price Cuts to Drive Out Entrants Are Not Predatory--and the Implications for Defining Costs and Market Power," *Yale Law Journal* 112 (2003): 681.

Elzinga, Kenneth G., and Thomas F. Hogarty "Utah Pie and the Consequences of Robinson Patman," *Journal of Law and Economics* 21 (1978): 427.

Epstein, Richard A. "The Pirates of Pennzoil," *Regulation* 9, no. 6 (Nov/Dec 1985): 18-24, 42.

Evans, Robert G. 1980. Professionals and the Production Function: Can Competition Policy Improve Efficiency in the Licensed Professions? Page 225 in *Occupational Licensure and Regulation*, edited by Simon Rottenberg. AEI Press.

Faigman, David L. "'Normative Constitutional Fact-Finding': Exploring the Empirical Component of Constitutional Interpretation," *University of Pennsylvania Law Review* 139 (1991): 541.

Fairman, Christopher M. "Heightened Pleading," *Texas Law Review* 81 (2002): 551.

Farmer, Susan Beth. "More Lessons from the Laboratories: Cy Pres Distributions in Parens Patriae Antitrust Actions Brought By State Attorneys General," *Fordham Law Review* 68 (1999): 361.

Finkelstein, Michael O., and Hans Levenbach "Regression Estimates of Damages in Price-Fixing Cases," *Law and Contemporary Problems* 46 (1983): 145.

Fisher, Franklin M. "Multiple Regression in Legal Proceedings," *Columbia Law Review* 80 (1980): 702.

Fisher, Franklin M., and R. C. Romaine. "Janis Joplin's Yearbook and the Theory of Damages," *Journal Of Accounting, Auditing, And Finance* 5 (1990): 145–158.

Fisher, George "The Jury's Rise as Lie Detector," *Yale Law Journal* 107 (2001): 575.

Fleming Jr., James, "Sufficiency of the Evidence and Jury-Control Devices Available Before Verdict," *Virginia Law Review* 47 (1961): 218.

Foster, William L. "Expert Testimony—Prevalent Complaints and Proposed Remedies," *Harvard Law Review* 11 (1897): 169

Gavil, Andrew I., "After Daubert: Discerning the Increasingly Fine Line Between the Admissibility and Sufficiency of Expert Testimony in Antitrust Litigation," *Antitrust Law Journal* 65 (1997): 663.

Goldfine, David A. J., and Kenneth M. Vorasi, "The Fall of the Kodak Aftermarket Doctrine: Dying a Slow Death in the Lower Courts," *Antitrust Law Journal* 72 (2004): 209.

Granitz, Elizabeth, and Benjamin Klein "Monopolization by 'Raising Rivals's Costs': The Standard Oil Case," *Journal of Law & Economics* 39 (1996): 1.

Guilfoil, John D. "Damage Determination in Private Antitrust Suits," *Notre Dame Lawyer* 42 (1967): 647–679.

Haddock, David D. "Basing-Point Pricing: Competitive vs. Collusive Theories," *American Economic Review* 72 (1982): 289.

Hamilton, Neil, and Virginia B. Come "Mitigation of Antitrust Damages," *Oregon Law Review* 66 (1987): 339.

Hand, Learned "Historical and Practical Considerations Regarding Expert Testimony," *Harvard Law Review* 15 (1901): 40.

Harrison, Jeffrey L. "Reconceptualizing the Expert Witness: Social Costs, Current Controls and Proposed Responses," *Yale Journal on Regulation* 18 (2001): 253.

Hastie, Reid, and Nancy Pennington "The O.J. Simpson Stories: Behavioral Scientists' Reflections on The People of the State of California v. Orenthal James Simpson," *University of Colorado Law Review* 67 (1996): 957.

Hausman, Jerry A. "Exact Consumer's Surplus and Deadweight Loss," *American Economic Review* 71 (1981): 662.

Hausman, Jerry A., and Whitney K. Newey "Nonparametric Estimation of Exact Consumers Surplus and Deadweight Loss," *Econometrica* 63 (1995): 1445.

Haveman, Robert H., Mary Gabay, and James Andreoni "Exact Consumer's Surplus and Deadweight Loss: A Correction," *American Economic Review* 77 (1987): 494.

Hjelmfelt, D. C., and C. D. Strother, Jr. "Antitrust Damages for Consumer Welfare Loss," *Cleveland State Law Review* 35, no. 4 (1991): 505–520.

Hockett, Christopher B., and Frank M. Hinman, "Admissibility of Expert Testimony in Antitrust Cases: Does Daubert Raise a New Barrier to Entry for Economists?," *Antitrust Law Journal* Summer (1996): 44.

Hovenkamp, Herbert "Fact, Value and Theory in Antitrust Adjudication," *Duke Law Journal* 1987, no. 5 (1987): 897–914.

Hovenkamp, Herbert "Post-Chicago Antitrust: A Review and Critique," *Columbia Business Law Review* 2001 (2001): 257.

Howard, Jeffrey H., and David Kaserman "Proof of Damages in Construction Industry Bid-Rigging Cases," *Antitrust Bulletin* 34 (1989): 359–393.

Hylton, Keith N., and Michael Salinger "Tying Law And Policy: A Decision-Theoretic Approach," *Antitrust Law Journal* 69 (2001): 469.

"Interview with Judge Kathryn Vratil," *Antitrust* (Spring 2003): 19.

Ippolito, Pauline M. "Resale Price Maintenance: Empirical Evidence from Litigation," *Journal of Law and Economics* 34 (1991): 263.

Joskow, Paul L. "Transaction Cost Economics, Antitrust Rules, and Remedies." *Journal of Law, Economics, and Organization* 18 (2002): 95.

Kaplan, Arthur M. "Antitrust as a Public-Private Partnership: A Case Study of the NASDAQ Litigation," *Case Western Reserve Law Review* 52 (2001): 111.

Kaplow, Louis "Rules Versus Standards: An Economic Analysis," *Duke Law Journal* 42 (1992): 557.

Katz, Ronald S. "The Kodak Case: Setting the Antitrust Agenda for the Nineties," *ALI-ABA* C695 (December 12, 1991): 28-29.

Kaye, D. H. "The Dynamics of Daubert: Methodology, Conclusions, and Fit in Statistical and Econometric Studies," *Virginia Law Review* 87 (2001): 1933.

Keeton, Robert E. "Legislative Facts and Similar Things: Deciding Disputed Premise Facts," *Minnesota Law Review* 73 (1988): 1.

Kirgis, Paul F. "The Problem of the Expert Juror," *Temple Law Review* 75 (2002): 493.

Klein, Benjamin. "Market Power in Antitrust: Economic Analysis after Kodak," *Supreme Court Economic Review* 3 (1993): 43.

Kleit, Andrew N. "Common Law, Statute Law, and the Theory of Legislative Choice: An Inquiry Into the Goal of the Sherman Act," *Economic Inquiry* 31 (1993): 647–662.

Kolasky, William J. "California Dental Association: The New Antitrust Empiricism," *Antitrust Law Journal* 14 (1999): 68.

Kolasky, William J. "U.S. and EU Competition Policy Cartels, Mergers, and Beyond" (2002), http://www.usdoj.gov/atr/public/speeches./9848.pdf.

Kolbe, A.L. (n.d.) "The Potential Value of the Option to Use the Ex Post Damage Methodology in Lawsuits," working paper in progress.

Kordana, Kevin A., and Terrance O'Reilly "Daubert and Litigation-Driven Econometrics," *Virginia Law Review* 87 (2001): 2019.

Kovacic, William E. "The Antitrust Paradox Revisited: Robert Bork and the Transformation of Antitrust Policy," *Wayne Law Review* 36 (1990): 1413.

Kovacic, William E. "Judicial Appointments and the Future of Antitrust Policy," *Antitrust* Spring (1993): 8.

Kutnjak Ivkovic, Sanja, and Valerie P. Hans "Jurors' Evaluations of Expert Testimony: Judging the Messenger and the Message," *Law and Social Inquiry* 28 (2003): 441.

Lande, Robert H. "Are Antitrust 'Treble' Damages Really Single Damages?" *Ohio State Law Journal* 54 (1993): 115.

Lande, Robert H. "Chicago Takes It on the Chin: Imperfect Information Could Play a Crucial Role in the Post-Kodak World," *Antitrust Law Journal* 62 (1993): 193.

Lande, Robert H. "Consumer Choice as the Ultimate Goal of Antitrust" *University of Pittsburgh Law Review* 62 (2001): 503.

Lande, Robert H. "Why Antitrust Damage Levels Should Be Raised," *Loyola Consumer Law Review* 16, no. 4 (2004): 329.

Landes, William M. "Optimal Sanctions for Antitrust Violations," *University of Chicago Law Review* 50 (1983): 652.

Lanzillotti, Robert F., and A. K. Esquibel. "Measuring Damages in Commercial Litigation: Present Value of Lost Opportunity," *Journal Of Accounting, Auditing, And Finance* 5, no. 1 (1990): 125–142.

Lanzillotti, Robert F., and James T. McClave "Comment: Meeting the 'Ambiguity' Test Under Daubert," *Antitrust* 17 (Spring 2003): 44.

Latin, Howard "Legal and Economic Considerations in the Decisions of Judge Breyer," *Law & Contemporary Problems* 50 (1987): 57.

Lavergne, Pascal, Vincent Requillart, and Michel Simioni "Welfare Losses Due to Market Power: Hicksian Versus Marshallian Measurement," *American Journal of Agricultural Economics* 83 (2001): 157.

Laycock, Douglas "The Remedies Issues: Compensatory Damages, Specific Performance, Punitive Damages, Supercedes Bonds, and Abstentation," *Review Of Litigation* 9, no. 3 (1990): 473–529.

Leland, Hayne E. "Quacks, Lemons, and Licensing: A Theory of Minimum Quality Standards," *Journal of Political Economy* 87 (1979): 1328.

Lempert, Richard "Juries, Hindsight, and Punitive Damage Awards: Failures of a Social Science Case for Change," *Depaul Law Review* 48 (1999): 867.

Leslie, Christopher R. "Trust, Distrust, and Antitrust," *Texas Law Review* 82 (2004): 515.

Lieblich, W. C. "Determinations by International Tribunals of the Economic Value of Expropriated Enterprises," *Journal Of International Arbitration* 7, no. 1 (1990): 37–76.

Lippitt, Richard "Intellectual Honesty, Industry and Interest Sponsored Professorial Works, and Full Disclosure: Is the Viewpoint Earning the Money, or Is the Money Earning the Viewpoint?," *Wayne Law Review* 47 (2001): 1075.

Lopatka, John E. "Antitrust and Professional Rules: A Framework for Analysis," *San Diego Law Review* 28 (1991): 301.

Lopatka, John E. "Solving the Oligopoly Problem: Turner's Try," *Antitrust Bulletin* 41 (1996): 843.

Lopatka, John E. and Paul E. Godek "Another Look at Alcoa: Raising Rivals' Costs Does Not Improve the View," *Journal of Law and Economics* 35 (1992): 311.

Lopatka, John E., and William H. Page "Posner's Program for the Antitrust Division: A Twenty-Five Year Perspective," *SMU Law Review* 48 (1995): 1713.

Lopatka, John E., and William H. Page "Monopolization, Innovation, and Consumer Welfare," *George Washington Law Review* 69 (2001): 367.

LoPucki, Lynn M., and Walter O. Weyrauch "A Theory of Legal Strategy," *Duke Law Journal* 49 (2000): 1405.

Los Mansmann, Carol. "Impact of GTE Sylvania on Third Circuit Jurisprudence," *Antitrust Law Journal* 60 (1991): 83.

MacIntosh, Jeffrey G. and David C. Frydenlund, "An Investment Approach to a Theory of Contract Mitigation," *University of Toronto Law Journal* 37 (1987): 113.

Masten, Scott E., and Edward Snyder "United States versus United Shoe Machinery Corporation: On the Merits," *Journal of Law and Economics* 36 (1993): 33.

May, James "Antitrust in the Formative Era: Political and Economic Theory in Constitutional and Antitrust Analysis, 1880-1918," *Ohio State Law Journal* 50 (1989): 257.

McChesney, Fred S. "Talking 'Bout My Antitrust Generation: Competition For and In the Field of Competition Law," *Emory Law Journal* 52 (2003): 1401.

McClintock, Michael D. "The Declining Use of Legal Scholarship by Courts: An Empirical Study," *Oklahoma Law Review* 51 (1998): 659.

McGee, John S. "Predatory Price Cutting: The Standard Oil (N.J.) Case," *Journal of Law and Economics* 1 (1958): 137.

Meese, Alan J. "Price Theory, Competition, and the Rule of Reason," *University of Illinois Law Review* 77 (2003): 83–84.

Miller, Richard B. "The Damages Dilemma in the Bet-the-Company Case," *Litigation* 17, no. 2 (1991): 12–16.

Milne, Robert A., and Jack E. Pace III "Conspiratologists at the Gate: The Scope of Expert Testimony on the Subject of Conspiracy in a Sherman Act Case," *Antitrust* 17, no. 2 (Spring 2003): 36.

Mnookin, Robert H., and Robert B. Wilson "Rational Bargaining and Market Efficiency: Understanding Pennzoil v. Texaco," *Virginia Law Review* 75, no. 2 (1989): 295–334.

Monahan, John, and Laurens Walker "Social Authority: Obtaining, Evaluating, and Establishing Social Science in Law," *University of Pennsylvania Law Review* 134 (1986): 477.

Nachwalter, M., W. J. Blechman, and S. E. Perwin. (1991) "Standing and Damages," Section of Antitrust Law, American Bar Association, Antitrust Fundamentals: Course Materials, 39th Annual Antitrust Spring Meeting, April 10, Washington, D.C.

Newberg, Joshua A. "The Narrative Construction of Antitrust," *Southern California Interdisciplinary Law Journal* 12 (2003): 181.

Noah, Lars "Civil Jury Nullification," *Iowa Law Review* 86 (2001): 1601.

Note. "Private Treble Damage Antitrust Suits: Measure of Damages for Destruction of All or Part of a Business," *Harvard Law Review* 80, no. 7 (1967): 1566–86.

Ohlbaum, Edward D. "Basic Instinct: Case Theory and Courtroom Performance," *Temple Law Review* 66 (1993): 1.

Page, William H. "The Scope of Liability for Antitrust Violations," *Stanford Law Review* 37 (1985): 1445.

Page, William H. "The Chicago School and the Evolution of Antitrust: Characterization, Antitrust Injury, and Evidentiary Sufficiency," *Virginia Law Review* 75 (1989): 1221.

Page, William H. "Ideological Conflict and the Origins of Antitrust Policy," *Tulane Law Review* 66 (1991): 1.

Parker, Alfred L., "Measuring Damages In Federal Treble Damage Actions," *Antitrust Bulletin* 17 (1972): 497–517.

Patell, James M., Roman L. Weil and Mark A. Wolfson "Accumulating Damages in Litigation: The Roles of Uncertainty and Interest Rates," *Journal of Legal Studies* 11 (1982): 341–64.

Peterman, John L. "The Brown Shoe Case," *Journal of Law and Economics* 18 (1975): 81.

Peterman, John L. "The International Salt Case," *Journal of Law and Economics* 22 (1979): 351.

Pitofsky, Robert "New Definitions of Relevant Market and the Assault on Antitrust," *Columbia Law Review* 90 (1990): 1805.

Pitofsky, Robert "Antitrust At The Turn Of The Twenty-First Century: The Matter of Remedies," *Georgetown Law Journal* 91 (2002): 169.

Polinsky, A. Mitchell, and Steven Shavell. "Should Liability be Based on Harm to the Victim or Gain to the Injurer?," Stanford Law School, Working Paper No. 109 (Dec. 1993).

Posner, Richard A. "Oligopoly and the Antitrust Laws: A Suggested Approach," *Stanford Law Review* 21 (1969): 1562.

Posner, Richard A. "Antitrust Policy and the Supreme Court: An Analysis of the Restricted Distribution, Horizontal Merger and Potential Competition Decisions," *Columbia Law Review* 75 (1975): 282.

Posner, Richard A. "The Chicago School of Antitrust Analysis," University of Pennsylvania Law Review 127 (1979): 925.

Posner, Richard A. "The Next Step in the Antitrust Treatment of Restricted Distribution: Per Se Legality," *University of Chicago Law Review* 48 (1981): 6.

Posner, Richard A. "The Law and Economics of the Economic Expert Witness," *Journal of Economic Perspectives* 13 (Spring 1999): 91.

Posner, Richard A. "Legal Scholarship Today," *Harvard Law Review* 115 (2002): 1314.

Posner, Richard A. "Reply: The Institutional Dimension of Statutory and Constitutional Interpretation," *Michigan Law Review* 101 (2003): 952.

Prentice, Robert A., and Jonathan J. Koehler "A Normality Bias in Legal Decision Making," *Cornell Law Review* 88 (2003): 583.

Project Committee on Antitrust Damages. "Proving Antitrust Damages: Legal and Economic Issues," *ABA Section of Antitrust Law*. Draft, November 15 (1993).

Reiffen, David, and Andrew N. Kleit "Terminal Railroad Revisited: Foreclosure of an Essential Facility or Simple Horizontal Monopoly?," *Journal of Law & Economics* 33 (1990): 419.

Rosengart, Matthew S. "The Motion In Limine: The Hidden Arrow in the Federal Litigator's Quiver," *The Federal Lawyer* 48, no. 5 (June 2001): 24.

Ross, Stephen F. "Network Effects and the Limits of GTE Sylvannia's Efficiency Analysis," *Antitrust Law Journal* 68 (2001): 945.

Rubinfeld, Daniel L. "Econometrics in the Courtroom," *Columbia Law Review* 85 (1985): 1048.

Salop, Steven C. "A Reassessment of Antitrust Remedies, Panel Discussion," *Antitrust Law Journal* 55 (1986): 123.

Scallen, Eileen A., and William E. Wiethoff, "The Ethos of Expert Witnesses: Confusing the Admissibility, Sufficiency and Credibility of Expert Testimony," *Hastings Law Journal* 49 (1998): 1143.

Schaefer, Elmer J. "Uncertainty and the Law of Damages," *William & Mary Law Review* 19 (1977–1978): 719.

Shores, David F. "Antitrust Decisions and Legislative Intent," *Missouri Law Review* 66 (2001): 725.

Sirico, Jr., Louis J. "The Citing of Law Reviews by the Supreme Court: 1971-1999," Industrial Law Journal 75 (2000): 1009.

Slobogin, Christopher. "The 'Ultimate Issue' Issue," *Behavioral Sciences and the Law* 7 (1989): 259.

Slobogin, Christopher. "The Structure of Expertise in Criminal Cases," *Seton Hall Law Review* 34 (2003): 105.

Stigler, George J. "The Economists and the Problem of Monopoly," *American Economic Review* 72, no. 2 (1982): 1–11.

Stigler, George J. "What Does an Economist Know?," *Journal of Legal Education* 33 (1983): 311.

Subrin, Stephen N. "How Equity Conquered Common Law: The Federal Rules of Civil Procedure in Historical Perspective," *University of Pennsylvania Law Review* 135 (1987): 909.

Sullivan, Allanna, and Anne Reifenberg. "Texaco To Take Charge Totaling $640 Million," *Wall Street Journal*, Monday, 11 December 1995.

Taurman, John D., and Jeffrey C. Bodington "Measuring Damage to a Firm's Profitability: Ex ante or Ex post?," *Antitrust Bulletin* 37, no. 1 (1992): 57–106.

Telser, Lester G. "Why Should Manufacturers Want Fair Trade?," *Journal of Law and Economics* 3 (1960): 86.

Telser, Lester G. "The Theory of Efficient Cooperation and Competition" (1987).

Turner, Donald F. "The Definition of Agreement Under the Sherman Act: Conscious Parallelism and Refusals to Deal," *Harvard Law Review* 75 (1962): 655.

Tye, William B., Stephen H. Kalos, and A. Lawrence Kolbe "How to Value a Lost Opportunity: Defining, Proving and Measuring Damages from Market Foreclosure," *Research in Law and Economics* 17 (1995): 83.

Wagner, M. J. "How Do You Measure Damages? Lost Income or Lost Cash Flow?," *Journal of Accountancy* February (1990): 28–32.

Wells, Catharine. "Situated Decisionmaking," *Southern California Law Review* 63 (1990): 1728.

Werden, Gregory J. "The History of Antitrust Market Delineation," *Marquette Law Review* 76 (1992): 123.

Werden, Gregory J. "The American Airlines Decision: Not with a Bang but a Whimper," *Antitrust* (Fall 2003): 32, 33.

Werden, Gregory J. "Economic Evidence on the Existence of Collusion: Reconciling Antitrust Law with Oligopoly Theory," *Antitrust Law Journal* 71 (2004): 719.

Whittington, Keith E. "Extrajudicial Constitutional Interpretation: Three Objections and Responses," *North Carolina Law Review* 80 (2002): 773.

Willig, Robert D. "Consumer's Surplus Without Apology," *American Economic Review* 66 (1976): 589.

Woolhandler, Ann, and Michael G. Collins, "The Article III Jury," *Virginia Law Review* 87 (2001): 587.

Zuckerman, Adrian A.S. "Law, Fact or Justice?," *Boston University Law Review* 66 (1986): 487–498.

Cases

Adventures Plus, Inc. v. City of Dallas, 2001 WL 1018732 (N.D.Tex. 2001)

Affiliated Capital Corp. v. City of Houston, 700 F.2d 226 (5th Cir. 1983)

Albrecht v. Herald Co., 452 F.2d 124 (8th Cir. 1971)

ALPO Pet Foods, Inc. v. Ralston Purina Company, 997 F.2d 949 (D.C. Cir. 1993)

Amarel v. Connell, 102 F.3d 1494 (9th Cir. 1996)

American. Booksellers Ass'n v. Barnes & Noble, Inc., 135 F. Supp. 2d 1031 (N.D. Cal. 2001)

American Column & Lumber Co. v. United States, 257 U.S. 377 (1921)

American Hospital Supply Corp. v. Hosp. Prods. Ltd., 780 F.2d 589 (7th Cir. 1986)

American Key Corp. v. Cole Nat'l Corp., 762 F.2d 1569 (11th Cir. 1985)

American Society of Mech. Eng'rs, Inc. v. Hydrolevel Corp., 456 U.S. 556 (1982)

American Tobacco Co. v. United States, 328 U.S. 781 (1946)

Amey v. Gulf Abstract & Title, 758 F.2d 1486 (11th Cir. 1985)

Andrx Pharm., Inc. v. Biovail Corp. Int'l, 256 F.3d 799 (D.C. Cir. 2001)

Anti-Monopoly, Inc. v. Hasbro, Inc., 958 F. Supp. 895 (S.D.N.Y.)

Arizona v. Maricopa County Med. Soc'y, 457 U.S. 332 (1982)

Arthur S. Langenderfer, Inc. v. S.E. Johnson Co., 792 F.2d 1050 (6th Cir. 1984)

Aspen Skiing Co. v. Aspen Highlands Skiing Corp., 472 U.S. 585 (1985)

Associated General Contractors of California, Inc. v. California State Council of Carpenters, 459 U.S. 519 (1983)

Atlantic Richfield Co. v. USA Petroleum Co., 495 U.S. 328 (1990)

Bailey v. Allgas, Inc., 148 F. Supp. 2d 1222 (N.D. Ala. 2000)

Ball Memorial Hosp. v. Mutual Hosp. Ins., 784 F.2d 1325 (7th Cir. 1986)

Barry Wright Corp. v. ITT Grinnell Corp., 724 F.2d 227 (1st Cir. 1983)

Bascom Food Prods. Corp. v. Reese Finer Foods, Inc., 715 F. Supp. 616 (D.N.J. 1989)

Bazemore v. Friday, 478 U.S. 385 (1986)

Beech Nut Nutrition Corp. v. Gerber Prods. Co., 69 Fed. Appx. 350 (9th Cir. 2003)

Bell Atlantic Business Sys. Servs., Inc. v. Hitachi Data Sys. Corp., 1995-2 Trade Cas. (CCH) P 71,259 (N.D. Cal. 1995)

Berlyn, Inc. v. Gazette Newspapers, Inc., 214 F. Supp. 2d 530 (D. Md. 2002)

Bigelow v. RKO Radio Pictures, Inc., 327 U.S. 251 (1946)

Blomkest Fertilizer, Inc. v. Potash Corp., 203 F.3d 1028 (8th Cir. 2000)

Blue Dane Simmental Corp. v. Am. Simmental Ass'n, 178 F.3d 1035 (8th Cir. 1999)

Blue Shield of Virginia v. McCready, 457 U.S. 465 (1982)

Board of Trade of Chicago v. United States, 246 U.S. 231 (1918)

Bob Nicholson Appliance, Inc. v. Maytag, 883 F. Supp. 321 (S.D. Ind. 1994)

Broadcast Music, Inc. v. Columbia Broad. Sys., Inc., 441 U.S. 1 (1979)

Brooke Group, Ltd. v. Brown & Williamson Tobacco Corp., 509 U.S. 209 (1993)

Brooks Fiber Communications of Tucson, Inc. v. GST Tucson Lightwave, Inc., 992 F. Supp. 1124 (D. Ariz 1997)

Brown Shoe Co. v. United States, 370 U.S. 294 (1962)

Brown v. Pro Football, Inc., 50 F.3d 1041 (D.C. Cir. 1995)

Brunswick Corp. v. Pueblo Bowl-O-Mat, Inc., 429 U.S. 477 (1977)

Business Electronics Corp. v. Sharp Elecs. Corp., 485 U.S. 717 (1988)

Calderone Enters. v. United Artists Theatre Circuit, 454 F.2d 1292 (2d Cir. 1971)

California Dental Ass'n v. FTC, 526 U.S. 756 (1999)

Callahan v. A.E.V., Inc., 182 F.3d 237 (3d Cir. 1999)

Cargill, Inc. v. Monfort of Colorado, Inc., 429 U.S. 104 (1986)

Carter Products, Inc. v. FTC, 323 F.2d 523 (5th Cir. 1963)

Chapin v. Brown, 48 N.W. 1074 (Iowa 1891)

Chicago Professional Sports Ltd. P'ship v. Nat'l Basketball Ass'n, 961 F.2d 667 (7th Cir. 1992)

City of Chanute v. Williams Natural Gas Co., 743 F. Supp. 1437 (D. Kan. 1990)

City of Detroit v. Grinnell Corp., 495 F.2d 448 (2d Cir. 1974)

City of Tuscaloosa v. Harcros Chemicals, Inc., 158 F.3d 548 (11th Cir. 1998)

City of Vernon v. Southern California Edison Co., 955 F.2d 1361 (9th Cir. 1992)

Clamp-All Corp. v. Cast Iron Soil Pipe Inst., 851 F.2d 478 (1st Cir. 1988)

Cleveland v. Viacom, Inc., 73 FED. APPX. 736 (5th Cir. 2003)

Coastal Fuels, Inc. v. Caribbean Petroleum Corp., 175 F.3d 18 (1st Cir. 1999)

Colorado v. Goodell Bros., Civ. A. No. 84-A-803, 1987 WL 6771 (D. Colo. Feb. 17, 1987)

Commonwealth v. Milk Indus. Mgmt. Corp., 812 F.Supp. 500 (E.D. Pa. 1992)

Com-Tel, Inc. v. Dukane Corp., 669 F.2d 404 (6th Cir. 1982)

Concord Boat Corp. v. Brunswick Corp., 207 F.3d 1039 (8th Cir. 2000)

Consolidated Metal Prods., Inc. v. Am. Petroleum Ins., 846 F.2d 284 (5th Cir. 1988)

Continental T.V., Inc. v. GTE Sylvania Inc., 433 U.S. 36 (1977)

Conwood Co. v. U.S. Tobacco Co., 290 F.3d 768 (6th Cir. 2002)

Copper Liquor, Inc. v. Adolph Coors Co., 624 F.2d 575 (5th Cir. 1980)

Daubert v. Merrell Dow Pharmaceuticals, Inc., 509 U.S. 579 (1993)

Dr. Miles Medical Co. v. John D. Park & Sons, 220 U.S. 373 (1911)

Drs. Steuer & Latham, P.A. v. Nat'l Med. Enters., Inc., 672 F. Supp. 1489 (D.S.C. 1987)

E.I. Du Pont de Nemours & Co. v. FTC, 729 F.2d 128 (2d Cir. 1984)

Eastern Auto Distributors, Inc. v. Peugeot Motors of Am., Inc., 795 F.2d 329 (4th Cir. 1986)

Eastman Kodak Co. v. Southern Photo Materials Co., 273 U.S. 359 (1927)

Elcock v. Kmart Corp., 233 F.3d 734 (3d Cir. 2000)

Eleven Line, Inc. v. North Texas State Soccer Ass'n, 213 F.3d 198 (5th Cir. 2000)

Engine Specialties, Inc. v. Bombardier Ltd., 605 F.2d 1 (1st Cir. 1979)

Federal Maritime Comm'n v. Aktiebolaget Svenska Amerika Linien, 390 U.S. 238 (1968)

Fishman v. Estate of Wirtz, 807 F.2d 520 (7nd Cir. 1986)

Fortner Enters., Inc. v. U.S. Steel Corp., 394 U.S. 495 (1969)

Frye v. United States, 293 F. 1013 (D.C. Cir. 1923)

FTC v. Abbott Labs., 853 F. Supp. 526 (D.D.C. 1994)

FTC v. Cement Inst., 333 U.S. 683 (1948)

FTC v. H.J. Heinz Co., 246 F.3d 708, 716 (D.C. Cir. 2001)

FTC v. Ind. Fed'n of Dentists, 476 U.S. 447 (1986)

FTC v. Staples, Inc., 970 F. Supp. 1066 (D.D.C. 1997)

FTC v. Superior Court Trial Lawyers Ass'n, 493 U.S. 411 (1990)

FTC v. Swedish Match, 131 F. Supp. 2d 151 (D.D.C. 2000)

FTC v. Tenet Healthcare Corp., 186 F.3d 1045 (8th Cir. 1999)

Gainesville Utils. Dep't v. Fla. Power & Light Co., 573 F.2d 292 (5th Cir. 1978)

General Electric Co. v. Joiner, 522 U.S. 136 (1997)

Graphic Products Distributors, Inc. v. Itek Corp., 717 F.2d 1560 (11th Cir. 1983)

Greene v. General Foods Corp., 517 F. 2d 635 (5th Cir. 1975)

Greenhaw v. Lubbock County Beverage Ass'n., 721 F.2d 1019 (5th Cir. 1983)

Hahn v. Rifkin/Narragansett S, Fla. CATV Ltd. P'ship, 941 F.Supp. 1196 (S.D. Fla. 1996)

Hall v. United Air Lines, Inc., 296 F. Supp. 2d 652 (E.D.N.C. 2003)

Hanover Shoe, Inc. v. United Shoe Mach. Corp., 392 U.S. 481 (1968)

Hawaii v. Standard Oil Co., 405 U.S. 251 (1972)

Healow v. Anesthesia Partners, No. 95-35241, 1996 WL 442524 (9th Cir. Aug. 5, 1996)

Heary Bros. Lightning Prot. Co. v. Lightning Prot. Inst., 287 F. Supp. 2d 1038 (D. Ariz. 2003)

Holiday Wholesale Grocery Co. v. Philip Morris, Inc., 231 F. Supp. 2d 1253 (N.D. Ga. 2002)

Illinois Brick Co. v. Illinois, 431 U.S. 720 (1977)

Image Technical Services, Inc. v. Eastman Kodak Co., 125 F.3d 1195 (9th Cir. 1997)

In *re Aluminum Phosphide Antitrust Litigation*, 893 F. Supp. 1497 (1995)

In *re Baby Food Antitrust Litig*., 166 F.3d 112 (3d Cir. 1999)

In *re Brand Name Prescription Drugs Antitrust Litig*., 186 F.3d 781 (7th Cir. 1999)

In *re Caere Corp. Sec. Litig*., 837 F.Supp. 1054 (N.D. Cal. 1993)

In *re Domestic Air Transp. Antitrust Litig*., 137 F.R.D. 677 (N.D. Ga. 1991)

In *re Flat Glass Antitrust Litig*., 385 F.3d 350 (3d Cir. 2004)

In *re High Fructose Corn Syrup Antitrust Litig*., 295 F.3d 651 (7th Cir. 2002)

In *re Industrial Gas Antitrust Litigation,* 681 F.2d 514 (7th Cir. 1982)

In *re Industrial Silicon Antitrust Litig*ation, No. 95-2104, 1998 WL 1031507 (W.D. Pa. Oct. 13, 1998)

In *re Japanese Electronic Products Antitrust Litig*ation, 631 F.2d 1069 (3rd Cir. 1980)

In *re Northwest Airlines Corp. Antitrust Litig*., 197 F. Supp. 2d 908 (E.D. Mich. 2002)

In *re Paoli R.R. Yard PCB Litig*., 35 F.3d 717 (3d Cir. 1994)

In *re Polypropylene Carpet Antitrust Litig*., 93 F. Supp. 2d 1348 (N.D. Ga. 2000)

In *re Verifone Securities Litig*., 784 F.Supp. 1471 (N.D. Cal. 1992)

In *re Visa Check/MasterMoney Antitrust Litig*., 297 F. Supp. 2d 503 (E.D.N.Y. 2003)

In *re Western Liquid Asphalt Cases*, 487 F.2d 191 (9th Cir. 1973)

Indiana Grocery, Inc. v. Super Valu Stores, Inc., 864 F.2d 1409 (7th Cir. 1989)

Instructional Sys. Dev. Corp. v. Aetna Casualty & Surety Co., 817 F.2d 639 (10th Cir. 1987)

International Boxing Club of N.Y., Inc. v. United States, 358 U.S. 242 (1959)

Interface Group v. Mass. Port Auth., 816 F.2d 9 (1st Cir. 1987)

Isaksen v. Vermont Castings, Inc., 825 F.2d 1158 (7th Cir. 1987)

J. Truett Payne Co., Inc. v. Chrysler Motors Corp., 451 U.S. 557 (1981)

J.T. Gibbons, Inc. v. Crawford Fitting Co., 704 F.2d 787 (5th Cir. 1983)

Kartell v. Blue Shield of Mass., Inc., 749 F.2d 922 (1st Cir. 1984)

Kelco Disposal, Inc. v. Browning-Ferris Indus., 845 F.2d 404 (2d Cir. 1988)

King & King Enterprises. v. Champlin Petroleum Co., 657 F.2d 1147 (10th Cir. 1981)

King v. Palmer, 906 F.2d 762 (D.C. Cir. 1990)

Kumho Tire Co. v. Carmichael, 526 U.S. 137 (1999)

Lantec, Inc. v. Novell, Inc., 146 F. Supp. 2d 1140 (D. Utah 2001)

Laurel Sand & Gravel, Inc. v. CSX Transp., Inc., 924 F.2d 539 (4th Cir. 1991)

Law v. NCAA, No. 94-2053-KHV, 1998 U.S. Dist. LEXIS 6640 (D. Kan. Apr. 23, 1998)

Leegin Creative Leather Products v. PSKS, Inc. d.b.a. Kay's Kloset, 2007 WL 1835892 (U.S.)

Lehrman v. Gulf Oil Corp., 500 F.2d 659 (5th Cir. 1974)

Litton Systems, Inc. v. AT&T, 700 F.2d 785 (2d Cir. 1983)

Lyons v. Westinghouse Elec. Corp., 222 F.2d 184 (2d Cir. 1955)

Malcolm v. Marathon Oil Co., 642 F.2d 845 (5th Cir. 1981)

Matsushita Electronic Industrial Co., Ltd. v. Zenith Radio Corp., 475 U.S. 574 (1986)

Metronet Services Corporation v. U.S. West Communications, 329 F.3d 986 (9th Cir. 2003)

MindGames, Inc. v. W. Publ'g Co., 218 F.3d 652 (7th Cir. 2000)

Minnesota Milk Producers Ass'n v. Glickman, 153 F.3d 632 (8th Cir. 1998)

Montreal Trading Ltd. v. Amax Inc., 661 F.2d 864 (10th Cir. 1981)

Multiflex, Inc. v. Samuel Moore & Co., 709 F.2d 980 (5th Cir. 1983)

National Farmers' Organization, Inc. v. Associated Milk Producers, Inc., 850 F.2d 1286 (8th Cir. 1988)

National Society of Professional Engineers v. United States, 435 U.S. 679 (1978)

National Treasury Employees Union v. Horner, 1987 WL 10106 (D.D.C. 1987)

NBO Industries Treadway Cos. v. Brunswick Corp., 523 F.2d 262 (3d Cir. 1975)

*NCAA v. University of Okla*homa, 468 U.S. 85 (1984)

Nelson v. Monroe Regional Medical Center, 925 F.2d 1555 (7th Cir.1991)

New York v. Nintendo of America, Inc., 775 F. Supp. 676 (S.D.N.Y. 1991)

New York v. Reebok International, Ltd., 903 F. Supp. 532 (S.D.N.Y. 1995)

New York v. Salton, Inc., 265 F. Supp. 2d 310 (S.D.N.Y. 2003)

Newman-Green, Inc. v. Alfonzo-Larrain R., 854 F.2d 916 (7th Cir. 1988)

Nordenfelt v. Maxim Nordenfelt Guns & Ammunition Co. [1894] A.C. p. 565, 6 Engl. Rul. Cas. 413

Northern Pacific Railway Co. v. United States, 356 U.S. 1 (1958)

Ohio ex rel. Montgomery v. Louis Trauth Dairy, Inc., 925 F. Supp. 1247 (S.D. Ohio 1996)

Ohio v. Louis Trauth Dairy, Inc., 925 F. Supp. 1247 (S.D. Ohio 1996)

Oil Spill by the Amoco Cadiz off the Coast of France on March 16, 1978 1992 U.S.A. LEXIS 833 (7th Cir.),

Olympia Equipment Leasing Co. v. Western Union Telegraph Co., 786 F.2d 794 (7th Cir. 1986)

Pennzoil v. Texaco, 17 LITIGATION 14 (1991)

People v. Milk Exchange, 39 N.E. 1062 (N.Y. 1895)

People v. Sheldon, 34 N.E. 785 (N.Y. 1893)

Petruzzi's IGA Supermarkets, Inc. v. Darling-Delaware Co., 998 F.2d 1224 (3d Cir. 1993)

Pierce v. Ramsey Winch Co., 753 F.2d 416 (5th Cir. 1985)

Pool Water Products v. Olin Corp., 258 F.3d 1024 (9th Cir. 2001)

R.S.E., Inc. v. Pennsy Supply, Inc., 523 F. Supp. 954 (M.D. Pa. 1981)

Radian Burners, Inc. v. Peoples Gas Light & Coke Co. 364 U.S. 656 (1961)

Rangen, Inc. v. Sterling Nelson & Sons, Inc., 351 F.2d 851 (9th Cir. 1965)

Re/Max Int'l, Inc. v. Realty One, Inc., 173 F.3d 995 (6th Cir. 1999)

Rebel Oil Co. v. Atl. Richfield Co., 51 F.3d 1421 (9th Cir. 1995)

Reiter v. Sonotone Corp., 442 U.S. 330, 343 (1979)

Remeron End-Payor Antitrust Litig., 2005 WL 2230314 (D.N.J. 2005)

Rintel v. Wathen, 806 F.Supp. 1467 (C.D. Cal. 1992)

Rossi v. Standard Roofing, Inc., 156 F.3d 452 (3rd Cir. 1998)

Ruiz-Troche v. Pepsi Cola Bottling Co., 161 F.3d 77 (1st Cir. 1998)

Sanderson v. Culligan International Co., 415 F.3d 620 (7th Cir. 2005)

Sanner v. Bd. of Trade of Chicago, No. 89 C 8467 (N.D. Ill. Sept. 28, 2001)

Security Systems Canada, Inc. v. Checkpoint Systems, Inc., 198 F. Supp. 2d 598 (E.D. Pa. 2002)

Seminole Tribe v. Florida, 517 U.S. 44 (1996)

Service Merchandise Co., Inc. v. Boyd Corp., 722 F.2d 945 (1st Cir. 1983)

Silver v. NYSE, 373 U.S. 341 (1963)

Southern Pacific Communications Co. v. AT&T, 556 F. Supp. 825 (D.D.C. 1982)

Stamatakis Industries, Inc. v. King, 965 F.2d 469 (7th Cir. 1992)

Standard Oil Co. v. Moore, 251 F.2d 188 (9th Cir. 1957)

State Oil Co. v. Khan, 522 U.S. 3 (1997)

Stearns Airport Equip. Co. v. FMC Corp., 170 F.3d 518 (5th Cir. 1999)

Story Parchment Co. v. Paterson Parchment Paper Co., 282 U.S. 555 (1931)

Sugar Institute v. United States, 297 U.S. 553 (1936)

Telecor Communication, Inc. v. Southwestern Bell Tel. Co., 305 F.3d 1124 (10th Cir. 2002)

Texaco Inc. v. Dagher, 126 S. Ct. 1276 (2006)

Thomas J. Kline, Inc. v. Lorillard, Inc., 878 F.2d 791 (4th Cir. 1989)

Todd v. Exxon Corp., 275 F.3d 191 (2d Cir. 2001)

United States v. Addyston Pipe & Steel Co., 85 F. 271 (6th Cir. 1898)

United States v. AMR Corp., 335 F.3d 1109 (10th Cir. 2003)

United States v. Arnold, Schwinn & Co., 388 U.S. 365 (1967)

United States v. BNS Inc., 848 F.2d 945 (9th Cir. 1988)

United States v. Bogan, 788 F.Supp. 433 (N.D. Cal. 1992)

United States v. Brown, 936 F.2d 1042 (9th Cir. 1991)

United States v. Call, 129 F.3d 1402 (10th Cir. 1997)

United States v. Capitol Serv., Inc., 756 F.2d 502 (7th Cir. 1985)

United States v. Connecticut National Bank, 418 U.S. 656 (1974)

United States v. Consolidated Laundries Corp., 291 F.2d 563 (2d Cir. 1961)

United States v. Container Corporation of America, 393 U.S. 333 (1969)

United States v. Downing, 753 F.2d 1224 (3d Cir. 1985)

United States v. General Motors Corp., 384 U.S. 127 (1966)

United States v. Marine Bancorporation, Inc., 418 U.S. 602 (1974)

United States v. Microsoft Corp., 84 F. Supp. 2d 9 (D.D.C. 1999)

United States v. MMR Corp., 907 F.2d 489 (5th Cir. 1990)

United States v. Pabst Brewing Co., 384 U.S. 546 (1966)

United States v. Sealy, 388 U.S. 350 (1967)

United States v. Socony-Vacuum Oil Co., 310 U.S. 150 (1940)

United States v. Suntar Roofing, Inc., 897 F.2d 469 (10th Cir. 1990)

United States v. Topco Assocs., Inc., 405 U.S. 596 (1972)

United States v. Trenton Potteries Co., 273 U.S. 392 (1926)

United States v. U.S. Gypsum Co., 438 U.S. 422 (1978)

United States v. VISA U.S.A., Inc., 344 F.3d 229 (2d Cir. 2003)

United States. v. Cooperative Theatres of Ohio, Inc., 845 F.2d 1367 (6th Cir. 1988)

Verizon Communications Inc. v. Law Offices of Curtis V. Trinko, 540 U.S. 398 (2004)

Virgin Atlantic Airways Ltd. v. British Airways PLC, 257 F.3d 256 (2d Cir. 2001)

Virginia Vermiculite, Ltd. v. W.R. Grace & Co., 98 F. Supp. 2d 729 (W.D. Va. 2000)

W.H. Hill Co. v. Gray & Worcester, 127 N.W. 803 (Mich. 1910)

W.W. Montague & Co. v. Lowry, 193 U.S. 38 (1904)

Walker Process Equip., Inc. v. Food Machinery & Chem. Corp., 382 U.S. 172 (1965)

Wallace v. Bank of Bartlett, 55 F.3d 1166 (6th Cir. 1995)

Warner Management Consultants, Inc. v. Data Gen. Corp., 545 F. Supp. 956 (N.D. Ill. 1982)

Webb v. Utah Tour Brokers Ass'n., 568 F.2d 670 (10th Cir. 1977)

Western Parcel Express v. United Parcel Service of Am., Inc., 65 F. Supp. 2d 1052 (N.D. Cal. 1998)

White Motor Co. v. United States, 372 U.S. 253 (1963)

Williams v. St. Joseph Hosp., 629 F.2d 448 (7th Cir. 1980)

Williamson Oil Co. v. Philip Morris USA, 346 F.3d 1287 (11th Cir. 2003)

Worldwide Basketball and Sports Tours, Inc. v. NCAA, 273 F. Supp. 2d 933 (S.D. Ohio 2003)

Yoder Brothers, Inc. v. California-Florida Plant Corp., 537 F.2d 1347 (5th Cir. 1976)

Zenith Radio Corp. v. Hazeltine Research, Inc., 395 U.S. 100 (1969)

Statutes

15 U.S.C. § 1 (2000)

15 U.S.C. § 15 (2000)

15 U.S.C.A. § 15c(c)

15 U.S.C.A. § 15c(d)(2)

15 U.S.C.A. § 15d

Clayton Act § 4, 15 U.S.C. § 15 (2000)

Clayton Act § 7, 15 U.S.C. § 18 (2000)

FED. R. EVID. 401

FED. R. EVID. 402

FED. R. EVID. 702

FED. R. EVID. 704(a)

Federal Trade Commission Act, 15 U.S.C. § 45

Sherman Antitrust Act, 15 U.S.C. §§ 1,2

U.S. Dep't of Justice & Federal Trade Comm'n, Horizontal Merger Guidelines, 57 Fed. Reg. 41

U.S. Dep't of Justice Merger Guidelines, 49 Fed. Reg. 26

About the Authors

Stephen H. Kalos, Ph.D. is Vice President of CRA International, a consulting firm providing expertise in economics, finance and business strategy. Dr. Kalos specializes in industrial organization, the economics of innovation, and intellectual property (IP). He has consulted to corporations, law firms, and government agencies for more than 30 years. His consulting practice includes three related areas: Economic Damages; IP and Technology; and Antitrust and Competition. Dr. Kalos has testified, published, lectured, and consulted extensively on economic damages. He has calculated damages and/or critiqued damage estimates in many legal disputes involving IP, antitrust, breach of contract, fraud, discrimination, and product liability issues. Dr. Kalos has testified and/or consulted on a number of litigation matters involving IP and technology, including patent infringement, patent misuse, trademark infringement and delimitation, and misappropriation of trade secrets cases. In these matters, he has analyzed damages, as well as competitive issues arising from IP rights. Dr. Kalos also consults to government and corporate clients on management and policy issues related to technology and IP. He served as principal investigator on several studies for the National Institute of Standards and Technology (then known as the National Bureau of Standards) and the National Science Foundation. Dr. Kalos also has extensive experience in the economics of antitrust and competition. He has provided economic counsel, analysis and/or testimony in many antitrust and merger cases. Dr. Kalos also analyzes competition in the context of defining the "but-for" world in his economic damages work. Dr. Kalos received a Ph.D. in Economics from Yale University in 1983, an M.A. in Economics from Yale University in 1975, and a B.A. in Economics and Mathematics from Wesleyan University in 1973.

A. Lawrence Kolbe, Ph.D. is a founding Principal of *The Brattle Group*, an economic consulting firm with offices in Cambridge (Massachusetts), San Francisco, Washington, Brussels and London. Dr. Kolbe's work focuses on financial economics, especially as it applies to rate regulation and project or asset valuation. Clients for this work have included federal, state/provincial and local government agencies; national research institutes; industry organizations; and private firms in a variety of industries. He is the co-author of three books and has published a number of articles. Dr. Kolbe has served as an expert witness in arbitrations in The Hague, London, and Melbourne; lawsuits in U.S. courts; federal and state/provincial regulatory proceedings in the U.S. and Canada, and U.S. commercial arbitrations. Dr. Kolbe received a Ph.D. in Economics from the Massachusetts Institute of Technology in 1979, and a B.S. in International Affairs (Economics) from the U.S. Air Force Academy in 1968.

Christopher R. Leslie, M.P.P., J.D. is a professor of law at the Chicago-Kent College of Law in Chicago, Illinois, where he teaches antitrust law. Professor Leslie has a degree in economics and political science from UCLA and a Masters in Public Policy from the Kennedy School of Government at Harvard University. He graduated from Boalt Hall School of Law, University of California at Berkeley, where he served as an Associate Editor on the California Law Review and was elected to the Order of the Coif. After clerking for Judge Diarmuid O'Scannlain on the Ninth Circuit Court of Appeals, he practiced law at Pillsbury Madison & Sutro and Heller Ehrman White & McAuliffe in San Francisco, concentrating on antitrust and complex business litigation. Prior to joining the faculty of Chicago-Kent, Professor Leslie taught Antitrust and Corporations at Boalt Hall. He has been a Visiting Professor of Law at Stanford Law School, at the NYU School of Law, and at the University of Texas School of Law. He will again be a Visiting Professor of Law at NYU School of Law in the spring of 2008. Professor Leslie's scholarship has appeared in the *Texas Law Review*, the *UCLA Law Review*, the *Minnesota Law Review*, the *William & Mary Law Review*, the *Wisconsin Law Review*, the *Harvard Civil Rights-Civil Liberties Law Review*, and the *Ohio State Law Journal*, among others. His research focuses on antitrust law and the intersection of antitrust law and intellectual property rights.

John E. Loptka, J.D., L.L.M. is currently the A. Robert Noll Distinguished Professor of Law at Penn State Dickinson School of Law. He joined the Dickinson School of Law from the University of South Carolina School of Law, where he was the Solomon Blatt Professor of Law. He began his full-time teaching career at the University of Illinois College of Law, where he was an associate professor. One of the nation's leading antitrust scholars, he has published over forty articles in the areas of antitrust, economic analysis of law, and regulated industries. With Professor Joseph Bauer of the University of Notre Dame Law School and Professor William Page of the University of Florida, Levin College of Law, he is a co-author of the multi-volume treatise, *Federal Antitrust Law*. He and Professor Page have also written *The Microsoft Case: Antitrust, High Technology, and Consumer Welfare*, which will be published by the University of Chicago Press in 2007. Professor Lopatka earned his juris doctor degree from the University of

Chicago and his master of laws degree from Columbia University, where he also served as an Associate in Law and Fellow in the Center for Law and Economic Studies. Apart from his career in teaching, he served as assistant director for planning for the Bureau of Competition of the Federal Trade Commission and practiced law with Donovan Leisure Newton & Irvine in New York City and Isham Lincoln & Beale in Chicago. Professor Lopatka is a member of the American Bar Association's Antitrust Section leadership and is a contributing editor of the section's *Antitrust Law Journal*. From 2001 until 2004, he was a consultant to the Office of General Counsel of the Federal Trade Commission.

Kevin S. Marshall, Ph.d., M.P.A., J.D. is an Associate Professor of Law at the University of La Verne College of Law where he teaches Antitrust Law and Law & Economics. Dr. Marshall also serves as an Adjunct Professor at the University of La Verne College of Business and Public Administration where he teaches courses in economics and finance. Dr. Marshall received the degree of Bachelor of Arts, *cum laude*, Phi Beta Kappa, with a major in Economics from Knox College in May 1982. Upon graduating from Knox College, he attended Emory University's School of Law in Atlanta, Georgia, where he was conferred the degree of Juris Doctorate in May 1985. In May 1991, he received the degree of Master of Public Affairs from the University of Texas at Dallas, and in December of 1993, he was awarded the degree of Doctor of Philosophy in Political Economy from the University of Texas, Dallas. Additionally, Dr. Marshall is certified in Quantitative Methods and Economic Analysis by the University of Texas at Dallas' School of Social Sciences for his academic achievement and coursework in Descriptive and Inferential Statistics, Costs-Benefits Analysis, Social Science Research Methods, Regression Analysis, Advanced Regression Analysis, and Econometrics. In 2004, Dr. Marshall accepted a tenured-track faculty position with the University of La Verne College of Law in Ontario, California. Dr. Marshall is also a practicing economist and serves as a Senior Fellow at the Institute for Policy Studies and Information Services (IPSIS), a for-profit organization founded for the purpose of promoting, preserving and enhancing the integrity of scientific methodology in the policy-making process. He is the editor of *The Earnings Analyst,* the annual publication of the American Rehabilitation Economics Association dedicated to the publication of quality manuscripts dealing with substantive research and practice issues in the areas of forensic vocational and economic evaluation and testimony. Dr. Marshall has served as both a testifying and consulting economic expert with respect to economic damages in antitrust, Robinson-Patman, complex commercial litigation, class-action, personal injury, wrongful death, breach of contract, wrongful termination, and employment discrimination cases. Dr. Marshall has published and presented numerous articles involving the interdisciplinary workings of law and economics.

Michele A. Molyneaux, J.D. is an associate with Sanders & Parks, P.C., in Phoenix, Arizona, where she practices in the areas of commercial litigation, construction law, insurance coverage, and insurance bad faith litigation. Ms. Molyneaux is admitted to practice in Arizona and before the United States District Court, District of Arizona. She earned a Bachelor of Science degree in Computer Science Engineering, *highest honors*, from California State University in 1992, and a Juris Doctor degree, *magna cum laude*, from Arizona State University in 2004. During law school, Ms. Molyneaux served as a Note & Comment Editor on the Arizona State Law Journal, a Teaching Assistant for Legal Method and Writing Class, and member of the Order of the Coif. Ms. Molyneaux won the *Arizona State Law Journal* Best Comment Award for her publication *Quality Control of Economic Expert Testimony: The Fundamental Methods of Proving Antitrust Damages*, 35 *Ariz. St. L. J.* 1049 (2003). She also served as a Judicial Clerk for the Hon. Roslyn O. Silver, United States District Court, District of Arizona.

William H. Page, J.D., L.L.M. is Marshall M. Criser Eminent Scholar at the University of Florida Levin College of Law. He has authored over fifty articles, book chapters, and other commentary, primarily on antitrust law and economics, and is co-author (with John Lopatka) of the *The Microsoft Case: Antitrust, High Technology, and Consumer Welfare* (University of Chicago Press 2007). He was a trial attorney with the Antitrust Division of the U.S. Department of Justice and has taught at Boston University and at Mississippi College, where he was the J. Will Young Professor of Law. He received his J.D. summa cum laude from the University of New Mexico and his L.L.M. from the University of Chicago.

William B. Tye, Ph.D. is an expert in economic analysis and public policy and has served as an economic consultant for over twenty years. He is currently a Principal with *The Brattle Group,* a public policy consulting firm located in Washington, D.C. Dr. Tye received a B.A. in economics from Emory University in 1965, and was conferred a Ph.D. in economics from Harvard University in 1970. Dr. Tye specializes in regulatory and antitrust issues. His clients have included regulatory bodies, firms in regulated industries, and law firms. He has authored or co-authored over one-hundred papers and publications, including five books.

Index

D

E

N

O

P

R

S

#4128 Measuring Loss in Catastrophic Injury Cases

Edited by Kevin Marshall, Thomas Ireland

This new reference work addresses the loss measurement issues confronted in catastrophic injury cases. The measurement of loss in such cases is an interdisciplinary effort involving the participation of many specialists including economists, rehabilitation counselors and therapists, health care providers, life care planners, attorneys, and others, including the patient and his or her family. This book is designed for all parties involved in catastrophic injury cases. Areas covered include the interdisciplinary nature of measuring loss, the role of the forensic economist in determining loss, working with life care planners and rehabilitation and vocational experts, impact of a reduced life expectancy, types of settlements including annuities, structured settlements and periodic payment judgments, and suggestions for building an expert damages team when working on this type of case. In this book, you'll find the information necessary to assess and derive a fair and accurate measurement that will, as fairly as possible, compensate the injured party and/or his or her family for his or her actual losses.

Topics Include

- Interdisciplinary nature of measuring loss
- The role of the forensic economist
- The roles of vocational and rehabilitation experts
- Overview of life care planning
- What is needed from life care planning experts
- Impact of reduced life expectancy
- Annuity contracts
- Structured Settlements
- Periodic payment judgments
- Building an expert damages team

Product Code: 4128 • ISBN: 1-933264-12-8
Softbound • 6" X 9" • Pages: 288

#6508 Emotional Distress: Proving Damages

by Jon R. Abele

The issue of emotional distress damages has perplexed the law for hundreds of years. While it was admitted that a person had both a physical and an emotional component, only one could be seen and examined. Courts over time have wrestled with these concerns, adopting rules and exceptions to the rules in an attempt to balance the competing interests of the parties, the court, and society in general.

Emotional Distress: Proving Damages provides a summary of emotional distress cases that have been litigated in jurisdictions throughout the country. You will read about the different categories of emotional distress and which categories are most accepted by courts and jurors. You will also learn about the limitations that the plaintiffs have in claiming emotional distress, such as their relationship to the victim and being in the "zone of danger."

After reading this book you will understand why some cases were successful and others failed.

Topics Include

- Basis of emotional distress claim
- Intentional infliction
- Negligent infliction of emotional distress
- Emotional distress as an element in tort
- Cause of action
- Limitations on emotional distress actions
- Potential plaintiffs
- Potential defendants
- Proof of injury
- Arguments
- Client interview checklist

Product Code: 6508 • ISBN: 1-930056-50-8
Softbound • 6" X 9" • Pages: 164

#6079 Assessment of Earning Capacity, Second Edition

by Michael S. Shahnasarian

In *Assessment of Earning Capacity*, Shahnasarian recommends standardization, objectivity, and consistency in vocational evaluations. He begins by introducing you to vocational expert services, guiding you through consultation and the standard methods to determining your clients' earning capacity. From there you will be taken through several comprehensive case studies examining common situations that may require vocational assessment, such as personal injury cases, family law, employment law, and an all new chapter on long term disability insurance. Finally, the author presents tips on appearing as an economic expert in court. Learn what is required for trial preparation, testimony, and be presented with sample deposition questions and tips to aid you in presenting a professional demeanor while undergoing intense cross examination.

Assessment of Earning Capacity contains many examples to help you understand the expert's job. This second edition has been extensively revised and contains an all-new chapter dealing with cases of long-term disability insurance.

Topics Include

- Vocational expert consultation
- Assess the value of earning capacity claims
- Investigate the integrity of vocational expert assessments
- Gain insight into the assessment process
- Methods of inquiry
- Career development potential
- Transferable skills
- Rehabilitation psychology
- Vocational rehabilitation surveys
- Client interview forms
- Sample clinicial interview
- Earning Capacity Assessment Form
- Examine the validity of opposing experts' opinions
- How to present vocational opinions

Product Code: 6079 • ISBN: 1-930056-99-0
Softbound • 8.5" X 11" • Pages: 324

#6338 A Daubert Hearing on the Admissibility of Hedonic Damage Testimony

Edited by Thomas R. Ireland

This CD comes from one of the country's leading expert economists. Using a straightforward case which challenged the admissibility of expert testimony, Thomas Ireland provides you with all relevant documentation to *Janice Christofferson v. City of Great Falls* and demonstrates how *Daubert* affected the decision to exclude expert testimony. This is an ideal case to study the *Daubert* decision and the admissibility of hedonic damage testimony. The two experts were the only witnesses in the hearing and the issue was straightforward—whether or not hedonic damage testimony met the scientific standards required for admissibility in the trial. The judge provided an extended narrative with his decision that hedonic damage testimony was not admissible. The briefs on both sides seem well focused on the issues at hand. Both sides developed their positions in a straightforward way and a decision was made on the basis of the positions that were presented without distracting side issues. A great resource for any lawyer or expert witness.

Product Code: 6338 • ISBN: 1-930056-33-8 • CD-ROM

These and many more products are available through our catalog:

Download a free catalog at www.lawyersandjudges.com

Lawyers & Judges Publishing Co., Inc.
PO Box 30040 • Tucson, AZ 85751
(800) 209-7109 • fax 800-330-8795
e-mail: sales@lawyersandjudges.com

L&J online
www.lawyersandjudges.com

L&J online
www.lawyersandjudges.com